The World-View of Prehistoric Man

Papers presented at a symposium in Lund, 5–7 May 1997, arranged by the Royal Academy of Letters, History and Antiquities along with The Foundation Natur och Kultur, Publishers

Editors: Lars Larsson and Berta Stjernquist

Konferenser 40

Kungl. Vitterhets
Historie och Antikvitets Akademien

Abstract

The World-View of Prehistoric Man. Papers presented at a symposium in Lund, 5–7 May, 1997, arranged by the Royal Academy of Letters, History and Antiquities along with The Foundation Natur och Kultur, Publishers. Kungl. Vitterhets Historie och Antikvitets Akademien. *Konferenser* 40. Stockholm 1998. 274 pp. ISBN 91-7402-279-2. ISSN 0348-1433.

This volume contains 14 papers on The World-View of Prehistoric Man from a symposium arranged by the Royal Academy of Letters, History and Antiquities along with The Foundation Natur och Kultur, Publishers, and with the support of The Royal Society of Letters at Lund. The symposium was dedicated to Gad Rausing on the occasion of his 75th birthday in 1997. The aim of the symposium was to have a broad perspective on the theme with contributions from archaeologists with different experiences and preferences as well as from representatives of other disciplines.

The contributions put forward critical viewpoints about the possibilities of capturing the mentality of prehistoric man and distinguishing between the world-view of prehistoric man and the archaeologist's own world-view. Despite this, different aspects of the world-view of prehistoric man were presented. Some authors have emphasized a social approach, others a celestial/symbolic or religious/symbolic approach, others a gender approach. Others have treated material illustrating a view of power. In addition there is a paper giving an overview of the research tradition with the connections between ethnology and archaeology.

Kungl. Vitterhets Historie och Antikvitets Akademien, Box 5622, S-114 86 Stockholm, Sweden.

© The authors 1998
ISBN 91-7402-279-2
ISSN 0348-1433
Distributed by Almqvist & Wiksell International AB, Stockholm, Sweden
Typesetting: Editorial Office, Uppsala University
Printed in Sweden by Gotab 1998

Contents

Lars Larsson and *Berta Stjernquist*, To Gad Rausing 5
Lars Larsson and *Berta Stjernquist*, Preface 7
Lars Larsson and *Berta Stjernquist*, Introduction 9
John Barrett, The Politics of Scale and the Experience of Distance:
   The Bronze Age World System 13
Ezra B. W. Zubrow and *Michael Frachetti*, Changing World-View of
   Prehistoric Populations 27
Evzen Neustupny, Otherness in Prehistoric Times 65
Bo Gräslund, The Biological Basis of Social Behaviour. 73
Alf Hornborg, Opposition, Hierarchy and Gender in Aboriginal South
   America: Linguistic and Architectural Homologies 93
Ulf Näsman, The Scandinavians' View of Europe in the Migration
   Period. 103
Richard Bradley, Directions to the Dead 123
Lars Larsson, Rock, Stones and Mentality: Stones that Unite, Stones
   that Subjugate—a Megalithic Tomb in Vale de Rodrigo, Southern
   Portugal 137
Berta Stjernquist, The Basic Perception of Religious Activities at
   Cult-Sites such as Springs, Lakes and Rivers 157
Michael Müller-Wille, The Cross as a Symbol of Personal Christian
   Belief in a Changing Religious World: Examples from Selected
   Areas in Merovingian and Carolingian Europe. 179
Gro Mandt, Vingen Revisited: A Gender Perspective on "Hunters' Rock
   Art" 201
Torsten Capelle, Man-Made Boundaries of World Views: Long-Distance
   Ramparts 225
Carl Nylander, The Mutilated Image: "We" and "They" in History—
   and Prehistory? 235
Nils-Arvid Bringéus, Ethnology as Archaeology 253
Gad Rausing—Bibliography 269
Addresses of the authors 273

To Gad Rausing

The symposium entitled "The World-View of Prehistoric Man" is dedicated to Gad Rausing on the occasion of his 75th birthday on 19 May 1997. The aim was to have a broad perspective on the theme, with contributions from archaeologists with different experience and preferences, as well as from representatives of other disciplines. This arrangement was inspired by Gad Rausing's very broad and unconventional research.

It is now 30 years since the issue of his doctor's thesis *The Bow: Some Notes on its Origin and Development*, where he applied a worldwide approach. Since then he has continued his interdisciplinary research, despite all his other activities. He has used every minute he could spare for archaeological work; the list of publications is long. Works such as *Archaeology and the Natural Sciences, Ecology, Economy and Man,* and *Prehistoric Boats and Ships of Northwestern Europe* are among them.

Gad's innovative research and commitment to archaeological research have been an inspiration to us. We wish to express our gratitude for this and our hope that he will long continue working in this spirit.

Lars Larsson *Berta Stjernquist*

Preface

From the 5th to the 7th of May 1997 a symposium entitled "The World-View of Prehistoric Man" was held at Lund. It was arranged by the Royal Academy of Letters, History and Antiquities along with the Foundation Natur och Kultur, Publishers, and with the support of the Royal Society of Letters at Lund.

The symposium was dedicated to Gad Rausing on the occasion of his 75th birthday on 19 May 1997.

The aim was to have a broad perspective on the theme with contributions from archaeologists with different experience and preferences as well as from representatives of other disciplines.

The symposium comprised two days of presentations to an audience consisting of Gad Rausing and his wife Birgit Rausing, Fil.dr h.c., along with the lecturers and a small number of scholars specially invited to take part in the discussions. The third day was devoted to an excursion in the Scanian landscape.

The Royal Academy of Letters, History and Antiquities honoured the symposium through the presence of its Secretary-General, Professor Staffan Helmfrid, who opened it and participated in the proceedings on the first day.

The symposium was organized by the undersigned with the help of Fil.kand. Ulla Karin Larsson and went off in a very positive fashion.

Manuscripts by participants who did not deliver lectures in their mother tongue have been revised by Alan Crozier and Roger Littleboy.

We should like to extend our sincere thanks to all those institutions and individuals who have contributed to the symposium and to the completion of this volume.

Lars Larsson *Berta Stjernquist*

Introduction

By Lars Larsson and Berta Stjernquist

Recent decades have seen a distinct change in archaeological research. Instead of distinguishing different forms of social expression, there is now a clear ambition to see the connections between these forms of expression. The way in which people perceive the world around them, whether the physical or the social environment, helps us to understand their reactions and relations. From dealing with the symbolic meaning of material culture, interest has been shifted to an analysis of man's mental perception of the landscape and his actions in time and space. An interpreted world-view is thus allowed to stand as an explanatory model for the actions of prehistoric society and of the individual.

The concept of world-view is diverse. The contributions to the symposium, however, have put forward critical viewpoints about the possibilities of capturing the mentality of prehistoric man. Two papers deal with the problem of drawing a dividing line between the world-view of prehistoric man and the archaeologist's own world-view. Despite this, various aspects of the world-view of prehistoric man have been envisioned and presented. The papers put forward different aspects, although they are not absolute or unmingled. Some authors have emphasized a social approach, others a celestial/symbolic or a religious/symbolic approach, others a gender approach, and others, finally, have treated material illustrating a view of power. One paper gives an overview of the research tradition.

John Barrett's contribution based on Bronze Age material presents a critical opinion. He *stresses the difficulties of discerning the world-view* of prehistoric man because of the scholar's confinement by his or her own world-view. The scholar draws his conclusions from his own point of view. The world-view we imagine is always coloured by our own. The world-view of prehistoric man was limited and temporarily formed by his limited experiences. Differences in space, however, speak for global systems during the Bronze Age, and we can therefore suppose the existence of global systems.

Ezra Zubrow and Michael Frachetti discuss *the problem of the world-view of prehistoric man* from different viewpoints of contemporary archaeologists expressed in models and problem definitions. They examine four aspects of the changing view of prehistoric populations. The first aspect takes up the tendency of the world's media as regards archaeology, the second the changing view of human ancestry from succession to contemporaneity and interaction. Prehistoric population movement, the third aspect, is analysed in depth. The changing view of migration is an important element. The fourth aspect is demographic stability. It is illustrated by a large number of experiments. The paper makes some suggestions about our changing ideas of the world-view of prehistoric society.

Because of the varying state of the concept of the world-view of prehistoric man, it is useful that *Evzen Neustupny* gives some definitions and develops the problem in his paper *Otherness in Prehistoric Times,* treating the Neolithic, Eneolithic and the Bronze Age. He is of the opinion that the world-view is a set of ideas adopted by prehistoric communities as regards *"what their social world was,* and *what kind of mutual relations they had with the external world."* He distinguishes the communal world, the strange world, and a third world which he has named the world of otherness. This world of otherness comprises relations of spatial and temporal kinds such as economic relations, kinship and warfare. The world of otherness helped to explain the unknown world outside the communities.

Bo Gräslund asks whether the problem of the world-view of prehistoric man can be illustrated through the behaviour of the animal world. In his interdisciplinary paper *The Biological Basis of Social Behaviour* he takes his starting-point in evolutionary population theory, which sees the ideas of kin selection and reciprocal altruism as central. He discusses a series of investigations of behaviour among animals and human beings. The result is that the *theoretical basis* of sociobiology's inexorably deterministic view of human social behaviour is partly wrong, which "opens prospects for better future understanding of biological aspects of human behaviour".

Alf Hornborg's contribution concerning *social conditions* in the northern part of South America focuses on comparative ethnography. He has studied architectural remains at sites in this area and compared their layouts. The basic principles of classification which he uses in his analysis are dual kin-affine opposition, age and gender. He has found that these principles underlie the settled conditions of social life. They are fundamental principles of Amerindian cosmology in large areas even in areas with very different natural conditions. Hornborg believes that they are universally human considerations and tell us about the world-view of prehistoric man.

Ulf Näsman takes up a large body of material from the Iron Age and the connections between Scandinavia and the world outside Scandinavia. The change of the rural system, social conditions documented for instance in votive finds, in the customs of awarding gold medals, and the shaping of women's dress are seen as influences from centres on the Continent. The background is the connections which can be traced from the Roman Iron Age down to the Viking period. The result is the development of Scandinavian society from a tribal grouping to an integrated society with power centres with rulers at the same level as the rulers of the *gentes* outside Scandinavia. This *change of social life* which took place in the Migration Period changed the world-view of the inhabitants in the north.

A *celestial/symbolic aspect* colours the contribution given by *Richard Bradley*. He recognizes and analyses this symbolic system of the megalithic monuments around the Irish Sea. It is expressed in the constructions of the passage-graves and in the systematic choice of rock: red, grey and pink, and white. The rising sun and the setting sun are marked in the construction. The author shows that the symbolic system of the monuments at the cemetery formed part of a wider cosmology. The directions of the dead are local in their cairns but perhaps also allied to an imagined homeland, Ireland. This gives fascinating aspects of the thinking and doing of the individuals who created the monuments.

A ritual *religious/symbolic aspect* can be traced in the contributions by Lars Larsson, Berta Stjernquist and Michael Müller-Wille. *Lars Larsson* discusses rock as a mass that contains potential values. An investigation of a megalithic tomb in southern Portugal has given knowledge of the construction and use of the megalithic graves and fundamental views of the societies building them. They are a form of cave where individuals can live. The choice of stone and the process of construction are a series of symbolic ritual activities. The development of the tomb from a simple to a complex form reflects the change of the society. The monuments have a symbolically charged role which changed during the time they were used. The stone groups can be seen as an actor in a changeable conceptual world.

In her paper *Berta Stjernquist* takes up water as a fundamental animated element in the world-view of prehistoric man. This conception is exemplified by the sacrificial site of Röekillorna Spring, with finds of archaeological objects and bones of domesticated animals and of human beings. Offerings and ritual meals are demonstrated from the early Neolithic to the Roman Iron Age. This activity can probably be associated with the everyday life of the agricultural community in the vicinity, a fertility cult. A human face and a phallic-shaped pole of wood have a symbolic meaning.

One can probably trace similar aims and actions of prehistoric man at different sites in different countries and at sites venerated during different periods. This may mean that man reacts in the same way in relation to water and uses the same symbols.

A religious/symbolic aspect is also documented by *Michael Müller-Wille*, who shows through a presentation of a large body of finds from settlement sites and graves of Merovingian and Carolingian Europe that the cross was used during the Iron Age as a symbol of Christian belief. The custom of wearing the cross was widespread from the Mediterranean to Scandinavia. The crosses and the cruciform brooches were of varying types but the symbolic meaning was the same. This speaks about the world-view of individuals.

The *gender aspect* in ritual activity is stressed by *Gro Mandt*. She has chosen Vingen, the largest rock-art site in southern Norway, for a critical discussion of the conventional interpretation of Scandinavian rock art. She is not so interested in the chronological problems and the problems of cultural tradition of the rock art. Instead she concentrates on a gender perception of the figures and their purpose. She stresses that the figures have a message about social life which relates to gender ideology and the relations between women and men.

The *aspect of power* is treated by Torsten Capelle and Carl Nylander. *Torsten Capelle* discusses a series of ramparts constructed as demarcation or as protection against attack from enemies and infiltration or to prevent escape. Many of these are well known, such as the Roman *limes,* the Great Wall of China, the wall systems around Hedeby, and the Iron Curtain. Walls around large settlements have the same purpose. All these ramparts indicate a position of power, which colours the world-view of the rulers as well as that of the controlled individuals. These ramparts can also indicate an ideological difference.

Carl Nylander has studied the damage to ancient sculpture and found that such damage is a systematically executed action against the enemies. It is very common for the nose to be mutilated. Nylander has followed this activity on pictures and sculptures from the seventh century BC through the sculpture of the antique world into Roman public art. Mutilations of pictures in modern time are also mentioned. He has found that the mutilations illustrate an antagonistic We—They relationship in the world-view of man, at least in historical times.

The last contribution to be discussed here is the paper in which *Nils-Arvid Bringéus* describes the connection between ethnology and archaeology. It is in the form of an *overview of the research tradition,* especially in Sweden. This is a background to the present-day ethnological research concerning mentality, which is of importance for archaeological research as well.

As we have seen, the different aspects of the world-view of prehistoric man covered by the symposium have given expression to basic needs and presented symbolic activities aimed at securing these needs. It is obvious and not surprising that as a rule the participants have chosen material from defined periods and defined areas, material with which they are acquainted through their research. They sometimes stress, however, that the results seem to be general.

The critical aspects of the contributions about the possibilities of capturing the world-view of prehistoric populations have given scholars special problems to think about.

The Politics of Scale and the Experience of Distance: The Bronze Age World System

By *John C. Barrett*

Introduction

There exists now a substantial archaeological literature drawing inspiration from the idea of world systems. Although originally formulated for the analysis of the modern world whose centre was dominated by Europe, others have seen a strength in an idea which they claim transcends its initial application. In other words, and despite some specific reservations, there is widespread acceptance that the analytical power of the concept is contingent not upon the specific historical condition analysed (it is not in itself only applicable in characterising the modern world) but is contingent upon general features inherent in all periods of social reproduction. Central to this is the recognition that 'cycles of reproduction are not necessarily bounded by individual societies' and that conceptually it is necessary to start with the issue of social reproduction, that is with tracing 'cycles through from production to consumption to new production in whatever social form.' This is a significantly different concern from the more traditional emphasis upon the identification and characterisation of social institutions, for these can be defined as fixed categories specific to particular and autonomous social configurations—the basis of functionalist analysis (Friedman 1994:7). Within total systems of social reproduction asymmetrical relations may be reproduced between different social configurations operating in different geographical localities. As initially conceptualised these asymmetries operate to accumulate wealth in particular core communities where that wealth has been derived from the exploitation of peripheral or dependant regions.

There are two points which need to be stressed at the outset for they will inform the development of my argument. First, although Wallerstein's concern was with the economic logic the modern world system, as a process of capital accumulation, others have stressed that global systems are concerned with the reproduction of political relations (Wallerstein 1974; cf. Edens & Kohl 1993). We should carry this argument to its logical conclusion, emphasising that we are not simply concerned with the reproduction of the material conditions of life but with the reproduction of human life itself and thus with the categories of humanity which that life recognises (in other words the ways in which that life knows of itself and of its relations to others). Obviously such categories of humanity are materially situated, they are not abstractions. The second point follows from this and it concerns the way that world systems theory has informed the development of a self-critical anthropology. Anthropology has now realised that it has never discovered an objective non-modern or non-capitalist 'other' existing beyond the edge of its world, instead what it always discovers is its own relationship with that other. That relationship is reproduced in the context of the modern world system to which both observer and participant belong. This world system, with all its structural inequalities and relationships of exploitation is partly reproduced through the anthropologists' own relationship with the traditional object of their studies.

Whilst the analysis of global systems thus allows us to chart the accumulation of wealth at certain locations within those systems, an accumulation which was the direct result of the functioning of the system through time, it must do more. Emphasis upon the total conditions for the reproduction of life must also examine the ways a practical and conscious engagement with the available material conditions differentially distributed across the system, reproduced different categories of humanity. This will mean the definition of different kinds of global system will be intimately connected with the reproduction of different forms of knowledge. To what extent is such a position applicable to the archaeology of the European Bronze Age?

The reproduction of knowledge

The fundamental dualism in the social sciences separates the observer and the observed. By examining the lives of other communities the social scientist seeks to understand those lives through a process of contextualisation. In other words the observer seeks to demonstrate that the meanings and values represented by other lives can be understood as either a product of, or as being constructed relative to, certain material, social and historical conditions. There is an important distinction here. When the emphasis is placed upon identifying conditions which supposedly *produce* other kinds of life the result tends to be the production of analyses which are of a highly deterministic kind whereby those whom the social scientist observes seem to merely play out roles pre-set for them by the conditions which that observer has identified. On the other hand if we accept that those lives are *constructed* relative to certain conditions, then a more active role is imparted to those other agents—they make their own lives although not under the conditions of their own choosing. This is a point to which we shall return below. The dualism between the observer and the observed is therefore constructed as differences in knowledge (where knowledge also necessarily empowers). I do not make this point as a prelude to questioning its validity; the views of the observer and the observed will always be different, the point of the social sciences is to explore these differences and through comparative research to learn something about human variability in general. Thus whilst the members of a particular community may understand themselves as social beings by seeing the actions of their own lives as conforming with a particular kind of given world order, the observers of that community will see those actions as being relative to one of a number of options concerning the practices of humanity. The question which interests the social scientist is why certain options rather than others emerge in certain places and at certain times. To the participant those chosen options normally appear as the inevitable consequences of their understanding of the conditions which they currently inhabit.

Bronze Age world systems

In enquiring as to what a Bronze Age world system might have looked like, Sherratt has recently set about charting the archaeological remains of such a system for Europe (Sherratt 1993). That process has involved mapping the scale and extent of the some of the material transformations of the period. In these we see the physical consequences of a number of material practices such as processes of material exploitation, production, exchange and consumption. Regional patterns emerge in the form of the material, in its range, and in the nature of its deposition. An overall 'logic' can thus be discerned in the ways in which materials whose origins lay in one part of Europe were consumed in another. We can even take the pattern further, claiming that certain regions appear to display greater levels of consumption than others implying that they had achieved some form of accumulative dominance within the operation of the overall system.

Archaeologists have often suggested that the strength of their discipline lies in their ability to establish a large scale view over which to chart the history of social and economic processes. They are thus capable, or so they claim, of tracing long term cycles of change which once operated over large distances. This is a scale of view and a form of knowledge which was not available to those who were embedded in the mechanisms of actually reproducing these social and economic systems. It is not therefore surprising to find archaeologists characterising the dualism between their own views of the past and the views of those who inhabited that past partly as a dualism of scale. For example Kristiansen comments:

'Looking at distribution maps of selected types of metalwork enables the archaeologist to discover both regional traditions and international connections and regularities that were unknown to prehistoric people, although they might have been aware of larger parts of such networks from combined personal experience and myth .... Their knowledge would thus be contextualised and localised within a social and ritual framework at a specific point in space within the network.' (Kristiansen 1993:143)

Clearly the matter extends beyond a contrast of scale, for it also encompasses the means by which knowledge is gained. There seems a clear distinction between the discovery of 'regional traditions and international connections' by the archaeological observer when compared with the knowledges gained from 'personal experience and myth' by the indigenous practitioner. Expressed thus the dualism of scale could appear as a dualism between the identification of real conditions and subjective experience.

Not all writers have treated the contrast in such terms and for many the difference in scale is simply a methodological issue concerning the most adequate scale upon which the archaeological observer should operate. Sherratt for example suggests that 'two competing forms of explanation' are available in 'the interpretation of European prehistory' (1993:1). One of these he terms 'evolutionary' or 'autonomist', which emphasises 'ecological factors, population growth, and agricultural change or the local development of technologies' as mechanisms with which to explain historical trajectories. This contrasts with 'diffusionist' or 'interventionist' explanations which emphasise 'outside contacts, trade, and the spread of ideologies' (Sherratt 1993:1). A factor which has created the analytical distinction between 'regional' studies and the 'broader continental perspective' has been the desire to examine historical change as driven by 'internal' or 'autonomous' processes rather than as a product of diffusionist contacts. In Bronze Age studies Renfrew's attempt to establish the autonomy of the copper age of south-east Europe is the classic example of this move (Renfrew 1969). In that well known study Renfrew sought to dislocate the cultural links traditionally established between the Aegean and the Balkans and in so doing identify a 'chronological fault line' which cut free the earliest representations of the Balkan chalcolithic from what others had claimed to be its Anatolian and Aegean origins. Renfrew's argument was that once that break is achieved it becomes necessary to identify mechanisms of social, economic and technological change which, operating within the Balkans, gave rise to metalworking independently of any external contact. The contrast was summed up by Renfrew:

'European prehistory has for long had a preoccupation with *origins* and with the way in which ideas and cultural traits were transmitted. Today it seems more fruitful to consider *processes* and the way in which such features were *invented*.'(Renfrew 1969:15 emphasis in the original)

The implication of Renfrew's argument was that an understanding of process and invention, as opposed to origins and transmission, required that archaeologists shift the scale of their analyses towards local or regional mechanisms of historical change (Renfrew 1974). There are problems, for the claim that it was essentially local mechanisms and conditions which drove historical change turned out to be little more than an assertion. Whilst we may doubt the usefulness of diffussionist explanations in which historical dynamics were assumed to have been instigated by some kind of external transmission from a distant source, this does not automatically require that we accept an entirely local genesis for all the historical trajectories which archaeologists observe. In the specific case of south-east Europe, Renfrew certainly demonstrated that the synchronisms traditionally assumed to exist between the cultural sequences of the Aegean and the Balkans and which grounded the diffusionist narrative were unsustainable, but this was not the same thing as establishing the operation of entirely local mechanisms for either the developing material conditions or the social process which brought metallurgy about.

Renfrew's approach towards conceptualising the spatial scale over which the mechanisms which drove cultural change operated is to assume that such mechanisms primarily operated through the systemic organisation of the 'basic social group' (Renfrew 1984:30 ff.). Human social organisation is recognisable in the archaeological record, according to Renfrew, because a simple cellular pattern in the territorial organisation of archaeological sites reflects the repeated modular distribution of similarly sized socio-political groups. In the case of relatively complex societies Renfrew terms these social groups 'polities', that is they are the autonomous or self-governing and politically independent units of a society. Whilst social evolution concerns the different degrees of complexity achieved by the internal organisation of these polities, and is therefore supposedly strongly driven by the internal development of specialist functions and increasing inhomogeneity, none the less polities still interact at different degrees of intensification with their neighbours. These processes of 'polity interaction' have resulted, again according to Renfrew, in the distribution of shared generalised cultural traits across a region along with the distribution of items widely traded from a single source. The result is an understanding of change in which:

'change is seen to emerge from the assemblage of interacting polities, that is to say it operates in most cases at the regional level. ... While analysis at the local level, in terms, for instance, of the intensification of production, is always necessary, and an assessment of the significance of long distance contacts equally desirable, it is suggested ... that in many cases it is the intermediate-scale interactions between local but independent communities which are perhaps the most informative... The significant unit is thus seen ... to be the larger community beyond the polity level, comprised of loosely related, yet politically independent, interacting groups. It is here, for instance, that the processes of ethnic formation must in may cases operate, and here too that the foundations for the later emergence of the nation state are laid.' (Renfrew 1986:6 f.)

Discussions such as this therefore tend to concern themselves with identifying spatially the social unit of production, and not the entire spatial conditions necessary for the reproduction of the total conditions of life.

An alternative approach has been to accept that a system of local social reproduction—the operation of Renfrew's 'basic social unit'—will always depend for the material conditions of its existence upon a system of exchange relations which extend well beyond that social unit. The conditions which operate external to the social group may therefore help to determine the history of the local processes of reproduction. In European Bronze Age studies this case was first made with considerable clarity by Kristiansen in his study of the deposition of Bronze Age metalwork in Denmark. Recognising that all the bronze deposited in Denmark, including that significantly deposited as part of ritual sacrifice in grave rituals, had to be procured from central southern Europe, Kristiansen proposed a relatively simple model by which local political structures were constructed through different exchange relations which united 'local' production with that from further afield. The political structure therefore distinguished between different types of exchange in which local relations were defined by the exchange of local products (such as agricultural products and food) and where long-distance exchange entered the local system at specific points, most probably through the contact established and controlled by elites. Thus a twofold process is envisaged by which the structuring of the local political unit through asymmetrical exchanges of local materials was further transformed by the elite's ability to enter into long distance exchange networks by which it procured exotic materials (including in the Danish case metals). These exotics then entered a limited and controlled circulation within the local system, reinforcing local political obligations and very often being consumed in acts of votive display (Kristiansen 1978).

There is a distinct evolutionary mechanism linked to a politics of scale which is assumed to have been operating in cases such as this (cf. Friedman and Rowlands 1977). A trajectory of increasing social complexity and ranking, the growth of hierachial systems, is linked directly with the ability of the local unit to grow to a point at which long-distance political alliances and exchange partners could be secured by the elite. These ensured the availability of exotic materials which were necessary for the elite to maintain its political dominance through specialist exchanges and sacrifice. The need to procure long-distance exchange partners would thus have driven forward local cycles of production and consumption (competitive displays in feasting for example) by which those elites maintained their local dominance in the face of their competitors. Such local consumption operated within given ecological limits. Kristiansen argued that regions with more fragile ecological systems would have failed to sustain the productivity necessary to service these local demands and in turn would have failed to sustain the political structures necessary to procure metals and other exotic materials. The effects of these failures are marked by the increasing use of old and worn items of metalwork in the graves of such regions during the Danish Bronze Age.

There is a degree of consensus in the archaeological literature concerning the operation of a European Bronze Age world system. The local social unit is taken as representing the basic unit of production, although the cycles through which that unit reproduced itself drew upon resources derived from a wider geographical and social world. This view accepts that the position occupied by the local social unit within the larger world system directed the history of that local unit in a far more deterministic way than is perhaps allowed for by Renfrew. The exchange networks which tied the social unit together internally, and those which bound that and other units into the regional components of the world system, not only represented contrasting geographical scales but different political values. For example, the political status of a local elite which was created from internal exchange obligations could be converted into an increasingly ritualised status by the appropriation of exotic materials and their use in votive display and consumption (Friedman & Rowlands 1977: Figs. 3 & 4). The conversion between the two different scales of exchange, local and regional, therefore embedded within it a procedure of political reproduction. The world system is effectively a system of political values. Renfrew's objection to the general applicability of these ideas would appear to turn upon the argument that a number of forms of contact between polities, including emulation and trade, did not function to structure political relations in the way implied by world systems analysis (Renfrew 1993:7). None the less it remains generally accepted that contacts did occur between polities, that these are directly represented in the distribution of materials which are recovered archaeologically, and that such contacts contributed to the historical development of the individual polities and to the overall development of the global system.

Critique

There are two strands operating in the current programme of archaeological analysis. The first is essentially empirical and it involves the spatial and temporal ordering of the material, essentially the construction of distribution maps. In these patterns it is possible to identify regionally comparable forms of material production and levels of consumption, as well as trace the movement of raw materials and some artefacts from a place of origin to another place of deposition. All these patterns are regarded as representing the material consequences of social processes.

The second strand involves the conceptualisation of those processes, and here a general consensus exists, at least at one level, for it isolates for analysis a basic social unit of habitual associations. Those associations between people functioned as the fundamental unit of production in which relations of rank, status and gender were practised as balanced or asymmetrical relationships of exchange. Such units were situated within a larger global system, the operation of which accounts fairly directly for the form of the archaeological record in the large scale distribution of sites and artefacts. The distinction thus drawn is between mechanisms of production and exchange which were 'internal' to the social unit and the processes of exchange which operated 'externally' and between these units. As Rowlands has noted, this position is 'characteristic of many general analyses' and is partly a reflection of our own understanding of the development of the modern nation state and the position of international trade as a mechanism of interaction between states (Rowlands 1987:3 f.). Social evolution is often charted as a path towards an increasingly 'complex' internal structure as characteristic of the social unit, and increasing levels and distances of exchange between these social units.

Such analyses represent our view of the lives of others. They are constructed out of the ways we synthesise the material consequences of those lives and chart their systemic regularities (the overall movement from one part of Europe to another of items which have been exchanged, for example). It is a view only made possible by the distance which now separates us from the conditions under which those material conditions were inhabited. From our position we appear to see the overall picture, an objectification of the 'international connections and regularities' that were 'unknown to prehistoric peoples'. The material from which this view is constructed seems real enough and unambiguous, indeed the whole purpose of archaeological analysis is to reduce ambiguity in the material, by detailed description, the analysis of stratigraphic context, and by physical and chemical characterisation. This is a reality, but it is our reality, one which we make in the construction of our academic discourse and through which we maintain our authority to operate within such a discourse. It is a politics of scale, and it is part of a contemporary politics, in the same way that the anthropological discourse is also situated in a contemporary world.

The problem with this perspective is the absence of that other human agency from any part of it. The patterns we record in the material remains become increasingly clear-cut and their significance almost self-evident to us. Thus:

'Horses reached temperate Europe in larger numbers as a result of the Pit-Grave expansion on the steppes, itself made possible by the use of wheeled vehicles. While the cultures of south-east Europe were immediately transformed, those of the north and west—where farming had been adopted more recently, and 'echo' phenomena were still occurring—absorbed them more selectively, and continued a megalithic pattern until the more radical changes with the spread of the Corded Ware and Bell-Beaker complexes, paralleled by the emergence of the Pit-Grave complex on the steppes. The large areas covered by these phenomena are symptomatic of a new scale of contacts, ...' (Sherratt 1993:16 f.)

All these processes appear relatively abstract, a history without the agents who created it. Our view of the totality enables us to characterise how the material conditions had come about, the consequences of long term processes certainly, but history was made because under those conditions people lived and acted on the basis of an understanding of their world which was constructed through the experiences available to them. Rowlands observes that:

'Those who adhere to a scientific, objectivist stance can never cope with the real emotional forces that shape people's perceptions of their own past and the role it plays in the present. And those who espouse a dogged subjectivism espouse a relativism that can make nothing of the ironies and unintended consequences of the history that impinge upon sentient human action.' (Rowlands 1987:2)

The presence of the social agent transforms our conceptualisation of the human social condition because we now have to accommodate conscious practice and strategic intention into our histories. The social institutions which we study were the consequence of routine strategic practices, what held those practices together over time and space, and the ways certain routines were challenged and alternatives became effective, are the issue of historical analysis. It is here that the crux of the matter lies, for the maintenance of routine by conscious beings was the maintenance of certain interpretations of, and expectations about, the inhabited world. And whilst certain interpretations may have achieved a dominant position against alternatives, their frailty may ultimately have been exposed. It was the existence of competing and alternative realities which defined a social condition enabling the available material conditions to be occupied and used. The routines of social action reworked those competing interpretations materially, giving the social system the particular form and historical trajectory which it followed. The significance of the material world was therefore inherently ambiguous and open to challenge, it is precisely this which defined its historical quality. That world thus represented a number of provisional and competing perspectives and realities for human inhabitation.

Global identities

An enormous number of structural modifications were made to the material conditions of temperate and Mediterranean Europe between the middle of the third and the middle of the first millennia BC, the period traditionally assigned to the Bronze Age. These modifications were on-going, whether they were the increasing diversification of crops, the management and clearance of woodland, processes of soil erosion, the design-modification and deposition of artefacts, population change, changes in settlement architecture, or changes in animal populations. We should stress this idea of a dynamic because by it we can begin to enquire into the agencies by which such a dynamic operated. Natural properties certainly played their part—the decay of materials, climatic change, the chemical depletion of soils, breeding cycles and fertility, and so forth—but even here the ways these properties operated in detail, the kinds of consequences which arose from them, were mediated by the agency of human beings.

The transformation of the material world and the reproduction of humanity were processes which were, indeed remain, intimately related. This relationship, between the emergent forms of the material and the conscious and knowledgeable actions of a self-aware humanity, has always been lived out as a knowledgeable occupation of the world upon which that humanity worked. If we believe that the different patterns of deposition recovered by archaeologists represent regional differences of political power (the 'core' and 'periphery' of a world system for example) then we also have to allow that those who inhabited and made those different patterns come into being, on a day by day basis, will have seen their world according to other logics. And in so doing they will also have known themselves in terms of those other logics. The difference between their ways of knowing the conditions which they inhabited and our ways of knowing those conditions should be one of the things which interests us, because it defines our relationship with a past out of which we create history. It does not define a difference between an objectively ordered reality and one which was merely glimpsed. Instead we are looking, as Rowlands argues, at different sides of the same coin.

Among the parameters out of which the world is known and our places within it are fixed are the parameters of time and space. One way of understanding the differences of the past in general, and of defining the Bronze Age in particular, is to recognise time and space not as fixed forms of description but as resources which could be structured and controlled, and through which differences in human identity could be created (cf Helms 1988).

There are perhaps three qualities of space as a resource which we might consider. The first is that quality through which it is possible to know of the existence of absent and distant places. This is the space which recedes to the horizon, it holds the places inhabited by strangers and maps the distances travelled. The references which may have been made to this quality of space as places currently occupied may have been through the presence of exotic materials, although such materials would have had to have been recognised and spoken of. These materials may have carried with them and made present, in the references which they made to other places, their history of origination and the stories of their movement. Archaeologists are used to considering the presencing of this spatial quality in artefact exchange and deposition, where the power of the object lay in its foreignness, and where such powers were also given to those who took part in these exchanges. What has not been so widely discussed is the ways objects of dress and personal decoration become increasingly aligned with these values during the Bronze Age. Complex bodily adornment which used exotic materials and geographically widespread forms of representation is most notably encountered in the grave assemblages of the period. These deposits are frequently taken as indicators of wealth and differences in ranked status. Alternatively we might look on such material as being one of the ways in which the body was a created as a cultural signifier whose referent was to a spatial quality of distance. In such cases the biographical histories of objects and of the body itself may have converged in such a way as to ensure that the body's identity was expressed in terms of distances travelled and of absent origins.

To claim membership or origin among a more far flung or distant community such as this brings me to the second quality of space which was reworked in the European Bronze Age. This is the quality of belonging, of finding one's place among a generalised and widely dispersed community of practices and appearances. These are the practices which suppressed the strangeness of travel and displacement and which enabled at least a certain level of relocation and comprehension among a recognisable if distant community. In face to face exchanges the essential processes for facilitating such relocation include the service and exchange of food and drink. By the late Neolithic a number of very widespread and relatively uniform traditions of service vessels emerged from northern Europe to the Mediterranean, they include the Beaker assemblages of central western Europe and the range of cups and pouring vessels distributed around the Aegean. A common set of vessel forms indicate widespread conventions of hospitality and disciplines of friendship, but these disciplines may have been firmly bounded, for whilst some may have been able to move widely and recognise a place for themselves over extensive distances, others may have been excluded at a local level.

Both these qualities of space were inhabited and experienced in ways which were autobiographical, they were the ways in which the body spoke of itself in terms of its identity, history, rights and obligations. Such systems of reference cut across the local social units upon which so much emphasis has been placed by archaeology. These other inhabited spaces introduced into the local political realm the absence of distant places and of personal histories, and they facilitated movement between these local communities. But if such spatial experiences made the body as a social being, giving it a history and place in which to reside, then the ability to monitor space and to define its value will have operated as a way of controlling those bodies. Political control is essentially a discourse of monitoring, and the third quality of space is that of a resource which is defined, mapped and ordered by a particular authority. Within the technologies of the Bronze Age the means for achieving such political control were limited. Where such control arose it was likely to have established the redefinition and re-ordering of distant places according to a single political logic by demanding the presence of people and of products from those places to submit to that logic. Unable to monitor and to map those other places in the ways which are available to the modern state, Bronze Age political control demanded that distance was collapsed and re-ordered under its domain by importing it to its own locale. In their discussion of the palaces of the Aegean Renfrew and Cherry have consistently attempted to set these structures into the central places of local polities (cf Cherry 1986). However the palaces of Crete lay on the southern margins of the Aegean archipelago and their role was perhaps more extensive. Their complex architecture of dramatic facades, processional entrances, open areas of congregation and enclosed cult centres, and the attendant store rooms and work-shops, may all have operated to 'call in' the people and products of distant places according to an order and a logic which was defined by those places alone. The times of submission, of processional entrance and the ordering of goods effectively collapsed distance and re-wrote it under a single political domain.

The interplay of the three qualities of space which I have outlined here, through the specific material conditions of the European Bronze Age and under the varying geographical conditions of Mediterranean and northern Europe, made a series of intercutting global systems in which categories of humanity were created and forms of political authority were reproduced. It was only by knowing the world in such ways that the practices of these varied and complex populations could operate to create the material residues which archaeologists study today. Such material does not speak for itself or represent an essential logic for archaeological scrutiny, rather it reminds us of the distance separating purposeful life and its residual consequences. It is that distance which maps the object of archaeological study.

References

Cherry, J. F. 1986. Polities and palaces: some problems in Minoan state formation. In Renfrew, C. & Cherry, J. F. (eds.), *Peer Polity Interaction and Socio-Political Change*. Cambridge, 19–45.

Edens, C. M. & Kohl, P. L. 1993. Trade and world systems in Early Bronze Age Western Asia. In Scarre, C. & Healy, F. (eds.), *Trade and Exchange in Prehistoric Europe*. Oxford, 17–34.

Friedman, J. 1994. *Cultural Identity and Global Process*. London.

Friedman, J. & Rowlands, J. M. 1977. Notes towards an epigenetic model of the evolution of 'civilisation'. In Friedman, J. & Rowlands, M. J. (eds.), *The Evolution of Social Systems*. London, 201–276.

Helms, M. W. 1988. *Ulysses' Sail*. Princeton.

Kristiansen, K. 1978. The consumption of wealth in Bronze Age Denmark: A study in the dynamics of economic processes in tribal societies. In Kristiansen, K. & Paludan-Müller, C. (eds.), *New Directions in Scandinavian Archaeology*. Copenhagen, 158–191.

— 1993. From Villanova to Seddin. The reconstruction of an elite exchange network during the eighth century BC. In Scarre, C. & Healy, F. (eds.), *Trade and Exchange in Prehistoric Europe*. Oxford, 143–151.

Renfrew, C. 1969. The Autonomy of the South-East European Copper Age. *Proceedings of the Prehistoric Society* 1969, No.35, 12–47.
— 1984. *Approaches to Social Archaeology*. Edinburgh.
— 1986. Introduction: peer polity interaction and socio-political change. In Renfrew, C. & Cherry, J. F. (eds.), *Peer Polity Interaction and Socio-Political Change*. Cambridge, 1–18.
— 1993. Trade Beyond the Material. In Scarre, C. & Healy, F. (eds.), *Trade and Exchange in Prehistoric Europe*. Oxford, 5–16.
Rowlands, M. 1987. Centre and periphery: a review of a concept. In Rowlands, M., Larsen, M. & Kristiansen, K. (eds.), *Centre and Periphery in the Ancient World*. Cambridge, 1–11.
Sherratt, A. 1993. What would a Bronze-Age world system look like? Relations between temperate Europe and the Mediterranean in later prehistory. *Journal of European Archaeology* 1993, No.1, 1–57.
Wallerstein, I. 1974. *The Modern World-System*. London.

Changing World-View of Prehistoric Populations[1]

By Ezra B.W. Zubrow and Michael Frachetti

Introduction

In the light of a pale dusk, *silhouetted* figures plod past a few thorny trees on distant horizon. They climb, spin, gavotte across the skyline's stage, and disappear never to rise again. Each commands the scene for only a brief moment. Then they are replaced by a seemingly endless progression of would be refugees. Our fascination with the 'marche' is not accidental. It speaks to one of the central events of our actuality—our ultimate movement through existence. Sometimes the marche has been to the slow beat of the stately waltz other times to the frantic pace of the highland fling. Individual marchers have performed acts of greatest heroism- ministering to their partners before collapsing exhausted to an unknown grave. Others have been universally condemned for plundering the homes of their fallen brethren and even the bodies of the silhouetted figures themselves. As one moves closer to the horizon, one sees groups of people struggling to move through a small gap—reaching for life itself (Fig. 1).

This paper cannot examine the entire scope of the changing world view of prehistoric population. The last half century has been a time of important theoretical, methodological and substantive innovations and discoveries. Rather, this paper will be examine four major topics. It is similar to a wine tasting. Not all wines will be tasted—nor will the taster completely drain the each glass. However, the taster is able to intuit a sense of the stock and the reader a sense of the changing world view. The four topics are:

- The Changing View of Prehistoric Data from Material to Population
- The Changing View of Demographic Contemporaneity
- The Changing View of Prehistoric Population Movement
- The Changing View of the Demographic Stability of the Village

Changing View of Prehistoric Data from Material to Population

The growth of the population concept

The single most important change in the archaeological literature in the last five decades has been the transformation from the "object" to the "person". It

Fig. 1. Reaching for life by Elka Kazmiercz.

is the change from the artifact, site, and culture oriented conception of archaeology to the person, village, and population oriented understanding of prehistory. This is the transformation from the object to the "person". Much of this change can be traced to the wide spread acceptance of the principles of both a "more scientific-processual" and a more "deconstructionist and post-processual" archaeology. With these came a concomitant interest in the person both as a member of a population and as an individual.

In the broader non-archaeological academic world, the last one hundred and fifty years may be divided into three approximately equal periods. One might describe the last half of the nineteenth century as the age of observation and biology—the great voyages of the Beagle (Darwin 1933) and the theories of Wallace (1870) and Darwin (1964, 1979) characterize the time. Archaeological studies either followed the format of history or were put into the service of the new views of the development of humankind.

The first half of this century could be describe as the "age of experiment and physics". It was the period of atomic fission and fusion as well as the theories of Einstein (1945) and Fermi (1956) and their application by Oppenheimer (1989) and others. Archaeological innovation focused on Libby's (1995) radiocarbon techniques and the revolution in time space systematics. This process of filling the gaps in the archaeological record was systematically applied to the artifactual materials around the world. The result of this "gapsmanship" was the generally agreed upon prehistory of the world. (Zubrow *et al.* 1974) To be truthful, it was agreed upon in broad strokes. The details frequently were a matter of bitter controversy. However, the development of a general prehistoric record resulted from being able to date more precisely archaeological sites and cultures.

The second half of the century may be characterized as the age of information and molecular genetics. The major discoveries of the systems theorists (1976) and their application to the processing of information by computers resulted in the information age and the globalization of information. Its archaeological correlate was first the "new" or "processual" archaeology (Clarke 1968; Binford 1972) and later the "post-processual" archaeology (Hodder 1987). The former focused on the system and the population's behavior; the latter focused on the information and the individual's knowledge. Simultaneously, the equally important revolution in genetics was undertaken by such scholars as Watson (1968), Crick (1992), Lederberg (1981), and Cavalli Sforza (1981, 1994). Analyzing the double helix, mapping genes, genetic patenting and the human genome had an impact on archaeological and anthropological studies. Scholars attempted to type DNA from prehistoric skeletal populations and to reconstruct ancestry from studies of mitochrondrial DNA.

The history of archaeology is ironic. During the seventies and eighties as the principles of a more scientific archaeology became generally accepted, the labels and "schools of thought" were rejected. "I am not a new archaeologist but I am studying hypotheses about Paleolithic adaptation". "I am not a post-processual archaeologist-I believe in history".

At the same time as the "scientific" aspects of the discipline were being rejected, the rise of post-processual archaeology took place. The importance of understanding the individual, their cognitive structures, of doing "reflexive" archaeology was a priority of the nineties. It could only be done in the context of changing the subject of archaeology from the "object" to the "person—a transformation from a "material field' to a "people field".

The changing world view of prehistoric data

The changes in the professional literature noted above are reflected in the popular view, the world view of archaeology. This world view partially has been created upon an increasing focus of the world's media on archaeology. Although great or sensational discoveries still make the news, there has been an increasing tendency for the press to put them in a broader context—a context that is frequently demographic. If one considers a small survey of 2300 journals undertaken at the beginning of 1997, several interesting trends occur.[2] They are sustained across differences in continent, class, or urbanity. There

Table 1. *The number of archaeological news stories from 2300 journals by date and type*

Type of News Stories (1)	Number of News Stories (2)	Number of News Stories with Population (3)	Percentage {(2)/(3)}* 100
Archaeological during the last two years	33,587	4,570	13.6
Archaeological prior to the last two years	76,586	8,777	11.4

Table 2. *Popular Archaeological News Stories from 2300 journals*

Type of News Stories (1)	Number of News Stories (2)	Number of News Stories with Population (3)	Percentage {(2)/(3)}* 100
Out of Africa	4,395	925	21
Iceman	202	59	29
Contemporaenous Neanderthals and **Homo sapiens sapiens**	401	169	42
Contemporaenous Neanderthals, **Homo erectus**, and **Homo sapiens sapiens**	152	71	47

was little variance whether one considered European, Asian, African or New World papers; nor whether it was the broadsheets or the tabloids, nor whether the venues were rural or urban. The results are shown in tabs. 1 through 3 and may be quickly summarized.

Five inferences may be drawn from these tables.

– The number of archaeological news stories is surprisingly high—more than 100,000.
– Furthermore, the number is increasing. During the last two years there were more than 75,000 stories, e.g. more than twice all the previous stories.
– There is an increasing percentage of stories that are concerned with demographic topics.
– During the last two years popular interest was greatest in the "Out of Africa", the "Iceman", and the contemporaneity of different hominids. Each has major demographic implications.
– Finally, the popular interest in the demographic aspects of prehistoric societies centres on the ageing of the population and the family rather than migration, fertility, and mortality.

Table 3 *News stories concerning prehistory concerned with demographic topics by demographic topic*[3]

Category of News Stories (last two years)	Number of News Stories (last two years)
Prehistory and ageing of population	4,361
Prehistory and family	3,123
Prehistory and migration	542
Prehistory and fertility	420
Prehistory and mortality	170

Changing View of Demographic Contemporaneity

The new contemporaneity and the new origins: succession versus interaction

Focusing on the penultimate topic, one might describe the broad change in the world view as the "New Contemporaneity". The traditional view of human succession was that *Homo erectus* was followed by *Homo sapiens neanderthalensis* who was followed in turn by *Homo sapiens sapiens*. Succession has been replaced by contemporaneity. This changing world view has come in two steps. First, were the relatively recent discoveries at Djebel Qafzeh and St. Cesaire. The dating of the sapiens and the Neanderthals at these sites have made *Homo sapien sapiens* and *Homo sapien neanderthalenis* contemporaries from approximately 100,000 years to 25,000 years ago.

The second step occurred this year with the dating of the Homo Erectus strata in Java. Until recently, most paleoanthropologists believed that *Homo erectus* was the "grandfather" of modern humans becoming extinct approximately 100,000 years ago. From this perspective they never coexisted with modern humans (*Homo sapiens sapiens*). However, the new date for the Ngandong fossil skulls by an international team of researchers places *Homo erectus* as late as 53,000 to 27,000 years ago.

By this new date, modern humans already had existed for 50,000 years and had colonized most of the world. *Homo erectus and Neanderthals are not our grandparents and parents but our siblings.* It is the evolutionary equivalent of going into a dance hall and seeing Queen Victoria doing the macarena.

If these dates "hold up" under scrutiny, the multiregional theory of human origins will be shaken. This theory proposes that modern humans evolved approximately simultaneously in Africa, Asia and Europe from populations of *Homo erectus*. In Southeast Asia the processes of hominid change evolutionary transition began as far back as two million years ago. The Ngandong fossils had been considered to be one of the best examples of this transition.

The new dates mean that sweeping migrations may populate the world instead of gradual in situ succession. It brings new meaning to the "Out of

Africa" hypothesis. The Indonesian discovery implies that *Homo sapiens* migrated to Asia from elsewhere in the world. Modern humans first evolved in Africa and later swept out of that continent to wipe out populations of less advanced Homo erectus, originally the Middle East and later in Asia. It must not have been easy. For there is an old lineage of *Homo erectus* that has been very successful having existed there for an incredibly long time. Only be another very determined hominid is capable of displacing the predecessor. In short, gradual evolution is replaced by punctuated equilibrium and Darwin slowly rolls over in his grave.

The demographic issues are many. It means a change of focus from succession to interaction. Coexistence implies competition for resources and for area. Success may be the result of more rapid fertility, less rapid mortality, an ability to migrate faster and easier, and perhaps an improved ability to fend off disease.

Having examined some broad generalities about the changing world view of prehistoric population, two more substantive examples will be discussed.

Changing View of Prehistoric Population Movement

Processual, post-processual, and cognitive archaeology: a changing view of migration

Traditionally, archaeologists have viewed migration through the prism of the changing distribution of artifacts on the landscape. If, however, one begins to examine migration through the lens of people moving through the countryside a very different picture emerges. The word migration is derived from "migrare" and means either a temporary or a permanent change of residence by one person or by a group of people. It may take numerous forms. The forms associated with sedentary populations are very distinct from the life-styles of the non-sedentary populations that follow the game or the herds.

Migration is partially a matter of perspective. The view of the migrant 'en route' differs from both 'those who are left behind' and 'those who already have arrived at the destination'. Some of these multiple perspectives are formalized. Thus, migration from the viewpoint of the place of origin results in analyses of emigration (outmigration) or conversely from the point of view of the destination in studies of immigration (inmigration). The 'en route' viewpoint is the least developed.

Migration has been one the most important prehistoric and historic processes impacting human activities. From prehistoric times and geographically throughout Asia, Europe, Africa, and the New World, there have been many mass migrations. "Out of Africa", "the adaptive radiation through Europe and Asia", the "invasion of Australia", "crossing Beringia", the Biblical "Exodus", the over running of the Roman Empire by the Huns, the Visigoths , the Vandals, as well as others, the continual invasions of Europe by Arabs, Mongols,

Franks, Vikings, Christian Crusaders, and Turks, the ten million slaves extracted from Africa during the 17th through the 19th centuries, and the sixty million people who left Europe to seek new homes during the 19th and 20th centuries are structurally similar in many ways.

Previous archaeologists have measured the similarity of artifacts to determine if they originate from a distant source or developed in situ. Perhaps, if one wishes to understand the past, one should ask what are the processes by which migration takes place and what are the decisions individual migrants make. What are the processes that differentiate refugees from migrants? Refugees reflect non-voluntary movement while migration is voluntary. Rather than ask whether sets of artifacts were traded or represent hoards abandoned by passing migrants, archaeologists might more relevantly contrast "determinate" from "non-determinate" migration. The former occurs when the refugee or migrant knows from where they are leaving and to where they are going. It frequently takes place when migrants move for economic reasons. "Non-determinate" migration transpires when the refugee or migrant knows from where they are leaving but has no idea regarding their destination. This frequently occurs when refugees are fleeing military actions.

One relates these contrasts of migrants to refugees and determinate to non-determinate migration to changes in archaeological theory. Among the tenets of both 'post processual' and 'cognitive archaeology' are the necessity of examining more fully the motivation and knowledge of individuals. The migration/ refugee contrast speaks to motivation while the determinate/ non-determinate speaks to the knowledge held by individuals. There are significant differences in motivation for movement between migrants and refugees and significant differences in the knowledge that individuals possess between those migrants who know where they are going and those who only know that they are fleeing where they are. These differences inform both processual and post processual archaeology. They are modeled in the next section.

Models

In this section of the paper, several models are described. They are called for ease of terminology:

– the pull model
– the push model
– the traveling center model
– the bi-nodal model

All of these models have the following assumptions and labels in common. Individuals are located in space. They may either reside at a location or move through space to another location. Individuals have "needs" that they wish to fulfil. They obtain their sustenance from the area in which they live or from

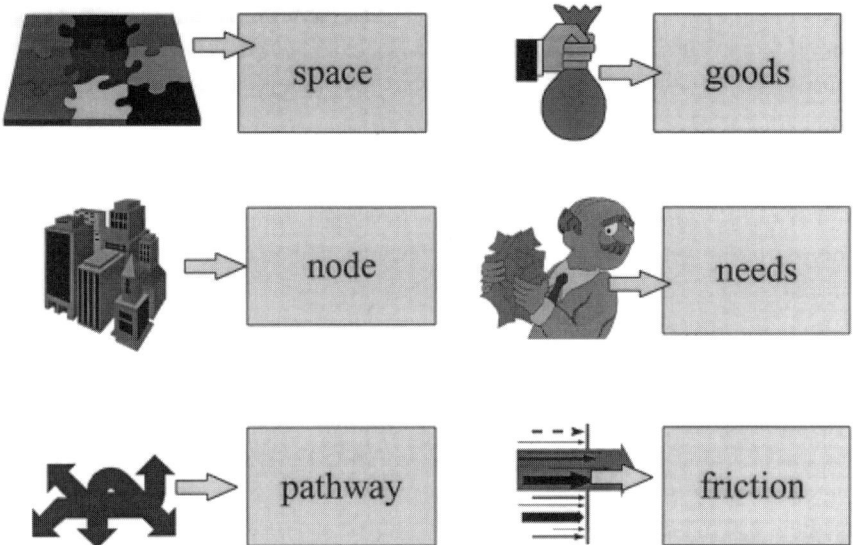

Fig. 2. Some standard elements of the models.

other areas. The spatial resolution at which these systems may be viewed may be changed. The number of individuals, the amount of sustenance, and the sum of the "needs" may be aggregated.

The various forms of property that people want and which fulfill various "needs" are labeled "goods". The term is used as in but not limited to "subsistence goods." The various individual "desires" are "needs." These include the usual "needs" for food, shelter, mates, social interaction, aesthetic and religious expression as well as numerous others. Some are reflections of individual idiosyncrasies; others are reflections of cultural norms. Some are the results of chance; others are reflections of norms beyond the control of individuals and their circumstances. Thus, individuals and their "needs" may be grouped, aggregated and analyzed. One may speak of "populations" whose aggregated "desires" may be expressed "demand"

The spaces that these individuals inhabit and through which they move are similarly constrained. The locations they inhabit whether rural or urban are termed "nodes". The routes that people or "goods" follow from one place to another will be labeled the "pathways". There is a cost for either individuals or "goods" to travel from "node" to "node." It is a reflection of distance and difficulty of travel. Each pathway imposes a certain degree of difficulty to the traveler which for standardization of meaning is labeled "friction". Finally, the traveler's ability to overcome this "friction" is designated "proficiency" (Fig. 2). [4]

The Pull model

The first model is the linear pull model with constant "demand" and increasing "proficiency". In this model, the "demand" for "goods" is set to a high constant. As a group's "proficiency" increases, they are able to travel longer and more difficult paths to satisfy their "needs". There is a relative reduction in "friction" costs as "proficiency" increases. The result is a growing enticement from "nodes" at ever greater distances to obtain "goods" to fulfill "needs". This pulls the group to move greater distances. Thus the "demand" is met through increased travel. Imagine an individual named Alanya who is located at a "node" called "Clevedon". She requires a relatively high, constant and continual need for "goods". As her "proficiency" for travel increases, the "goods" located at ever further "nodes' such as Tickenham, Nailsea, and even Bristol will be seen as reasonable places to satisfy her "demand". Whether she makes the trip to the new destination is determined by what Alanya knows is available at a distance and by her increased "proficiency". She is being *pulled* by the knowledge of available "goods" at a more distant location. It is the determinant, post processual case.

The Push Model

In this model, the "demand" is variable and increasing. However, the "proficiency" and the "ease of travel" is a constant. One imagines the population of a "node" growing rapidly. As the "needs" of the group of people living at the node increases each individual is pushed to travel further and further to get the items that are necessary for survival. In other words, more and more of the population are *pushed* out of the "node" to find their "needs" met at further and further distances. Imagine a second individual named Alexis who is located at a "node" called "Weston". As the population grows faster and faster, there is not enough "goods" to support him in the style that he wishes. He leaves the "node" searching for "goods" elsewhere. The "push" model has a very different orientation than the "pull" model. It is non-determinant and processual.

In both the above models the movement is from one "node" only. This constraint will be relaxed in following models.

The Traveling Center (Sequential or Step Model)

Both the "proficiency" and the demand is constant in the traveling center model. It is a step process across space and a sequential process through time. A very common set of migratory events is represented. For example, a migrant wishes to move from west to east. First, he attempts to reach the "node" furthest from his "node" of origin. Usually, the migrant chooses the path that allows him to maximize the distance toward his goal. However, he may have more than one choice of "path". He picks the "path" based upon prior knowledge of the amounts of "goods" at the "nodes" and the amounts of "friction" of the "pathways". However, he may make mistakes. In some cases, the "path" selected does not supply sufficient "goods" or the migrant's "proficiency" was inadequate to overcome the "path's" friction. In this case, the migrant is forced to return to the previous "node", and select a different route in hope of meeting the "demand." Once the new "node" is reached it becomes the "node" of origin. The process is repeated until the entire west to east trip is completed. In short, the population recursively moves along the routes to the most peripheral center constrained by both the migrant's "proficiency" and the necessity of meeting "demand".

The Bi-nodal Model

Two bi-nodal models are discussed. They are based upon the same assumption base as the single nodal models. The difference is there are two migration streams. The migrants leave simultaneously from two nodes rather than one.

– Traveling Center Model

The bi-nodal "traveling center" model is similar to the sequential traveling center model above but portrays a slightly more complex set of interactions. The "bi-nodal" model's migration originates at two "nodes" simultaneously. The end points of the models are also different. The sequential single "node" model was stopped after a full west to east tour was completed. The bi-nodal model was stopped when the two migratory parties meet—one traveling east the other traveling west.

– Constant Center Model

The bi-nodal "constant center" model resembles the "push" model where the "proficiency" is set very high. The "demand" is also set sufficiently high that the system is full. The model is stopped when the two groups of migrants "meet". This procedure also reveals the *least cost* path between the two centers.

The Human Settlement of Åland

The models were simulated in a limited Scandinavian test region—the Åland islands. They lie between Finland and Sweden. Today, a semi-autonomous province of Finland, there are strong linguistic and cultural ties to Sweden. A long history testifies to various populations moving through the islands for it is a natural routing for the small boats crossing the Bothnia. A brief timeline of the settlement of Åland will illustrate the value of this data as well as its appropriateness as a "laboratory".

The first settlers who arrived on Åland appear to be members of the Comb Ceramic culture stemming from mainland Finland. The earliest sites date to the late fifth millennium BC. The shallow culture layers and the lack of contemporaneously available exploitable resources indicate these dwellings were semi-permanent. Both Swedish and Finnish archaeologists speculate that the first settlements were bases for seasonal sealing expeditions from the Finnish mainland (Alhonen and Väkeväinen 1980). These settlers were followed by people who belonged to the Pitted Ware culture emigrating from the Swedish mainland. They are distinguished by ceramic style and by permanent settlements.

Agriculture and the domestication of livestock occurred in the archipelago during the subsequent Bronze Age (Nuñez 1986a, 1990). The flat meadows along the sounds provided excellent grazing land and the inland plateaus supplied land for tillage. The broad spatial extent of the settlement conforms to the necessities of a pastoral economy with a population of active shepherds. The scarcity of metal resources on Åland meant stone was still the primary material for tool construction during this and later periods.

The Iron Age was a period of florescence. It saw the greatest increase in human population and activity. There was a great influx of immigration from the west and the southwest. Partially, it was the result of increasing land area due to uplift. The land surface was more than two times greater than the land that greeted the first Ålanders. Agriculture flourished (Fries 1963) Increased land, increased agriculture, and the use of iron resulted in prehistoric settlements reaching their apex at the end of the first millennium AD.[5] Åland lost its reclusive nature and became a hub for Bothnian maritime activity. Its locality, the short maritime reaches, and its inherent nature as an archipelago made it very conducive for seafaring economies.

To minimize temporal inconsistency the models were simulated using only Iron age site locations. These date approximately 500 BC–500 AD. The sites are burial mounds which are marked by cairns. A network of pathways providing a prehistoric route system were generated from these. There was no apriori loading of the settlement hierarchy.

Åland's geography is particularly appropriate for these models. The universe is relatively constrained; the relatively short distances between sites conforms to how most scholars currently visualize most prehistoric migration; and the geographic size and the number of sites are manageable. The decay functions for numbers of migration and number of people migrating with distance are thought to be very steep. Furthermore, it should be noted that the constantly changing geographical conditions did not radically change the spectrum of human activities. Rather, they simply changed the location of the activities for "the environmental zones were seldom destroyed, they merely shifted" (Nuñez 1995).

Results

The results may be examined either visually or statistically. In this paper visual results are presented for they have the advantage of ease of understanding.

38 *Ezra B. W. Zubrow and Michael Frachetti*

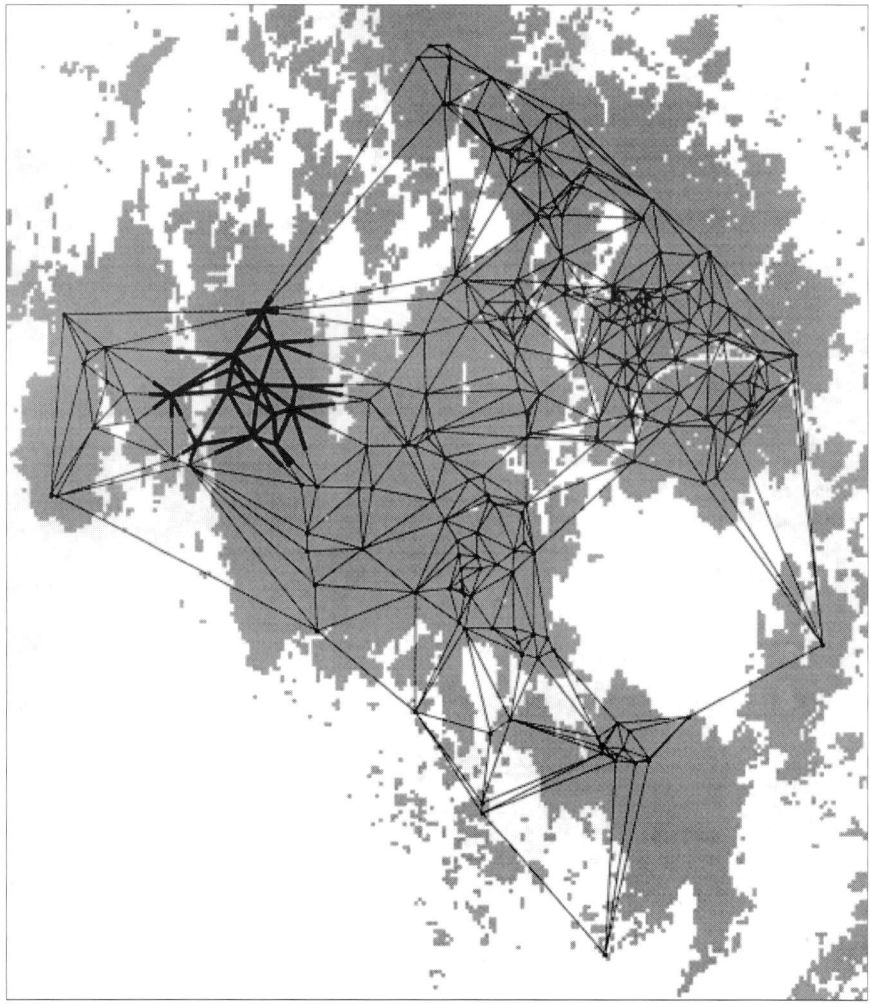

Fig. 3 a. Simulation of the pull model of migration for the Åland islands.

The Pull Model

Fig. 3 a, b, and c show the development of a route system for a single moving population under the conditions of the Pull Model. The map shows the Åland islands as a grey archipelago on a white sea. North is towards the top of the page. The black dots are the sites. They are connected by potential routes which are indicated by the thin black lines. The heavier lines show the routings actually taken. In figs. 3 a. b. and c. There was a constant demand for resources. Fig. 3a shows the initial spread of the population. The spread is relatively small and many routes were not completed. However, as the migrants'

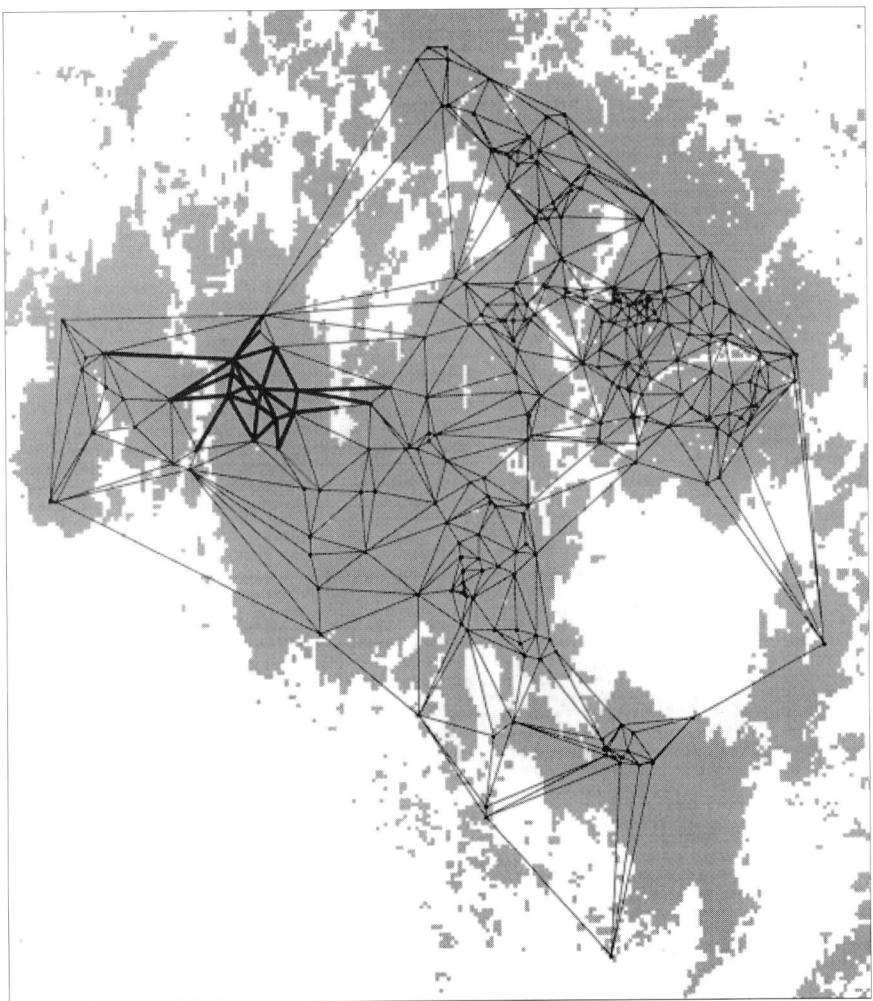

Fig. 3 b. Simulation of the pull model of migration for the Åland islands.

travel "proficiency" began to increase, their ability to overcome the friction of travel increased, and the pull of goods from further places began to occur. Fig. 3b shows that some of the routings had been rejected and that other routes which are further out have been completed. Fig. 3c shows the same process recursively continuing. One sees the expansion of one route to the west.

The Push Model
Fig. 4 a–d shows the routing for a push model that has a constant "proficiency" of travel and a sequentially increasing demand for resources. It begins with a

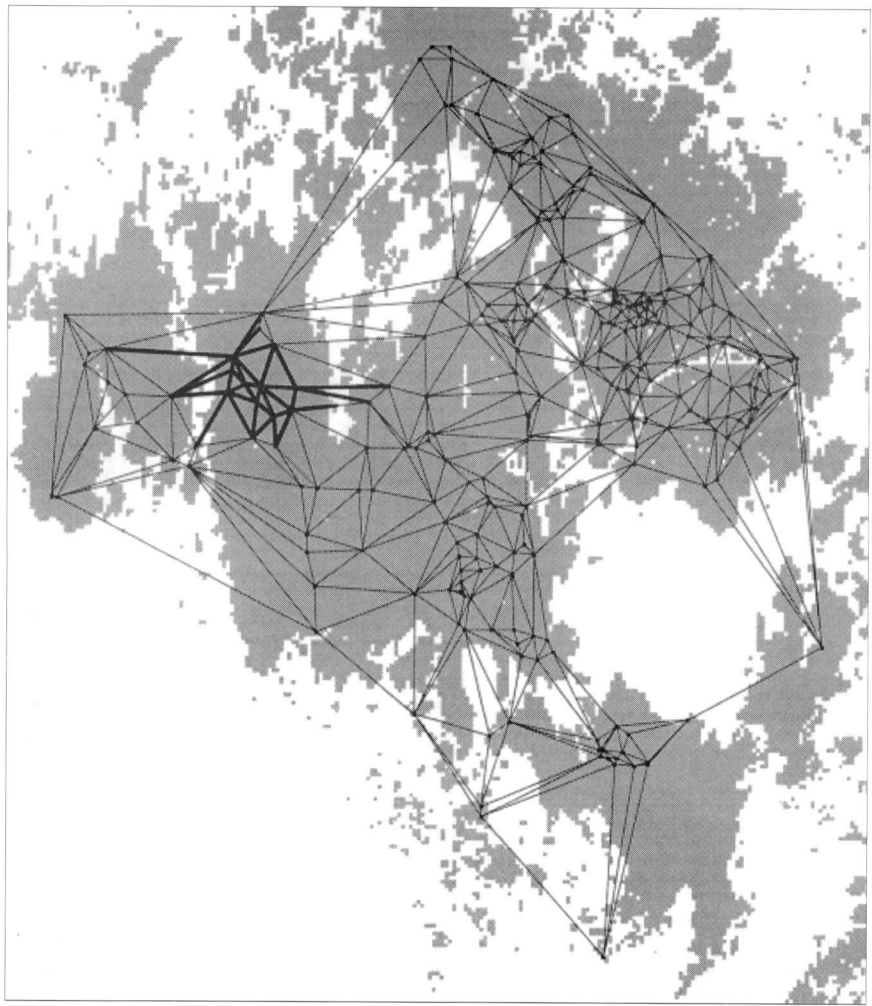

Fig. 3 c. Simulation of the pull model of migration for the Åland islands.

very small amount of population being pushed out of their local area because they cannot be sustained locally. Moreover, they are required to travel only a very small distance to satisfy their needs. Fig. 4b. shows the case for an increased demand. The expansion is approximately the same as the "pull model". In fig. 4c and fig. 4d one can see the further extension of the migration as greater numbers of people are "pushed" out of their homes and into the migration stream. By fig. 4d the migration stream has reached approximately eighty per cent of the "nodes".

Fig. 4 a. Simulation of the push model of migration for the Åland islands.

The Traveling Center (The Sequential or Step Model)

Fig. 5 a–d shows the development of a single moving population under the constraints of a constant "demand" and a constant "proficiency". In this model the population moves in steps across the space and sequentially through time. They reach out as far as necessary to support the population and then the process continues recursively from this new peripheral "node". What will surprise most readers are two aspects of the migratory stream apparent in these figures. First, although the direction is generally west to east, it is surprising how many blind turns and incomplete migrations that take place. Second is the fragility of the network

42 *Ezra B. W. Zubrow and Michael Frachetti*

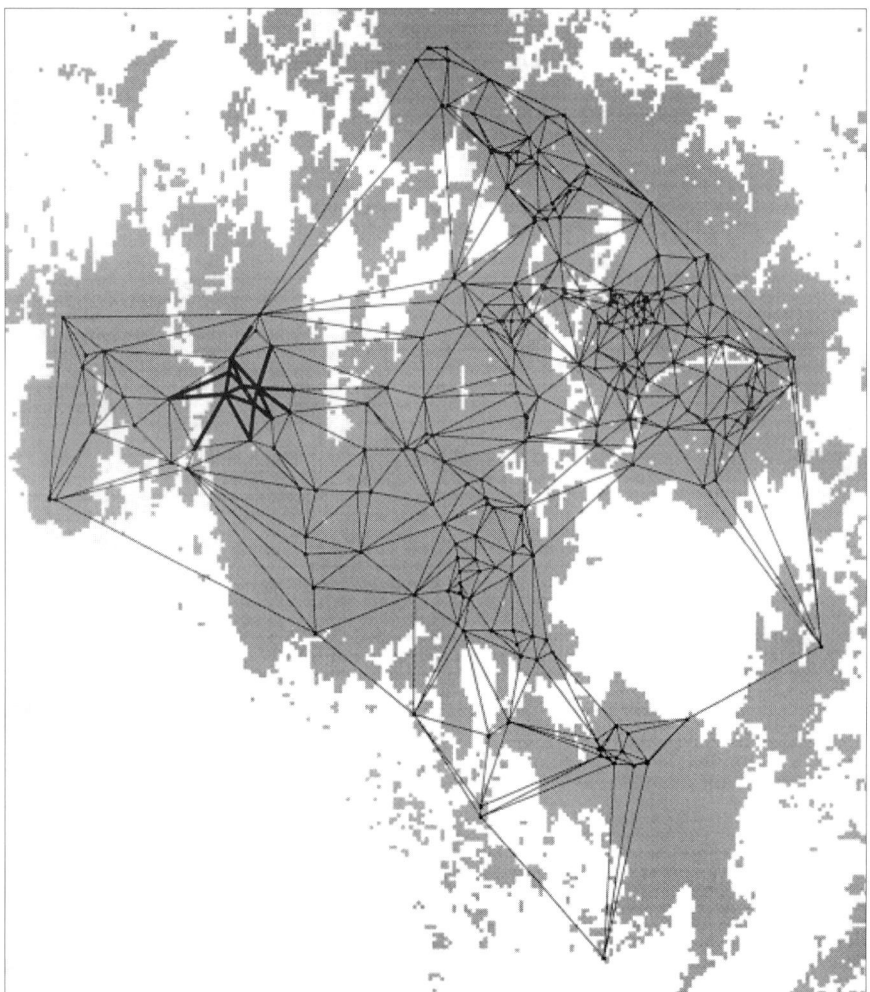

Fig. 4 b. Simulation of the push model of migration for the Åland islands.

The Bi-nodal Model

– Traveling Center Model

Fig. 6 a–d shows the results of applying the traveling center model to two different migrating populations simultaneously. There are many differences between fig. 5 and 6. However, perhaps most important are the differences in the fragility and the routings. The bi-nodal model is less fragile in that there are frequently multiple routings taken between nodes. Thus, even if one of the routes collapses, the migration is able to continue. The other major difference is in the central and eastern part of the routing. The bi-nodal model turns north more centrally than the traveling center model.

Changing world-view of prehistoric populations 43

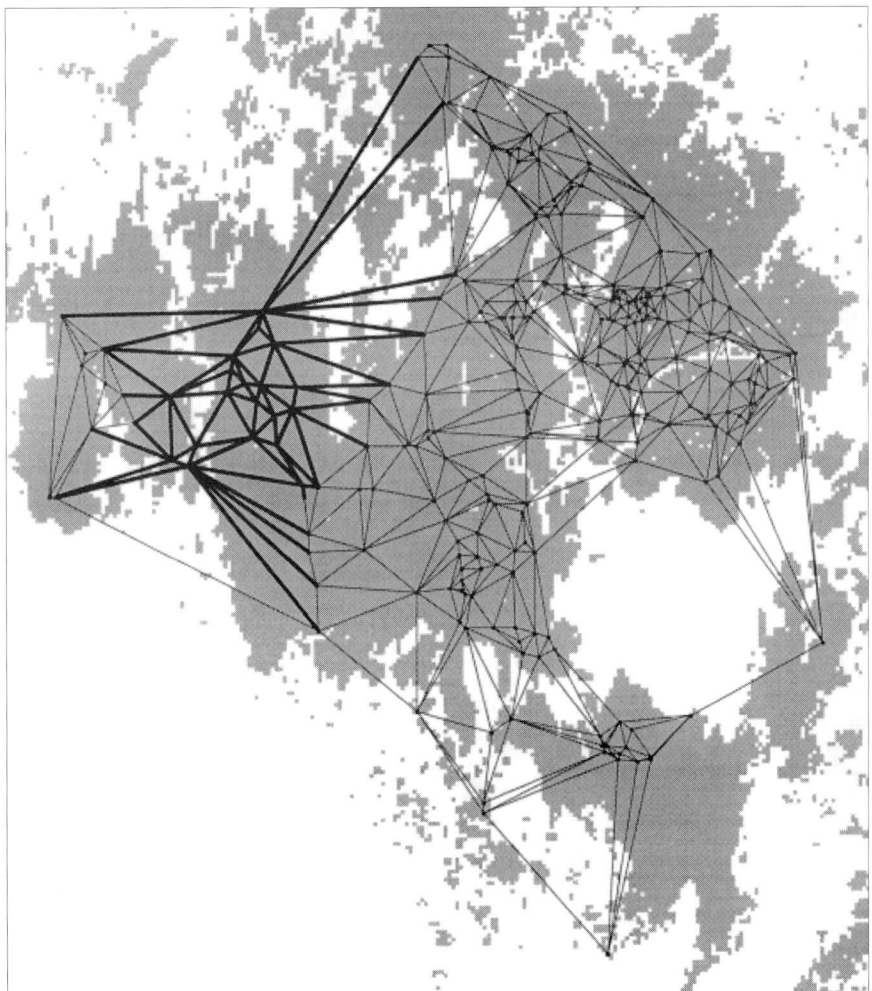

Fig. 4 c. Simulation of the push model of migration for the Åland islands.

– Constant Center Model
  Fig. 7 shows the result of applying the push model to two nodes simultaneously. Each population was operating under a "push' system of migration with demand increasing. The amount of resources necessary for the two-"node" system to span the network is approximately one quarter of that of a single "node" migration. In this model the ease of travel is constant.

44 *Ezra B. W. Zubrow and Michael Frachetti*

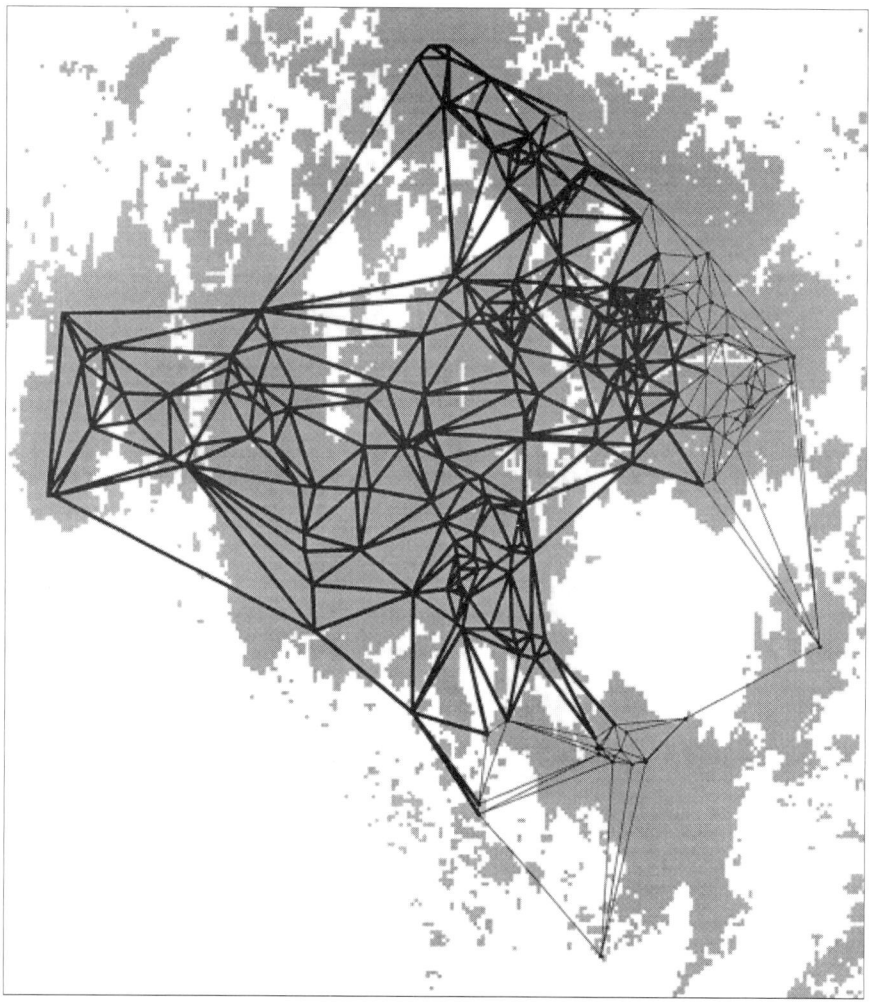

Fig. 4 d. Simulation of the push model of migration for the Åland islands.

Comparison of Push and Pull Models

Figs. 8 and 9 provide a comparison of the "Pull" and "Push" models. Each plots the results of numerous simulations. Fig. 8 shows the "ease of travel" in the "pull model" by the number of site locations ("nodes") reached by the migrating population. Fig. 9 shows the "push' model in which "demand" is plotted by number of site locations ("nodes") reached by the migrating population. One should note that the scales are different. The pull models fit into a small section of the push models near the origin. Regression analysis on the data restates what the graphs show. Namely, the pull models are stronger mi-

Changing world-view of prehistoric populations 45

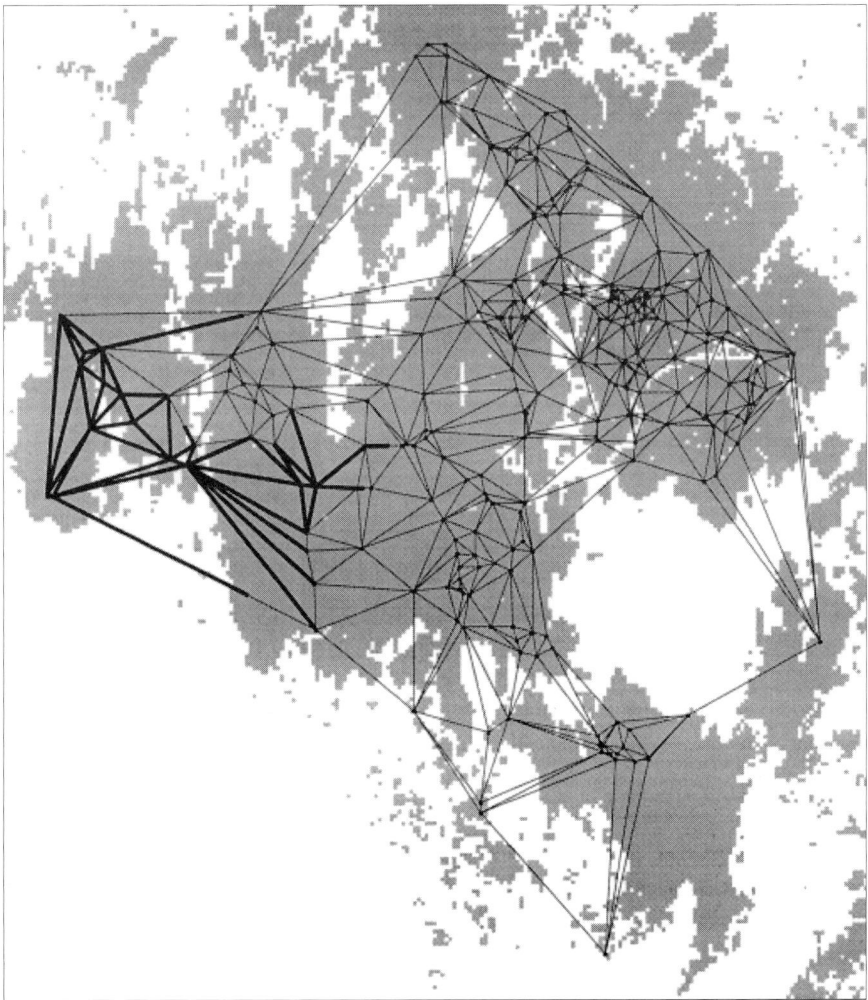

Fig. 5 a. Simulation of the travelling centre model of migration for the Åland islands.

gratory models than the push ones. An increase of one unit in the ease of travel parameter is approximately three times stronger than a similar increase in demand. This shows that *given other aspects being equal the forces of "motivation and individual decision" are stronger than the forces of "demand and population surplus"*. The forces suggested by post processual archaeology are stronger than those put forth by processual archaeology

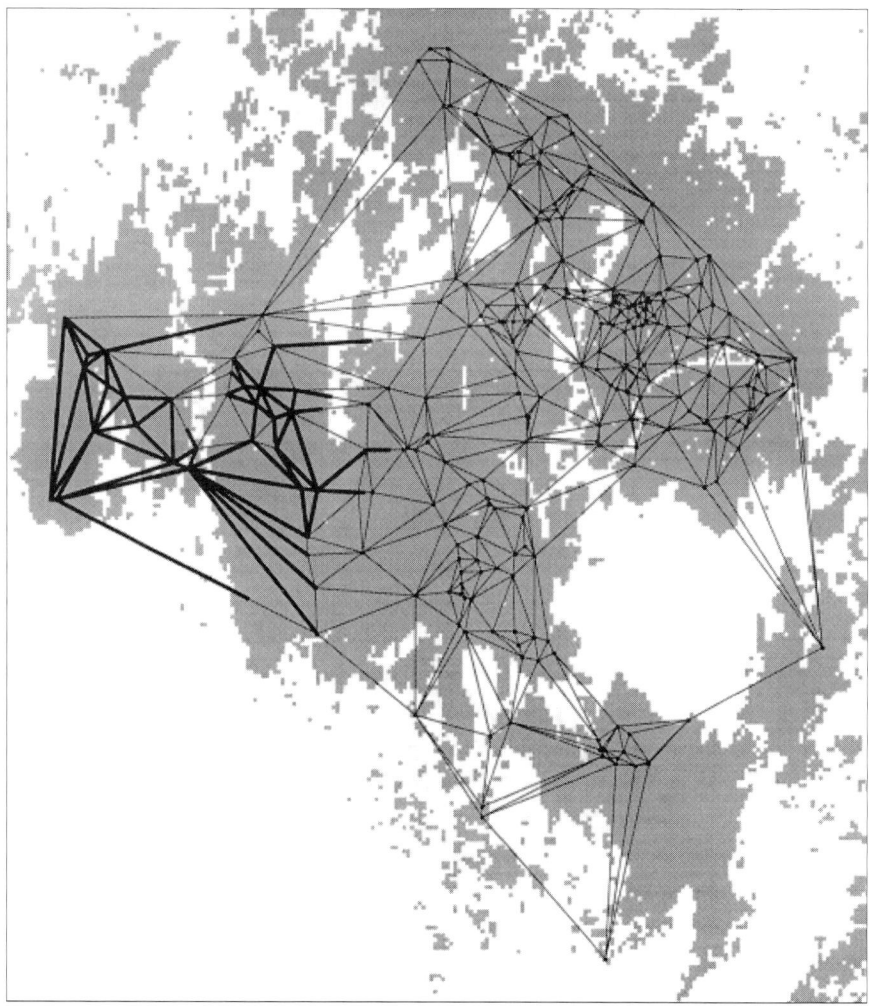

Fig. 5 b. Simulation of the travelling centre model of migration for the Åland islands.

Changing View of the Demographic Stability of the Village

There has been a long term interest in the impact that chance has on the growth of small populations (Ward & Weiss 1976; Zubrow 1976; Welinder 1979; Hassan 1981). It was suggested in the early 1960's that all other things being equal the time to extinction of small populations (i.e. less than 150) is relatively short. Conversely, once a population reaches a larger size such as 1000 the time to extinction is almost infinite.

It has been important for a variety of reasons. Most scholars believe the transition from "hunting and gathering" to successful agriculture was not only

Changing world-view of prehistoric populations 47

Fig. 5 c. Simulation of the travelling centre model of migration for the Åland islands.

a technological but a demographic revolution. The size of communities is thought to increase from approximately 100 to more than 1000 with a concomitant reduction in the probability of extinction. Increasing fertility resulting in larger families is a method of guaranteeing continuing survival for small populations [6]. In other words, the question that may be asked is do small populations have a high probability of going extinct under the early agricultural demographic conditions.

48 *Ezra B. W. Zubrow and Michael Frachetti*

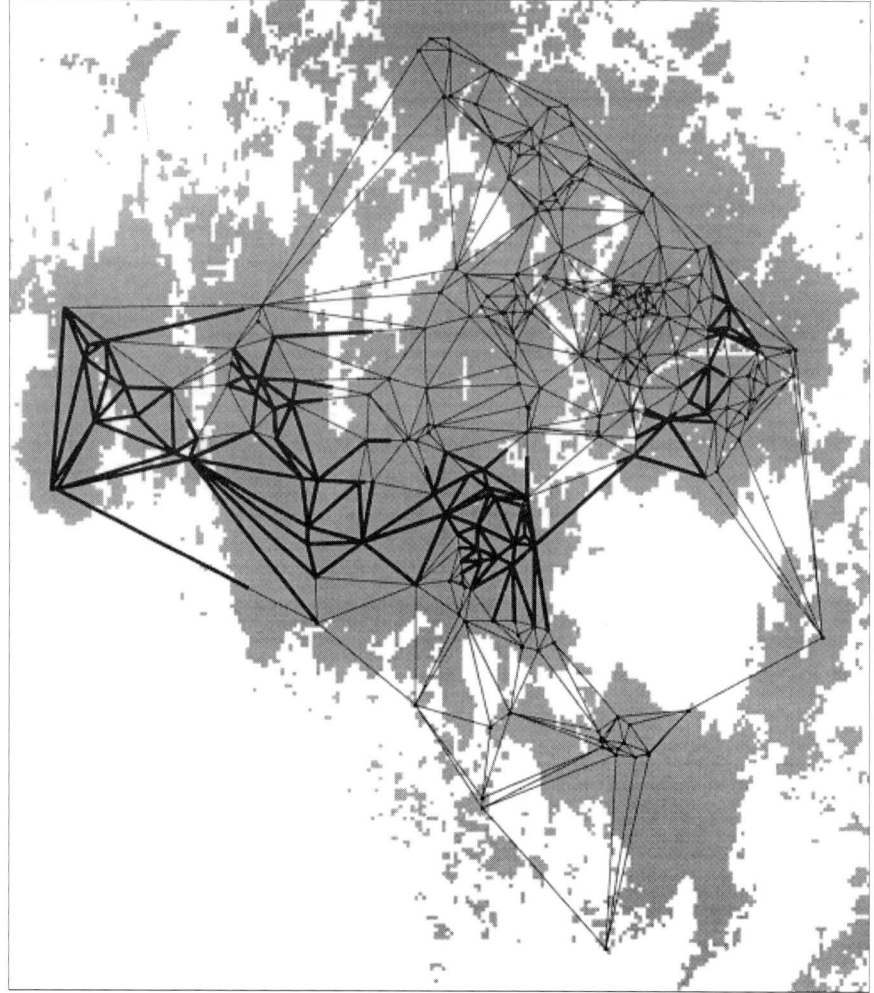

Fig. 5 d. Simulation of the travelling centre model of migration for the Åland islands.

Methodology

The methodology used is direct and robust. It consists of undertaking a large number of experiments under different demographic scenarios through simple simulations. The units of study are small villages with different initial sizes. One imposes large amounts of chance variation to fertility, mortality, in-migration and out-migration rates and tracks the outcomes over thousands of years. [7]

The Model

All simulations were programmed in IDL. The model used is a simple demographic accounting model that may be reduced to two do-loop expressions.

Changing world-view of prehistoric populations 49

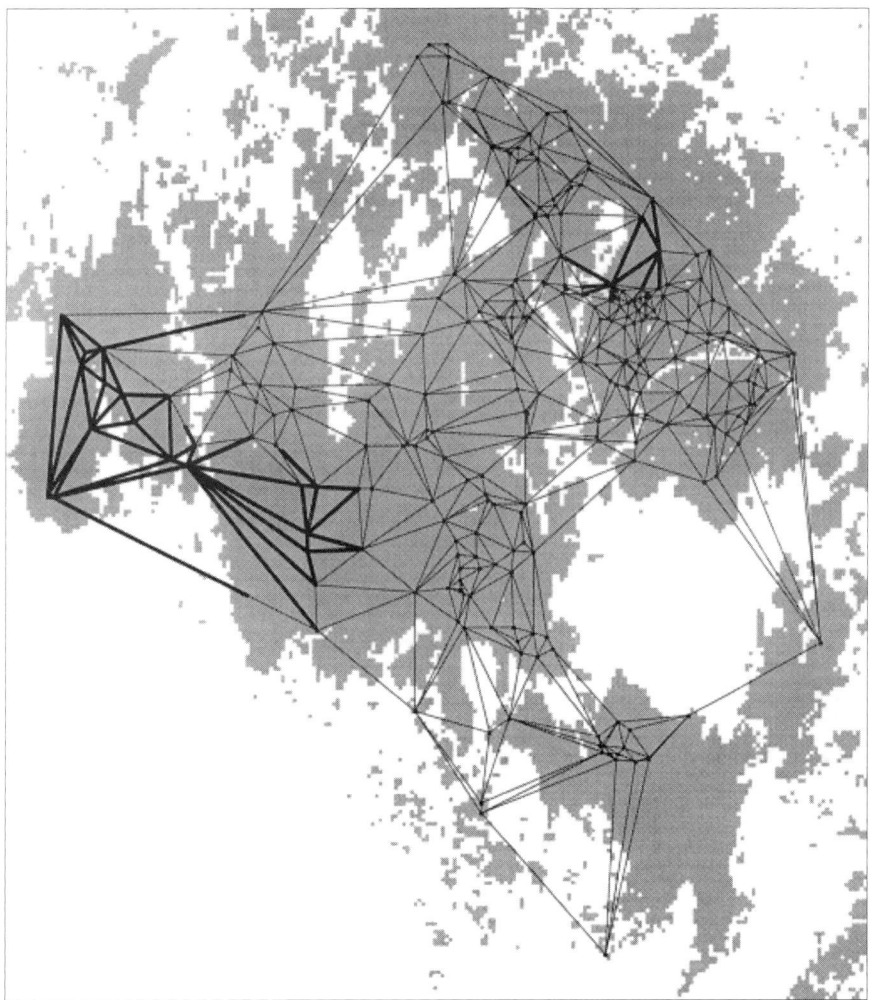

Fig. 6 a. Simulation of the bi-nodal travelling centre model of migration for the Åland islands with two simultaneously migrating populations.

Base fertility, mortality, inmigration, and outmigration rates are provided to the program as is the beginning size of the hamlet or village. These initial values are based upon ethnographic and archaeological estimates. They are made to vary randomly on an annual basis through multiplication by r, a draw from a uniform distribution between 0.5 and 1.5. This draw applied to the fertility, mortality, inmigration, outmigration, and population using different random series. The process is repeated annually and for different initial values for village population.

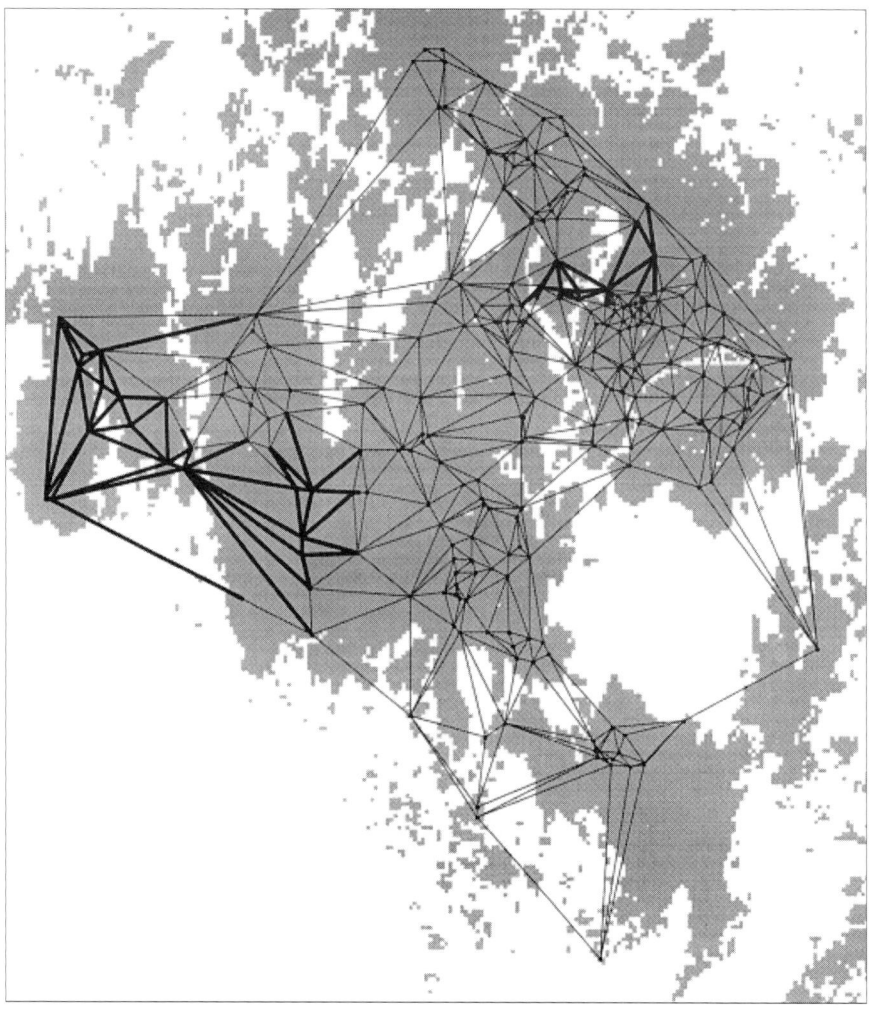

Fig. 6 b. Simulation of the bi-nodal travelling centre model of migration for the Åland islands with two simultaneously migrating populations.

Parameter estimation was based upon a variety of data including rural European growth rates[8] from the early part of this millennium as well as the highest documented rates of fertility known. These occurred among a European religious sect named the Hutterites [9] Given these parameters as approximate limits i.e. +/– .02 for growth and +/– .01 for fertility, we set the ranges of fertility from .033 to .044. Consequently, mortality ranges from .033 to .055, immigration from .033 to .055, and outmigration from .033 to .055. Historically, most of the settlements were less than 150 people.

Changing world-view of prehistoric populations 51

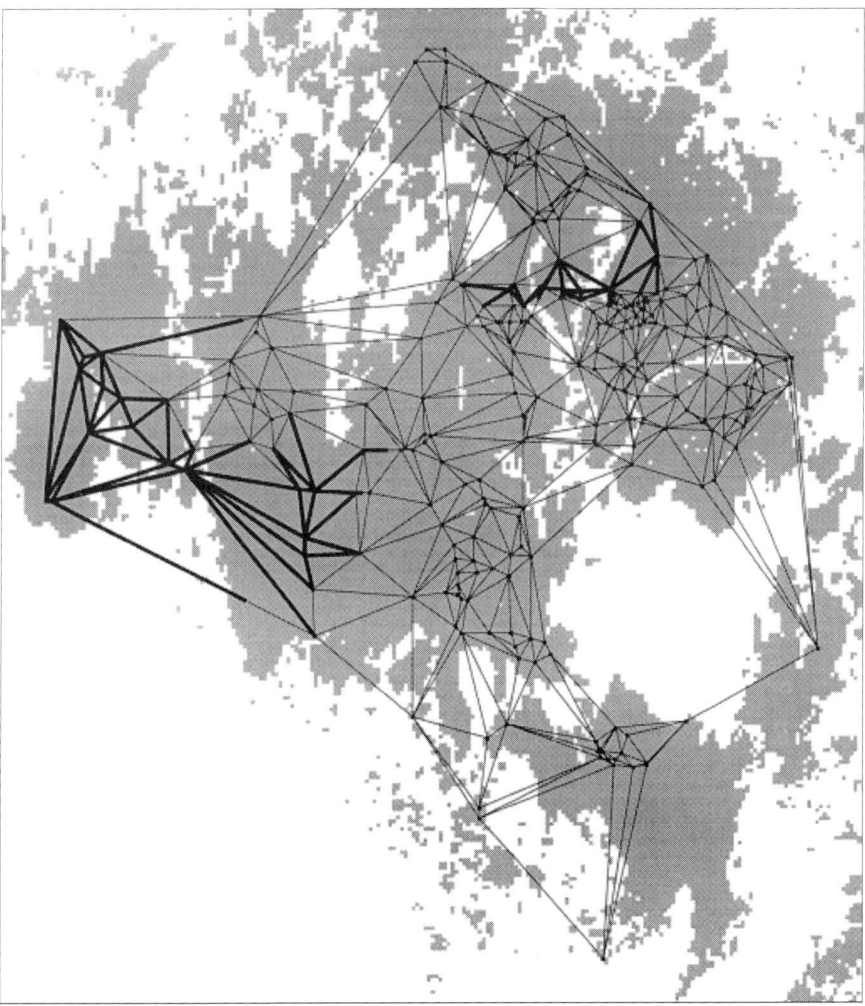

Fig. 6 c. Simulation of the bi-nodal travelling centre model of migration for the Åland islands with two simultaneously migrating populations.

The Results

The results of the model simulations were originally considered in a series of scenarios of increasing size and complexity. First studies were done of individual villages varying the parameters of size, growth, fertility, mortality in-migration and out-migration as well as time. Second, simulations of multiple villages with varying parameters were analysed. Finally, chance was constrained to a patterned time structure rather than being universal.

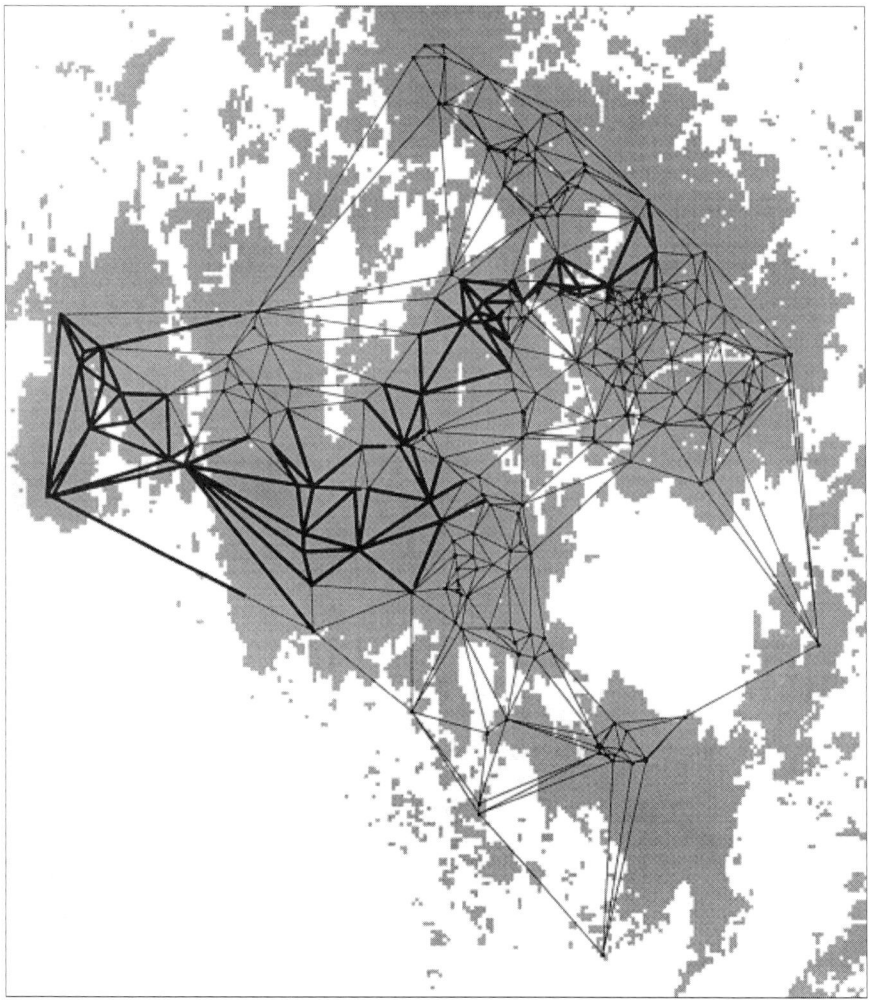

Fig. 6 d. Simulation of the bi-nodal travelling centre model of migration for the Åland islands with two simultaneously migrating populations.

Individual Villages

Although most of the simulations will be described—only a few exemplary scenarios will be shown graphically. Fig. 11 shows population change for a village whose initial population is 100 and whose fertility, mortality, immigration, and outmigration are initially set to .04. All the demographic change was taking place by chance events. In this particular case chance causes the population to begin a slow decline.

Increasing the length of time that the village may last to 1000 years with the same fertility, mortality, migration and mortality rates results in the population

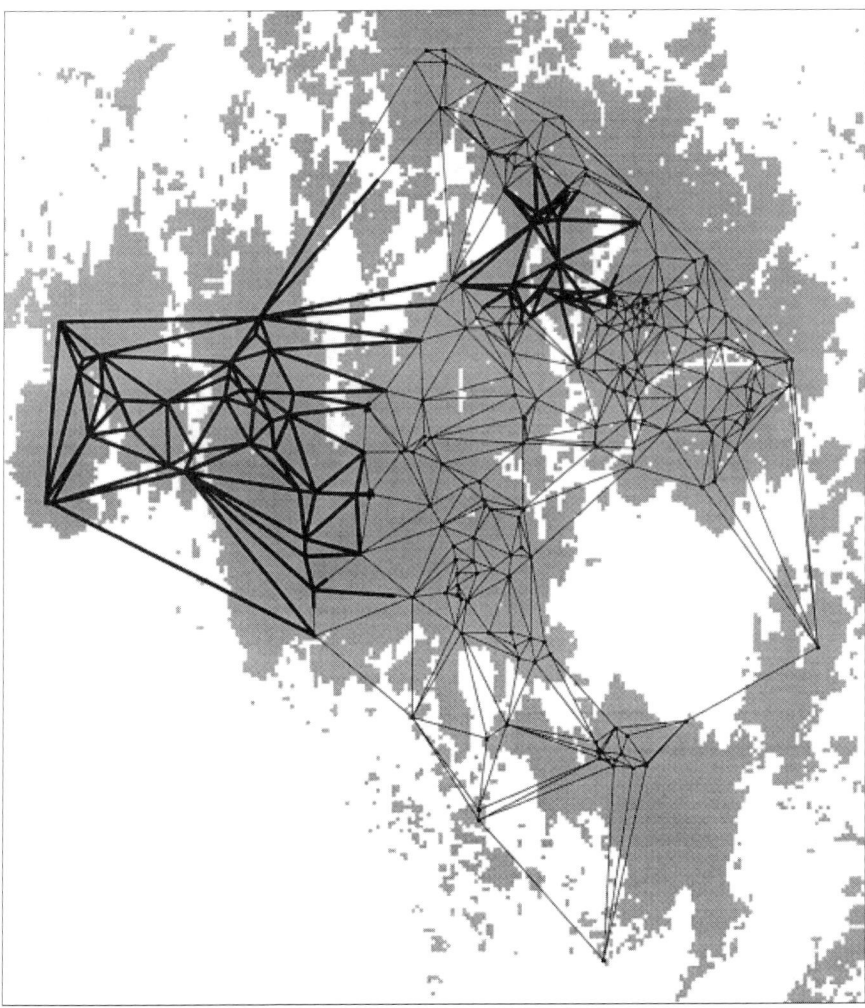

Fig. 7. Simulation of the bi-nodal push model of migration for the Åland islands with two simultaneously migrating populations.

following an irregular path. It reaches 120 people in 100 years and 190 people in 1000 years.

A frequent scenario is caused by or reflects colonization. It occurs when fertility is slightly greater than mortality resulting in a surplus population. This surplus is reduced by outmigration being greater than immigration. In the following example initial fertility is set at .0441, mortality at .038, but, outmigration .0442 is greater than inmigration at .38. The result is colonization taking place that eventually impacts the donor village. This is shown in fig. 12 where after 200 years the population of the donor village begins to seriously decline

Pull model:

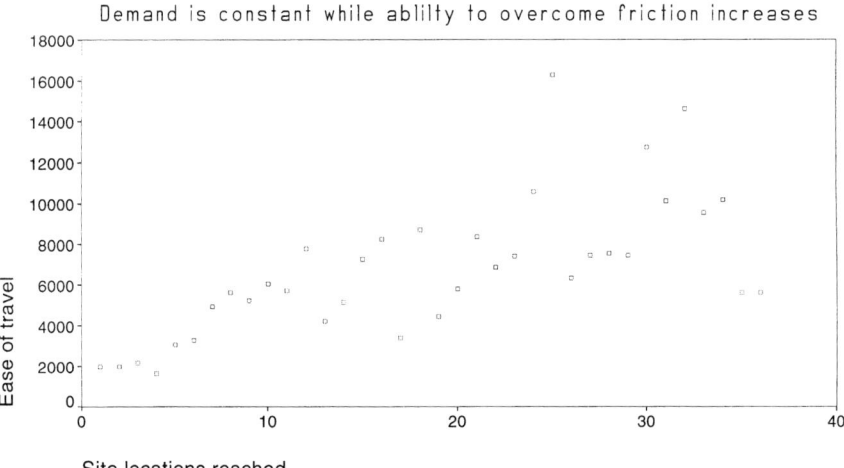

Fig. 8. The relationship between ease of travel (proficiency) and number of site locations reached for the pull model.

to about 40. However, it does not become extinct due to chance events. In other runs the population was able to maintain itself near 100.

Growth[10] and extinction scenarios[11] also were explored. Typically in the former the population would grow to almost 380 before dropping back to 300.

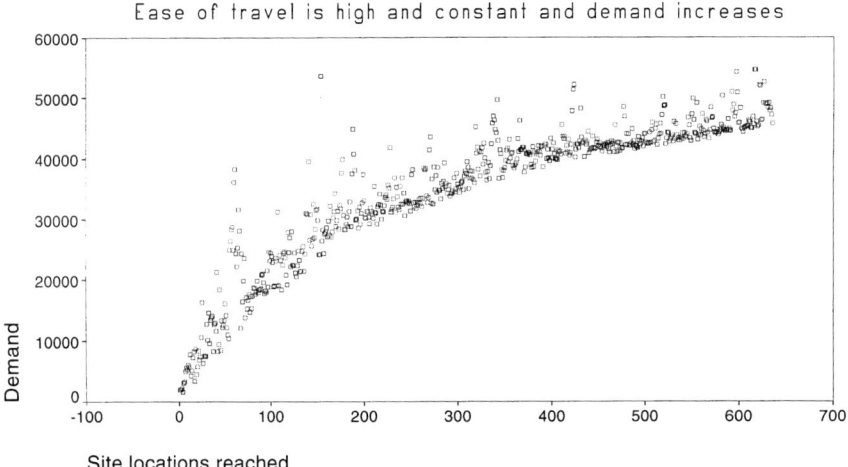

Fig. 9. The relationship between demand and number of site locations reached for the push model.

The Simple Population Model with robust Chance Applied

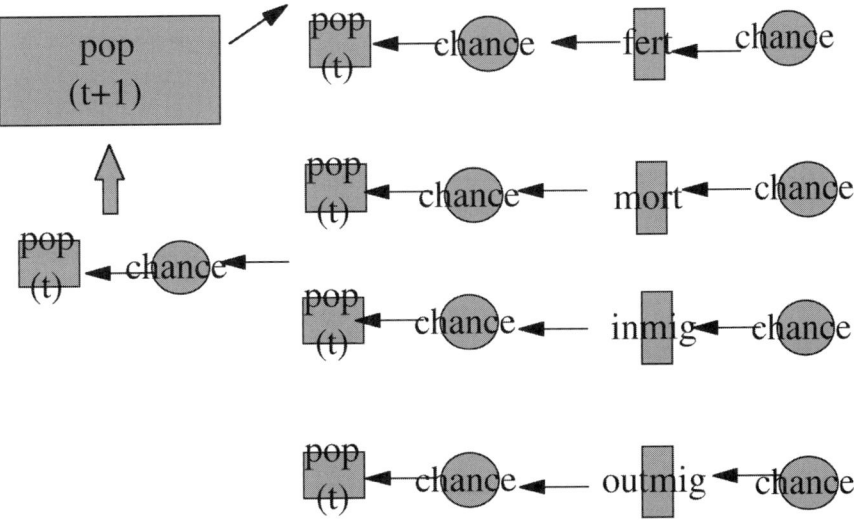

Fig. 10. The simple population model with robust chance applied.

The growth pattern is irregular with two or three large cycles each lasting approximately two centuries. In the extinction scenario, depopulation takes place rapidly during the first few centuries but then continues to decline at a much slower rate and in some periods the depopulation is actually halted and even reversed.

Multiple Villages

A large prehistoric region was considered next. In it there would be a large number of villages of different sizes. In this case there were 50,000 villages distributed so that there were ten thousand villages with a population of 100, ten thousand with 200, ten thousand with 300, ten thousand with 400, and ten thousand with 500. The fertility, mortality, immigration and outmigration rates were set equal at .040., just below Hutterite norms. The simulations were allowed to run for 1000 years. Fifty thousand simulations later not one of the 50,000 villages went extinct. In fact, initial size made no difference.

The author was concerned whether the results were an artifact of the relatively high vital and migration rates or initial village size. Thus, simulations were run for another 40,000 villages for 1000 years with the vital and migration rates set for .01 for 10,000 villages, .02 for 10,000 villages, .03 for 10,000 villages, and .04 for 10,000 villages. In each of these cases, the villages were distributed 1000 villages with 100 people, 1000 villages with 200 people ini-

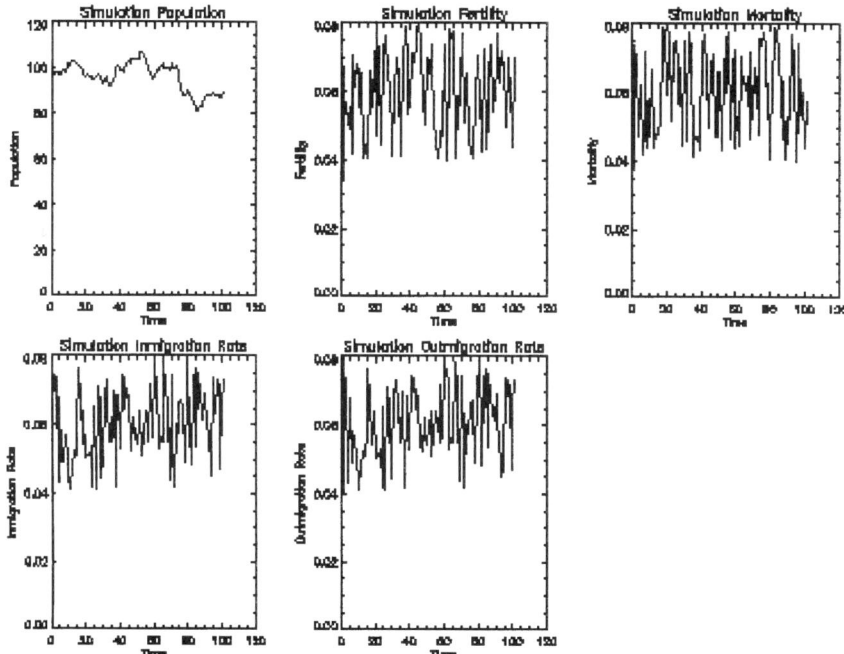

Fig. 11. 100 years of growth for even parameters of fertility .04, mortality .04, inmigration .04, outmigration .04. 11a Simulated village population by time; 11b fertility rates by time; 11c mortality rates by time; 11d in-migration rates by time; 11e out-migration rates by time.

tially, etc. It made no difference. Chance was not sufficient to create any extinctions. Essentially, the same pattern of growth and decline was seen.

In general, the number of declining villages was greater than the number of growing villages. Typically, there was a 60 to 40 ratio. Thus, the most common experience of people living in small villages was demographic decline with its concomitant problems in the economic sector due to lack of labor and in the social sector due to lack of mates. There were a larger number of villages with smaller populations, a smaller number of towns, and an even smaller number of cities. There was a Christmas tree shaped hierarchy for both the number and sizes of hamlets, villages, towns, and cities.

Village populations roll dice with nature. Thus, one might ask whether these villages are so robust demographically because chance was applied randomly. This may have been an error for one frequently hears that luck is ordered in the agricultural world. There is a string of bad weather followed by a string of good. One believes that there will be several years of "good luck" that will be followed by several years of "bad luck" or vice versa. In other words the

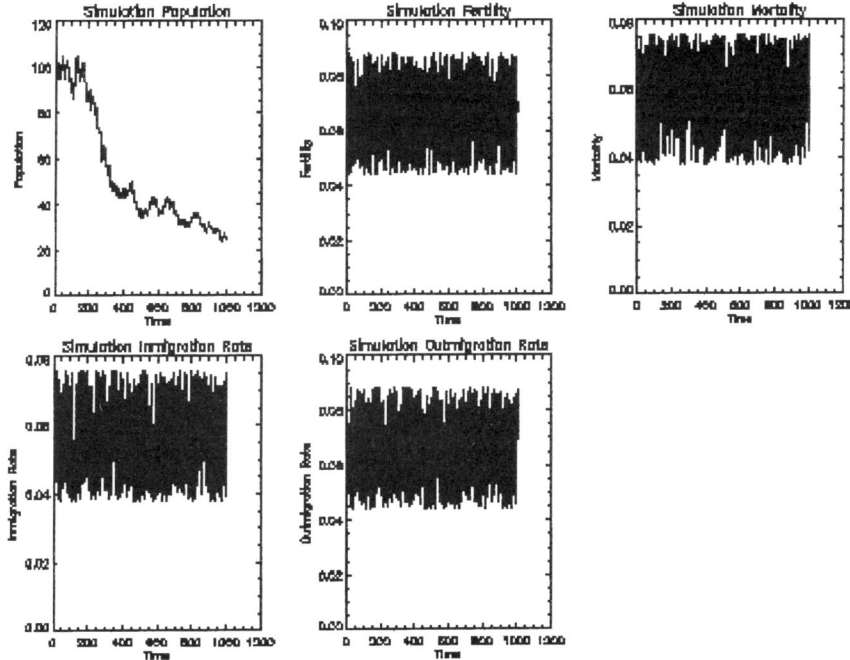

Fig. 12. The colonising scenario for 1000 years where outmigration is critical. The parameters are fertility .0441, mortality .038, in-migration .038, out-migration .0442. 12a Simulated village population by time; 12b fertility rates by time; 12c mortality rates by time; 12d in-migration rates by time; 12e out-migration rates by time.

application of chance is not totally random but systematic and sequenced. As the bible states

"In the seven years of plenty the earth brought forth in heaps…and the seven years of famine began to come according as Joseph had said and their was famine in all the lands…" Genesis ch. 41 verses 47 and 54.

To model Genesis series of simulations were run examining the impact that the amplification and patterned oscillation of chance would have on both the demographic parameters and the village populations. A total of 16,000 villages were simulated for 1000 years. There were four scenarios—high balanced parameters .04, low balanced parameters .01, low parameters with fertility raised, and low parameters with mortality raised. For each scenario four chance environments were simulated. They were non-patterned, patterned with a 10 year sine wave applied to fertility, patterned with 10 year sine wave applied to net increase, and patterned with an asynchronous 10 year sine wave applied to all the parameters. Thus, for each cell with numbers in the following

Table 4. *The number of village extinctions for 16,000 villages caused by different types patterned chance*

	Scenario-high balanced	Scenario-low balanced	Scenario-raised fertility	Scenario raised mortality
Parameters f., m. i., o.	.04, .04, .04, .04	.01, .01, .01, .01	.0125, .01, .01, .01	.01, .0125, .01,01
Number extinctions without patterned chance	2	0	0	0
Number extinctions with patterned chance on fertility	10	0	0	0
Number extinctions with patterned chance on net growth rate	26	0	0	0
Number extinctions with asynchronous patterned chance on all parameters	157	0	0	0

table 1000 villages were simulated. The results were startling. The assumption had been the repetitive high birth rates or high mortality rates, as Joseph's periods of plenty and famine, would destabilize the village demography. However, the structure is extraordinarily robust. Periodic frequent increases in mortality are saved by frequent periodic increases in fertility and vice versa. Only in the case of high balanced scenario does one find a significant increase in the number of extinctions when one adds patterned chance.

In short, one must conclude that chance does not play the role that anthropological demographers have suggested. In other words, a major conclusion is that village extinction for small populations is far more rare than the archaeological and anthropological literature suggests. In fact a robust chance model shows that for large numbers of small villages over long time periods, chance is not sufficient to cause extinction. Once a village is located and reaches a population of 100, there is a far better possibility that it will continue to exist and increase or decrease, rather than become extinct. It would appear that village extinction is more probably caused by cultural reasons, disease, or warfare. It is not caused by the law of small numbers.

Conclusions

The world view of archaeology changes over time. Furthermore, the world view of the archaeologist changes. This paper makes some suggestions about our changing world view of prehistoric society. It examined four topics. They were the changing view of archaeology from studies of material culture to studies of prehistoric population; the changing view of human ancestry from an evolutionarily successive view to an interactive, demographic contemporaneous view ; the changing view of prehistoric population movement from a processual to a post-processual perspective; and the changing view of the stability of the prehistoric village from a high unstable to a stable demographic phenomena.

The transformation from the object to the "person" has been a result of both processual and post-processual archaeology. It has been reflected in the popular press. Of the more than 100,000 stories examined, there was an increasing percentage of demographic stories with the greatest emphasis on the "Out of Africa" hypothesis, the contemporaneity of different hominids, and the Iceman. The most important popular demographic interests in the aging of the population and in the family rather than in migration, fertility, and mortality.

One aspect of this changing world view is the new contemporaneity. The general world view has been a concept of genera and species succession e.g. Homo follows Australopithecines, Cro-Magnon follows Neanderthals, etc. The details varied but succession was important. The new view based on new finds and redating of old finds is to allow the possibility of contemporaneity of *Homo erectus*, *Homo sapiens neanderthalenis*, and *Homo sapiens sapiens*. It upsets the multi-regional theory of human origins. It implies a change of focus from succession to interaction and suggests that successful adaptation may result from coexistence.

Another aspect of this changing world view is the re-examination of the concept of migration. If one examines migration from the point of view of the migrants, the donor populations or the receiving populations rather than through the prism of artefacts on the landscape, a different world view emerges as one asks what are the processes by which migration takes place and what are the decisions migrants make. The contrasts of determinant and non-determinant migration and voluntary and involuntary movements become important and may be used to illuminate and test contrasting ideas of processual and post processual archaeology. Pull, push, travelling centre, and bi-nodal models of migration were described and then tested on the Åland islands. The results show that the pull models which are based upon individual perception of the gains to be obtained at the receiving settlement are stronger than the push models which are based upon increasing demand caused by surplus population. An increase of one unit in the ease of travel parameter is approximately three times stronger than a similar increase in demand. This suggest that post processual forces are stronger than processual ones for the same phenomena.

Finally, the paper has examined the changing view of the demographic stability of the village. Generally, it has been believed that village life was precarious. All other things being equal the time to extinction of small populations (i.e. less than 150) is relatively short. Conversely, once a population reaches a larger size such as 1000 the time to extinction is almost infinite. This paper reports on a study in which a large number of experiments applying robust chance to small villages under different demographic scenarios were simulated. More than 100,000 villages were simulated for over 1000 years. In some cases they grew; in some cases they decreased. Chance was applied randomly and systematically. One must conclude that chance does not play the role that anthropological demographers have suggested. Once a village is located and reaches a population of 100, there is a far better possibility that it will continue to exist and increase or decrease, rather than become extinct. It would appear that village extinction is not caused by the law of small numbers.

The 'danse' continues.

Notes

1. This paper benefited from the help of numerous people who are gratefully acknowledged. Patrick Daly and Jennifer Robinson contributed significantly to the thinking and writing of the sections on Åland and the demography of the village. The "Changing Stability of the Village" is partially based upon a joint paper by Ezra Zubrow and Jennifer Robinson that is to appear in a publication of the Populus project. Eric Thurston and Daniel Finkler provided production support. Elka Kazmiercz painted the image "Reaching for Life" and Heather Schneider did some of the hand drawn illustrations. The other illustrations were the result of computer programs including ARC-INFO (ESRI 1997), a GIS software product copyrighted by the ESRI corporation of Redlands, California and IDL (1996), an interactive data language, copyrighted by Research Development Systems of Boulder, Colorado. Support for this paper includes support from the Laboratory for Applied Social Systems, the Departments of Anthropology and Geography of SUNY Buffalo, the National Center for Geographic Information, the Populus project, the Geography department, and the Center for Mediterranean Studies of Bristol University as well as Academy of Science of Sweden. Particular thanks go to Institute for Advanced Studies of Bristol University that provided me with an intellectual and professional home while this paper was being written.
2. This data base includes journals in all the major scientific languages but is biased toward English. However, its Swedish coverage was sufficient to note the Sjöbo affair.
3. Please note the discrepancy between the tab. 1 and tab. 3. In tab. 1 there are 4570 archaeological stories with population interest over the last two years. In tab. 3 there are a total 8815 prehistoric stories that consider different aspects of population. This discrepancy is caused by two factors. First, there is a difference between archaeology and prehistory in the categorization. Second, and what is more important there is double counting in tab. 3. If a story considers both family and migration, it would be counted twice.
4. For a more complete discussion of such network schemata see Abler, Adams, and Gould (1971) or Haggett (1977) and for a more detailed discussion of their operationalization into geographic models see ESRI ARC-INFO network module (Esri 1990, 1997). The models discussed here are particular operationalizations of these more general models.
5. The resident population is estimated between 3600–6000 people during the Iron Age (Nuñez 1993).

6. For example, Goody (1976) shows that under reasonable mortality conditions there is one chance in five that there will be no surviving children. For example consider the following scenario. If there is a .3 probability of a child dying before the father and the family size is 2.5, there is almost 1 chance in 5 that there will be no surviving children. On the other hand, if one increases the family size to 6, the percentage decreases to 2 %.
7. Initially, age specific rates were used but it was found that over long periods of time that crude rates were as effective.
8. Grigg (1980) suggests that the largest crude rates of population increase in rural Europe range from 1.1 % per annum to –.12 % per annum from 1450 AD to 1600 AD. He suggests rates .25 % to .82 % for the later centuries. These figures correspond with many figures developed by Wrigley (1996, 1969), Wall (1983), Laslett (1965, 1972) and others at the Cambridge Group for the study of Population and Social History as well as Le Bras (1993, 1996) for the analogous European populations. In addition they correspond to Colin Clark's (1967) population of Europe 1000–1900. Thus, we will limit our rates of change to being no more than .02 % and more frequently .01%.
9. The highest known rates of fertility are documented from the Hutterite populations (Hostetler & Huntington 1980; Hostetler 1983). These rates range from .04 to .044 with family size often reaching 11 or more children.
10. An example of the growth scenario has the parameters set initially at fertility .040, mortality .037, inmigration .040 outmigration .040. The initial population is 100 and the simulation is allowed to run for 1000 years.
11. An example of the extinction scenario has the parameters set initially at fertility .037, mortality .040, inmigration .038 outmigration .038. The initial population is 100 and the simulation is allowed to run for 1000 years.

References

Abler, R., Adams, J. S. & Gould, P. 1971. *Spatial organization; the geographer's view of the world.* Englewood Cliffs.
Alhonen, P & Väkeväinen, L. 1980. Diatom analytical studies of Comb ceramic vessels. *Suomen Museo* 67–77.
Ammerman, A. J. & Cavalli-Sforza, L.L. 1984. *The neolithic transition and the genetics of populations in Europe.* Princeton, N.J.
Binford, L. R. 1972. *An archaeological perspective.* Studies in archeology. New York.
Bossel, H., Klaczko, S. & Muller, N. (eds) 1976. *Systems theory in the social sciences: stochastic and control systems, pattern recognition, fuzzy analysis, simulation, behavioural models.* Interdisciplinary systems research. Basel.
Cavalli Sforza. L. L & Feldman, M. W. 1981. *Cultural transmission and evolution : a quantitative approach.* Monographs in population biology 16. Princeton, N.J.
Cavalli-Sforza, L. L., Menozzi, P. & Piazza, A. 1994. *The history and geography of human genes.* Princeton, N.J.
Clark, C. 1967. *Population growth and land use.* London.
Clarke, D. L. 1968. *Analytical archaeology.* London.
Crick, F. 1981. *Life itself: its origin and nature.* New York.
Darwin, C. 1933. *Charles Darwin's diary of the voyage of H.M.S. "Beagle".* Edited from the ms. by Nora Barlow. New York.
— 1964. *The descent of man, and selection in relation to sex.* 2d ed. London.
— 1979. *On the origin of species.* Cambridge, Mass.

Einstein, A. 1945. *The meaning of relativity.* Princeton, N.J.
Environmental Systems Research Institute 1977 *ARC-INFO A software product.* Redlands Ca.
Environmental Systems Research Institute 1990 *Understanding GIS : the ARC/INFO method.* Redlands Ca.
Fermi, E. 1956. *Thermodynamics.* New York.
Fries, M. 1963. Pollenanalysis pa Åland *Åländsk Odling* 24.
Goody, J. 1976. *Production and reproduction : a comparative study of the domestic domain.* Cambridge studies in social anthropology 17. Cambridge.
Grigg, D. 1980. *Population growth and agrarian change : an historical perspective.* Cambridge geographical studies 13. Cambridge.
Haggett, P., Cliff, A. D. & Frey, A. 1977. *Locational Analysis in human geography.* 2d ed. New York.
Hodder, I. (ed.) 1987. *The Archaeology of contextual meanings.* New directions in archaeology. Cambridge.
Hassan, F. A. 1981. *Demographic archaeology.* Studies in archaeology. New York.
Hostetler, J. A. & Huntington, G. E. 1980. *The Hutterites in North America.* Case studies in cultural anthropology. New York.
Hostetler, J. A. 1983. *Hutterite life.* Scottdale, Pa.
IDL 1996 A software product of Interactive Data Language inc. Boulder Colorado
Laslett, P. (ed.) 1972. *Household and family in past time; comparative studies in the size and structure of the domestic group over the last three centuries in England, France, Serbia, Japan and colonial North America, with further materials from Western Europe.* Assisted by Richard Wall. Cambridge.
Laslett, P. 1965. *The world we have lost.* New York.
Le Bras, H. 1993. *La Planete au village : migrations et peuplement en France.* Avec la collab. de Morgane Labbe. [Paris]: DATAR. Monde en cours. Serie Prospective et territoires. La Tour d'Aigues.
— 1996. *Le peuplement de l'Europe.* Documentation francaise, Recherches. Paris.
Lederberg, J. 1992. *Encyclopedia of microbiology.* San Diego.
Libby, W. F. 1995. *Radiocarbon dating.* 2d ed. Chicago.
Nunez, M. 1990 Människa och miljö i den åländska skärgården under stenåldern. *Skärgård* 13:3, 42–47.
— 1993 Searching for a structure in the late Iron Age settlement of the Åland Islands, Finland. *Karhunhammas* 15, 61–75.
— 1994 Agrarian colonization of the Åland Islands in the first millenium AD. *Fennoscandia Arcahaeologica.*
Nunez, M. & Vinberg, A. 1991. Determinations of anthropic soil phosphate on Åland. *Norwegian Archaeological Review* 23, 128–130.
Oppenheimer, J. R. 1989. *Atom and void : essays on science and community.* 1st Princeton science library ed. print. Princeton, N.J.
Swisher, C.C III., Rink, W. J., Anton, S. C., Schwarcz, H. P., Curtis, G. H., Suprijo, A. & Widiasmoro, T. 1996. Latest Homo erectus of Java: potential contemporaneity with *Homo sapiens* in Southeast Asia. *Science* 1996: v274, nu. 5294.
Wall, R. (ed.) 1983. *Family forms in historic Europe.* With Jean Robin and Peter Laslett Cambridge Group for the History of Population and Social Structure. Cambridge.
Wallace, A. R. 1870. *Contributions to the theory of natural selection.* London.
Ward, R. H. & Weiss, K. M. 1976. *The Demographic Evolution of Human Populations.* New York.
Watson, J. D., 1968. *The double helix; a personal account of the discovery of the structure of DNA.* New York.

Welinder, S. 1979. *Prehistoric demography.* Acta archaeologica Lundensia, Series in 8o minore. Lund.
Wrigley, E. A. (ed.) 1966. *An introduction to English historical demography from the sixteenth to the nineteenth century.* Cambridge Group for the History of Population and Social Structure. Publication no. 1. New York.
Wrigley, E. A. 1969. *Population and history.* World University Library. New York.
Zubrow, E. B. W. 1976. *Demographic anthropology: quantitative approaches.* Advanced seminar series. Albuquerque.
Zubrow, E. B. W., Fritz, M. C. & Fritz, J. M. (eds.) 1974. *New World archaeology: theoretical and cultural transformations.* Readings from Scientific American, San Francisco.

Otherness in Prehistoric Times

By Evzen Neustupny

If the term "world view of prehistoric people" is analysed word by word, it appears to be a set of ideas adopted by prehistoric communities on what their social world was, and what kind of mutual relations they had with the external world.

I am going to exploit the concept of otherness for the discussion of the world view of prehistoric communities. This means considering how people came into contact with other people in areas other than their own, and how they created symbolic systems (texts) which operated in the other world.

I am going to limit my deliberations to later periods of prehistory in Central Europe, mainly to the Neolithic and Eneolithic Periods, and to the Bronze Age. Many of my remarks may also be valid for other periods and for other regions, but certainly not universally.

The Model

The social world of human beings can be systemized in many ways. One of them is to look at the world as consisting of three major subdivisions:

The first of them is the *communal world,* i.e. the world of one's own community, consisting of members of the community, the artefacts, institutions and symbolic texts created by the community, and the community area—a structured set of activity areas exploited by the community (cf. Neustupný 1986, 1991a and 1994).

The second subdivision is *the strange (foreign, alien, unknown) world* which consists of supposed but largely unknown territories and foreign beings occupying those territories. One's own community has no regular contact with these creatures, who are possibly dangerous. It is intensely perceived as something improper to have contacts with the strange world.

The third subdivision is the *world of otherness* which occupies the place between the communal world and the outer strange world. It consists of human and other beings who do not belong to our own community, but who share artefacts and symbols with "us"; they and we live in the same culture which is mutually understandable, and in a territory which is close to "ours". People and possible supernatural beings with such characteristics may also have lived in times different from the present, and now be in the other world. One's own community has regular contacts with this world of otherness.

The concept of otherness (cf. Neustupný 1997) seems to be able to supply a useful insight into the minds of prehistoric people. However, it does not exhaust prehistoric world view entirely. As the community is an important constituent of the social world, world view is also formed inside communities, and individuals have their own world views as well. I am not going to touch on these aspects of the problem.

Modern people might assume that all the three worlds are perceived by any human being as a matter of course, but this is clearly not the case. As we know from written documents, the strange (unknown) world was constantly shrinking in historical times. The world known to ancient Greeks was still fairly limited, and it was even more so with ancient Egyptians. Ethnography tells us that many people structurally close to prehistoric Europeans knew little in addition to a few nearest villages.

There are two basic kinds of otherness: spatial and temporal.

Spatial Otherness

I assume that the division of space into the three spheres was not a matter of *theoretical rumination* of prehistoric people on the universe, but rather the matter of *social experience,* or purposeful activity (not necessarily "practical").

I am interested in social and ideological relations, not in the casual experience of individuals. Visiting foreign countries does not lead automatically to the establishment of the relationship of otherness. Millions of modern people travel abroad each year, returning with the vision of some historical monuments or natural beauties, but the world view of such people remains unchanged.

The intercommunal contacts proceeded along several lines. The first of them are economic relations by means of exchange of either commodities or labour.

As most prehistoric communities were self-sufficient in the procurement of the basic necessities of life, most economic relations with other communities were more or less dispensable. It can be argued that prehistoric people had very reliable and productive economies able to generate abundance in most particular situations. Therefore, economic relations with "other" communities were aimed at creating social ties, their motivation not being material necessity (Neustupný 1995b:646). I do not assume that economic contacts were necessary for the survival of humans as natural beings in their presumed fight with Nature.

Economic relations outside the immediate community are frequently believed to be recognizable on the basis of distribution maps, mainly of nonalimentary products assumed to be traded. Such maps, however, almost never testify to direct trading partners, they only exemplify how far certain products could get after passing a certain (unknown) number of intermediate links.

If archaeologists want to discover how trade flowed from one community to another, and to delimit the circuits of otherness in this way, they have to look for products that are most likely to have been traded directly to the final consumer in one single step. Many types of prehistoric pottery are not resold and thus can serve as markers of trade relations. It is mostly difficult, however, to recognize pottery traded over short or medium distances.

We are better off in the case of long-distance trade. It implies that people travelled long distances, establishing positive links with geographically distant populations. However, the argument that a foreign-looking artefact has travelled from its homeland in several intermediate steps nearly always applies. The use of pottery that was not resold may help in some instances.

The second category of intercommunal contacts were based on social relations by means of marriage and war (leading to people being relatives, allies or enemies). These relations are non-economic.

It can be assumed that individual communities were largely exogamous. The set of communities related by blood tended to be closed, that is, marital relations with the foreign (strange) world around were restricted. In fact, marriage was the main, if not the only, regular social mechanism for the physical inclusion of "other" people into one's own community (but cf. the case of "migrations by infiltration"—Neustupný 1982).

I have already argued that the purpose of most economic relations in the sphere of otherness is not to provide necessities of life but rather to create an abstract society. Such economic relations, however, do not substantially differ from what is traditionally described as social relations in general.

Economic relations are considered to be positive relations: they influence the society so as to enhance its cohesion. Warring covers a group of social relations assumed to have negative influence upon the cohesion of human society. Its role is clearly different from economics, but in assessing its real importance we should not consider it from the point of view of the Charter of Human Rights. It must be kept in mind that a war implies not only the existence of enemies but also of allies (an undoubtedly positive aspect), and the relation of war brings the warring parties into the world of otherness, thus selecting them from the greyness of the strange. In this sense, war is a socializing factor.

The reason for prehistoric wars cannot be seen either in the instinct of aggression or in avid economic greed for seizing material items. This is born out by the fact that wars were mostly ceremonial acts in which people did not die in great numbers, although a considerable number of persons may have been killed over a longer period of time (Shnirelman 1994) as warring was a more or less permanent social condition.

A naive modernizing view of prehistoric warring in the traditional paradigm was that warlike conflicts had occurred (mainly or exclusively) between different ethnic groups usually represented by different archaeological cultures.

The model presented in this paper explains prehistoric warring in very different terms. It conceives of wars as relations in the world of otherness, that is, relations operating on communities that are spatially close and that form together a kind of abstract society. Warring was a more or less permanent condition of prehistoric life.

The third kind of relations of individual communities are relations with the other world. All living human groups had some kind of relationship with their own mental products, expressed and externalized by means of symbols and often endowed with supernatural powers. These supernatural forces and beings were sometimes located outside community areas, that is, in the other world.

The other world, like any sphere of otherness, was accessible to prehistoric people: it could be contacted by means of appropriate rituals. Some of them may have been performed by anybody in the early phases of human culture, but there is conclusive evidence that at least since the Eneolithic period and especially in the Iron Age the supernatural forces were approached by a specialized group of persons.

A special, and very important, group of inhabitants of the other world were the ancestors, who lived in the world of otherness from the chronological point of view. Considering the usual location of cemeteries in Central Europe, however, it seems likely that the ancestors remained within the communal world at least in some periods of prehistory, as the burial areas often form a part of the community (settlement) area. The ancestors and the other supernatural beings got outside the communal world, however, when they moved to heaven or to the underworld (this may have happened in the Iron Age).

Temporal Otherness

While the realization of spatial otherness stresses the importance of other territories occupied by other people, the idea of temporal otherness emphasizes the importance of the past (Neustupný 1997). Time, like space, can also be conceptualized in three layers. One of them is the present time, in which communities perform their functions. The present may also include events that take place in the grammatical past tense; unless they represent something that opposes the present structurally, such events can hardly be understood as representatives of a real past.

To recognize the past in this sense is not a matter of chronometry. Many people assume that the concept of the past was always known to any human society. However, an event that does not differ structurally from the present, is a present event irrespective of whether it is described in the past tense or in the present tense.

Prehistoric people expressed their thoughts by means of artefacts and symbols—usually artefacts with a symbolic loading, but also by means of symbols such as linguistic signs. It is most natural that the new status of human memory reflecting the structural past became symbolized by means of artefacts. As one way of creating highly symbolic artefacts was to erect constructions high above the ground, it was only natural that the concept of the past was materialized in the form of durable artefacts, and nothing was more appropriate for the purpose than graves, megalithic graves in particular. In this way, megalithic graves became the first carriers of major importance of what I would describe as material memory. Memories of prehistoric communities were externalized and eternalized by being expressed in large blocks of stone.

The situation in which the idea of the past originated seems to be rather late. I find no archaeological evidence earlier than the beginning of the Central European Eneolithic period, which is equivalent to the beginning of Neolithic in Scandinavia and in the British Isles (roughly the middle of the 5th millennium BC—Neustupný 1991b).

Some Explanations

The thoughts that I have so far developed constitute a theoretical model which cannot be considered to be the end product of my research. The goal of archaeological inquiry should be the understanding of particular past situations.

I am not going to discuss methodological problems now. I shall only point out that explanation is achieved by comparing the model with structures of an archaeological context (for more details cf. Neustupný 1993).

In the next few paragraphs I am going to make a sketch of prehistoric warfare on the basis of my model. However, my example will not use all aspects of the preceding model.

There are two major groups of evidence for prehistoric warfare in Central Europe. One group is formed by graves with weapons, the other group consists of so-called fortifications. It has been found that these two sorts of evidence are mutually exclusive: in those phases of prehistory that produce graves with weapons, there are no defences and vice versa (J. Neustupný 1968).

Following many colleagues, I am inclined to believe that many prehistoric weapons of the Eneolithic period and the Bronze Age could hardly serve for fighting: they most probably had symbolic significance (Zápotocký 1994). I do not deny, however, that some of the weapons could kill people and were in fact used for that purpose.

At the same time, I could also argue that the so-called fortifications may have been symbolic artefacts rarely, if ever, employed for defence during actual fighting (Neustupný 1995a). Here again, the fortifications could be used against human enemies from time to time.

All this, if accepted, throws a new light upon the warfare of this period. There remains a very limited space for devastating wars. On the contrary: everything in any way connected to war clearly points to what should rather be termed "military ceremonies" or, possibly, ritual or ceremonial warfare. This kind of warring, however, demonstrates that those who waged such wars were somehow related to each other: the warring parties apparently accepted certain ceremonial rules for which symbolic weapons were appropriate. A devastating war, aimed at killing and robbing, would require a different set of weapons such as clubs and spears and possibly simple stockades.

The choice of either weapons or fortifications appears to be a puzzle in the case that the social meaning (i.e. the "practical" use of fighting) is accepted for the weapons and the fortifications.

Ceremonial fighting by means of ceremonial weapons was an occasion for individuals to display their bravery (this was a secondary social meaning of the weapons). Ceremonial warring was also expressed by so-called fortifications. In this case there is some chance to reconstruct the circuits of otherness that contributed to the individual fortifications, as most of them do not belong just to one but clearly to several (or many) communities.

Prehistoric activities at the fortified sites were most varied. Some of them were possibly used as trading places (markets) for a number of neighbouring communities within their circuits of otherness. But mainly they were centres for rituals.

I have already argued that the (frequently) unritually disposed skeletons in the ditches and other parts of some "hillforts" (e.g. Mercer 1980, Salas 1990, Bertemes 1991, Hrala, Sedláček and Vávra 1992 etc.) are too many to be explained as slain or sacrificed inhabitants of the fortified place itself. It is tempting to explain their presence in the ditches as the result of repeated ritual slaughters of enemies, possibly prisoners of war. In my view, there is hardly any other explanation.

Conclusions

It can be concluded that the opposition of the communal world and the world of otherness determined the way in which prehistoric people viewed the great world outside their communities. This world was backed mainly by economic relations, kinship and warfare. Warfare was one of the tools that helped to wrest some surrounding communities out of the unknown world of strangeness and brought them into the orbit of human society.

Acknowledgement

The work was supported by Grant No. 404/95/0523 of the Grant Agency of the Czech Republic. I thank Martin Kuna for reading a draft of this article.

References

Bertemes, F. 1991. Untersuchungen zur Funktion der Erdwerke der Michelsberger Kultur im Rahmen der kupferzeitlichen Zivilisation. In Lichardus, J. (ed.), *Die Kupferzeit als historische Epoche: Symposium Saarbrücken und Otzenhausen 6.–13.11.1988*, 441–464. Teil 1. Bonn.

Hrala, J., Sedláček, M. & Vávra, M. 1992. Velim: a hilltop site of the Middle Bronze Age in Bohemia. *Památky archeologické* 83, 288–308.

Mercer, R. J. 1980. *Hambledon Hill—a Neolithic Landscape*. Edinburgh.

Neustupný, E. 1982. Prehistoric migrations by infiltration. *Archeologické rozhledy* 34, 278–293.

Neustupný, E. 1986. Sídelní areály pravěkych zemedelcu—Settlement areas of prehistoric farmers. *Památky archeologické* 77, 226–234.

— 1991a. Community areas of prehistoric farmers in Bohemia. *Antiquity* 65, 326–331.

— 1991b. Zum Begriff des mitteleuropäischen Äneolithikums. In Lichardus, J. (ed.), *Die Kupferzeit als historische Epoche: Symposium Saarbrücken und Otzenhausen 6.–13.11.1988*, 747–752. Bonn.

— 1993. *Archaeological Method*. Cambridge.

— 1994. Settlement area theory in Bohemian archaeology. *Památky archeologické*—Supplementum 1, 248–258.

— 1995a. The significance of facts. *Journal of European Archaeology* 3:1, 189–212.

— 1995b. Úvaha o specializaci v pravěku—Thoughts on specialisation in prehistory. *Archeologické rozhledy* 47, 641–650.

— 1997. Uvedomování minulosti. *Archeologické rozhledy* 49, 217–230.

Neustupný, J. 1968. Otázky pravěkého osídlení ceskoslovenského území—Some problems of the settlement of Czechoslovak territory in prehistory. *Sborník Národního muzea v Praze,* rada A—historie XXII/2, 61–119.

Salaš, M. 1990. To the problem of human skeletal remains from the Late Bronze Age in Cézavy near Blučina. *Anthropologie* (Brno) 28, 221–229.

Shnirelman, V. 1994. *Voyna i mir v ranney istorii chelovechestva*. Moskva.

Zápotocký, M. 1992. *Streitäxte des mitteleuropäischen Äneolithikums*. Quellen und Forschungen zur prähistorischen und provizialrömischen Archäologie, Acta humaniora 16.

The Biological Basis of Social Behaviour
By Bo Gräslund

Introduction

Charles Darwin explained biological evolution and its basic mechanism, natural selection acting through genetic variation (Darwin 1859), and Gregor Mendel demonstrated the fundamental laws of inheritance (Mendel 1866). From this basis Ronald Fisher explained how natural selection is generally regulated through the mechanism of reproductive fitness, which means that an individual with a tendency to have and raise more viable offspring will have its genes and thereby this tendency spread in the population (Fisher 1930).

Yet some main contradictions in evolutionary population theory remained to be explained, for example, that animals to some extent also help other relatives than offspring. Then in a famous paper of 1964, "The Genetical Evolution of Social Behaviour", William Hamilton argued that individuals by helping relatives in reality favour their own genetical survival. Since parents and offspring share 50% of their varying genes, siblings 50%, half-siblings 25%, as do grandparents with their grandchildren and uncles/aunts with their nephews/nieces, and cousins share 12.5% and second cousins 6.25%, Hamilton predicted that help is generally given according to these coefficients of relatedness, provided that the genetic cost does not exceed the profit. For instance, if a mother sacrifices her own life to save three of her offspring, she promotes the survival of her own genes more than if she survives herself and her offspring die, and so her tendency to help relatives will be evolutionarily favoured. Since Hamilton's explanation included other relatives than offspring, he called this concept *inclusive fitness* (Hamilton 1964), soon also known as *kin selection* (Maynard Smith 1964).

Still one serious contradictory problem remained to be understood. How come that in such a world of genetic self-interest, also non-kin are observed to help each other? Then Robert Trivers proposed his idea of *reciprocal altruism*. From the observation that support among non-kin animals is, in the long run, often reciprocal, Trivers argued that help given on one occasion and repaid on another will actually further the reproductive success of both parts (Trivers 1971). In this way also social group-living in general was finally explained as basically a mechanism of genetical self-interest.

Such was the starting-point for sociobiology, as advocated especially by Edward O. Wilson and Richard Dawkins, and for its argument that altruistic behaviour is nothing but an expression of genetic selfishness, in principal also among humans (Wilson 1975; Dawkins 1976). The contradictory fact that some true unselfishness does occur among humans at first led Wilson to point out altruism as biology's most important theoretical problem (Wilson 1975). However, in what seems to have been a half-hearted attempt to satisfy a sour public opinion, Dawkins and soon also Wilson declared that a unique co-evolution of genes, culture and intelligence, as an exception to the rule, had allowed for true social altruism together with more complex social structures to appear in humans (Dawkins 1976; Wilson 1978).

Thus the main objections to the selfish gene theory were eliminated. Since then the ideas of kin selection and reciprocal altruism have been seen as the backbone of evolutionary population theory, explaining almost all social behaviour in the animal world as genetically selfish.

All this may sound convincing. None the less, there is something in the presumptions of the theory which does not make full sense.

The theory of kin selection presupposes that animals, in a statistical sense, behave as though they can identify their genetic kin, determine the degree of this kinship, and estimate whether help to relatives is genetically profitable or not. Initially, when very little data was available, it was assumed that this was carried out basically through some sort of genotypic kin recognition or phenotype matching (Hamilton 1964; Maynard Smith 1964). Phenotype matching is the idea that kin recognition is performed by some instinctive matching of the helper's observable characteristics as determined by the genes, the relationships between the alleles and the interaction of the genes with the environment. Today, kin recognition is also often thought to be learned directly from parents or nestmates and from environmental features or to be the result of location communion and living together in general, Sometimes kin recognition is also seen as an effect of social learning through early familiar proximity, what I here will call early close contact. (Dawkins 1989; Maynard Smith & Szathmáry 1995; Krebs & Davies 1997).

Kin selection is not just a matter of straight coefficients of relatedness. The assessing of the total genetic gains and costs in helping actions is often such a complex affair that gifted scholars have to make use of advanced mathematics to understand what dull animals have to instinctively estimate in seconds.

Since animals generally behave as if to confirm the idea of kin selection, kin recognition is often seen as a magic mechanism which does not need empirical demonstration. But the lack of empirical evidence confers an almost metaphysical vagueness on descriptions of genotypic and phenotypic kin discrimination. Further, little is said about the proportions in which the various mechanisms occur in which type of taxa or species in higher animals or what kind of mechanism is in operation behind kin discrimination based on social learning.

Finally, how could reciprocal altruism, or any permanent group-living between non-kin, have ever evolved if social discrimination had been generally based on allelic kin discrimination or phenotype matching, mechanisms which exclude non-kin from permanent mutual positive sociality? The mere existence of social group-living between non-kin, as in mammals and birds, in fact suggests that social discrimination among higher animals is basically regulated in some other way.

Functions of Kin Discrimination

The ability to discriminate between kin and non-kin is important not only for cooperative behaviours such as kin altruism, reproductive altruism, other helping actions, and for social group-living in general. First and foremost, kin discrimination is the basic prerequisite of mating avoidance. Since inbreeding avoidance is a fundamental condition of genetic variation, which is in turn a basic condition of evolutionary dynamics, it must be under evolutionary control. The fact that all sexually reproducing animals (Greenwood 1980; Dobson 1982; Waser & Jones 1983), even plants (Pfennig & Sherman 1995; Barrett & Harder 1996), generally avoid close inbreeding is thus only to be expected. Hence, the mechanisms for kin discrimination for inbreeding avoidance can also be supposed to be under genetic control.

It can be assumed that evolution makes use of the same basic method of kin discrimination among higher animals and humans for nepotism as for the avoiding of kin mating, at least within species.

Little Evidence for Direct Kin Discrimination

Despite a large number of studies of animal reproduction and behaviour, and despite much research on this specific subject (Fletcher & Michener 1987; Hepper 1991), there is still a startling lack of convincing evidence for allelic and phenotypic kin discrimination in higher animals (Wilson 1987; Walters 1987; Grafen 1990; Alexander 1990b; Bernstein 1991; Pfennig & Sherman 1995; Keller 1997; Kempenaers & Sheldon 1996; Krebs & Davies 1997). Considering that many studies have explicitly tried to verify the existence of direct kin recognition and discrimination, this absence is striking. Had allelic kin recognition and phenotype matching been important mechanisms for kin discrimination in higher animals, data should have been abundant.

The only data presented for genetic kin discrimination among bigger mammals, for rhesus and pig-tailed macaques, has not endured close scrutiny (see Gouzoulez & Gouzoulez 1987).

Even in the rare cases when some genetic kin discrimination by means of odour has been supposed for smaller animals, as for mice (Kareem & Barnard 1982, Boyse *et al.* 1987) and various ground-squirrels (Holmes & Sherman 1982, Davis 1982, Holmes 1986) it seems, at least as a regulator of social life, to be subordinate to the mechanism of imprinting through early close contact. Individual odour recognition among mice and ground-squirrels may to some degree benefit cooperation between kin. Among mice and several other vertebrates MHC-induced odours seem to be operating in the promoting of kin recognition to avoid inbreeding (Potts & Wakeland 1993). Similar observations have been made for lower animals such as tadpoles of frogs (Blaustein & O'Hara 1982) and of toads (Pfennig 1990), and certain ants (Keller 1995). Even if honeybee workers seem under certain experimental conditions to be able to discriminate between supersisters and halfsistsers, there is no evidence that they use this ability in natural conditions to increase their inclusive fitness according to kin selection theory (Kryger & Moritz 1997). In fact, there seems to be little evidence for genetic kin recognition among social insects (Keller 1997).

It seems that body scents, whether genetical or environmental, and various learned templates such as bird song often serve as instruments for individual recognition necessary for inbreeding avoidance and for positive and negative social discrimination as regulated by imprinting by early close contact.

Inbreeding Avoidance

It is generally agreed that natal dispersal (exogamy) plays an important role in the avoidance of close inbreeding in higher animals. Natal dispersal is generally male among mammals and female among birds. Monogamous and some polygamous mammals apply both female and male dispersal (Pusey 1987; Wolff 1997). But since one of the sexes in most cases stays in the natal group, natal dispersal only solves half of the inbreeding problem.

As yet there are few systematic studies of the mechanisms regulating kin discrimination for inbreeding avoidance in higher animals. But studies of human societies (Alexander 1990a, 1990b, 1991; Wolf 1995) and of different wild primates (Greenwood 1980; Wilson 1987; Pusey & Packer 1987; Hepper 1991), as well as experiments with and studies in the wild of Damaraland mole-rats and naked mole-rats (Jarvis *et al.* 1994; Jacobs & Jarvis 1996), prairie dogs (Hoogland 1995), thirteen-lined ground-squirrels (Holmes 1984), spiny mice (Porter *et al.* 1981) grey-tailed voles (Boyd & Blaustein 1985), Orkney voles (Lambin & Mathers 1997) and prairie voles (Getz & Carter 1996), not to mention birds (Greenwood 1980), all directly or indirectly point to the limited importance of genetical kin discrimination and to the importance of imprinting through early close contact (cf. Holmes & Sherman 1983). There are also examples among insects, such as paper wasps (Pfennig *et al.* 1983). Evidence also suggests that the colony-living and eusocial naked mole-rats are unable to discriminate between familiar and unfamiliar kin and that they, like many insects and ants, discriminate between colony and non-colony members through a unique colony odour (Jacobs & Jarvis 1996).

In fact, it seems that newborn offspring of higher animals can be socially imprinted on any conspecific individual with whom they live in close physical contact, regardless of kinship.

Among birds, parents can ignore their own offspring if it is moved outside the nest, yet at the same time care for a foreign offspring that has been placed in the nest. This is not just a matter of spatial communion but also one of imprinting over time. Bank swallows will accept other offspring that have experimentally been placed in their nest, if the latter are not older than fifteen days (Beecher *et al.* 1981; Beecher *et al.* 1981). A female herring gull will care for any unrelated offspring that happens to be in her nest, provided it is not older than one or two days. At the same time she can attack and devour the offspring in a neighbouring nest, if it is older than two days (Parsons 1971). Among Belding's ground-squirrels, a female will accept a foreign offspring if it is not older than twenty-two days (Sherman 1981). In the case of spiny mice, siblings of the same litter learn to recognize each other and form social ties within fourteen to fifteen days (Porter 1978; Porter & Wyrick 1979; Porter *et al.* 1981). Among black-tailed prairie dogs social imprinting seems to occur regardless of kinship up to the time of sexual maturity (Hoogland 1995). Thus, the basic social bonding here seems to occur in the form of imprinting through early close physical contact, regardless of whether the parties are related by kin or not.

In 1891, on the basis of ethnographic and sociological data, the Finnish sociologist Edward Westermarck presented his controversial idea that the unspoken and formal taboos against sexual contact within the human family, which are found in all societies, are based on an innate inhibition which is activated when small children grow up close to each other and adults live close to small children, in the way that children and mothers, sisters and brothers and, in general, children and fathers normally do (Westermarck 1891). This so-called Westermarck effect corresponds completely to what I here call imprinting through early close contact.

On the basis of data from 2,769 genetically unrelated men and women who from an early age grew up together in Israeli kibbutzim, Shepher was able to show that they consistently avoided sexual relations and marriage with each other, a highly improbable correlation under other circumstances. The rare exceptions concerned persons who had not lived together before the age of six. He drew the conclusion that close contact over a total of four years between birth and the age of six, especially the first three years, is enough to instil strong inhibition about future mutual sexuality in humans (Shepher 1983).

In the traditional Sim-Pua marriages in Taiwan, brides were placed at a tender age in foster-families with a boy of the same age. These children grew up almost as twins, but despite close friendship they often resisted strongly when it was time to marry. The marriages were largely failures, not least sexually, and showed a high rate of adultery and divorce (Wolf 1970, 1995). The same is shown by a study of marriages between cousins in a Lebanese ethnic group, where the parties from an early age grew up together almost as siblings. The marriages, which were seldom initiated by the young people themselves, resulted in four times as high divorce rates and twenty-three per cent fewer children than normal (McCabe 1983).

The effectiveness with which early close contact raises psychological barriers against further sexual contact is also demonstrated by innumerable adoptions of small children. The same is valid when animals adopt or kidnap young unrelated offspring (Hepper 1991; Pfennig & Sherman 1995).

Another example of the ability of early close contact to raise barriers against mutual sexuality is the observation that female Japanese macaques in oestrous, who live a highly matrifocal social life (Wolfe 1979; Chapais & Mignaux 1991), systematically exclude close kin from their lesbian interactions. The same applies to homosexual human twins. Despite the fact that twins normally uphold close social relations and that homosexuality is genetically harmless, twins of the same sex, if they have grown up together, consistently avoid each other homosexually (Whitam *et al.* 1993). A striking contrast are the bonobos, among whom normally all females in a group maintain lesbian contacts. This can in my opinion only be explained by their consistent female exogamy (de Waal 1997), which eliminates the sexual inhibitions between adult females that in matrifocal primates are provided by early close contact.

Among monogamous and such polygamous animals where males live close to their daughters, strong sexual inhibitions normally develop between fathers and daughters. Males otherwise, as in some primates, often lack permanent close social relationships with mothers and offspring. Mothers, on the other hand, always live close to their young sons, often until these are sexually mature. As a result, imprinting of strong lifelong mating inhibitions generally develops between mothers and sons. Mating inhibitions through early close contact are often weaker between fathers and daughters but still normally strong enough to prevent inbreeding, not only in monogamous but also in many polygynous groups (Wolff 1997).

Thus, at the same time as male natal dispersal dominates among mammals, mating inhibitions are stronger between mothers and sons than between fathers and daughters. This indicates that mental inhibitions against mating through early close contact are an important force behind natal dispersal—in combination with male competition, which in mammals is always stronger than that in females (cf. Wolff 1997).

Chimpanzees and bonobos are interesting exceptions in that these polygynandrous apes consistently apply female natal dispersal. This can be explained by the much weaker sexual inhibitions between males and daughters (due to limited social contact between males and females with their offspring) than between mothers and sons (due to years of intimate early contact). The strength of the sexual inhibition between mothers and sons stands out clearly against the very free sexual habits exhibited by chimpanzees and bonobos. This applies especially to the super-sexy bonobos, among whom, according to Takayoshi Kano (de Waal 1997:60), males moreover often live close to their mothers as adults.

As we have seen, it is generally unproblematic that higher group-living animals do not understand the genetic risks of close inbreeding, or that males do not "know" which young females are their daughters. Imprinting through early close contact together with natal dispersal is normally enough to avoid close inbreeding.

Incest and Infanticide

Daley and Wilson showed that most of the men in a large group who had committed incest had been absent from the home for lengthy periods of time and little involved in the care of their daughters during their first three years. In contrast, a random control group of men without incest tendencies had lived close to their daughters during the same period. It is also remarkable that the tendency in both cases was the same for genetic fathers as for genetically non-related stepfathers and adoptive fathers (Daley & Wilson 1994).

Sigmund Freud's theory of the Oedipus complex maintained that incest in humans is basically a reflection of an atavistic instinct inherited from a pre-cultural stage of human evolution, when reproduction was wholly promiscuously incestuous. One can hardly imagine an explanation of the incest phenomenon as impossible in evolutionary terms as Freud's idea. Such a reproductive system is not found in the animal world.

The fact that incest is statistically least common between mother and son, then between sister and brother and finally between father and daughter, is in complete agreement with the average degree of closeness in human and most primate family relationships. From this perspective, the often discussed universal spread of the Oedipus myth can be explained by the similar universal background of its basic motif: the very lack of early close contact when a child at an early age is separated from the parent with whom incest is later committed.

Thus, incest, infanticide and violence against small children are statistically committed mainly by men who have not lived close to the child in question during its early years. That they are more often stepfathers than genetic fathers is usually seen as an expression of kin selection. At the proximate level, however, it can be explained by the fact that stepfathers generally have experienced the least amount of early close contact with the children in question.

Among primates, the degree of physical/social closeness between males and the young varies according to species and population. But even when contact is less direct, it is normally enough to maintain inhibitions about assaulting infants, provided there is social security in the group. So, as a rule, male animals treat the young well. Nevertheless, infanticide mainly committed by males has been observed among several primates and other mammals, for instance like lions, prairie dogs, dwarf mongooses, ground-squirrels and various other rodents (Hausfater *et al.* 1984; Parmigiani & vom Saal 1994; Struhsaker & Leland 1987). Also infanticide committed mainly by females occurs, e.g. among black-tailed prairie dogs (Hoogland 1995) .

Special attention has been paid to polygynous groups with a dominant harem male, where infanticide is committed by an outside male who tries to establish himself as the leader of the group. like lions and hanuman langurs. Among certain hanuman langurs in India, a group of females with offspring is for several years dominated by a single male who has exclusive sexual rights to the females and hence is normally the father of their offspring. The other sexually mature males are forced to live in celibacy on the periphery. Every third or fourth year such a celibate male group attacks the harem and drives away the leader. It is at this point or shortly after that the new leader kills young offspring. The mother then stops nursing, resumes ovulation, comes into heat, and the new leader immediately mates with her.

Often this type of infanticide, like that among lions and some other carnivores, is interpreted as an expression of the male's instinct to increase his inclusive fitness: he kills the suckling offspring to whom he is not related in order to conceive his own offspring with its mother. The same is said to be valid when he kills offspring born some time after he has taken over leadership, as he cannot be their father either. In this way genes for male infanticidal behaviour are supposed to spread in the population (Hrdy 1977; Sommer 1994, 1996). From the proximate perspective, however, it is decisive that males who commit infanticide have been isolated from mothers and young for a lengthy period, and that they have long lived in a mood of social tension and aggression and under chronic sexual frustration. Nor have their inhibitions about assaulting the young ever been activated by early close contact. If no female happens to be in heat when the new leader takes over, no one is willing to have sex with him. Since every langur male knows that a nursing female is uninterested in sex, the suckling infant appears as the final hindrance for the new leader to enjoy a sexual life. He thus fulfils all conditions for a potential child-killer: he is in an aggressive mood, he is socially stressed, he is sexually frustrated, he has the motive, he has the opportunity, and not least, he lacks the inhibition against assaulting infants which early close contact normally provides.

If it was only a question of favouring his own genes, the new male leader would also kill the next youngest and still mother-dependent offspring, in fact all offspring who are not his. But he seldom does so. The fact that he sometimes kills an infant born a short time after he has taken over does not imply that he "understands" that he is not the father, but that he realizes that a suckling offspring will for a long time foil his chances of sex with the mother. That he does not kill his own offspring when they are born does not mean that he instinctively understands that he is the father, but that his social and sexual tensions have at that time been relieved through long co-existence with the females, and that close contact with his offspring since they were born has inoculated him against violence against them.

A great number of studies have shown primate males to be completely incapable of direct paternal recognition and discrimination (Gouzoulez & Gouzoulez 1987; Pusey 1987; Bernstein 1991; Wolff 1997). It can further be noted that many other langurs of the same species live in socially harmonious polygynandrous groups, where all the males live close to the young offspring and mothers, have their erotic needs satisfied, are seldom aggressive, treat their young well and do not commit infanticide. The fact that these differences are also related to environmental differences indicates that infanticide in langurs is mainly an expression of social stress caused by changes and restrictions in the environment. If infanticide was basically a natural evolutionary outcome of kin selection it should have been the general norm among all hanuman langurs irrespective of biotope—not to say among higher animals in general.

Another impressive example of infanticidal behaviour is seen in the North American black-tailed prairie dog. According to Hoogland, 36% of their offspring die by infanticide during the six weeks they stay in their underground burrows. Remarkably, the killers are most often close kin, sisters, daughters and mothers of the offspring's mother and are themselves often nursing mothers. Sometimes males commit infanticide as well and can then happen to kill offspring whom they have themselves conceived but never met. However, as soon as the infants come up into daylight, all females change their behaviour into a tender collective nursing and care of all the infants in the group, even those they might earlier have tried to kill.

This suggested to Hoogland that kin selection theory could not sufficiently explain infanticide in the prairie dog (Hoogland 1995). In my opinion, the reason that female prairie dogs do not hesitate to kill closely related offspring is that these are kept isolated in dark underground burrows so that no other adults than their mother come under influence of early close contact with them. That all females change their behaviour when the young appear above ground suggests that imprinting through early close contact in this species mainly come about via visual impressions. The infanticidal behaviour of the prairie dog thus indicates a general absence of genotypic and phenotypic kin discrimination and a corresponding complete dominance of a social imprinting through early close contact.

That monogamous and even polygamous fathers normally behave as the fathers they usually are to the offspring in the family and do not kill them may be in line with the theory of kin selection. But at the proximate level it reflects that early close contact has a particularly powerful effect on monogamous and harem-polygamous fathers, regardless of whether they are genetic kin or unrelated to the infant due to philandery, a widespread behaviour among monogamous birds, harem mammals, not to mention humans. The background of infanticide in animals is often complex, but the main proximate mechanism, at least among humans and non-human primates, seems to be social and/or sexual frustration in combination with weakly developed inhibitions about assaulting infants due to insufficient early close contact.

The imprinting of inhibitions about sexual relations through early close contact operates on an individual level. A male who has been imprinted with inhibitions about assaulting a certain young can commit violence against another with whom he has not had early close contact, kin or not.

Accordingly, infanticide is more common among polygamous than among monogamous and polygynandrous animals. It can also be noted that infanticide and incest in humans are dominated by the same categories as among non-human primates, that is, socially and sexually frustrated stepfathers and adoptive fathers, sometimes genetic fathers, who have been insufficiently imprinted on the child by early close contact.

Helping Behaviour and Reproductive Altruism

Among many monogamous species of birds, 25–30% of the offspring can be the result of extra-pair copulation (Westneat *et al.* 1990; Birkhead & Möller 1992; Wagner *et al.* 1996; Stutchbury *et al.* 1997). A study of Canadian tree swallows under natural conditions showed that as many as 84% of the nesting females obtained fertilization from extra-pair males, who actually fathered as much as 69% of all nestlings (Barber *et al.* 1996). Extra-pair offspring are common also among many other monogamous and polygynous animals, including humans, and DNA studies have revealed an astonishing amount of extra-group paternity among West African chimpanzees (Gagneux *et al.* 1997). This means that a substantial number of males unwittingly feed and care for other males' offspring as if they were their own. The effect is even more dramatic when birds lay eggs in nests that belong to other birds of different or even the same species. For swallows and starlings, respectively, 3–31% and 5–46% of the nests have been estimated to be affected in this way (Petrie & Möller 1991). But despite the great reproductive loss, both females and males show parental behaviour towards the young to which they are not related. Even though genetic profits and losses may balance out during an individual's lifetime, this hardly applies to the majority of males and not in connection with intraspecific brood parasitism. This behaviour demonstrates that birds are more or less incapable of allelic kin discrimination and of acting as though they could judge whether or not their behaviour directly favours their reproductive success according to the idea of inclusive fitness. On the proximate level, this can only be understood in the light of the ability of early close contact to imprint positive social behaviour regardless of genetic kinship.

Reproductive altruism is known among several hundred species of birds, one hundred and twenty species of mammals and many types of fish. If the young bird is not ready to breed or fails to find a mate or an adequate territory in the vicinity of its parents, it often chooses to stay close to them, on which it has been strongly imprinted socially through early close contact. Its instinct to care for young offspring is then in a natural way directed towards the newly hatched infants in its parent's nest, who are normally its siblings, sometimes half-siblings, in another brood, but who can also be unrelated to it due to inter- and intra-specific brood parasitism.

Thus, even if individuals involved in reproductive altruism are often close kin, there is no hindrance at all for reproductive altruism to affect non-kin. Hence it seems that reproductive altruism does not operate through allelic identification but through discrimination based on imprinting by early close contact. On the proximate level, reproductive altruism should rather be seen as a combined effect of the ability to identify individuals, the instinct to care for the young, imprinting through early close contact, and perhaps also the helper's desire to increase its social prestige and thereby its reproductive success (Armitage 1987; Barnard 1991; Zahavi 1995).

Among insects and other lower animals, kin recognition and kin discrimination is often a complex affair, involving genetic, locational and social factors. Earlier evidence for kin recognition by genetic cues among social insects has not endured close examination (Keller 1997). It seems that in social insects and ants—as in various types of wasps (*Polistes*) (Michener 1987)—imprinting for positive sociality and against inbreeding often occurs by means of odours, for example, from the environment where they are bred or some basic food. Laurent Keller has shown that two newly hatched, unrelated litters from different ant colonies, which were experimentally mixed with each other, after a few months coordinated their smell to one common odour. The aggression they would normally have shown each other was replaced by mutual friendliness as if they had been close kin. It thus seems that kin discrimination in some social insects and ants can be regulated by a combination of imprinting through early close contact and environmental factors.

Sterile workers among eusocial insects, ants and termites, and some eusocial mammals, are often said to be infertile as a result of kin selection for the purpose of assisting the queen in producing and raising all her offspring, to which they are closely related. As I see it, the proximate key factor is the mass reproduction of close relatives in a secluded nest. The close spatial communion creates the frame for early physical contact which imprints its inhabitants for mutual positive social behaviour and against mutual mating, while the common odour of the nest acts as the means of group identification. Since the risk of inbreeding within the nest remains, large-scale sterility is developed, for example through reproductive suppression. The fact that sterile females help offspring that are not their own only reflects that they have retained their instinct to care for offspring, which chemical odours tell them that they belong closely to, regardless of the degree of kinship. However, the genetic unity among social insects and ants is not as great as was formerly thought (Keller 1995; Arnold *et al.* 1996; Strassmann *et al.* 1994; Oldroyd *et al.* 1995), and current evidence does not suggest differences in altruistic behaviour between different degrees of relatives. Similar mechanisms may well regulate the "selfless" suicidal behaviour of worker bees, which has often been seen as the definite proof for the theory of kin selection. Furthermore, non-reproductive helping behaviour in animals may, just as in low-technical human societies, serve as an instrument in population control.

The observation that eusocial naked mole-rats show greater aggression towards uncles and aunts than towards offspring and siblings has aroused attention considering the very little genetic difference between these two groups (Reeve & Sherman 1991). However, from the perspective of imprinting through early close contact, less aggressive behaviour towards offspring and siblings than towards uncles and aunts in a mammal would make good sense even if the parties had been genetically identical.

Warning cries and alarm signals are another classic example of kin selection. As kinship within the group is often great, the warning animal is seen as reaping a genetic profit even at the cost of its own death. Of course warning cries have an evolutionary value, but little is known about the risks of giving warning cries, and if a mother dies as a consequence of her warning, her offspring will probably dramatically decrease in fitness. The fact that warning cries are often directed from mothers to offspring or otherwise between close kin could rather be seen as an outcome of parental instincts and as the result of an evolutionary selection for warning cries between individuals affected by positive imprinting through early close contact.

There is also good evidence that imprinting by early close social is associated with inbreeding avoidance by means of reproductive suppression of females among insects, rodents, carnivores, horses and primates (Wolff 1997).

Conclusions

The assumption behind Hamilton's theory of inclusive fitness is the observation that animals behave positively to each other roughly according to their degree of kinship. But this observation in fact reflects realities which are basically the outcome of imprinting through early close contact. The success of Hamilton's rule has thus effectively blinded us to the importance of imprinting through early close social contact as an evolutionary mechanism.

The fact that imprinting through early close contact occurs in widely different animal taxa demonstrates its great evolutionary age. In humans it is most likely regulated by the limbic system.

Imprinting through early close contact between infants, and between infants and adults, seems to create permanent positive social relations as well as permanent mental barriers against sexual contact. Normally the parties are close kin, but imprinting through early close contact affects non-kin with the same force. The duration and time for the imprinting process vary according to the rate of life development of the species.

Hence, parental care as such in higher animals is not dependent on genetic kinship in itself. Apart from hormonal changes in the new mother, and the instinct of infant care, parental care is discriminated for by early close contact. For mothers, nursing and the physical intimacy of infant care seem to imply such strong social imprinting that, for instance, a primate mother and her adult child will always recognize their roles as mother and child, as do normally males and children who have lived close together in, for instance, monogamous relations. But there is no proof that males have any direct means of recognizing their own genetic offspring. Since the male notion of his own fatherhood is wholly dependent on imprinting through early close contact, it is indirect and genetically unquestionable only when fathers live close to mother and infant in monogamous or polygamous relations free from extra-pair matings.

This sharp contrast between maternal and paternal possibilities to recognize own genetic offspring illustrates the general inability among higher animals to identify close kin by means of genetic cues or phenotype matching. It also demonstrates the central role for kin discrimination of imprinting through early close contact. Therefore, and as an effect of male dispersal, kin discrimination among mammals often follows matrilineal patterns, and therefore male mammals do not often come into a position where they can favour their inclusive fitness by helping grandchildren, cousins or aunts.

The fact that most social mammals apply male natal dispersal and matrilocality means that sisters, as an effect of early close contact, often keep together even as mothers. Hence the imprinting through early close contact among females often occurs beyond the level of siblings, and hence the favouring of relatives in social mammals especially appears between female cousins, between females and their aunts and between grandmothers and grandchildren. For male birds, such imprinting beyond the sibling level is limited due to female natal dispersal and to the system of separate nests.

Since primates normally bear only one offspring, which is dependent on its mother or parents for a long time, older and younger siblings often become socially imprinted on each other through early close contact. But among socially monogamous birds, siblings from different broods are not imprinted on each other by early close contact. Thus full siblings from different broods could only favour their inclusive fitness by helping each other in the form of reproductive altruism, as when older siblings, often brothers, help younger siblings of later broods. Since natal dispersal among birds is most often female, the same conclusion applies to adult female full siblings within and between broods. Hence, if kin selection follows coefficients of relatedness, the effect will differ for different sexes.

It can thus be said *a priori* that the operational range of kin selection is restricted by various social factors and that it should be of different relevance for different taxa, species, populations and sexes.

If kin discrimination in higher animals is basically non-allelic, then kin selection is indirect. What it is about is a selection of genes which promote positive imprinting through early close contact, which in turn most often affect kin. Hence the term kin selection is not fully adequate.

Eusocial insects provide an interesting contrast to mammals and birds. The mere fact that eusocial insects and ants live together in such great numbers limits their possibilities for individual recognition based on appearance. Instead, they are resigned to chemical signals to distinguish kin from non-kin, friend from foe, and sexually neutral individuals from potential mating partners. This makes permanent co-existence between unrelated individuals impossible. For the sake of reproduction, eusocial insects and ants therefore make use of sexual pheromones, which temporarily overrule the recognition odours that normally block contacts between individuals from unrelated colonies. As a consequence, their social life includes neither the permanent living together of unrelated adults, nor reciprocal altruism, nor reproductive altruism between non-kin, nor the adoption of non-kin. This means that eusocial insects and ants lack full social complexity, and that their value as models for the understanding of social life among higher social animals has been erroneously overplayed.

Thus, social complexity in the true sense postulates permanent co-existence between reproductive males and females who are not close kin, as in most birds and mammals. Hence mammals and birds would scarcely have developed in the way they have, had allelic recognition or self-referential phenotype matching been their main instrument for social discrimination. The fact that kin discrimination in higher animals is basically non-allelic stands out as a precondition for the evolution of the permanent living together of non-kin adults, as in monogamous and polygamous social relations. It is also a precondition for positive social interactions in the form of reciprocal altruism and reproductive altruism between non-kin, as well as for the evolution of phenomena such as adoption, adultery, extra-pair copulation, and inter- and intra-specific brood parasitism.

No doubt, better knowledge of the mechanism of early close contact would promote better insight into human social life in general. In particular it provides a useful instrument for analysing, and to some extent also for preventing, social problems such as incest and infanticide.

By intertwining positive sociality and inhibitions from sexual intercourse, and by excluding allelic recognition as a means of kin discrimination, the mechanism of early close social contact stands out as a basic code for the understanding of the evolution of social order and social norm systems among complex, group-living animals and humans. Social complexity and flexibility as expressed by strategic alliances, reciprocal altruism and social altruism between non-kin, including all that we call friendship, sympathy, empathy, love, unselfishness, gratitude, guilty conscience, sense of responsibility, sense of justice, and so on, between unrelated individuals, would never have evolved in humans, had kin been generally discriminated through allelic recognition or phenotype matching.

Thus non-allelic imprinting through early close contact can be seen as a prerequisite for the evolution of full social complexity. A useful way of separating "lower" and "higher" animals would then be to distinguish between those who can and cannot, by means of the absence of allelic kin recognition and by the presence of imprinting through early close contact, organize their reproductive and social life according to permanent non-kin monogamous, polygamous and polygynandrous relations.

Together with such evolutionary deep-rooted mechanisms as survival instinct, sexual drive, instinctive infant care, ability to recognize individuals, and, among mammals, nursing, imprinting through early close social contact should explain much of the proximate behaviour in higher animals that is interpreted as an ultimate expression of kin selection.

Thus, if there is no evidence for selection of genes for altruism aimed exclusively at genetic kin in the form of direct kin selection, the theoretical objections against the possible evolution of social altruism, which have been raised by classical sociobiology on the basis of kin selection theory, cannot be upheld. The "altruistic paradox" is not that paradoxical. Not surprisingly, a certain moral behaviour is to be found, not only among humans but also among some other higher animals (de Waal 1996, 1997). But since true altruism—like true selfishness—theoretically cannot be regarded as a stable evolutionary strategy (Maynard Smith 1964; Wilson 1968), social altruism can then be assumed to appear and reappear without ever becoming dominant, precisely as seems to be reflected by human societies.

If the theoretical basis of sociobiology's inexorably deterministic view of human social behaviour can thus be shown to be partly wrong, the criticism against it can also be said to have been misdirected. This opens prospects for better future understanding of biological aspects of human behaviour from the part of humanists and social scientists.

Acknowledgements

I thank Lars Berg, Karl Fredga, Jan Ekman, Hans Ellegren, Sara Gräslund, Andreas Kindmark, Dan Larhammar and Thomas Ljungberg for helpful comments and discussions.

References

Alexander, R. D. 1990a. *How did humans evolve? Reflections of the Uniquely Unique Species.* Ann Arbor, Michigan.
Alexander, R. D. 1990b. Social learning and kin recognition. *Ethology and Sociobiology* 11, 241–303.
Alexander, R. D. 1991. Social learning and kin recognition: An addendum and reply to Sherman. *Ethology and Sociobiology* 12, 387–399.
Armitage, K. 1987. Social dynamics of mammals: reproduction success, kinship and individual fitness. *Trends in Ecology and Evolution* 2, 279–284.
Arnold, G., Quenet, B., Cornuet, J.-M., De Shepper, B., Estoup, A. & Gasqui, P. 1996. Kin recognition in honeybees. *Nature* 378, 498.
Barber, C. A., Robertson, R. J. & Boag, P. T. 1996. The high frequency of extra-pair paternity in tree swallows is not an artefact of nestboxes. *Behavioral Ecology and Sociobiology* 38, 425–430.
Barnard, C. 1991. Kinship and social behaviour: The trouble with relatives. *Trends in Ecology and Evol*ution 6, 310–312.
Barrett, S. C. H. & Harder, L. D. 1996. Ecology and evolution of plant mating. *Trends in Ecology and Evolution* 11, 73–79.
Beecher, M. D., Beecher, I. M. & Hahn, S. 1981. Parent–offspring recognition in the bank swallow (*Riparia riparia*): development and acoustic basis. *Animal Behaviour* 29, 95–101.
Beecher, M. D., Beecher, I. M. & Lumpkin, S. 1981. Parent–offspring recognition in the bank swallow (*Riparia riparia*): I. Natural history, *Animal Behaviour* 29, 86–94.
Bernstein, I. S. 1991. The correlation between kinship and behaviour in non-human primates. In Hepper, P. G. (ed.), *Kin recognition*, 6–29. Cambridge.
Birkhead, T. R. & Möller, A. P. 1992. *Sperm competition in birds: Evolutionary causes and consequences.* London.
Blaustein, A. R. & O'Hara, R. K. 1982. Kin recognition in Rana cascadae tadpoles: maternal and paternal effects. *Animal Behaviour* 30, 1151–1157.
Boyd, S. K. & Blaustein, A. R. 1985. Familiarity and breeding avoidance in the gray-tailed vole (*Microtus canicaudus*). *Journal of Mammalogy* 66, 348–352.
Boyse, E. A., Beauchamp, G. K. & Yamazaki, K. 1987. The genetics of body scent. *Trends in Genetics* 3: 4, 97–102.

Chapais, B. & Mignaux, C. 1991. Homosexual incest avoidance among females in captive Japanese macaques. *American Journal of Primatology*, 23:3, 175–179.
Daley, M. & Wilson, M. 1994. Some differential attributes of lethal assaults on small children by stepfathers versus genetic fathers. *Ethology and Sociobiology* 15, 207–217.
Darwin, C. 1859. *On the Origins of Species by Means of Natural Selection, or, the Preservation of Favoured Races in the Struggle for Life*. London.
Davis, L. S. 1982. Sibling recognition in Richardson's ground-squirrels, *Spermophilus richardsoni*. *Behavioral Ecology and Sociobiology* 11, 65–70.
Dawkins, R. 1976 *The selfish gene*. Oxford.
Dawkins, R. 1989. *The selfish gene*, New edition, 95–108. Oxford.
Dobson, F. S. 1982. Competition for mates and predominant juvenile male dispersal in mammals. *Animal Behaviour* 30, 1183–1192.
Fisher, R. 1930. *The genetical evolution of natural selection*. Oxford.
Gagneux, P., Woodruff, D. & Boesch, C. 1997. Furtive mating in female chimpanzees. *Nature* 387, 22 May 1997, 358–359.
Getz, L. L. & Carter, S. 1996. Prairie-vole partnerships. *American Scientist* 84, 54–62.
Gouzoulez, S. & Gouzoulez, H. 1987. Kinship. In Smuts B., Cheney, D., Seyfarth, R., Wrangham, R. & Struhsaker, T., (eds), *Primate Societies*. Chicago, 299–305.
Grafen, A. 1990. Do animals really recognize kin? *Animal Behaviour* 39, 42–49
Greenwood, P. J. 1980. Mating systems, philopatry and dispersal in birds and mammals. *Animal Behaviour*, 1140–1162.
Hamilton, W. D. 1964. The genetical evolution of social behaviour I–II. *Journal of Theoretical Biology* 7, 1–52.
Hausfater, G. & Hrdy, S. Blaffer (eds) 1984. *Infanticide. Comparative and evolutionary perspectives*. New York.
Holmes, W. G. 1984. Sibling recognition in thirteen-lined ground-squirrels: Effects of genetic relatedness, rearing association, and olfaction. *Behavioral Ecology and Sociobiology* 14, 225–233.
Holmes, W. G. 1986. Identification of paternal half siblings by captive Belding's ground-squirrels. *Animal Behaviour* 34, 321–327.
Holmes, W. G. & Sherman, P. W. 1982. The ontogeny of kin recognition in two species of ground squirrels. *American Zoologist* 22, 491–517.
Holmes, W. G. & Sherman, P. W. 1983. Kin recognition in animals. *American Scientist* 71, 46–55.
Hoogland, J. L. 1995. *The Black-Tailed Prairie Dog. Social Life of a Burrowing Animal*. Chicago.
Hrdy, S. Blaffer. 1977. *The Langurs of Abu: Female and male strategies of reproduction*. Cambridge, Mass.
Jacobs, D. S. & Jarvis, J. U. M. 1996. No evidence for the work-conflict hypothesis in the eusocial naked mole-rat (*Heterocephalus glaber*). *Behavioral Ecology and Sociobiology* 39, 401–409.
Jarvis, J. U. M., O'Riain M. J., Bennett, N. C. & Sherman, P. W. 1994. Mammalian eusociality: a family affair. *Trends in Ecology and Evolution* 9, 2, 1994, 47–51.
Kareem, A. M. & Barnard, C. J. 1982. The importance of kinship and familiarity in social interactions between mice. *Animal Behaviour* 30, 594–601.
Keller, L. 1995. Social life: the paradox of multiple-queen colonies. *Trends in Ecology and Evolution* 10, 355–360.
Keller, L. 1997. Indiscriminate altruism: unduly nice parents and siblings. *Trends in Ecology and Evolution* 12, 99–103.

Kempenaers, B. & Sheldon, B. C. 1996. Why do male birds not discriminate between their own and extra-pair offspring? *Animal Behaviour* 51, 1165–1173.
Krebs, J. R. & Davies, N. B. 1997. *Behavioral Ecology. An evolutionary approach.* Fourth ed. Cambridge.
Kryger, P. & Moritz, R. 1997. Lack of kin recognition in swarming honeybees (*Apis mellifera*). *Behavioral Ecology and Sociobiology* 1997, 40, 271–276.
Lambin, X. & Mathers, C. 1997. Dissipation of kin discrimination in Orkney voles, *Microtus arvalis orcadensis*: a laboratory study. *Annales Zoologici Fennici* 34, 23–30.
Maynard Smith, J. 1964. Group selection and kin selection. *Nature* 201, 1145–1147.
Maynard Smith, J. & Szathmáry, E. 1995. *The major transitions in evolution.* New York.
McCabe, S. 1983. FBD-marriage: Further support for the Westermarck hypothesis of the incest taboo? *American Anthropologist.* 85, 50–69.
Mendel, G. 1866. Versuchen über Pflanzenhybriden. *Verhandlungen naturforschender Verein in Brünn. Abhandlungen.* Brünn.
Michener, C. 1987. Kin recognition in primitively eusocial insects. In Fletcher, D. J. C. & Michener, C. D. (eds), *Kin recognition in animals*, 209–242. Chichester.
Oldroyd, B. P., Smolenski, A. J., Cornuet, J.-M., Wongsiri, S., Estoup, A., Rinderer, T. & Crozier, R. H. 1995. Levels of polyandry and intercolonial genetic relationships in *Apis florea*. *Behavioral Ecology and Sociobiology* 37, 329–335.
Parmigiani, S. & vom Saal, F. S. (eds) 1994. *Infanticide and parental care.* Chur.
Parsons, J. 1971. Cannibalism in herring gulls. *British Birds* 64, 528–537.
Petrie, M. & Möller, A. P. 1991. Laying eggs in other's nests: intraspecific brood parasitism in birds. *Trends in Ecology and Evolution* 6, 310–312.
Pfennig, D. W. 1990. "Kin recognition" among spadefoot toad tadpoles: A side-effect of habitat selection. *Evolution* 44, 785–798.
Pfennig, D. W., Gamboa, G. J., Reeve, J. S. & Ferguson, I. D. 1983. The mechanisms of nestmate discrimination in social wasps (*Polistes, Hymenoptera: Vespidae*). *Behavioral Ecology and Sociobiology* 13, 299–305.
Pfennig, D. W. & Sherman, P. W. 1995. Kin recognition. *Scientific American*, June 1995, 68–73.
Porter, R. H., Tepper, W. J. & White, D. M. 1981. Experimental influences on the development of huddling preferences and "sibling" recognition in spiny mice, *Developmental Psychobiology* 14, 375–382.
Porter, R. H. & Wyrick, M. 1979. Sibling recognition in spiny mice (*Acomys cahirinus*): influence of age and isolation. *Animal Behaviour* 27, 761–766.
Porter, R. H., Wyrick, M. & Pankey, J. 1978. Sibling recognition in spiny mice (*Acomys cahirinus*). *Behavioral Ecology and Sociobiology* 3, 61–68.
Potts, W. K. & Wakeland, E. K. 1993. Evolution of MHC genetic diversity: a tale of incest, pestilence and sexual preference. *Trends in Genetics* 9, 408–412.
Pusey, A. 1987. Sex-biased dispersal and inbreeding avoidance in birds and mammals. *Trends in Ecology and Evolution* 2, 295–299.
Pusey, A. & Packer, C. 1987. Dispersal and philopatry. In Smuts B., Cheney D., Seyfarth, R., Wrangham, R. & Struhsaker, T., (eds), *Primate Societies*. Chicago, 250–266.
Reeve, H. K. & Sherman, P. W. 1991. Intracolonial aggression and nepotism by the breeding female naked mole-rat. In Sherman, P. W., Jarvis, J. U. M. & Alexander, R. D. (eds), *The biology of the naked mole-rat*, 337–357. Princeton.
Shepher, J. 1983. *Incest: A Biosocial View.* New York.
Sherman, P. W. 1981. Kinship, demography, and Belding's ground squirrel nepotism. *Behavioral Ecology and Sociobiology* 8, 251–259.

Sommer, V. 1996. *Heilige Egoisten—Die Soziobiologie indischer Tempelaffen.* München.
Strassmann, J., Hughes, C., Turilazzi, S., Solis, C. & Queller, D. 1994. Genetic relatedness and incipient eusociality in stenogastrine wasps. *Animal Behaviour* 48, 813–821.
Struhsaker, T. T. & Leland, L. 1987. Colobines: Infanticide by adult males. In Smuts B., Cheney, D., Seyfarth, R., Wrangham, R. & Struhsaker, T., (eds), *Primate Societies*, 83–97. Chicago.
Stutchbury, B., Piper, W. H., Neudorf, D., Taroff, S., Rhymer, J., Fuller, G. & Fleischer, R. C. 1997. Correlates of extra-pair fertilization success in hooded warblers. *Behavioral Ecology and Sociobiology* 1997, 40, 119–126.
Trivers, R. 1971. The evolution of reciprocal altruism. *Quarterly Review of Biology* 46, 35–37.
de Waal, F. 1996. *Good natured: On the origins of right and wrong in humans and other animals.* Cambridge, Mass.
de Waal, F. & Lanting, F. 1997. *Bonobo: The forgotten ape.* Cambridge, Mass.
Wagner, R., Schug, M., Morton, E. 1996. Confidence of paternity, actual paternity and parental effort by purple martins. *Animal Behaviour* 1996, 52, 123–132.
Walters, J. R. 1987. Kin recognition in non-human primates. In Fletcher, D. J. C. & Michener, C.D. (eds), *Kin recognition in animals*, 359–393. Chichester.
Waser, P.M. & Jones, W. T. 1983. Natal philopatry among solitary mammals. *Quarterly Review of Biology* 58, 355–390.
Westermarck, E. 1891. *The history of human marriage.* London.
Westneat, D. F., Sherman, P. W. and Morton, M. L. 1990. The ecology and evolution of extra-pair copulations in birds. *Current Ornithology* 7, 330–369.
Whitam, F. L., Diamond, M. & Martin, J. 1993. Homosexual orientation in twins: a report on 61 pairs and three triplet sets. *Archive of Sexual Behavior* 22, 187–206.
Wilson, E. O. 1975. *Sociobiology: The new synthesis.* Cambridge, Mass.
Wilson, E. O. 1978. *On human nature.* Cambridge, Mass.
Wilson, E. O. 1987. Kin recognition: An introductory synopsis. In Fletcher, D. J. C. & Michener C. D. (eds), *Kin recognition in animals*, 7–18. Chichester.
Woodruff D. S. & Boesch, C. 1997. Furtive mating in female chimpanzees. *Nature* 387, 1997, 358–359.
Wolf, A. P. 1970. Childhood association and sexual attraction. *American Anthropologist* 70, 503–515.
Wolf, A. P. 1995. *Sexual attraction and childhood association: A Chinese brief for Edward Westermarck.* Stanford.
Wolff, J. 1997. Population regulation in mammals: an evolutionary perspective. *Journal of Animal Ecology* 1997, 66, 1–13.
Wolfe, L. M. 1979. Behavioral patterns of estrous females of the Arashiyama West troop of Japanese macaques (*Macaca fuscata*). *Primates,* 525–534.
Zahavi, A. 1995. Altruism as a handicap—the limitations of kin selection and reciprocity. *Journal of Avian Biology* 26:1, 1–3.

Opposition, Hierarkchy and Gender in Aboriginal South America: Linguistic and Architectural Homologies

By Alf Hornborg

Introduction

For many years my research was focused on the comparative ethnography of the Amazon Basin (Hornborg 1988, 1993, in press). Like several others who have penetrated the systems of classification and symbolism of this region, I sensed that there were interesting connections between the indigenous cosmological systems that could be documented ethnographically in the lowlands, on the one hand, and those that could be traced ethnohistorically to the ancient civilizations of the Andes, on the other.[1] The most intriguing similarities were certain aspects of spatial organization that were not immediately apparent to the eye, but that emerged in ethnographical and ethnohistorical explications of their cosmological significance. The challenge was to bring ethnography, ethnohistory and archaeology together, and, not least, to account for the widespread distribution of recurrent patterns and principles throughout South America. In the early eighties, I found the concept of "ethnoarchaeology" adequate for what I was trying to do, even if my competence was more in the "ethno-" than in the archaeology.[2]

Now that this symposium offers me an opportunity and an incentive to return to this topic, I recall how little explicit thought I had given to issues of methodology. I had allowed various bits and pieces of ethnographical, historical and archaeological information to fall upon me, and, to be honest, finally relied on whatever capacity for *Gestalt* perception I may have had to integrate it all. From a purely archaeological point of view, this is probably inexcusable, but the heterogeneity of the material then seemed to leave me little choice. I nevertheless arrived at six structural principles that appeared to organize social space in several cultures in both the highlands and lowlands, which I shall recapitulate shortly. I realize that these abstract, spatial "principles" in themselves might simply reflect universal inclinations of the human mind[3], but the particular substance of the parallels in certain contexts still strikes me as being idiosyncratic enough to suggest cultural and historical continuities. In this paper, I would like to review some of my earlier observations on spatial symbolism in aboriginal South America, and then go on to relate them to the principles of social classification evident in the type of kinship terminology that has been predominant throughout much of the continent. Where this puts me in the current polemic between "post-processual" and "cognitive-processual" archaeology (Renfrew 1994), I leave it to others to judge. I myself would like to think that if similar principles of classification can be discovered in architecture and language, this might represent a small step toward increased scientific precision.

Architecture and World-View

A very basic point of departure is that, in the "traditional" or "premodern" cultures that we are talking about, there is no distinction between practical function and symbolic meaning (cf. Hodder 1986). All human action and all material culture (including what we would classify as architecture and technology) was embedded in cosmological significance. A realm of pure, material instrumentality emerged only with modernity, or with what Ellul called "the technological society." This is definitely not to say that modern material culture is practical function and nothing else (cf. Sahlins 1976), but that the concept of the technical and instrumental has been detached from an all-encompassing symbolic scheme, or world-view. It is perhaps the absence of a pervasive cosmology—and the preoccupation with a decontextualized instrumentality—that more than anything else defines the modern condition. The modern mind is trained to think of material causality as devoid of deeper significance. Premodern material culture, in contrast, can generally be *expected* to say something about world-views.

Another point of departure is that the human mind can harbour implicit, cosmological "deep structures" that are communicated along with the explicit details and that can generate various manifestations in different contexts. In this regard, I remain faithful to the structuralist project in anthropology. The basic elements of cosmologies are principles for classification, metaphors and symbols. At the most abstract levels, cosmologies can persist over long periods of time and, through migration, reach wide geographical distribution.

With these two points of departure as a baseline, it would be justifiable (a) to look to architectural remains for evidence of world-views, and (b) to consider the possibility of far-reaching continuities in time and space. I have thus compared various indigenous site layouts throughout the northern half of South America, with particular attention, of course, to the native explications that have been documented through ethnographical or ethnohistorical research. Thanks to the religious zeal of Spanish chroniclers such as Bernabé Cobo (cf. Rowe 1979), the cosmological principles underlying the layout of sixteenth century Inca towns are almost as accessible to us as those of Indian villages contacted in the twentieth century. The geographically far-flung comparisons that I am suggesting, ranging from highland Peru to eastern Brazil, are not as arbitrary as it may seem, for highland and lowland populations may be closer related linguistically than we have assumed. The center of Chiripa in the Titicaca Basin, built around 200 B.C., and considered to be the prototype of Tiwanaku, Wari and Inca sites throughout the southern Andes (Conklin & Moseley 1988:160 ff.), may have been inhabited by Arawak-speakers ancestral to the Chipaya (Browman 1980:110 ff.; Ruhlen 1987:373). Arawak is a language family that, emerging from the lower Amazon about 3000 B.C., spread widely across lowland South America and up along the eastern flanks of the Andes (Lathrap 1970).

Arawak- and Gé-speaking groups in eastern Brazil still build villages the underlying principles of which are reminiscent of Inca centers such as Cuzco (Zuidema 1964; Rowe 1979), Huánuco Pampa (Morris 1980) and Inkawasi (Hyslop 1985). Similar principles seem to have been internalized in the layout of longhouses in lowland Colombia (Hugh-Jones 1977:207) and roundhouses in Venezuela (Wilbert 1981). This is not the place to reiterate all the details of these widespread redundancies and correspondences. Let me rather recapitulate the principles themselves:

"The formal argument is that several cultures in both the highlands and lowlands express, in their architecture, a mental template by which space is organized in terms of (1) an absolute centre, located on (2) one or two axes achieving a bi- or quadripartition, and geared to (3) a circular perimeter yielding (4) a radial distribution of social and cosmological categories. Where native elucidation is accessible, recurrent features include (5) a mirror-image asymmetry, produced by the projection of an hierarchical dimension parallel to the central axis, i.e. perpendicular to the diametric opposition achieved by this axis, and (6) a conflation of space and time, so that the circular perimeter is imbued with calendrical significance" (Hornborg 1990:84).

To give an indication of the kind of specific parallels that have been documented, we might briefly review a comparison between sixteenth century Cuzco (Fig. 1) and a Bororo village of eastern Brazil (Fig. 2), described a few decades ago.

Cuzco was divided into the two moieties Hanan (Upper, in the north) and Hurin (Lower, in the south), and subdivided by a second axis into four quarters (suyu). The idea of an absolute center was manifested in monuments on or near the central plaza like the *ushñu* platform, the Sunturwasi observatory, and the Coricancha (The Temple of the Sun). It has been suggested that the Hanan side of the central plaza was associated with male activities and the Hurin side with the feminine domain (Isbell 1978:275). The social categories of the city were associated with distinct directions of the compass through a system of ritual sight lines *(ceques)* radiating from its center and serving as a calendar, with the Hanan and Hurin sets of *ceques* representing different seasons. These lines and attendant social categories were ideally arranged in twelve groups of three. The three *ceques* in each group were ranked according to a standard set

96 Alf Hornborg

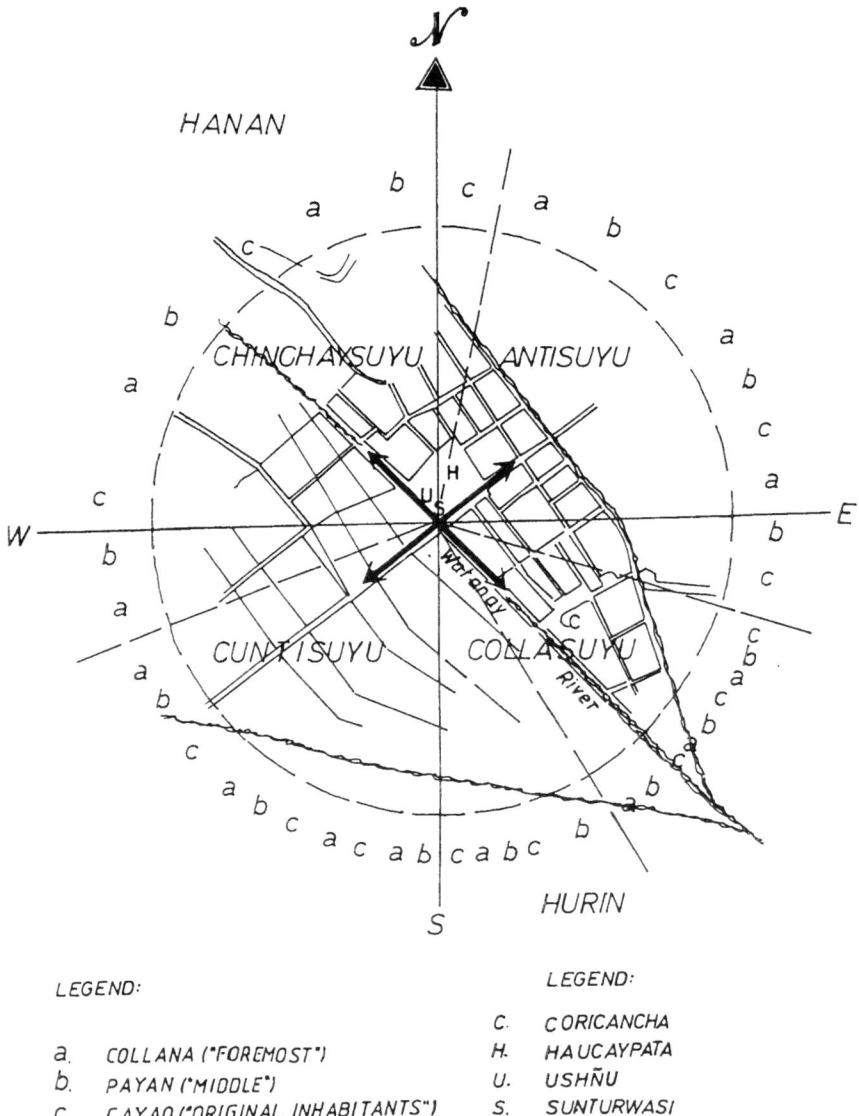

Fig. 1. The four divitions of the *ceque* system superimposed on a plan of Inca Cuxco.

of categories (Collana, Payan, and Cayao, translated as Foremost, Middle, and Lower [or "Original inhabitants"]). Six of the twelve groups belonged to the northern moiety, the other six to the southern. The projection of rank order was clockwise in the northern moiety, counterclockwise in the southern. The highest ranked (Collana) *ceque* in each group of three was thus always located furthest to the west, irrespective of moiety, producing mirror-image hierarchies

Opposition, hierarkchy and gender in aboriginal South America 97

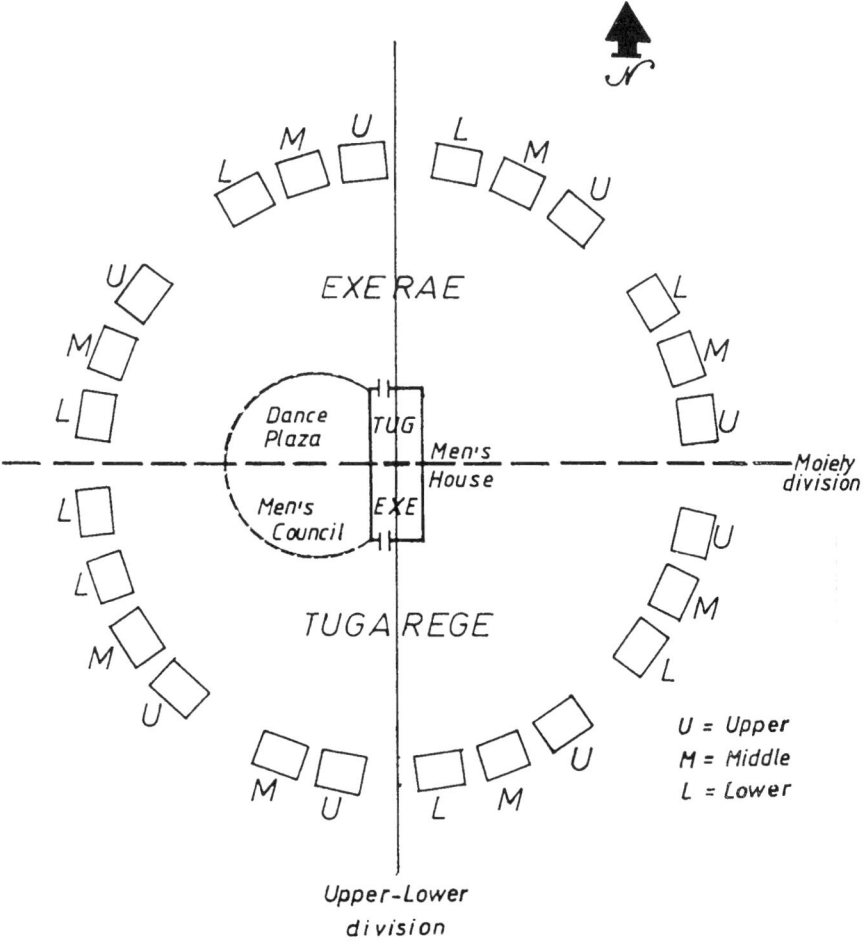

Fig. 2. Plan of a Bororo village (adapted from Crocker 1971).

along the perimeters of the two moieties, with categories of similar rank facing each other across the town axis.

The Bororo village is similarly subdivided by two perpendicular axes (Crocker 1969:57 f.; Lévi-Strauss 1973:74 f., 81). One of the axes distinguishes the two exogamous moieties Exerae (in the north) and Tugarege (in the south), and early data suggest a second set of moieties, called Upper and Lower, cross-cutting these to yield a quadripartition (Lévi-Strauss 1936:270 ff.; Lowie 1946:421, 427). The central men's house and dance plaza is surrounded by a circle of matrilineal clans to which paths radiate like the spokes of a wheel. The village center is associated with male activities, while the perimeter is a feminine domain. There are four named clans in each of the

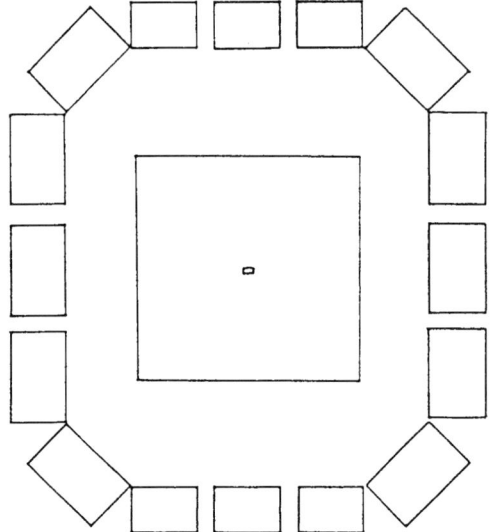

Fig. 3. Plan of Chiripa at the beginning of the Early Intermediate Period, around 200 B.C. (adapted from a reconstruction by W. J. Conklin; cf. Conklin & Moseley 1988:161). A "ring" of houses surround a sunken plaza with a stone pillar in the centre.

exogamous moieties, and each is ideally subdivided into three ranked sections (Upper, Middle, and Lower; Crocker 1971). The tripartite hierarchy, which appears to be conceived in terms of relative age, i.e. older vs. younger siblings (Crocker 1971:391), is arranged clockwise in one moiety and counterclockwise in the other. The highest ranked (Upper) section is always located furthest to the east, irrespective of moiety, so that social categories of similar rank face each other in mirror-image fashion across the village axis. Finally, the circular villages of eastern Brazil are often reported to serve as calendars, sun dials, or other modes of reckoning time (cf. Gregor 1977:36 f.), and the moieties are often associated with different seasons (Nimuendajú 1946; Lave 1979:27 f.).

Before moving on, let us briefly return to the ancient site of Chiripa in the Titicaca Basin. We have suggested that it may represent a link between the Andean civilizations and the populations of the Amazonian lowlands. It is ancestral to Tiwanaku and Inca, but was built by speakers of an Arawakan language distantly related, for instance, to that of the Mehinaku of Brazil, whose circular villages resemble those of the Bororo. The layout of Chiripa (Fig. 3) indeed seems intermediate to the circular villages of the lowlands and the quadrangular plazas of the highland civilizations. It may in fact represent a point of transition between them.

Architecture and Kinship Terminology

It is difficult to decide whether the architectural parallels listed above say something specific about the cosmologies of aboriginal South America or the

Gen.	Male			Female		
+ 2	FF MF			FM MM		

	KIN		AFFINES	
	Male	Female	Male	Female
+ 1	F FB MZH	M MZ FBW	WF MB FZH	WM FZ MBW
0	B FBS MZS WZH	Z FBD MZD WBW	WB MBS FZS ZH	W MBD FZD BW
− 1	S BS ZDH	D BD ZSW	DH ZS WBS	SW ZD WBD

	Male	Female
− 2	SS DS	SD DD

Fig. 4. Alignments of kin in a two-line (Dravidian) system of kin classification.

New World, or whether identical spatial arrangements have been documented widely enough to suggest that they are projections of more general principles. In any case, there seem to be certain fundamental congruities between the set of principles which generated these architectural layouts, on the one hand, and that which has governed most Amerindian kinship terminologies, on the other. In so-called Dravidian terminologies (Dumont 1953; Trautmann 1981), the basic components of categorization are (1) a dual, kin-affine opposition, (2) hierarchy conceived in terms of generation and relative age, and (3) gender. A pure Dravidian system can be reduced to these three, generative principles. The basic regularity which defines it is the merging of cross-collateral relatives and affines in the three medial generations, producing only four kinship categories in Ego's own generation and those immediately above and below it (Fig. 4). These four categories are male kin, female kin, male affines and female affines. Commonly, also, Ego's same-generation, male and female kin are divided into elder and younger "brothers" and "sisters". Three or at most four specifications will thus suffice for a componential analysis of any individual term in the Dravidian system. For example, the category including male Ego's brothers-in-law (WB, ZH) and male cross-cousins variously removed (MBS, FZS, etc.) can be defined simply as (1) affine, (2) same generation, and (3) male.

Sometimes referred to as a "two-section" or "two-line" relationship terminology, the Dravidian system has long been recognized as fundamental to the indigenous cultures of lowland South America (Rivière 1973). Moreover, it has been characterized as logically primordial, i.e. as the simplest possible starting-point (Needham 1967:45; Overing Kaplan 1975:194). If the fundamental classificatory principles which it expresses can be said to constitute a "deep structure" of aboriginal Amerindian cosmology, it should not be surprising to find it manifested also in architecture. As we have seen, dual opposition, age hierarchy and gender are pervasive considerations in the organization of South Amerindian site layouts. Paradoxically, they seem to be particularly pronounced in areas where kinship terminologies deviate most from the simple Dravidian template, including the savannas of eastern Brazil and the Andean highlands. These are areas where settlements are generally much larger than in the rainforest, where single or small groups of *malocas* are the rule. Smaller groups are more easily integrated by the transitive, kin-affine logic of the Dravidian system, according to which the affine of an affine is automatically a kinsman. In larger groups, this logic tends to break down, producing various kinds of Iroquois, Crow-Omaha or Hawaiian patterns (Hornborg, in press). But precisely where the Dravidian terminology is abandoned, its underlying principles are all the more emphasized in architecture. It is as if the larger and more stratified settlements have required a more concrete externalization of these principles, so as to withstand the threat of chaos. From now on, it becomes vitally important to *literally* "know your place" in the social scheme. In anthropological jargon, an egocentric dualism is replaced by a sociocentric dualism (i.e. dual organization and concepts of unilineal descent.)

As is immediately evident in the designation itself, Dravidian terminologies are not confined to South America. They have also been widely documented in Asia, Australia, Oceania, and North America (cf. Trautmann *et al.*, in press).[4] There is no question, then, that the three principles of classification inherent in Dravidian terminologies have a tremendous time depth. They probably do tell us something about the world-view of prehistoric man. If principles of dual opposition, hierarchy based on relative age, and gender have been in some sense universally human considerations, it should not be totally misguided to expect them to have manifested themselves not only in language, but in material culture as well. The point of juxtaposing linguistic and architectural data would be to try to ground ethnoarchaeological interpretations of spatial symbolism in cognitive anthropology, so as not to devise "structural principles" completely out of thin air. A subsequent challenge would be to systematically compare the specific ways in which different cultural traditions externalize fundamentally similar principles of classification. It is in the specifics of such comparisons that we can discover family likenesses suggesting cultural and historical continuities.

Notes

1. Pioneering observations along these lines have been made by Lowie (Nimuendajú & Lowie 1937:578), Lévi-Strauss (1945:41, 1963:107), Zuidema (1964:xiii), and Lathrap (1970:133, Lathrap *et al.* 1975:43 ff., Lathrap *et al.* 1977:10 f.).
2. My argument on highland-lowland parallels was originally presented as a paper at the 44th International Congress of Americanists in Manchester in 1982. A revised version was published in *Folk* (Hornborg 1990).
3. Set in another discussion, such a conclusion would be no less relevant to cognitive archaeology. It would be interesting to know what cognitive science might have to say on the matter.
4. In fact, it was the discovery of similarities between Ojibwa terminologies from North America and Tamil terminologies from India that in 1858–1859 inspired Lewis Henry Morgan to "invent" the comparative, anthropological study of kinship (cf. Trautmann 1987). The schedules which Morgan mailed to missionaries and others throughout the world (including one to be forwarded to "Dr. Livingstone in Africa") listed a total of 234 kinship positions. He first sought to prove the unity and the Asiatic origin of all Amerindians (what he called the Ganow†nian family, from Iroquois words for "bow" and "arrow".) This conclusion was based on interpreting the widespread, classificatory pattern as an "artificial", arbitrary construct with a single, historical origin. In the process of comparison, Morgan expanded contemporary philology by discovering structural (semantic, rather than lexical) affinities between kin terminologies in different cultures. In part stimulated by the suggestions of his close friend, the Rev. Joshua Hall McIlvaine, Morgan began to see the various terminologies as reflections of historically successive marriage practices. No longer as artificial as they first had seemed, they were to become the foundation of his "conjectural history of the family." Although this historicist interpretation was, in Trautmann's words, "an intellectual house of cards," it bore the seed of structural analysis in anthropology.

References

Browman, D. L. 1980. Tiwanaku Expansion and Altiplano Economic Patterns. *Estudios Arqueológicos* 5:107–120.

Conklin, W. J. & Moseley, M. E. 1988. The Patterns of Art and Power in the Early Intermediate Period. In Keatinge, R. W. (ed.), *Peruvian Prehistory.* Cambridge, 145–163

Crocker, J. C. 1969. Reciprocity and Hierarchy among the Eastern Bororo. *Man* (n.s.) 4:44–58.

— 1971. The Dialectics of Bororo Social Inversions. *Akten XXXVIII Amerikanistenkongress* 3:387–391.

Dumont, L. 1953. The Dravidian Kinship Terminology as an Expression of Marriage. *Man* 53:34–39.

Gregor, T. 1977. *Mehinaku: The Drama of Daily Life in a Brazilian Indian Village.* Chicago.

Hodder, I. 1986. *Reading the Past: Current Approaches to Interpretation in Archaeology.* Cambridge.

Hornborg, A. 1988. *Dualism and Hierarchy in Lowland South America: Trajectories of Indigenous Social Organization. Uppsala Studies in Cultural Anthropology* 9. Stockholm.

— 1990. Highland and Lowland Conceptions of Social Space in South America: Some Ethnoarchaeological Affinities. *Folk* 32:61–92.

— 1993. Panoan Marriage Sections: A Comparative Perspective. *Ethnology* 32:101–108.

— in press. Serial Redundancy in Amazonian Social Structure: Is There a Method for Post-Structuralist Comparison? In Trautmann, T. R., Godelier, M. & Tjon Sie Fat,

F. (eds.), *Transformations of Kinship Systems: Dravidian, Australian, Iroquois and Crow-Omaha.* Washington.
Hugh-Jones, S. 1977. Like the Leaves on the Forest Floor...: Space and Time in Barasana Ritual. In Albert, B., Baudez, C.-F., Galarza, J., Guyot, M. & Soustelle, G. (eds.), *Actes du XLIIe Congrès International des Américanistes II.*. Paris, 205–215.
Hyslop, J. 1985. *Inkawasi, the New Cuzco. Cañete, Lunahuaná, Peru.* British Archaeological Reports, International Series 234. New York.
Isbell, W. H. 1978. Cosmological Order Expressed in Prehistoric Ceremonial Centers. In Albert, B., dÁns, A.-M. & Guyot, M. (eds.), *Actes du XLIIe Congrès International des Américanistes* IV. Paris, 269–297.
Lathrap, D. W. 1970. *The Upper Amazon.* London.
Lathrap, D. W., Collier, D. & Chandra, H. 1975. *Ancient Ecuador: Culture, Clay and Creativity 3000-300 B.C.* Chicago.
Lathrap, D. W., Marcos, J. G. & Zeidler, A. 1977. Real Alto: An Ancient Ceremonial Center. *Archaeology* 30:1:2–13.
Lave, J. C. 1979. Cycles and Trends in Kríkatí Naming Practices. In Maybury-Lewis, D (ed.), *Dialectical Societies: The Gé and Bororo of Central Brazil.* Cambridge, 16–44.
Lévi-Strauss, C. 1936. Contribution à l'étude de l'organisation sociale des Indiens Bororo. *Journal de la Société des Américanistes* 28:269–305.
— 1945. On Dual Organization in South America. *America Indigena* 4:37–47.
— 1963. *Structural Anthropology.* London.
— 1973. *Structural Anthropology 2.* Harmondsworth.
Lowie, R. H. 1946. The Bororo. In Steward, J. H. (ed.), *Handbook of South American Indians I: The Marginal Tribes.* Bureau of American Ethnology Bulletin 143. Washington, 419–434.
Morris, C. 1980. Architecture and the Structure of Space at Huánuco Pampa. Manuscript to be published in *Cuadernos,* Instituto Nacional de Antropolog•a (Festschrift for A. Rex González), Buenos Aires.
Needham, R. 1967. Terminology and Alliance II: Mapuche; Conclusions. *Sociologus* 17:39–53.
Nimuendajú, C. 1946. *The Eastern Timbira.* Berkeley.
Nimuendajú, C. & Lowie, R. H. 1937. The Dual Organizations of the Ramkokamekra (Canella) of Northern Brazil. *American Anthropologist* 39:565–582.
Overing Kaplan, J. 1975. *The Piaroa, A People of the Orinoco Basin: A Study in Kinship and Marriage.* Oxford.
Renfrew, C. 1994. Towards a Cognitive Archaeology. In Renfrew, C. & Zubrow, E. B. W. (eds.), The Ancient Mind: Elements of Cognitive Archaeology. Cambridge, 3–12.
Rivière, P. G. 1973. *The Lowland South America Culture Area: Towards a Structural Definition.* Paper presented at the 72nd Annual Meeting of the American Anthropological Association. New Orleans.
Rowe, J. H. 1979. An account of the shrines of ancient Cuzco. *Nawpa Pacha* 17:1–80.
Ruhlen, M. 1987. *A Guide to the World's Languages, Volume 1: Classification.* Stanford.
Sahlins, M.D. 1976. *Culture and Practical Reason.* Chicago.
Trautmann, T. R. 1981. *Dravidian Kinship.* Cambridge.
— 1987. *Lewis Henry Morgan and the Invention of Kinship.* Berkeley.
Wilbert, J. 1981. Warao Cosmology and Yekuana Roundhouse Symbolism. *Journal of Latin American Lore* 7:1:37–72.
Zuidema, R.T. 1964. *The Ceque System of Cuzco: The Social Organization of the Capital of the Inca.* Leiden.

The Scandinavians' View of Europe in the Migration Period

By Ulf Näsman

Introduction

Scandinavia during the first millennium A.D. was a periphery of Europe, at least in the view of the classical world. Modern Scandinavian archaeological research is deeply marked by a Mediterranean perspective and the general assumption that all good things come from the south. Only barbarism was once domestic, to quote a famous Swedish author of the nineteenth century. And of course this still today seems to be true to us, but I doubt that this world-view was evident for our forefathers and foremothers, the Hyperboreans. In their perspective, from a point somewhere between the North Sea and the Baltic, the world may have looked more different than we usually consider.

Of course, the centre-and-periphery dichotomy is mainly a modern construct, a way of understanding the world that was created by the modern scholar in his or her attempts to comprehend the relations between different societies that vanished so long ago (for example Hedeager 1987), and in my thesis I significantly included a map that demonstrates the distance *from* the Roman borders *to* Scandinavia, and *not* the distances *to* the Roman border *from* the site I wrote about, Eketorp on Öland (Näsman 1984:map 13). Naturally, archaeologists have to compare different societies with one another in order to understand them. Sometimes the societies under comparison are distant from each other, and a classical example is of course the relation between the Roman Empire and the Nordic tribes. But is a centre-and-periphery dichotomy the only way of describing this relation? The application of the centre-periphery concept may clarify some aspects but I suspect that it does not give us a proper understanding of the world-view of the inhabitants of Scandinavia.

Distribution maps of imported Roman bronze and glass vessels in Scandinavia (Lund Hansen 1987) do of course demonstrate the enormous Roman impact on Scandinavia in the first four centuries A.D., and the influx of Roman vessels seems strongest during the third and fourth centuries. But behind the dots on the map we will find sites that in fact reveal a material culture which in all its main traits is very Nordic. Of course it is related to other Barbaric cultures in northern Europe, especially a number of those peoples that spoke a Germanic language but also some peoples speaking Finno-Ugrian or Baltic languages; still it is distinctly Nordic. In contrast, we will see that the Roman impact was very superficial. Besides, the distribution maps demonstrate primarily in which areas a burial custom was practised which resulted in an archaeological record of Roman vessels. Probably also densely settled regions in Germanic Scandinavia lacking graves with Roman vessels took the same part in the Roman import as regions with wasteful burial customs.

Fortunately, we have other ways of illustrating the Roman impact, and in combination with the grave finds they give a more balanced picture. For instance, a series of distribution maps prepared by Frands Herschend (1991) demonstrates a variation in the number of different types of coins that have been found in each region from the second century B.C. to the sixth century A.D. (it is not the number of coins or the number of find-sites with coins that are illustrated, since these figures are so dependent on burial and hoarding practices as well as on the modern population's willingness to deliver finds to museums). His maps clearly show that the regions to the west and south had the largest number of coin types and thus very likely the closest contact to the Roman Empire. South Jylland (Jutland) is one of these regions. Some of the areas that have given many rich graves with Roman imports are not represented with equally many coin types, for instance both Fyn and Sjælland have a lower number than Jylland, and thus our opinion about their relation to the Roman Empire has to be modified. This comparison of the distribution of wealthy graves and the number of coin types demonstrates that we must not use too simple models when we wish to evaluate the position of a region in the pan-European network of social relations.

After the collapse of the Roman empire, the exchange network that furnished Scandinavia with luxuries was directed towards the new powers that took over after the Romans. Especially the relations to some other Germanic-speaking *gentes* became important (on the *gens* concept, see Wenskus 1961 and Wolfram 1988). For instance, relations between Scandinavian polities and the Anglo-Saxon kingdoms in England developed in a way unparalleled before the Germanic conquest of the former Roman province Britannia. A map produced by the late Hayo Vierck (1970) shows how the relations between Anglo-Saxon England and south-west Scandinavia were more or less direct, demonstrated by the fact that we here find several Anglo-Saxon originals among the finds, but further to the north in present-day Sweden and Norway we find mainly imitations of the Anglo-Saxon objects, an observation strongly suggesting that these regions rather had an indirect relation to England, probably passing through Denmark.

Furthermore, it is of considerable interest that it is not until now—in the Migration Period—that the Roman impact can most clearly be observed in the domestic craft products of Scandinavia. A well-known and most convincing example is the rapid adaptation of the Roman imperial medallions to local

Fig. 1. A series of a Roman medallion, a barbaric imitation, and bracteates of the so-called C- and D-types illustrates the transformation from Roman original to Nordic original as an *interpretatio Scandinavica*. (a) The Roman medallion for emperor Valens, who was defeated by the Visigoths in the battle at Adrianople in 378, was found at Hjortshøj near Århus in Jylland (Mackeprang 1952 no. 4). (b) The barbaric, presumably Nordic, imitation of a medallion for emperor Constans, was found on Godøy in west Norway (Hauck 1985 no. 256). (c) The C-type bracteate is from Ågedal, Vest Agder, South Norway (Mackeprang 1952 no. 140; Hauck 1985 no. 1). (d) The D-type bracteate is from Djurgårdsäng, Västergötland, Sweden (Mackeprang 1962 no. 269; Hauck 1989 no. 418).

customs, and soon the Roman motifs were given a local interpretation in the shape of the gold bracteates (Fig. 1). The iconographic and ideological content of the bracteates is a phenomenon that I will return to soon, but already now it should be noted how the ideological manifestations of the Scandinavian leaders closely followed Roman imperial propaganda.

We must not forget another remarkable phenomenon of the Migration Period, the fact that this period saw a stronger Scandinavian impact on the continental and insular cultures than at any time before or after: not even the Vikings—still today so celebrated by many—in reality made an impact on the material culture of others that is comparable to that of the Migration period Scandinavians. The distribution of cast relief brooches of Nordic types—and the continental and insular imitations as well—demonstrates the Europe-wide impact of Nordic culture in the Migration period (Fig. 2). Also the distribution of Nordic bracteates is wide, and the pictorial content of these religious amulets makes it probable that the distribution in foreign territories such as Thuringia, Frisia, Kent and the Anglian parts of England reveals very close relations to South Scandinavia (maps in for instance Andrén 1991).

Of course, the main continental power, the Frankish Merovingian kingdoms, had a marked impact on Scandinavian material culture, as illustrated for example by the distribution of Frankish-made jewellery with garnet inlays (Arrhenius 1985), and in reality one can say that it was the Merovingians that during the sixth–seventh centuries replaced the Romans as the main source of new impulses in Scandinavian culture (Vierck 1981:94; Steuer 1987:224 f.).

Important conclusions of these few observations are:

Pro primo: that in the Roman period there existed a distribution network that supplied also Scandinavia with Roman vessels—and weapons as well. As recompense, we have to suggest military service, diplomatic support, slaves, and raw materials of various kind: amber, furs, skin, wool, women's hair, etc. have been suggested. It is not likely that any of this exchange was directly with the Romans but that it took place via middlemen's hands, primarily partners among other Germanic-speaking peoples.

Pro secundo: that the network was considerably strengthened in the Migration period, and that the communication now became much more of a two-way exchange. To use a modern phrase, one could say that a kind of world-wide-web was created and it worked for a century or two. Of course, the close relations are easily explained by the relative similarity between Germanic peoples wherever in Europe they had settled, a situation quite different from that of the preceding period in which the network was based on the unequal relation between the Germanic tribes and the Roman state. But we have remember not to overemphasize Germanic coherence, and we must admit that an assumed Germanic similarity is too simple an explanation.

Some of the Scandinavian objects probably travelled as belongings of moving persons, and since most of the objects are women's jewellery, many finds may represent the property of brides of Scandinavian descent. But this cannot explain the frequent imitation of Nordic art styles and prestigious jewellery—the wide distribution of Scandinavian objects must have a deeper cause. Certainly the Nordic art is part of a broader Germanic heritage, in paradoxical

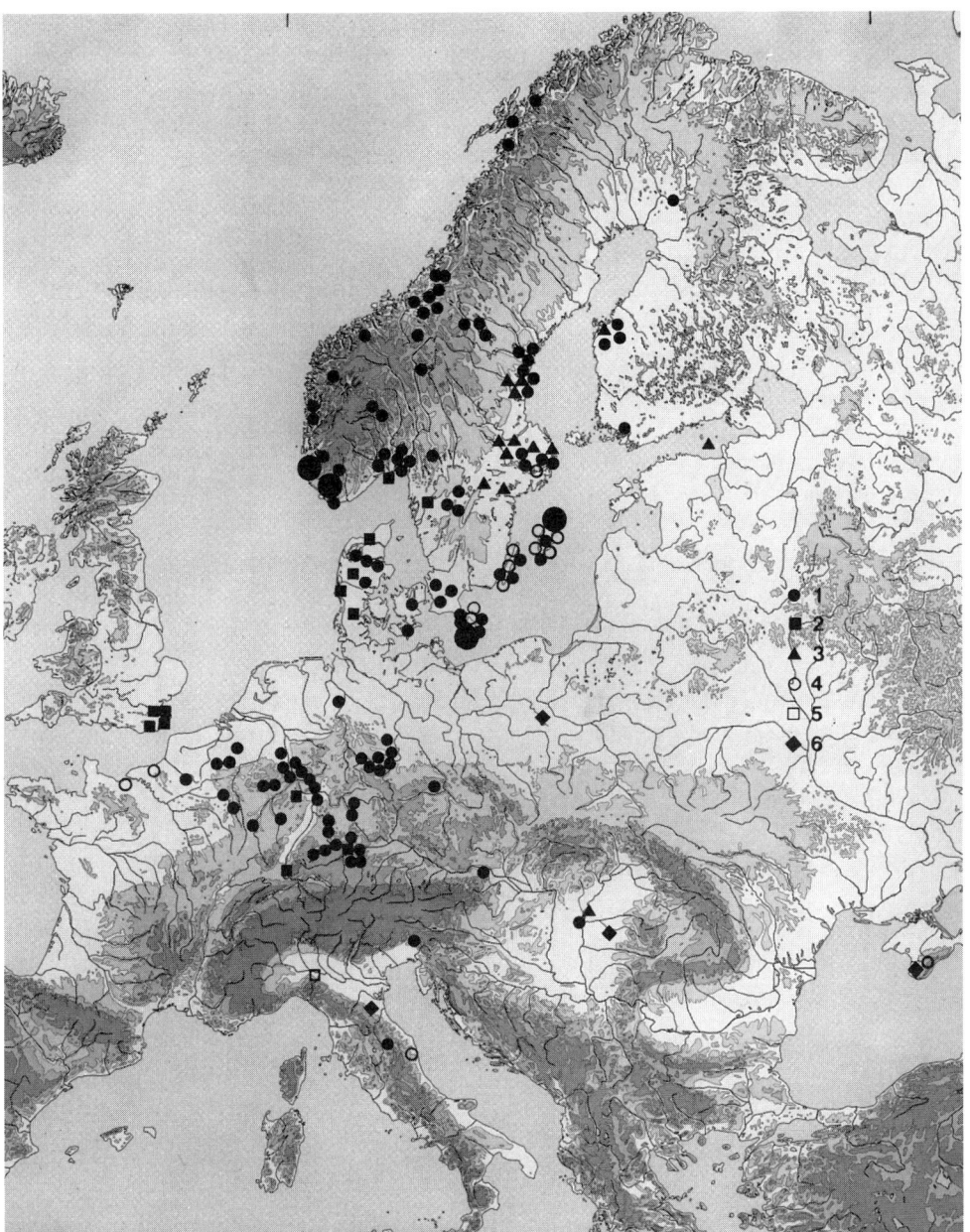

Fig. 2. On this map the distribution of Nordic relief brooches as well as continental and insular copies demonstrates the Europe-wide impact of Nordic material culture during the Migration period. (1) Various Nordic types. (2) The so-called Jutish type. (3) Equal-armed brooches of central and north Swedish type. (4) Brooches decorated with birds' heads, common on Bornholm, Gotland, and Öland. (5) Buckles with decoration of birds' heads. (6) Buckles with Nordic animal style I. (After Näsman 1984, 1991a, based on Haseloff 1985).

contrast and adaptation to the overwhelming legacy of the Classical world that streamed out over most parts of Migration period Europe.

Thus, the contrast between the two very different situations, that of the Roman period and that of the Migration period, seems to imply a change in world-view of the Scandinavians. The Roman impact on the regions of the Germanic-speaking peoples was naturally significant, and in Scandinavia a major shift in settlement pattern around A.D. 200 may be explained by this pressure, as I will explain shortly. But still, Scandinavian culture remained mainly barbaric and peripheral. The mutual relations that we find in the Migration period between Germanic-speaking *gentes* in Scandinavia on one hand and on the Continent and in England on the other, represent, however, a major step towards a European integration in linking the Baltic regions and the Mediterranean world. In this period, not only Goths and Franks adopted to the ideals of the classical world, but also the Scandinavians *gentes* did, albeit more slowly and hesitatingly. Certainly, the use of Nordic art styles among some Germanic peoples on the Continent and in England can be seen as an attempt by them to mark their non-Roman identity (Lotte Hedeager recently reminds us of this point (1996), in a paper that however precariously exaggerates the significance of a common Germanic/Nordic heritage).

Nevertheless, I will argue that the most important conclusion to be based on the Scandinavian objects of art is that they demonstrate that the barbaric *gentes* of Scandinavia now in the Migration period took a major step towards civilization.

Changes in the Rural Economy

In order to understand the change of world-view in the Migration period, we have to look very quickly at some results of recent settlement and landscape archaeology in South Scandinavia (recent surveys in Hvass 1988, 1993; Hedeager 1992). In the best investigated region, Jylland, we can see two major changes of the rural settlement pattern in the first millennium A.D.: c. 200 and c. 700. Both are interconnected with other changes, primarily in the economic sphere. A new field system was introduced in the late Roman period and agricultural equipment improved. A settlement contraction took place, and many small, widely distributed sites were now agglomerated into fewer, larger and more regulated hamlets, some with ten or more contemporary farms. Rotating quern stones and improved iron production are other technical improvements.

Another major change is the occurrence of an increasingly large number of sites that represent a new type of social centre, sites that we in Danish archaeology today call "central places", without too much consideration of the original definition by Christaller (recent discussion to be found in e.g. Näsman 1991a; Jensen & Watt 1993; Callmer 1994; Fabech & Ringtved 1995; Jørgensen 1995). The earliest seem to appear shortly after the shift around 200, followed by a slow increase in the number of new sites till a rapid growth in number during the seventh-eighth centuries. In the course of the Viking Age they were replaced region by region with proto-urban sites and early towns like Hedeby and Ribe (cf. summary by Jensen 1993).

The reasons for the change c. 200 are, as far as I can see today, mainly to be found in the economic sphere. The political and military impact of Roman power on the relations within and between barbaric polities was considerable. It certainly increased the social stress among Germanic societies. Their military capacity was strained and thus a rapid development of new structures of military and political leadership was triggered off. The supply of a surmised new military leadership called for an increased surplus of agrarian produce, and this I suspect, is the main cause of the new agrarian settlement structure after c. 200 (cf. Näsman 1991b:168).

Warfare

The increased social hierarchization that followed in the wake of the Roman political infiltration of Germanic societies naturally led to social conflicts. The contradictions between old tribal elites and new military elites, as well as the competition between the new elites in different societies, resulted in a protracted period of more or less endemic warfare (on this concept, see Halsall 1989). And due to a particular ritual behaviour among South Scandinavian tribes, this can be closely studied in South Scandinavia.

During the first to fourth centuries the many encounters between the Roman army and Germanic warrior groups usually ended with the defeat of the latter, in spite of the fact that they were fairly well organized according to the norm of tribal warfare. As may be expected, this led eventually to a considerable change among the Germanic *gentes*. A reorganization of the structure of Germanic military forces resulted in an increasing pressure against the Roman *limes*. Consequently the Roman army had to adapt to the new threat. Not only did the military organization and the weapons and armour change, but a conspicuous mixture of Roman and Germanic took place (summarized for instance by Roth 1979:27 f.). All this is of course current knowledge, and quite well studied and nothing I need to dwell upon in this context. But it is perhaps less well-known outside Scandinavia that the mutual military adaptation between the Roman and Germanic military systems also had considerable effects in the North.

For instance, the painted shields with rich decoration of gilded silver mounts that have been found in a large sacrifice of spoils-of-war in the Illerup bog in Jylland resembles the shields depicted in the *Notitia dignitatum* (colour illustrations in Carnap-Bornheim & Ilkjær 1996 (Illerup) and *Gallien in der*

Spätantike (1980:30 f.) (*Notitia dignitatum*). Roman swords are found in the Danish weapon sacrifices in large numbers (Lønstrup 1986). But not all weapons were imported; hundreds of projectile points were lost during the battles and most were locally made. Scandinavian weapon production was of course not on the scale of the Roman *fabricae* but certainly it took place at a professional level in specialized workshops, as indicated by fabrication marks in runes, probably the name of the blacksmith, on a couple of lance-heads from Illerup in Jylland, dated to c. 200 A.D. (Moltke & Stoklund 1982).

The men's costume among the Germanic elite was certainly in part traditional tribal, but also strongly influenced by Roman uniforms and officials' dress (Nockert 1991). A comparison between the dresses of three men, the reconstructed costumes of a Norwegian leader of the fifth century, based on a grave find from Evebø, and the Frankish king and Roman military leader Childeric, and a contemporary depiction of the Vandal Stilicho, who was *patricius* and served as *magister utriusque militiae* in the West Roman Empire, certainly demonstrates great similarities in spite of the social, political, and geographical distances (Périn & Feffer 1987:134; Dixon 1976:16; Magnus 1983). So we have to consider the information given by Jordanes about the Ranii, i.e. possibly the inhabitants of Romsdal in Norway, "over whom king Roduulf was king not many years ago. But he despised his own kingdom and fled to the embrace of Theoderic, king of the Goths, finding there what he desired" (after Mierow 1915), a story that clearly reveals that the upper echelons of the Scandinavian tribes could adapt to the Mediterranean civilization.

Scandinavian military strong-points are mostly relatively primitive hill-forts in mountainous landscapes and ring-forts in the plains, but nevertheless some influence from the Roman defences is traceable in the Öland ring-forts (Näsman 1989), perhaps most convincingly in the portcullis found at Eketorp (Herschend 1985). And the many fifth–sixth century solidus hoards on Bornholm, Gotland, and Öland are probably evidence of warriors returning with their pay from the war scene of central Europe (Herschend 1980; Kyhlberg 1986). So at least as an idea in the mind of the Öland soldiers and their enemies, the permanently settled Öland forts must have been associated with the late Roman border forts with their permanent settlement and social as well as economic functions (cf. Werner 1949). But we must not ignore the fact that the level of martial sophistication is not at all comparable (Fig. 3).

Social Change

The four maps in fig. 4 summarize the distribution of South Scandinavian votive deposits of war booty, bog finds with lots of weapons. At many of the sacrificial sites two or more offerings have been made, revealing that more than one battle had been fought in the neighbourhood. Together they cover

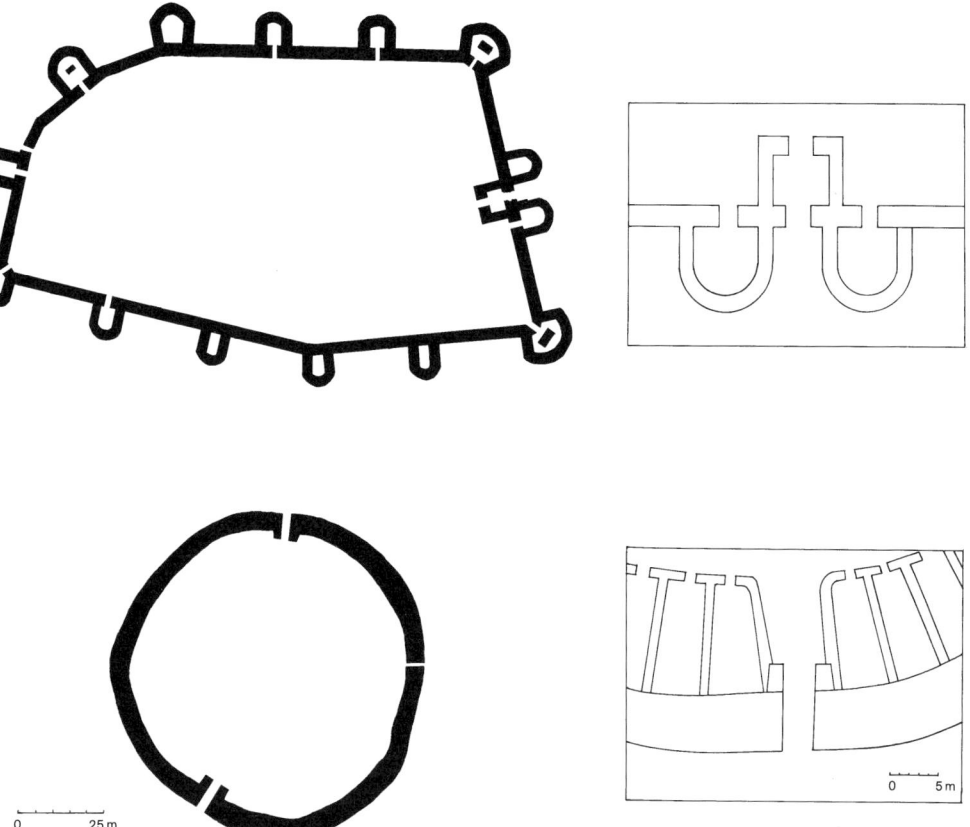

Fig. 3. A comparison of the contemporary forts of Eketorp on Öland and Dinogetia, a Moësian Danube fortress, clearly reveals the great difference in military strength and thus gives an indication that the military organization was correspondingly different. After Näsman 1989, 1997.

roughly three hundred years from 200 to 500, and they represent about 50 battles. The more than three centuries long period of seemingly endemic warfare was plausibly about control over men, land and communication channels, especially the Danish straits. In the long run it resulted in an amalgamation of the many small tribal areas that archaeologists believe can be distinguished in the material culture of the Roman Iron Age (for instance Ringtved 1988a, 1988b), and with the support of information found in works by Tacitus, Pliny and Ptolemy we get an impression of the number of polities. A new geographical and demographic scale of polities is found at the turn to the Migration period. Uniform material culture represents larger regions than before, and the few written sources mention only few ethnic groups in South Scandinavia, the

112 *Ulf Näsman*

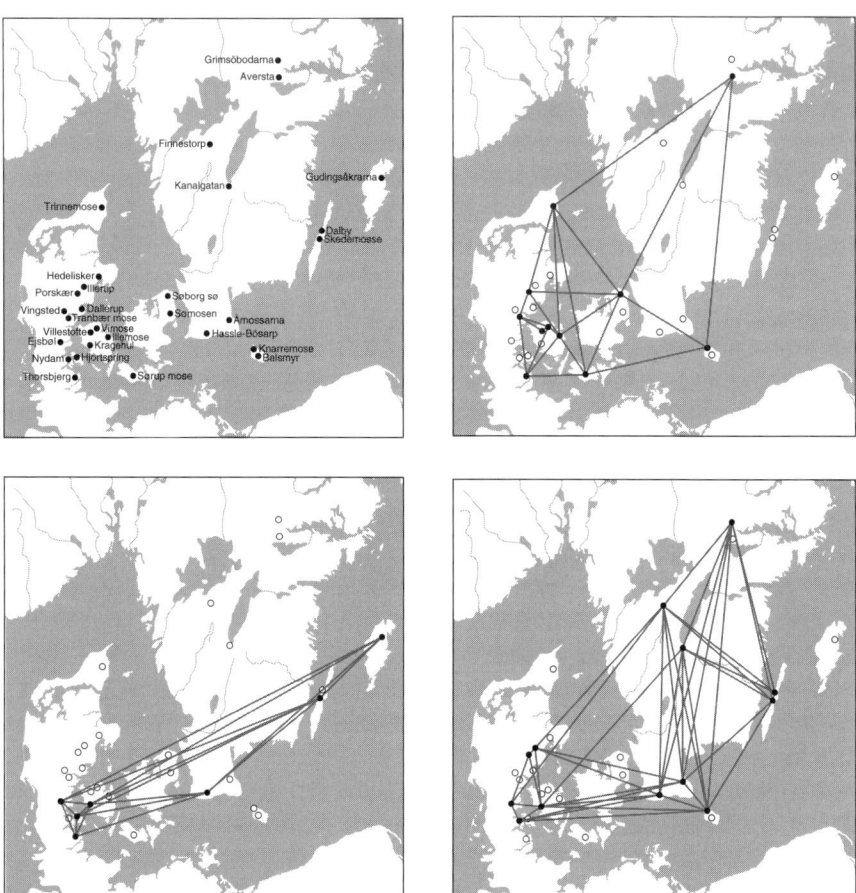

Fig. 4. A map of all sites recorded where the booty of one or more battles was sacrificed in a lake. Top left: all sites dated from the late first to the fifth century A.D. Top right: sites dated to the years around 200 A.D. Bottom left: sites dated to the years around 300 A.D. Bottom right: sites dated to the fifth century A.D. They demonstrate which areas were in conflict in three different periods. After Fabech 1996.

Danes and the Jutes being the dominating powers. On analogy of what happened on the Continent, this change can be described as a shift from tribes to *gentes*. This means also new needs of leadership. For continental Germanic peoples, for which we have better evidence in written sources, historians believe that a shift took place from old sacral leaders to a new elite based on warlords (Wenskus 1961; Schlesinger 1973; Wolfram 1971; 1988; Wood 1977). On the basis of the archaeological record of Germanic Scandinavia, you can argue that a similar development should be surmised here.

At the cessation of the custom of offering the booty of the battlefields, around 500 A.D., we also see a general abandonment of wet areas (lakes and bogs) for sacrifices, and cult finds are primarily found in a settlement context during the Merovingian and Viking periods (Fabech 1991). New pagan centres appear that are more or less identical with the residences of the new lords, and the sites of Gudme in Fyn and Uppåkra in Skåne are certainly two of these new sites (Nielsen *et al.* 1994; Stjernquist 1995). Archaeology has even been able to identify the hall of the lord in which the cult and other ceremonies took place (Herschend 1993). And eventually, 500 years later or more, it was at these residences that the first churches were built after the Christianization of the kingdoms of Denmark, Norway, and Sweden (Fabech 1994; Fabech & Ringtved 1995; Brink 1996). The change in cult from a wet to a dry setting included much more, as illustrated by the contemporary shift from golden bracteates to gold-foil figures, and by a change in the iconography of Gotlandic picture stones (Ellmers 1986). So in a way the change in cult that took place around 500 in South Scandinavia may be seen as a phenomenon parallel to the Christianization of Germanic peoples on or near former Roman territory (cf. Steuer 1989; Brink 1990:75 ff.). The common factor is the institutionalization of the people's cult practices in the hands of the elite, at their residences. In the south this change had a Christian disguise, up here it was embedded into a changing pagan religious universe, later to be better recognizable in the medieval Icelandic sources.

In a way the year 500 appears as a hinge in Scandinavian history, and the two centuries preceding and following year 500 are mounts that fasten the hinge to history. Before 500 we have tribal barbaric Scandinavian societies, after 500 we find a new, more or less civilized and national Scandinavia.

Imitatio imperii—interpretatio Scandinavica—imitatio regni Francorum—Scandinavia libera

In the course of the Roman Iron Age the Roman impact on Scandinavian material culture increased, especially during the third and fourth centuries. But the real breakthrough of the Roman influence did not take place before the Migration Period. The very rich material we have from this period reveals, however, that the world-view had now become fairly Romanized, at least among the elite. An example *par excellence* is the famous golden horns from Gallehus in South Jylland which probably were the holy objects of a Jutish tribal kingdom. Their astonishing pictorial content demonstrates clearly how a deep knowledge of Roman iconography could be reused and adapted to fit in a pagan tribal context (Voss 1967).

The Roman emperor's gift-giving of medallions to Germanic rulers and war-lords was obviously an attractive act and was rapidly accepted and imitated by the barbaric leaders of the fourth–fifth centuries. This is evidenced by barbaric medallion imitations that are spread as far as Scandinavia (Fig. 1a–b).

Probably they were used here in the ceremonies of a barbaric society, and in one way or the other the Scandinavian ceremonial probably corresponded to the Roman practice. The barbaric medallion imitations are clearly an example of *imitatio imperii*. So to me it also seems likely that the barbaric givers of gold medallions acted in their own view as a kind of local emperors.

Behind the custom of using golden pendants in Scandinavia we have to expect specific social needs. So it should be no surprise to us if the barbaric imitations, with a pictorial content entirely Roman, could not fulfil the purpose for long. Thus the designers and goldsmiths soon abandoned imitating the Roman medallions, and instead they created a new type of golden pendant, with similar but certainly Scandinavian motifs: the golden bracteate (Fig. 1c). As has been more or less convincingly argued by several scholars, and most energetically by Karl Hauck (1985–89), a Nordic pagan mythology is the basis of the bracteate images. Obviously the core area of the bracteate production was South Scandinavia, an area in which bracteates are only found in hoards, surrounded by a distribution—and eventually also a production—in a periphery where many bracteates are found in women's graves as well. As Anders Andrén has convincingly argued (1991), the runic inscriptions on many bracteates are made as an *interpretatio Scandinavica* of the Latin inscriptions of the Roman medallions. Thus our case is strengthened that the bracteates were used in a similar way, or rather in a ceremonial context that in Scandinavian society resembled the situations when the Roman emperor gave medallions.

This also means—in my opinion—that the personal name on the runic bracteates does not—as it is traditionally believed (e.g. Moltke 1985)—give us the name of the goldsmith or rune carver, but the name of the ruler who had the bracteate made. And thus geographical links between bracteates made for the same lord demonstrate diplomatic links in the same was as die-links do (Fig. 5). On the basis of the many bracteates imitating Roman medallions, it is possible to suggest that the Roman emperor at an early stage was equalled to the high god of the pagan Germanic pantheon, plausibly Odin. But of course, it seems also probable that the Germanic high god was related to the supreme Germanic ruler, the king (Schjødt 1991). This means, I think, that the Scandinavians in fact saw their own ruler as an equal to the Roman emperor. So the concept "the high" as written in runes on one of the famous bracteates found on Fyn (Mackeprang 1952, no. 50; Hauck 1985, no. 58), was perhaps not only a *noa*-name for the powerful and dangerous god, but also the title of a Scandinavian leader.

But soon bracteates were produced that had given up the Roman prototypes entirely, and pendants with an animal as motif become very popular (Fig. 1d). This so-called D-bracteate can be regarded as an indication that the Scandinavians now had the necessary self-consciousness and disrespect for the classical civilization to express their own pagan myths, but still in the same pictorial

The Scandinavians' view of Europe in the migration period 115

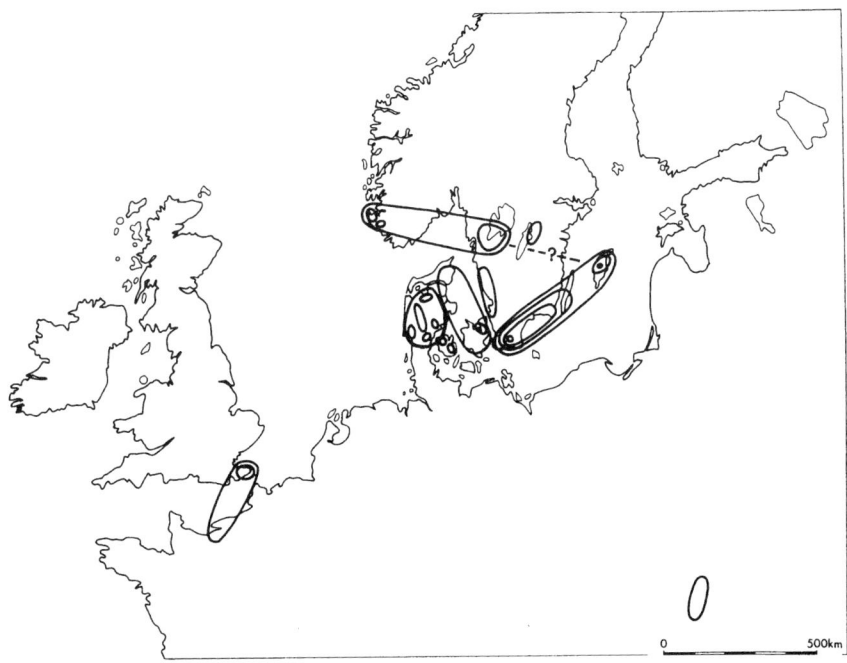

Fig. 5. A map of die-linked bracteate sites. Compiled by Andrén 1991 (on the basis of Mackeprang 1952; Hauck 1985–89; Axboe 1982).

idiom. As demonstrated by Hayo Vierck in excellent papers (1978b; 1981), several of the motifs on the golden pendants in Scandinavia can be traced back to Roman prototypes (Fig. 6; an obvious phenomenon observed earlier by e.g. Holmqvist 1955:73 f.).

The use of golden rings as symbols seems to be a Celtic custom that was continued by the Germanic peoples (Schramm 1954–56). Vierck has cleverly demonstrated how the Roman emperor's gesture with the *mappa* is replaced in Scandinavian pictures by the high god's holding a ring as sign of dignity, and that the use of rings was part of large complicated ritual ceremonies is revealed by the Gotlandic picture stones, for instance, in scenes in which a dead warrior is approaching Valhalla with his retainers, all with a raised ring in the hand (Lindqvist 1941–42:fig. 86). The various motifs with horsemen in classical art can also have been inspiring for similar pictures among the Scandinavians, and certainly the ceremonials depicted on the figure foils on Anglo-Saxon and Scandinavian helmets from the sixth–seventh centuries seem to be based on a Nordic interpretation of ceremonials at the Roman-Byzantine and later also Merovingian court. An argument similar to Vierck's is presented by Detlev Ellmers (1980) in connection with an analysis of the significance of the *adventus* motif in understanding the Danish funerary rituals of the Viking Age.

Fig. 6. A barbaric medallion imitation from Vika, Nord-Trøndelag, Norway, the obverse and reverse of which can be compared to two Roman versions of the *adventus* motif. But details carefully analysed by Vierck clearly show that the imitation has been given a local interpretation. After Vierck 1978b.

The close imitation of Mediterranean ideals was not an entirely male phenomenon, and as demonstrated, also by Vierck, traits in Scandinavian women's costume can easily be traced back to the Byzantine court, probably via the Merovingians, and the Viking Age pendant from Aska in Östergötland, in its naïve portrayal of a self-important Götic woman—or is it a goddess?—can be related to 400 years older portrait of another Germanic women, Amalsuintha, the daughter of the East Gothic king Theoderic the Great (Fig. 7).

All these examples show how Scandinavians in their material culture demonstrated that they thought of themselves as *distinct* from but also *equal* to the Romans. Later Scandinavian culture reveals similar attitudes towards the peoples of the Germanic successor kingdoms. So paradoxically, one can say that the Scandinavians demonstrated their distinctive character on the one hand and a European togetherness on the other.

Thus the strong kingdoms that developed during the wars of the third to fifth centuries legitimized in pictorial propaganda their hardening grip over their earlier peer polities by references both to the rulers of a pagan pantheon and to the Roman emperor as the paramount ruler of the world. In many respects they chose a way similar to the East Goths under their charismatic king Theoderic, *Flavius Theodericus rex,* who claimed to be both king of the Goths and a ruler on behalf of the Roman emperor in Byzantium (Wolfram 1988:284 ff.).

After the fall of the West Roman empire, however, the importance of the Roman heritage soon decreased, and the Germanic successor states rapidly replaced the Roman Empire as the most important prototype of an ideal society in the eyes of the Scandinavians. So it is not accidental that archaeologists in Norway and Finland call the period the Merovingian Iron Age. From the early sixth century we see how a Frankish or rather Merovingian impact re-

The Scandinavians' view of Europe in the migration period 117

Fig. 7. A gold-foil figure depicting a dressed Germanic woman from the early Merovingian period and a silver pendant showing a seated Viking woman, both dressed in an originally Byzantine fashion as demonstrated by a ivory diptych of the 400 years older Amalsuintha, the daughter of the East Gothic king Theoderic the Great. Gold-foil figure from the settlement fort at Eketorp on Öland and dating to the sixth century after Stenberger 1973, Viking Age pendant from Aska in Östergötland after Vierck 1978a and diptych after Dixon 1976.

placed the Roman influence, and one can say that the *imitatio imperii* was replaced by an *imitatio regni francorum* (Vierck 1981:94).

The Merovingian society became the ideal of the Scandinavian elite, illustrated by the many finds of Frankish sword pommels, gifts from Frankish to Scandinavian leaders (Arrhenius 1985). The Danish rulers used the period to strengthen and expand their hegemony over the cross-roads between Scandinavia proper and the Continent, as well as over the channels between the Baltic and the North Sea. Gudme was certainly central in this process, and I guess that the dominating position of the Danes will be revealed also by the seventh–eighth century finds at Uppåkra.

The relation to the dominating Merovingian realm was in a Danish perspective to be characterized as competitive emulation between rival kingdoms (for the concepts, see Renfrew & Cherry 1986). The incident related by Gregory of Tours that a Danish king Hugleik attacked the Franks and eventually was defeated by the Merovingian army demonstrates that they really put this conviction to test—but of course they lost (on this and other sources about Danish–Frankish encounters, see Wood 1983). The position of a Danish prime minister today is formally the same as that of his French counterpart, but the real strength of Denmark and France is—and was—something quite different.

When a North Sea market began to develop in the seventh century, the

Danish society soon took full part in the economic boom, and the foundation of the first urban community in Ribe demonstrates the increasingly close integration of the Danish kingdom in a west European civilization (Bencard et al. 1990; Feveile 1994).

To begin with this process ran without obvious difficulties, but not all groups of South Scandinavian society were ready for this rapid change, and in my opinion many of the disruptions of the early Viking Age are to be explained by the tensions created between two forces in action: the centripetal force of the Danish kingdom that in the long run resulted in a radical transformation of South Scandinavia into a European power, and centrifugal conservative powers based on regional elites, who clung to old values and an old structure. So when the Anglo-Danish king Knud the Great in a letter dated in 1027 used the title *rex totius Anglie et Denemarcie et Norreganorum et partis Suanorum* (Christensen 1969/1977:262) this does not reveal a tribal understanding of rulership but is a clear demonstration of the political ambitions of a modern European king. An event symbolizing the final transition of Denmark into a European power, equal to anyone, is the marriage in A.D. 1036 between king Knud's daughter Gunhild and Henry III, son of the German emperor Konrad II (Christensen 1969/1977:266).

But this transition had started centuries before, in the early post-Roman period, when the Danes and other Germanic speaking peoples in Scandinavia changed from a passive import and simple imitation of some classical culture elements to an active interpretation of the foreign prototypes. They adapted the motifs as well as the use of them in domestic ritual, so that the loans today appear as fully integrated elements of the material culture of late prehistoric Scandinavia.

References

Andrén, A. 1991. Guld och makt—en tolkning av de skandinaviska guldbrakteaternas funktion. In Fabech, C. & Ringtved, J. (eds.), *Samfundsorganisation og regional variation. Norden i romersk jernalder og folkevandringstid.* Jysk arkæologisk selskabs skrifter 27, 245–256.
Arrhenius, B. 1985. *Merovingian garnet jewellery.* Stockholm.
Axboe, M. 1982. The Scandinavian gold bracteates. *Acta Archaeologica* 51 (1981), 1–100.
Bencard, M., Bender Jørgensen, L., & Brinch Madsen, H. (eds.) 1990. *Ribe excavations 1970–76,* 4. Esbjerg.
Brink, S. 1990. *Sockenbildning och sockennamn.* Studier till en svensk ortnamnsatlas 14.
— 1996. Political and social structures in early Scandinavia. *Tor* 28, 235–281.
Callmer, J. 1994. Urbanization in Scandinavia and the Baltic region c. AD 700–1100. In Ambrosiani, B. & Clarke, H. (eds.), *Developments around the Baltic and the North Sea in the Viking Age: The Twelfth Viking Congress.* Birka studies 3, 50–90.

Carnap-Bornheim, C. v. & Ilkjær, J. 1996. *Illerup Ådal 5–7. Die Prachtausrüstungen.* Jysk arkæologisk selskabs skrifter 25/5–7.
Christensen, A. E. 1969 (1977). *Vikingetidens Danmark.* Copenhagen.
Dixon, P. 1976. *The making of the past: Barbarian Europe.* Oxford.
Ellmers, D. 1980. Fränkisches Königszeremoniell auch in Walhall. *Beiträge zur Schleswiger Stadtgeschichte* 25, 115–126.
— 1986. Schiffsdarstellungen auf skandinavischen Grabsteinen. In Roth, H. (ed.), *Zum Problem der Deutung frühmittelalterliche Bildinhalte.* Sigmaringen, 341–372.
Fabech, C. 1991. Booty sacrifices in Southern Scandinavia: a reassessment. *Sacred and profane.* Oxford University. Committee for archaeology. Monograph 32, 88–94.
— 1994. Society and landscape: From collective manifestations to ceremonies of a new ruling class. In Keller, H. & Staubach, N. (eds.), *Iconologia sacra.* Universität Münster. Arbeiten zur Frühmittelalterforschung 23, 132–143.
— 1996. Booty sacrifices in Southern Scandinavia—a history of warfare and ideology. *Roman Reflections.* Rome, 135–138.
Fabech, C. & Ringtved, J. 1995. Magtens geografi i Sydskandinavien. In Resi, H. G. (ed.), *Produksjon og samfunn: Om erverv, spesialisering og bosetning i Norden i 1. årtusind e.Kr.* Universitets Oldsaksamling. Varia 30, 11–37.
Feveile, C. 1994. The latest news from Viking Age Ribe. In Ambrosiani, B. & Clarke, H. (eds.), *Developments around the Baltic and the North Sea in the Viking Age: The Twelfth Viking Congress.* Birka studies 3, 91–99.
Gallien in der Spätantike: Von Kaiser Constantin zu Frankenkönig Childerich. Mainz (Ausstellungskatalog) 1980. French ed. A l'aube de la France. Paris 1981.
Halsall, G. 1989. Anthropology and the study of pre-conquest warfare and society: the ritual war in Anglo-Saxon England. In Hawkes, S. C. (ed.), *Weapons and warfare in Anglo-Saxon England.* Oxford, 155–177.
Hansen, U. Lund 1987. *Römischer Import im Norden.* Nordiske fortidsminder B 10.
Haseloff, G. 1981. *Die germanische Tierornamentik der Völkerwanderungszeit* 1–3. Berlin.
— 1984. Stand der Forschung: Stilgeschichte Völkerwanderungs- und Merovingerzeit. *Festskrift til Thorleif Sjøvold.* Universitetets oldsaksamlings skrifter, nr. 5, 109–124.
— 1986. Bild und Motiv im Nydam-Stil und Stil I. In Roth, H. (ed.), *Zum Problem der Deutung frühmittelalterliche Bildinhalte.* Sigmaringen, 67–110.
Hauck, K. (ed.) 1985–89. *Die Goldbrakteaten der Völkerwanderungszeit* 1–3. Münstersche Mittelalterschriften 24/1–3.
Hedeager, L. 1987. Empire, frontier and the barbarian hinterland: Rome and northern Europe from AD 1–400. In Rowlands, M., Larsen, M. & Kristiansen, K. (eds.), *Centre and periphery in the Ancient World.* Cambridge, 125–140, refs. pp. 141–153.
— 1992. *Iron-Age Societies.* Oxford.
— 1996. Myter og material kultur: Den nordiske oprindelsesmyte i det tidlige kristne Europa. *Tor* 28, 217–234.
Herschend, F. 1980. Två studier i öländska guldfynd. *Tor* 18 (1978–1979), 33–294.
— 1985. Fällgallerporten i Eketorp-II, Öland. *Tor* 20 (1983–1985), 165–216.
— 1991. Om öländsk metallekonomi i första hälften av första årtusendet e.Kr. In Fabech, C. & Ringtved, J. (eds.), *Samfundsfundsorganisation og regional variation.* Jysk Arkælogisk Selskabs skrifter 27, 33–46.
— 1993. The origin of the hall in southern Scandinavia. *Tor* 25, 175–199.
Holmqvist, W. 1955. *Germanic art during the first millennium A.D.* KVHAAs Handlingar 90.

Hvass, S. 1988. The status of the Iron Age settlement in Denmark. Bierma, M., Harsema, O. H. & van Zeist, W. (eds.), *Archeologie en landschap*. Festschrift to H. T. Waterbolk. Groningen, 97–132.
— 1993. The Iron Age and the Viking Period: Settlement. In Hvass, S. & Storgaard, B. (eds.), *Digging into the past*. Copenhagen, 187–194.
Jensen, S. 1993. Early towns. In Hvass, S. & Storgaard, B. (eds.), *Digging into the past* Copenhagen, 202–205.
Jensen, S. & Watt, M. 1993. Trading sites and central places. In Hvass, S. & Storgaard, B. (eds.), *Digging into the past*. Copenhagen, 195–201.
Jørgensen, L. 1995. The warrior aristocracy of Gudme? The emergence of landed aristocracy in Late Iron Age Denmark. In Resi, H. G. (ed.), *Produksjon og samfunn: Om erverv, spesialisering og bosetning i Norden i 1. årtusind e.Kr.* Universitets Oldsaksamling. Varia 30, 205–220.
Kyhlberg, O. 1986. Late Roman and Byzantine solidi. In Lundström, A. & Clarke, H. (eds.), *Excavations at Helgö 10: Coins, iron and gold*. Stockholm, 13–126.
Lindqvist, S. 1941–42. *Gotlands Bildsteine* 1–2. Stockholm.
Lønstrup, J. 1986. Das zweischneidige Schwert aus der jüngeren römischen Kaiserzeit im freien Germanien und im römischen Imperium. *Studien zu den Militärgrenzen Roms* III. Forschungen und Berichte zur Vor- und Frühgeschichte in Baden-Württemberg 20. Stuttgart, 747–749.
Mackeprang, M. 1952. *De nordiske guldbrakteater*. Aarhus.
Magnus, B. 1983. How was he dressed? New light on the garments from the grave at Evebø/Eide in Gloppen, Norway. *Studien zur Sachsenforschung* 4, 293–313.
Mierow, C. C. 1915. *The Gothic history of Jordanes*. Princeton, NJ.
Moltke, E. 1985. *Runes and their origin*. Copenhagen.
Moltke, E., & Stoklund, M. 1982. Runeindskrifterne fra Illerup Mose. *Kuml* 1981, 67–79.
Näsman, U. 1984. *Glas och handel i senromersk tid och folkvandringstid*. Aun 5.
— 1989. The gates of Eketorp-II: To the question of Roman prototypes of the Öland ringforts. In Randsborg, K. (ed.), *The birth of Europe: Archaeology and social development in the first millennium A.D.* Analecta Romana Instituti Danici. Supplementum 16, 129–139.
— 1991a. Some comments on the symposium "Social organization and regional variation", Sandbjerg Manor, April 1989. In Fabech, C. & Ringtved, J. (eds.), *Samfundsfundsorganisation og regional variation*. Jysk Arkælogisk Selskabs skrifter 27, 328–333.
— 1991b. Det syvende århundrede. In Mortensen, P. & Rasmussen, B. (eds.), *Fra stamme til stat i Danmark. 2 Høvdingesamfund og kongemagt*. Jysk arkæologisk selskabs skrifter 22/2, 165–177.
— 1997. Strategies and tactics in Migration Period defence. In Nørgård Jørgensen, A. (ed.), *Military Aspects of Scandinavian Society in a European Perspective AD 1–1300*. Copenhagen, 146–155.
Nielsen, P. O., Randsborg, K., & Thrane, H. (eds.) 1994. *The archaeology of Gudme and Lundeborg*. Arkæologiske studier 10.
Nockert, M. 1991. *The Högom find and other Migration Period textiles and costumes in Scandinavia*. Archaeology and environment 9.
Périn, P., & Feffer, L.-C. 1987. *Les Francs 1: A la conquête de la Gaule*. Paris.
Renfrew, C., & Cherry, J. F. (eds) 1986. *Peer polity interaction and socio-political change*. Cambridge.
Ringtved, J. 1988a. Jyske gravfund fra yngre romertid og ældre germanertid. *Kuml* 1986, 95–231.

— 1988b. Regionalitet. Et jysk eskempel fra yngre romertid og ældre germanertid. In Mortensen, P. & Rasmussen, B. (eds.), *Fra Stamme til Stat i Danmark*. 1 *Jernalderens stammesamfund*. Jysk Arkæologisk Selskabs Skrifter 22/1, 37–52.

Roth, H. 1979. *Kunst der Völkerwanderungszeit*. Propyläen Kunstgeschichte. Supplementband 4.

Roth, H. (ed.) 1986. *Zum Problem der Deutung frühmittelalterliche Bildindhalte*. Sigmaringen.

Schjødt, J. P. 1991. Fyrsteideologi og religion i vikingeiden. In Iversen, M. (ed.), *Mammen: Grav, kunst og samfund i vikingetid*. Jysk arkæologisk selskabs skrifter 23, 305–310.

Schlesinger, W. 1973. Über germanisches Heerkönigtum. *Das Königtum*. Vorträge und Forschungen 3, 105–141. First published in *Beiträge zur deutschen Verfassungsgeschichte des Mittelalters* 1. Göttingen 1963, 53 ff.

Schramm, P. E. 1954–56. *Herrschaftszeichen und Staatssymbolik* 1–3. Schriften der Monumenta Germaniae historica 13/1–3.

Steuer, H. 1987. Helm und Ringschwert. *Studien zur Sachsenforschung* 6, 189–236.

— 1989. Archaeology and history: proposals on the social structure of the Merovingian kingdom. In Randsborg, K. (ed.), *The birth of Europe: Archaeology and social development in the first millennium A.D*. Analecta Romana Instituti Danici. Supplementum 16, 100–122.

Stjernquist, B. 1995. Uppåkra, a central place in Skåne during the Iron Age. *Lund archaeological review* 1, 89–120.

Vierck, H. 1970. *Zum Fernverkehr über See im 6. Jahrhundert*. In Hauck, K. Goldbrakteaten aus Sievern, 355–395. München.

— 1978a. Die anglische Frauentracht. In Ahrens, C. (ed.), *Sachsen und Angelsachsen*. Hamburg, 245–253.

— 1978b. Religion, Rang und Herrschaft im Spiegel der Tracht. In Ahrens, C. (ed.), *Sachsen und Angelsachsen*. Hamburg, 245–253.

— 1981. Imitatio imperii und Interpretatio Germanica vor der Wikingerzeit. In Zeitler, R. (ed.), *Les Pays du Nord et Byzance*. Figura N.S. 19, 64–113.

Voss, O. 1967. Tvende bekendte ældgamle guldhorn. *Skalk* 1967/6, 18–27.

Wenskus, R. 1961. *Stammesbildung und Verfassung*. Cologne (2nd ed. 1977).

Werner, J. 1949. Zu den auf Öland und Gotland gefundenen byzantinschen Goldmünzen. *Fornvännen* 44, 257–286.

Wolfram, H. 1971. The shaping of the early medieval kingdom. *Viator* 1 (1970), 1–20.

— 1988. *History of the Goths*. Los Angeles. (Rev. Engl. ed. of 2nd German ed. 1980 (1st ed. 1979), *Geschichte der Goten*. Munich).

Wood, I. N. 1977. Kings, kingdoms and consent. In Sawyer, P. & Wood, I. (eds.), *Early medieval kingship*, 6–29. Leeds.

— 1983. *The Merovingian North Sea*. Alingsås.

Directions to the Dead

By Richard Bradley

Introduction

There are two different ways of thinking about the world-views of people in the past. One is to work at the largest possible scale, drawing together elements from the archaeology of a considerable area. That is the approach taken, for example, in the work of Marija Gimbutas. The other method is to focus on the details of human behaviour at particular places and times, building outwards by a process of comparison until we reach the limits of the phenomena being studied. In this paper I shall take the second approach, considering, first, the symbolic system epitomised by one megalithic cemetery in the north of Scotland and then extending the argument to a wider network of relationships between communities around the Irish Sea.

The colour red

It is troubling how little we notice when we study megalithic tombs. We speak of their mass, their height or the problems of entering them, but that may be all we observe. Apart from quite exceptional occurrences, like the quartz around the entrance of Newgrange (O'Kelly 1982), we take little note of their colour.

This reflection arises directly from one experience at one megalithic tomb, but this does not mean that the entire paper will be concerned with minutiae, for I shall use this example to study the organisation of an entire cemetery before considering that evidence in its wider context.

My case study concerns the cemetery at Balnuaran of Clava, near Inverness (Henshall 1963:chapter 1). The starting point is one of the well preserved passage graves on the site. The kerb of this monument is virtually complete but fieldwork in 1995 discovered further stones in the filling of an early excavation. Recently we re-erected them. One was dull grey in colour, enlivened by bands of quartz; the other was the colour red.

Why is this observation of interest? It is because we were taken aback by the brightness of the red kerbstone. It had not been exposed to sunlight for over a hundred years, and the surfaces were not covered with lichen like the stones in the rest of the monument. Since the raw material for these monuments was

124 *Richard Bradley*

 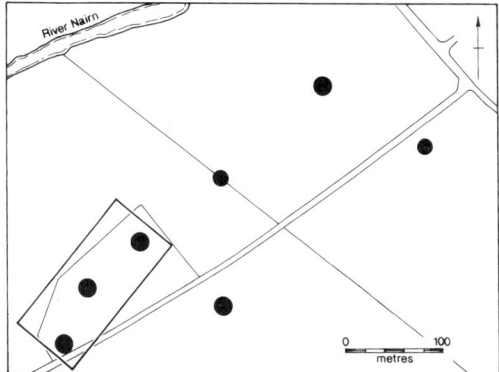

Fig. 1. (Left) The location of the Clava Cairns; (Right) Outline plan of the cemetery at Balnuaran of Clava. The box encloses the three cairns depicted in Figure 2. Drawing: Margaret Mathews.

extracted from the local gravel in a very similar manner to our excavation, it follows that originally the entire monument might have been brightly coloured. The same argument should extend to the cemetery as a whole.

That brought to mind some observations that we had been making about the use of raw materials in several of the cairns, but, whilst we had been recording them as part of the standing structure, their symbolic properties had never been discussed systematically. The experience of raising the fallen kerbstones opened a new agenda for work on these tombs.

The Clava Cairns consist of fifty or so monuments, all of which take a similar form (Henshall 1963:chapter 1), but rather than embark on an abstract description of such sites, I would like to begin by describing how these structures are organised in relation to the viewer. I shall confine myself to the cemetery at Balnuaran of Clava (Fig. 1). Three monuments are of immediate interest: two passage graves of the same basic design as those in southern Scandinavia, and a ring cairn which can be characterised as an unbroken circular enclosure defined by a rubble wall (Fig. 2).

Many of the Clava Cairns are located in valleys, which constrain the pattern of movement through the landscape, and their construction usually echoes that alignment (Phillips 1996). Their focal point is generally to the south-west, for it is here that the kerbstones are tallest. The cairns are enclosed by stone circles which follow the same convention, and in the case of the passage graves this is the side on which the entrance is found (Fig. 2). Thus the monuments have a front and a back. Our starting point is the observation that, viewed in relation to the local topography, the cairns are most conspicuous from behind (ibid).

The Balnuaran cemetery capitalises on this feature. It is located on a low ridge in the middle of a river valley, and the monuments within it fall into two

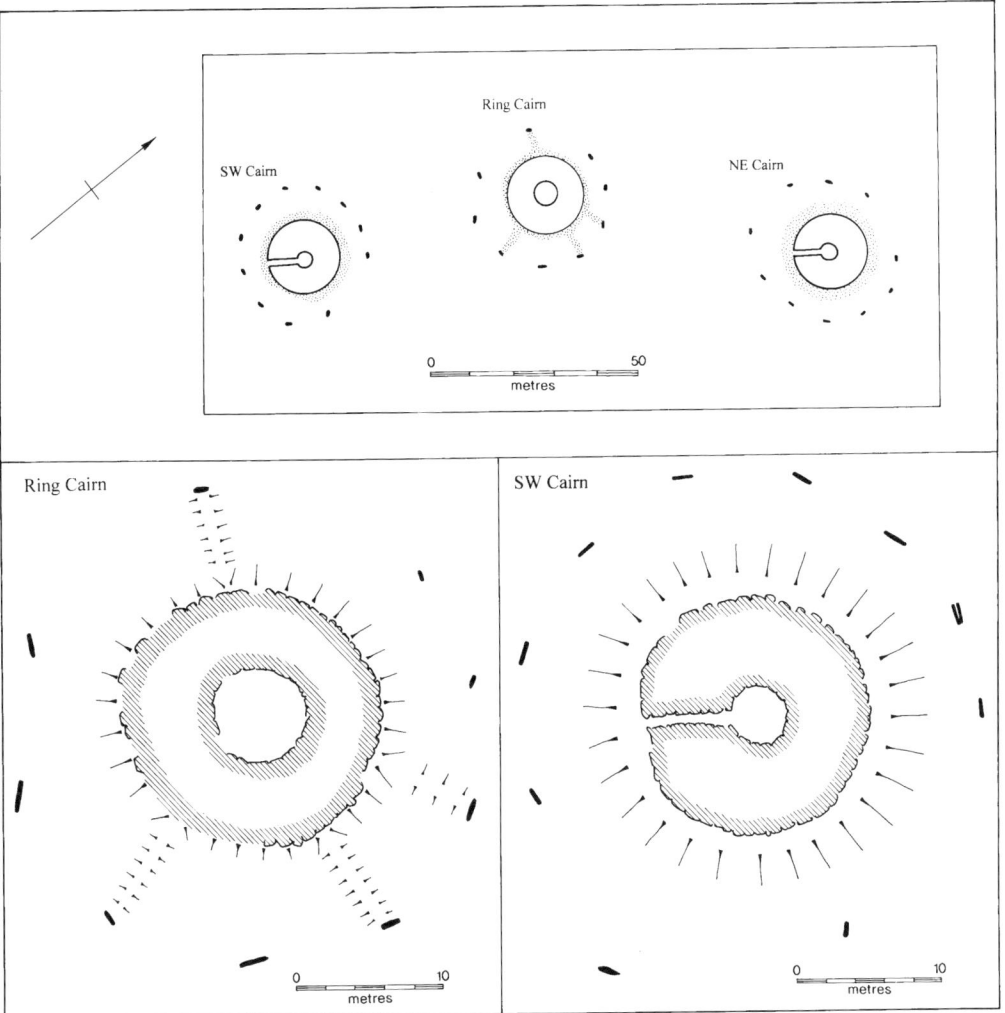

Fig. 2. (Above) The three best preserved cairns at Balnuaran of Clava. (Below) detailed plans of the central ring cairn (left) and south-west passage grave (right) Drawing: Margaret Mathews.

distinct groups, towards either edge of the higher ground (Figs. 1 and 2). They form two lines converging on a well-preserved passage grave (the south-west cairn) which is aligned on the midwinter sunset. The other intact passage grave (the north-east cairn) has the same axis and is orientated on the position of that tomb. The result was to create a complex visual effect. From the tomb at the pivotal point of the cemetery, the sun can be observed setting behind a nearby hill (Fig. 3). From the other passage grave the view is less straightforward.

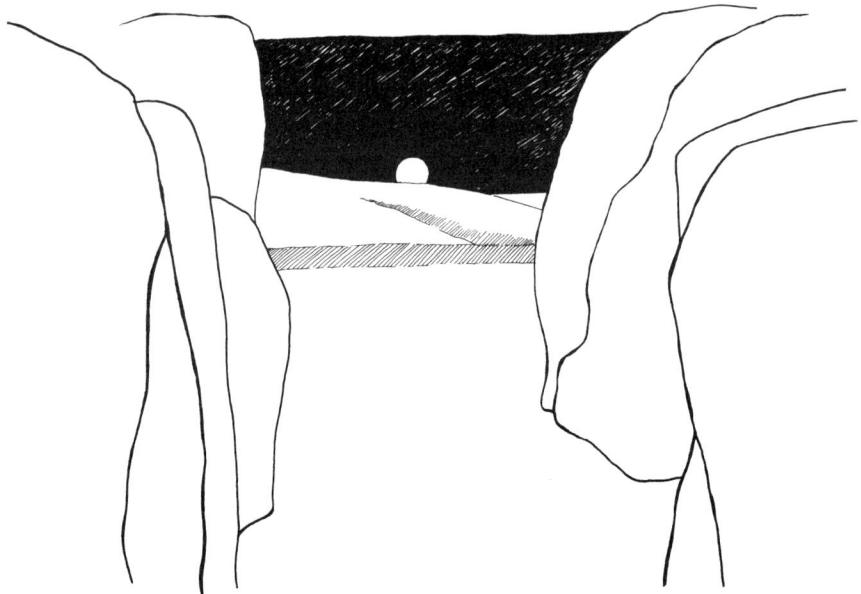

Fig. 3. The view of the midwinter sunset from the passage of the south-west cairn at Balnuaran of Clava. Drawing: Aaron Watson.

Observed from the central chamber, the midwinter sun would have set on top of the south-west cairn where it converges with the horizon (Fig. 4). The ring cairn that was constructed in between these two tombs was offset from that alignment so that the view was not obstructed.

We can consider the grouping of the monuments according to two distinct axes. The layout of the cemetery focuses on the passage grave with a view of the midwinter sunset. In the opposite direction we are looking towards the position of the midsummer sunrise. Those opposing axes are fundamental to the way in which the monuments are organised.

It is curious that studies of megalithic architecture—the architecture of great stones—take so little account of the raw material from which this phenomenon takes its name. At Clava these stones have three main characteristics: their height, their shape and their colour. They are the elements that conditioned the experience of using these monuments. Their sources are entirely local. The boulders that form a major component of the monuments were obtained from the glacial gravel on which the cemetery is built. The same applies to the rounded cobbles which form the outer skin of these cairns. The tallest uprights were slabs of sandstone quarried on the bank of a river 150 metres away. Although the cemetery contains eight monuments, I shall confine this discussion to those which are well preserved.

Directions to the dead 127

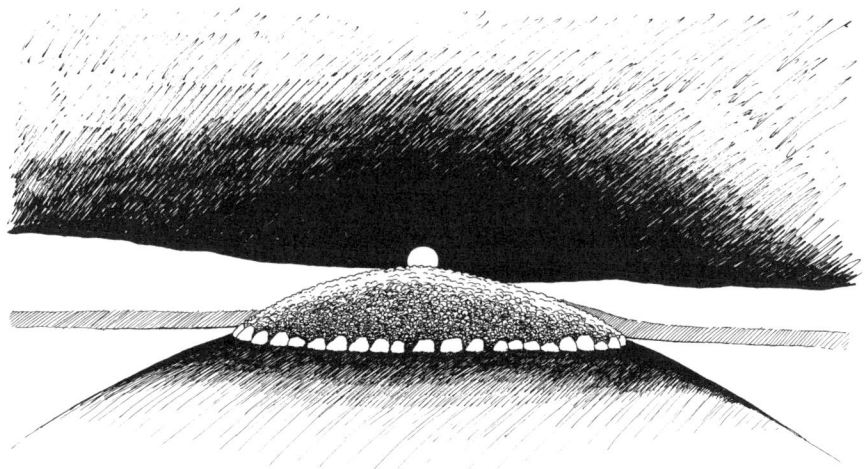

Fig. 4. The view of the midwinter sunset from the entrance to the north-east cairn at Balnuaran of Clava. Drawing: Aaron Watson.

On all three of these cairns the uprights of the stone circles are graded so that they are lowest to the north-east and highest to the south-west (Figs. 5 and 6). This also applies to the kerbstones and to the orthostats that provide the foundation for the chamber wall in both the passage graves; the inner kerb of the ring cairn follows the same convention. In each case this has a similar effect, for the entire monument seems to rise to meet the last rays of the midwinter sun.

For someone approaching the cairns from behind, the structures would increase in scale from the back kerb to the entrance. In that sense the configuration of the stones would parallel the movement of the rising sun. At the same time, the shape of these stones would change. In two of these monuments the taller stones of the circle have flat or rounded tops whilst the lower monoliths are pointed. To some extent this detail is reproduced in the grading of the kerbs, and at all three of the monuments we can identify cases in which individual stones have been selected because they are virtually the same shape or texture as their counterparts in the outer circle.

Such links are also identified by the colour of the stones, which can vary from white or grey to dark red according to the character of the rock. Again there were powerful conventions governing the choice of materials in the stone circles. It is towards the rear of the monuments, especially the north-east cairn which would have faced the midsummer sunrise, that more pieces of quartz are found. These become steadily less frequent as we approach the south-west passage grave with its orientation on the midwinter sunset.

128 *Richard Bradley*

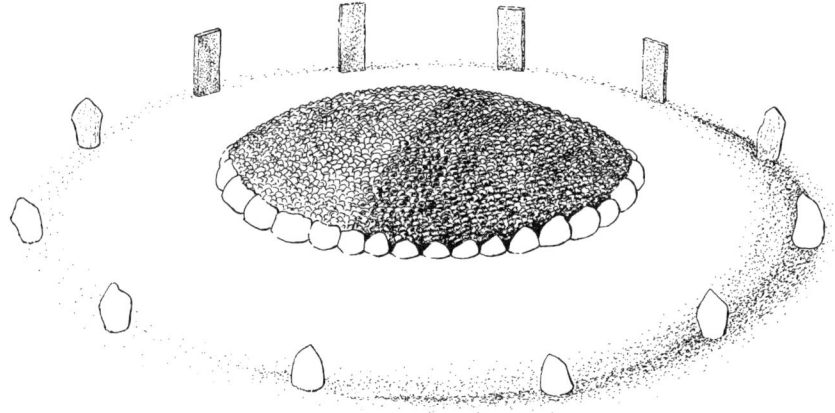

Fig.5. The basic structure of a Clava passage grave viewed from the back. Drawing: Aaron Watson.

The easiest way to describe the effect of these monuments on the observer is to imagine walking along the axis of the cemetery. First, I shall consider the changes that occur as we follow the rays of the rising sun as they extend across the site from the east. Then I shall describe how the monuments are related to the light from the setting sun.

Moving from east to west, the first cairn we encounter has a complex carving towards the rear of the kerb, and in the same length there is clear evidence that other stones were carefully selected. That kerb is composed from alternating sections of different raw materials. They change from red to white on the axis of the midsummer sunrise. The monoliths that surround the cairns follow a similar pattern, with stones that reflect the light towards the back of the monument. These contain large amounts of quartz and are either white or pink. Towards the entrance the stone circle is coloured red.

Much the same is true of the ring cairn in between the two passage graves. This time the stones of the outer circle were linked to those of the inner and outer kerbs and these connections were made explicit by radial divisions built into the structure of the monument. Again there is evidence of patterned stonework where the outer kerb was lowest. We can recognise a striking alternation between three different kinds of rock: red conglomerate, grey banded gneiss and quartz which is either pink or white; and again the colour of the kerbstones changes on the axis of the midsummer sunrise. The monoliths containing quartz were all confined to one section of the circle. They were restricted to the back of the monument, suggesting an association with the rising sun.

This pattern changes when we reach the cairn at the end of the cemetery where the two rows of monuments converge. Perhaps this is because that mon-

Directions to the dead 129

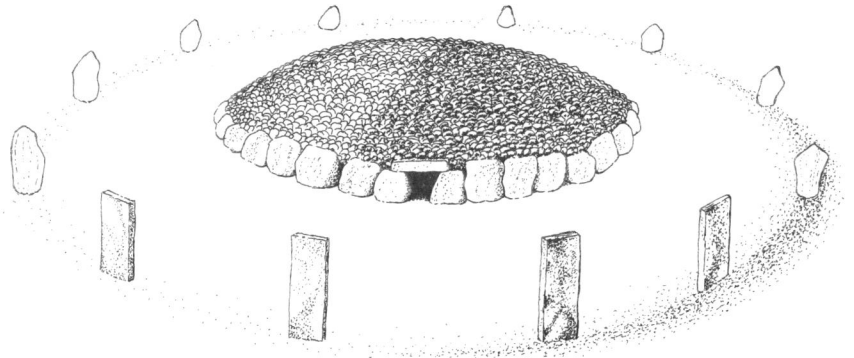

Fig. 6. The basic structure of a Clava passage grave viewed from the front. Drawing: Aaron Watson.

ument was directed towards the midwinter sunset. From this point we experience a radically different perspective. It is usually thought that the two passage graves were identical to one another. This is not the case. Almost all the monoliths enclosing this particular cairn were quarried for the purpose. With one exception, they consist of red sandstone slabs, and in contrast to their counterparts elsewhere in the cemetery, they have flat tops. The kerbstones, on the other hand, show rather less patterning, although those flanking the entrance are red and those on the opposite side of the monument are generally white and include pieces of quartz.

The passage and the central chamber share some unusual features. Unlike its counterpart, the roof of this passage slopes down towards the interior of the monument, directing the attention of anyone inside the cairn to the section of the sky where the sun sets at midwinter. At the junction of the passage and the chamber there is an orthostat with complex carved decoration. Its only counterpart is on the kerb of the other passage grave, where it is towards the back of the monument. Most important of all, the rear wall of the burial chamber employs a large amount of red sandstone which would have been illuminated by the midwinter sunset. A significant number of these stones had been decorated with cup marks before they were used in the building, but all of these 'hidden' carvings are in the area that would be highlighted by the setting sun.

The south-west passage grave has one other feature which distinguishes it from its counterpart in the same cemetery. All three well preserved cairns have an outer skin of rounded boulders obtained from the glacial gravel on the site. The cairn which faces directly into the midwinter sunset is unlike the other two because the boulders that provide this capping have been selected for their colour. More than two thirds of them are red whilst the others are grey. In the other passage grave each colour accounts for exactly half the material.

Now we shall follow the rays of the *setting* sun across the cemetery, investigating the front face of these three monuments. As we do so, the pattern changes yet again. The ring cairn still confronts the viewer with an arc of massive red slabs, which must have been quarried for the purpose, but towards the rear of the monument none of the monoliths comes from the same source. The stones of the outer kerb follow the same configuration, with several large red stones to the south-west and a more varied pattern along other parts of its perimeter where long sections of the kerb are restricted to a single colour: red or pink or white. By the time we reach the second passage grave on the site there is even less evidence that the front of the monument was treated in a special way. The only slabs of red sandstone are four monoliths close to the entrance itself. There is another upright of red conglomerate, but for the most part this setting consists of glacial erratics of other colours. The kerbstones emphasise these contrasts even further, for very few of them appear to have been quarried, although red stones do occur in several sections of the kerb. They are also found on either side of the entrance.

In effect the surviving portion of the cemetery has two distinct axes, and each of these is signalled in symbolic form. Approached from the direction of the rising sun, the cemetery consists of two rows of monuments converging on a single passage grave. This approach features the backs of the monuments. Here some of the kerbstones are highlighted by the use of quartz, and in one case by carved decoration. Approached from the other direction, the cairns emphasise the midwinter sunset, and this accounts for the alignment of both the passage graves and for the importance that was clearly attached to the south-western sector of these monuments. This is signalled by the grading of the kerbstones and rings of monoliths, but, above all, by the fact that so many of these stones had been quarried. There are more of these in the south-west cairn which is directed towards the setting sun. This is the only cairn where all the standing stones had been shaped and it is also the only monument with a capping of boulders selected for their colour. Almost all the major elements of this building made use of the colour red so that the entire structure would have glowed during the midwinter sunset. Less use was made of red stone with increasing distance from this cairn.

This suggests a basic duality in the organisation of these structures, in which the *rising sun* was associated with stones that increased in height, with unshaped erratics including pieces of quartz, and sometimes with the colours white, pink or grey. These stones include minerals that reflect the light. The *setting sun,* on the other hand, was linked with stones that decreased in height away from the main axis of the monuments, with slabs of rock that had been quarried for the purpose, and with the colour red. There were pieces of sandstone or conglomerate that seem to absorb the light.

A similar experience could be created by moving *around* the monuments, for the changing character of the stones displays the same kinds of patterning on a more local scale. The grading of the kerb towards the entrance to the tomb seems to imitate the passage of the sun from midwinter to the midsummer solstice. The progressively smaller stones towards the backs of these monuments would complete that cycle as the participants returned to their original point of departure. The organisation of the monoliths could have had the same effect, as if the sequence of sizes and shapes embodied in each of the stone circles stood for the progress of the seasons over the course of the year.

It is in this way that the fabric of the cemetery seems to have connected the dead inside their tombs with the movement of the sun that would remain constant across the generations. The emphasis on midwinter may have had a special significance, for in such northern latitudes the shortest day of the year is very short indeed. Not only did the winter solstice mark the moment when the hours of daylight began to increase, it might also have signalled the rebirth of the natural world. Perhaps rather similar ideas extended to the community's dead.

In the mind's eye

Some of the same beliefs may have been important over a wider area, and in the last part of this paper I would like to consider whether the symbolism so apparent at Balnuaran of Clava formed part of a wider cosmology.

There are three elements to discuss: the use of distinctive colours to symbolise the rising and setting sun; the principles that governed the orientation of individual tombs; and the ways in which links between these different monuments may have found expression. Having offered a study of one particular cemetery, I shall extend the discussion to further sites in Scotland, Ireland and Wales (Fig. 7).

The first point to consider is the use of colour in passage graves and other monuments. This is not peculiar to the Clava Cairns, and what seems to be essentially the same code can be recognised at sites over a much wider area. The association between quartz and passage graves is well documented in Ireland and is particularly obvious at Loughcrew (McMann 1994) and in the Boyne Valley (Eogan 1986:chapter 4). In both cases the use of quartz is particularly strongly associated with monuments orientated on the sunrise, although at Knowth, where the main mound contains two passages, they are associated with both the sunrise and sunset.

As so often, it may be the exception that proves the rule, for a recently discovered passage grave at Knockroe is also orientated on the midwinter sunset (O'Sullivan 1996). Again this is a site containing two distinct tombs, both of them associated with deposits of quartz, but the other passage does not appear to have any astronomical orientation. The excavator has commented on

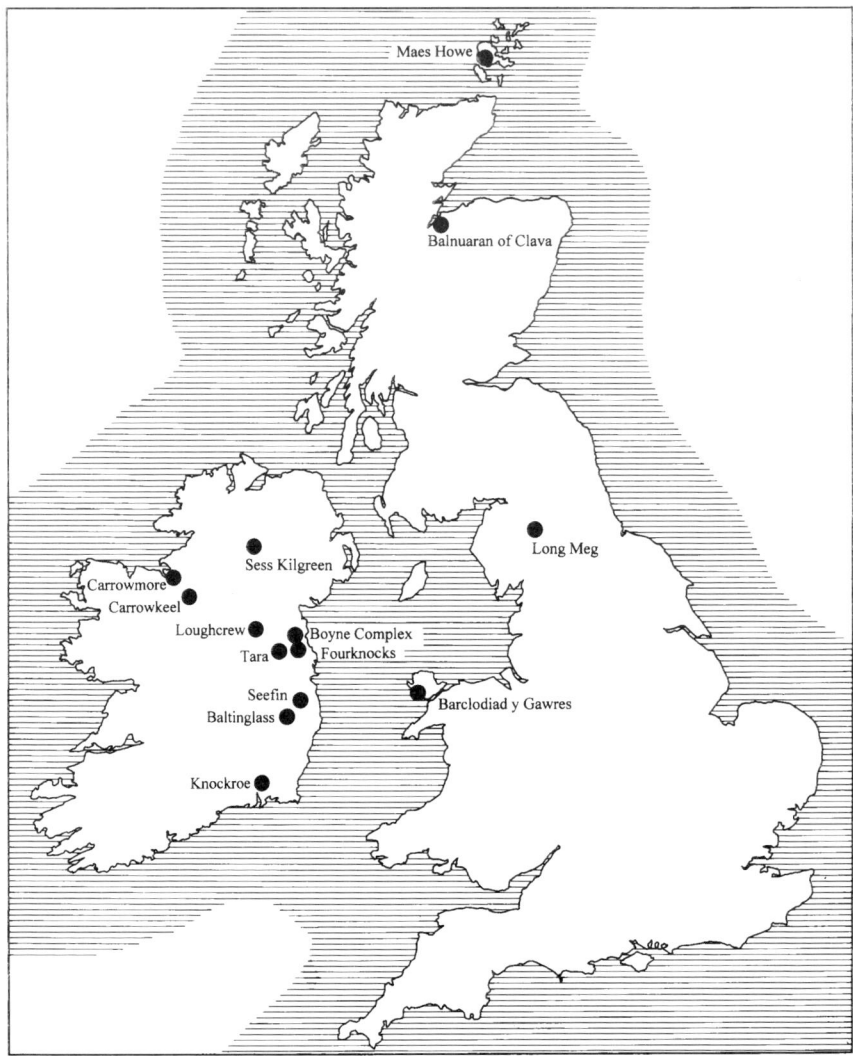

Fig. 7. Map of Britain and Ireland showing the monuments referred to in the text. Drawing: Margaret Mathews.

a curious feature of the passage grave that faces the midwinter solstice, for in the chamber there is an upright of red sandstone which plays no obvious role in the structure of the monument. Its appearance on the site recalls the evidence from Clava. The passage tomb at Knockroe is relevant for a different reason, for this is a cairn whose kerb was built out of stones of more than one colour (Muiris O'Sullivan pers. comm.). Again its perimeter included pieces of Old

Red Sandstone, and, as we saw at Balnuaran of Clava, the kerbstones seem to have changed their composition along the axis of the midwinter sunset.

On the opposite side of the Irish Sea there are two other monuments with well attested alignments on the setting sun at the shortest day of the year. Both show the same association with red stones. Maes Howe, the most impressive monument in Orkney, is actually built out of red sandstone (Davidson & Henshall 1989:142 ff.), but this may not be significant since it is the main building material in that area. What is more striking is the discovery that the chamber walls had been carefully dressed by picking. This practice is otherwise limited to Ireland, and it would have enhanced the colour of the monument at the time of the midwinter sunset (Eogan 1992:123 f.).

The other site is a stone circle in north-west England: Long Meg and her Daughters. This setting has one massive outlier which is unusual because it is decorated in the same style as Irish passage graves. It has long been recognised that it is located on the axis of the midwinter sunset, viewed from the centre of the site (Burl 1994). That observation takes on an added significance when we realise that the monolith is of red sandstone which must have been brought to the site from some distance away. It is the only piece of its kind in the monument.

Although the evidence is limited, it suggests that the cemetery at Balnuaran of Clava was not the only place to symbolise the rising and setting sun by the use of coloured stones: white quartz to reflect the rising sun, red sandstone towards the sunset. In each case there was the same emphasis on the shortest day of the year.

There also seem to be differences between the monuments found on either side of the Irish Sea. The passage graves in Ireland with astronomical alignments are more often directed towards the rising sun (Brennan 1983). The evidence from Scotland and northern England reveals an emphasis on the sunset. The sample is too small to be entirely convincing, but it suggests a reciprocal relationship between the monuments on ether side of the water. Irish monuments tended to face the sunrise, with the result that they would also face towards England and Scotland. The sites directed towards the sunset would be facing towards Ireland.

That relationship might seem fanciful, but it recalls an observation that has long been accepted in Ireland where the main passage grave cemeteries were orientated on one another (Patrick 1975; Bergh 1995:chapter 7). At first sight there is nothing remarkable about this idea, since so many of these monuments are on hilltops, but in fact these orientations may extend between monuments that could not have been observed over such long distances. In other cases, any views would been obscured by the presence of higher ground. Thus tombs at Loughcrew, Baltinglass and Seefin may be directed towards the Boyne Valley (Patrick 1975); six of the cairns at Loughcrew point at Fourknocks (McMann 1994:537); whilst the passage grave at Tara may also be orientated on that site

(Patrick 1975). In the same way, the tombs at Carrowkeel are aligned on those at Carrowmore (Bergh 1995:chapter 7).

The connections between these monuments are emphasised by the use of imported materials. Thus there are seashells from the passage graves at Loughcrew, even though the site is located 60 km from the coast (Herity 1974:172). Some of the stones deposited around the entrances of Newgrange and Knowth come from areas about the same distance away (Mitchell 1992). Among these are the Wicklow Mountains, where the passage graves at Seefin and Baltinglass are aligned on those in the Boyne Valley.

This suggests one further level of comparison. Almost all the passage graves in mainland Britain have easterly orientations, although none seems to be directed towards the midwinter sunrise. There are, however, a few important exceptions which face the other way. This is true of all the passage graves of the Clava tradition and also of Maes Howe. In Wales the same applies to the chambered tomb at Barclodiad Y Gawres, which is orientated towards the north west (Powell & Daniel 1956). What these sites share are close affinities with megalithic monuments in Ireland. As we have seen, the pick dressing at Maes Howe is shared with Newgrange and Knowth; the Clava Cairns are enclosed by stone circles much like that at Newgrange; and Barclodiad Y Gawres is decorated with a series of carvings that can hardly be paralleled outside Irish megalithic art. Only a small proportion of these sites are actually aligned on the sunset. Might the westerly alignment of the other monuments be a reference to their connections with Ireland?

I have called this paper 'directions to the dead'. Those directions may be significant for several reasons. On one level they are the directions taken by the rising and setting sun as it lights the ancestral tombs at special times of year. I have already suggested that the shortest day is the ideal moment for symbolising rebirth and renewal. The association between the dead and the workings of the heavens suggests that the ancestors may have played a part in a more complex cosmology.

On another level, it is likely that this symbolic system was particularly closely allied to the communities who built the main passage tombs in Ireland. These sites may have provided a source of inspiration for the British monuments—or rather the latter may have made an explicit reference to the principles of order embodied in those monuments. Is it possible that the westerly alignment of these particular structures was an acknowledgement of that relationship? Was Ireland conceived as the source of origin, real or imagined, of the people who constructed these tombs? And was it to Ireland that they might seem to return? The light of the midwinter sun provided directions to the dead in their great stone cairns; and the alignment of those buildings led them further, towards an imagined homeland in the west. The history of the people who had created these great stone monuments was played out year after year in the movements of the sun. The architecture of the tombs brought these ideas together in a powerful synthesis. It was one that reached back into an ancestral past. Only we can know how far it would extend into the future.

Acknowledgements

I am grateful to Margaret Mathews and Aaron Watson for the figure drawings. Margaret Mathews supervised the planning of the cairns at Balnuaran of Clava and the following people helped to record the colours of the stones: Heather Jackson, Andy Jones, Hannah Sackett, David Trebarthen and Aaron Watson. I must also thank Muiris O'Sullivan for information on the chambered cairn at Knockroe.

References

Bergh, S. 1995. *Landscape of the Monuments.* Riksantikvarieämbet Arkeologiska Undersöknigar. Stockholm.
Brennan, M. 1983. *The Stars and the Stones. Ancient Art and Astronomy in Ireland.* London.
Burl, A. 1994. The stone circle of Long Meg and her Daughters, Little Salkeld. *Transactions of the Cumberland and Westmorland Antiquarian and Archaeological Society* 94, 1–11.
Davidson, J. & Henshall, A. 1989. *The Chambered Cairns of Orkney.* Edinburgh.
Eogan, G. 1986. *Knowth and the Passage-tombs of Ireland.* London.
— 1992. Scottish and Irish passage tombs: some comparisons and contrasts. In Sharples, N. & A. Sheridan (eds), *Vessels for the Ancestors.* Edinburgh, 120–127.
Henshall, A. 1963. *The Chambered Tombs of Scotland,* volume 1. Edinburgh.
Herity, M. 1974. *Irish Passage Graves.* Dublin.
McMann, J. 1994. Forms of power: dimensions of an Irish megalithic landscape. *Antiquity* 68, 525–44.
Mitchell, F. 1992. Notes on some non-local cobbles at the entrances to the passage graves of Newgrange and Knowth, County Meath. *Journal of the Royal Society of Antiquaries of Ireland* 122, 128–45.
O'Kelly, M. 1982. *Newgrange. Archaeology, Art and Legend.* London.
O'Sullivan, M. 1996. A platform to the past. Knockroe passage tomb. *Archaeology Ireland* 10.2, 11–13.
Patrick, J. 1975. Megalithic exegesis—a comment. *Irish Archaeological Research Forum* 2.2, 9–14.
Phillips, T. 1996. *Circular Monuments in a Linear Landscape.* Unpublished MA thesis, Reading University. Reading.
Powell, T. & Daniel, G. 1956. *Barclodiad y Gawres: the excavation of a megalithic chamber tomb in Anglesey.* Liverpool.

Rock, Stone and Mentality
Stones that unite, stones that subjugate—a megalithic tomb in Vale de Rodrigo, southern Portugal
By Lars Larsson

When it comes to our conceptual world, we find no difficulty in perceiving the loose layers of earth as a self-evident aspect of our conceptual world. You sow seed, and up comes a crop. We are buried, and in the Christian burial ritual the mortal nature of the transformation of the body is marked with three scoops of earth. Water, through its significance as an element in which sacrifices are made, has an acknowledged role as a mental sphere. Both earth and water have an important role as a sphere for life on this planet. We find it more difficult, on the other hand, to perceive rock as a mental mass. One example of its lack of significance is the quotation from the Bible, "... which fell on stony ground." (Luke 8,6). Rock is only meaningful to us as a surface that can exhibit three-dimensional changes and yet is still perceived as providing a clear boundary to our room for manoeuvre.

Rock as a mass that contains potential values is clearly identified through mining activities, for instance. There is evidence dating back to the Middle Palaeolithic of extensive mining of flint and red ochre (Dart & Beaumont 1969), for example. A further example of long continuity in the utilization of rock is the mining of certain types of rock, for example in Norway, for axe manufacture during the Mesolithic (Alsaker 1987). The search for metal has imbued rock with a special meaning since the Early Neolithic, when the extraction of copper began (Magnusson Staaf 1996). The potential of rock has thus been known, prospected and utilized for a very long time. Such awareness ought to have been incorporated into the conceptual world so as to impart even greater significance to the rock mass.

Like earth and water, rock may have been perceived as a plastic material. The fact that rock concealed forces that were difficult to restrain would have been very clear to people who inhabited areas with extensive volcanic or high earthquake activity and with extensive land elevation.

We are also not unfamiliar with concepts along the lines that mythological beings, such as giants and trolls, lived inside the mountains. Even to this day, road building operations in Iceland will avoid rocks which, according to popular belief, are considered to be inhabited by spirit beings. Notions that rock is inhabited by beings may well derive from the awareness that the rock contained cavities and caves. Caves played an important part in the conceptual world of humans, which can be appreciated not least from the fact that they were objects both for artistic expression and sacrificial rituals.

The Portuguese case

As already mentioned, people began to remove part of the rock mass at an early stage. The ability to split large stones from the mass appears to date back to the same period as the oldest megalithic tombs.

Megalithic tombs along the coastal zone of Western Europe show shared general features, as well as regional and sometimes local distinctive features. To consider the general in relation to specific conditions was the aim of our collaborative project with the Lisbon office of the German Institute concerning a group of megalithic tombs in southern Portugal, which was started in 1991.

According to radiometric datings, megalithic tombs in Portugal begin to appear around 4500 BC (Kalb 1981; 1989), but it is still uncertain whether these dating samples come from the initial phase of burial in the tombs or date secondary burials during the time when the megalithic tomb was in use.

Some scholars think that the building of megalithic tombs began during a preceramic phase with very distinct Mesolithic traditions, while others date the initial phase to a later stage (Leisner & Leisner 1943, 1951, 1965; Morais Arnaud 1982, 1990; Lubell *et al.* 1989; Strauss 1991; Zilhão 1990, 1992, 1993). Some researchers regard the small, simple structures like cists as the oldest, and those with a more complex structure as somewhat later. Against this view there is the evidence that even megalithic tombs of an advanced structure contain categories of artefacts which correspond to those found in the simple tomb forms.

The problem is not in the first instance a question of chronology or typology; it concerns fundamental views of the societies that built the megalithic tombs. A slow development of the tomb forms, from simple to complex, would be characteristic of a society evolving slowly towards increasingly complex social patterns. The fact that complex types begin to appear simultaneously with, or very shortly after the introduction of megalithic tombs reflects a society in rapid change, perhaps with significant social conflicts. The manifestation of this tomb building with such variation and such advanced technique can be perceived as the result either of an extremely innovative environment attaching low value to traditional ideas, or of a society accepting external influence as regards both a changed conceptual world and purely practical knowledge about stone-building techniques and architecture.

Knowledge of the society that built the megalithic tombs can only be based to a small extent on investigations of settlement sites, simply because there are so few of them (Ribé *et al.* 1997). The main parts of the sites are big and sometimes fortified with ramparts. They can be related to an advanced stage of the use of megalithic tombs, but not to the phase when they were built (Jorge & Jorge 1997). For this reason, they can scarcely be viewed retrospectively as representative of the form of settlement which can be associated with the megalith-building society.

Another decisive question is why megalithic tombs were built? To answer this question it is essential to know where these monuments were erected— they are not evenly distributed in the landscape. To use the terminology of nuclear physics, we get the impression that a "critical mass" is necessary if a need to build monuments is to arise. Unlike nuclear physics, however, it is not a question of the accumulation of one component, but rather of a mixture of several different components. One of the ingredients is the geographical conditions. This is obvious from the fact that megalithic tombs are completely absent in certain regions. Mostly they are concentrated in areas with an ecologically varied zonation. Another ingredient is population density, which should not be confused with population growth, although there is often a certain association. A third ingredient is the scope of contact with other social groups. Further ingredients are the shaping of traditions as regards the social structure and hence the structure of the conceptual world, the composition of the economic base, and the mental capacity, charisma, or cunning of particular individuals to consolidate or suppress a lust for power.

This does not mean that exactly the same mixture was necessary on every occasion for the "critical mass" to arise. Nor should this be taken as evidence that the custom of building megalithic tombs arose independently in several different areas. It is most likely that they had a common origin. On the other hand, we must reckon with different combinations and varying significance for the above variables for the custom to have been adopted outside the area of origin. Some general ideas may have existed, but we should not, therefore, ignore the conditions and conceptions that were specific to each region. In a comparative study such as this project, viewpoints about both general and specific features of megalith building are worth examining more closely.

Megalithic tomb Vale de Rodrigo 2 and its content

During the years 1991–96 excavations were conducted at one of the four megalithic tombs located near the farm of Vale de Rodrigo, in the province of Alentejo in southern Portugal (Fig. 1) (Dehn *et al.* 1991; Silva & Parreira 1992; Becker 1994; Kalb & Höck 1994, 1995; Larsson 1995, 1997).

Tomb (Monument) 2, the excavation of which was the Swedish contribution to the international co-operation project, consists of an almost oval chamber defined by seven orthostats which have no capstone today (Fig. 2). Some stones have been broken off, and there are clear marks of the use of wedges. Of

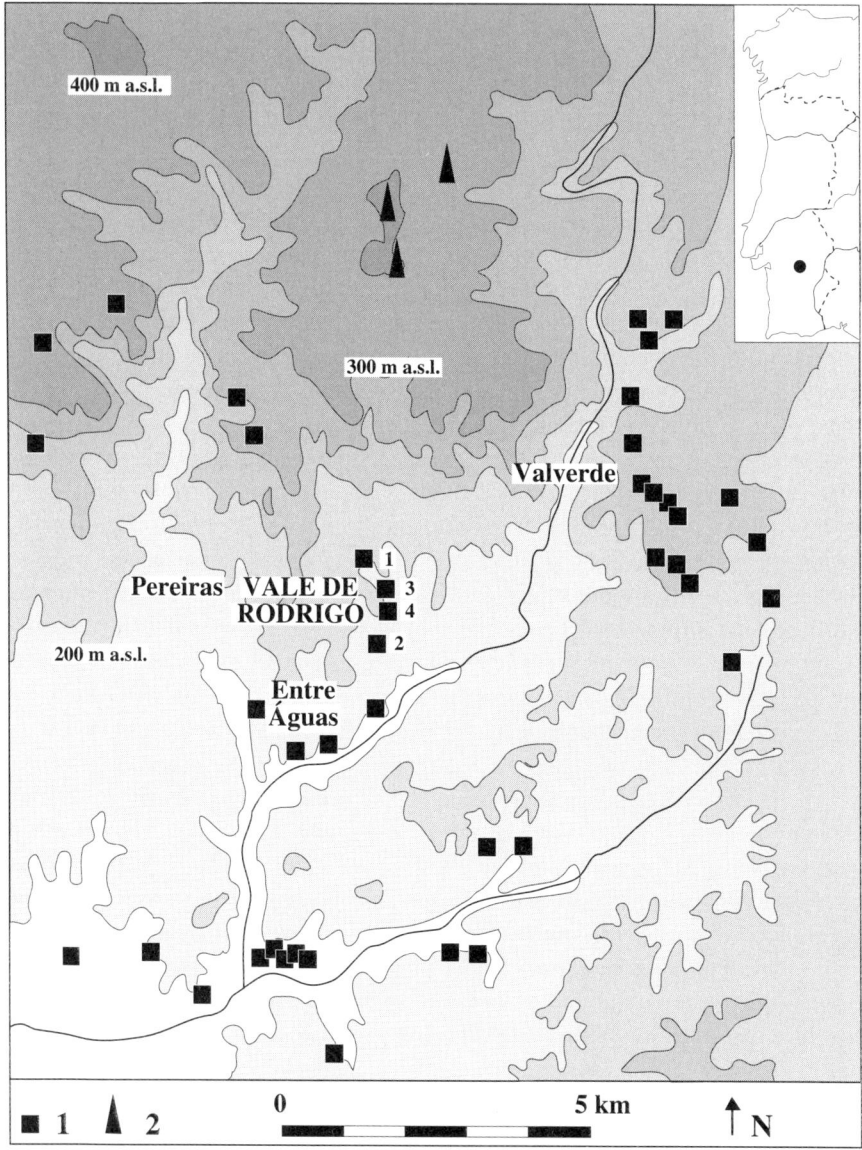

Fig. 1. The investigation area—Vale de Rodrigo—and its surroundings. Legends: 1: megalithic tombs and 2: menhirs. The map to the upper right marks the location of the investigation area within Portugal.

the passage, two capstones are visible above the tomb. The tomb, which has more or less the form of a passage grave, is located on a rise in the terrain about two metres high situated on a south-east slope.

The aim of the investigation was to study the method of construction and the

Rock, stone and mentality 141

Fig. 2. Vale de Rodrigo, monument 2 seen from the east. The stone at ground level in the foreground is a capstone of the passage.

use of the megalithic grave. This is why most of the investigated area was concentrated to trenches outside the stone chamber (Fig. 3).

The undisturbed orthostats stand roughly human height above the ground surface. This gave the impression of a comparatively small megalithic grave constructed on a natural mound, and we had expected to have to dig down roughly a metre to find the base of the wall. By investigating a section immediately outside the chamber, it turned out that the orthostats were almost 4 metres tall (Fig. 4). This shows that the ground where the tomb was built was originally level (Fig. 3). The builders had dug trenches more than half a metre deep in the crumbling bedrock, in which the orthostats were anchored with the aid of stone packing. The orthostats were fixed more firmly in position by being slightly overlapped. In places where the orthostats had somewhat irregular sides, the space between was filled with pillar-like stones.

A clear ground horizon could also be identified. It was of a slightly darker colour and contained fragments of clay pots and worked quartz of a size which allow us to interpret it as a human-influenced horizon.

More than half of the surface of the chamber, roughly ten square metres, has been investigated. The chamber filling contained a great many stones, and there were artefacts at all levels, the youngest of which belong to the Late Bronze Age.

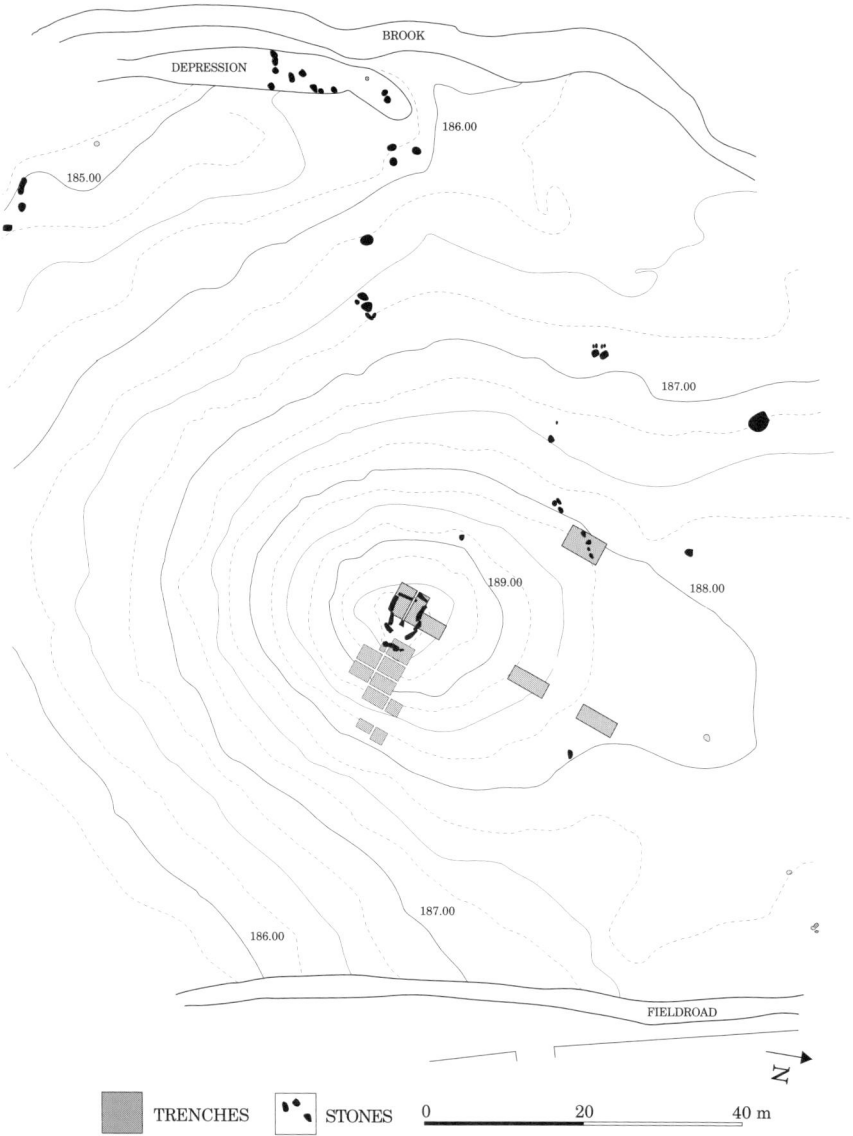

Fig. 3. Topographic conditions of Vale de Rodrigo, monument 2 and the position of the excavated areas.

An original division of the chamber was obvious from two slabs fixed between the orthostats at right angles to the wall. These stones, which appear to belong to the original structure of the chamber, divide the chamber into two cells of roughly equal size.

The bottom layer of the chamber, which was on the same level as the origi-

Fig. 4. A part of the outside of the megalithic chamber after its excavation with almost four metres high orthostats.

nal ground level, consisted of a very hard material which was probably spread to level the surface, after which it was subjected to a natural transformation. This material covered the bottom and reached part of the way up the orthostats. In at least two areas the bottom layer had been dug up in conjunction with secondary burials. There was some disturbance of the original find distribution. Because of the acid mineral soil, all that remained was the colouring of the bones of the deceased, which could be documented on only a few occasions. Assemblages of artefacts, for example the fact that the parts of the same flint blade lay close together, as did a couple of slate plates in another part of the excavated area, marked the individual burial spots.

The mound
The mound around the tomb was of considerable size. In the trench at the foot of the mound there were remains of a ring of bordering stones, of which only a

very limited section was intact (Fig. 3). Judging by the shape of this stone ring, the mound had a diameter of some 45 metres. Magnetic measurements reveal indistinct markings, however, which may suggest that there was yet another ring of bordering stones.

That the mound reached considerably higher than it does today is clear from the fact that the passage that is at the same height as the ground surface was totally filled with mound filling which had seeped down. The entrance area in this part reaches a height of two metres. This indicates that the covering of the tomb was significantly thicker than it is today. This suggests that the chamber was covered up to the capstone, when the mound reached a height of roughly four metres.

From the trench immediately outside the chamber it was possible to obtain insight into the structures adjoining the chamber. It was possible to document stone rings bordering the chamber. It cannot be ascertained whether these rings were built as stages in a continuous building process, or were built at long intervals. In the filling of the mound it was not possible to discern any darker horizon, which is usually the surest sign that the filling was added in stages at such long intervals that a plant cover had time to form. The absence of covered plant horizons inside the filling suggests that the entire filling was spread during a limited period of time. Small sections of other stone structures were found, such as a small cairn in the bottom level of the filling, which was built before the mound.

A clear ground horizon outside the chamber could be identified. It was of a slightly darker colour and contained fragments of clay pots and worked quartz in numbers which allow us to interpret it as a settlement area. It is uncertain what these human activities should be related to. Similar find conditions are known from other megalithic tombs, such as Anta de Zambujeiro (Ph. Kalb, personal communication). One suggested explanation is that they are the remains of a period spent in a camp as part of the construction of the tomb. However, their location right beside the tomb makes such an explanation difficult to understand. The area of the tomb should have been kept free of camps, for both practical and religious reasons. The fact that the find-bearing layer reaches all the way to the tomb, and was cut off when the channels were cut out for the orthostats, suggests that the finds should be related to a settlement that existed before the tomb was built.

Samples were taken from the original ground level for pollen analysis. Although the preservation conditions were poor, a small number of pollen types was identified. The majority were from oak and heather which formed a typical macchia vegetation (Regnell 1994). This shows that the landscape when the megalithic tomb was built was relatively open, probably grazed, while tillage, if there was any, was on a limited scale. No pollen from cultivated plants has been identified, but this may be because of the limited number of pollen grains

Rock, stone and mentality 145

Fig. 5. The passage and part of the forecourt of monument 2 with two rows of stones marking the edges of a rampart.

found. The pollen analysis also shows the occurrence of trees such as lime and hazel, which probably grew beside a small stream about a hundred metres west of the tomb. Today the area is covered with grassland with thin stands of oaks of different species. Only areas that have not been ploughed are still overgrown with heather today. The rich occurrence of microscopic charcoal may suggest deliberate burning by man to improve the grazing.

The entrance
The passage had a length of more than three metres (Fig. 5). The building of the passage took place in different phases. In the first of these, large orthostats supported three capstones, two of which remain. In a later phase, the passage was extended, with the width simultaneously being reduced. The northern orthostat side increased, with a couple of stones continuing the same line, while the stones on the opposite side were obviously moved inwards from the former line. This reduced the width by about 0.5 m.

The investigation of the chamber and the passage clearly showed that they had been filled up in different ways. The chamber was filled with a layer rich in stones, which had been placed there in different stages. In the passage most of the filling consisted of sand mixed with clay but with no stones—mound filling which had seeped down between the stones. A certain stratification

Fig. 6. Part of the passage and the forecourt of monument 2 with the paved area along the northern side of the forecourt.

indicates that this happened in stages. The only stones were a small number found in the bottom section. In addition, there were clearly distinguishable floor layers here consisting of hard-trodden clay. One of the capstones had been broken into three parts, which had fallen down into the passage. From their position it is evident that the passage was not entirely filled when this collapse occurred.

Assemblages of slates, rock crystals, clay pots, and beads of slate and/or arrowheads were found in the passage. Their combination with human dental enamel shows that these are burials.

The forecourt

To obtain a better idea of what the entrance section was like, trenches were dug outside and close to the passage (Fig. 3). Three stone slabs, which sealed the entrance, rested on stone paving (Fig. 6). The excavation of the passage showed that the floor layers were about 1 m lower than the base of the slabs covering the entrance. This means that significant layer formation had occurred outside the opening of the passage before it was sealed. A thick layer of stones had been laid on the surface outside the entrance. Large stones formed a transverse boundary. Present within this were stones at different levels, which formed a stairway leading down to the entrance. The sunken area directly adjacent to the entrance had been filled, however, before the passage was sealed.

Besides burials, we documented two rows of stones in several layers, which started from the corner of the passage opening and ran obliquely outwards (Fig. 5). These rows have been interpreted as the rampart of a court which led up to the opening of the passage. The court adjoined the edge marking of the mound. The ramparts extend as far as stones further inside the passage, which provides additional evidence that the passage had been extended at a later date.

A stone setting in the form of a paved section roughly 1.5 metres wide can be followed along the northern part of the forecourt (Fig. 6). Since the investigation has not been completed, it is somewhat uncertain how many stages of change affected the passage and the court. It was clear, however, that burials were found only within the paved area. Here there were assemblages of artefacts and dental enamel more than nine metres outside the entrance to the passage.

The layer sequence shows that the ramparts marked the edge of the mound filling, which was thus delimited down to the original ground surface. At a later stage parts of the court were filled and the paving was added. The mound filling was then extended to cover the southern part of the court. The mound filling was thereby delimited by the width of the paving.

The area in front of the passage proved to have a rich content of both finds and structures. The area outside the passage was covered by stone paving. A considerable number of artefacts, such as arrowheads, beads, slate artefacts and pots, was found on and inside this paving. The distribution of the finds and occurrences of dental enamel suggest that these are remains of true burials. They are not evenly distributed, and a combination of slate plates, vessels, and a piece of rock crystal was documented on a few occasions (Fig. 7). Judging by the stratigraphic conditions, this burial occurred after the tomb had been sealed.

Find conditions inside the forecourt

The richness of the finds from the area outside the passage, taken here to be a forecourt, may not be due exclusively to a number of burials outside the passage. The distribution of things like pottery and arrowheads shows that these are also traces of deliberate deposition. It is evident that the find categories have different distributions both horizontally and vertically. An example of this is the arrowheads, which increase in number with the distance from the entrance. In addition, in the trench furthest from the opening, it can be noted that arrowheads were found at a slightly higher level than the pottery. As we saw above, there is a considerable difference in level between the bottom of the passage and the level of the stone paving immediately outside the entrance. Since only the top level has been investigated so far, it is not possible to

Fig. 7. Find situation from the pavement outside the passage with slate plaques, a vessel and a piece of rock crystal indicating a burial.

determine whether or not there are more stone layers with assemblages of artefacts.

As regards the distribution of finds, one cannot avoid drawing parallels with the find conditions outside the entrance to several South Scandinavian graves, where the finds are interpreted as traces of repeated sacrificial acts, with a certain structure being visible as regards both the find categories and the times of the sacrifices (Strömberg 1968, 1971; Shanks & Tilley 1987). In only a few cases have excavations of megalithic tombs in southern or central Portugal included the section outside the entrance. It is therefore impossible to ascertain whether remains like these are unusual or frequent. What is clear from the excavation of monument 2, however, is that the archaeological approach, inspired by experiences from megalithic tombs in southern Scandinavia, has helped to give a new dimension to the use of Portuguese megalithic tombs.

Symbols in stone—petrified traditions

The execution of the megalithic tomb and its use provides rich opportunities to discuss the significance of rock and stones in the world-view of prehistoric man. Here we encounter the phenomenon of the cave once again. Early Neolithic burials on the Iberian peninsula are found in natural caves. The megalithic tombs—the artificial cave constructions—can be seen as a direct consequence of changing one's surrounding world (Bradley 1989b).

The rock is represented by orthostats that are hewn directly from solid rock. As can be appreciated from their form, several of these have also been reworked. The whole sphere of nature was to be subjected to society, and one expression which this took was the splitting of huge stone blocks. The hewing of stones from rock may have possessed important symbolic significance, since it was related to the ability to command and change the most resistant part of the landscape. The monuments expressed society's claim to power over nature.

The choice of stone and the origin of the raw material were guided by norms prevailing in the particular society. Different raw materials were used. The large orthostats originate from an area to the west approximately 2 km from the grave. The distance is short, although the area in between is undulating, which must have made transport more difficult.

Like the other megalithic graves in Vale de Rodrigo, however, monument 2 also contains a stone of porific grandiorite, which was collected from an area some 6 km distant (Dehn *et al.* 1992; Kalb 1996). This was used in monument 2 as the capstone in the original opening of the passage. The fact that the characteristics of this stone were not particularly good from the point of view of its use in construction can be appreciated from the fact that it is the only capstone in the passage that had subsequently cracked. The same exotic stone material is found in all the megalithic graves in Vale de Rodrigo, which points to the symbolic significance of the stones. The area would appear to have had major significance in the conceptual world of the megalith builders, for example as a marker of origin or a symbol of affinity.

Concerning the cracked cap stone, some of the megalithic tombs in the area in question have fractured capstones and/or orthostats that are not the results of influence at a later time. One possible explanation is that severe earthquakes caused the destruction, which in some cases may have led to the abandonment of all or parts of the stone chamber. More extensive earthquakes, which affected the stone monuments of an entire region, may have contributed to a changed view not only of the use of individual burial chambers, but also of deeper perceptions as to how the higher powers valued the building of monuments and the use of monuments by humans.

Menhirs have been interpreted in some cases as axe symbols, and are also regarded as metaphorical expressions for the human body (Thomas & Tilley 1993). We now have sound evidence from Brittany showing that menhirs were broken up and incorporated as parts of the building in megalithic graves (L'Helgouach 1983). The axe symbol has become part of the megalithic grave. In the area with which we are concerned here, the menhirs are found to have a distinct form, which agrees closely with axes of round or oval cross-section contained in the graves. The graves also contain axes with a flat form (Fig. 8: 4). If one examines the orthostats of the megalithic graves, it emerges that the nature of their hewing into trapezoidal form with a broad base harmonizes very closely with this form of axe and has symbolic links to the human body. A grave such as monument 2 would, in respect of its structural details, point to

Fig. 8. Artefacts found during the excavation of monument 2. 1–3: decorated slate plaques and 4: stone axe. Drawing: Eva Koch. 1:2.

Rock, stone and mentality 151

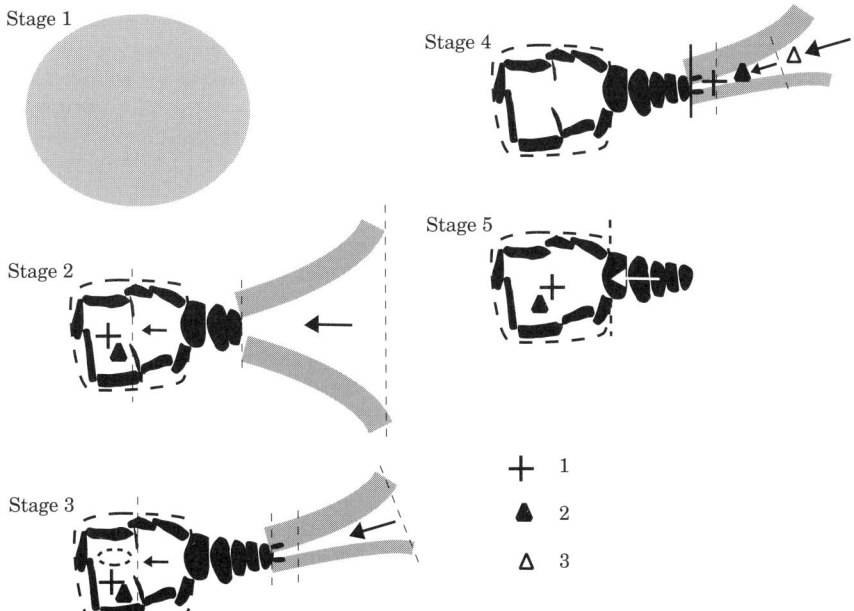

Fig. 9. Different stages of activites before, during and after the building of the megalithic tomb Vale de Rodrigo, monument 2. The arrows mark access, and the lines mark screening or delimitation of the tomb. Legends: 1: burial, 2: grave good deposition and 3: sacrificial deposition.

the repeated reproduction of the body—a room in which to house bodies constructed from bodies.

A further stage in this association chain can be followed. A later stage of the period of use of megalithic graves yields an abundance of decorated slate plates, which are interpreted as stylized human bodies partly because of the representation of eyes which they bear (Fig. 8: 1–3). Interestingly enough, these slabs exhibit a slightly marked trapezoidal form closely resembling both axes and orthostats.

In their construction and their detailed features, it is possible to follow a process in which access and screening are predominant themes (Bradley 1993; Barrett 1994). A megalithic grave is constructed on an earlier site (Fig. 9: Stage 1)—here the predominantly profane is incorporated with a clearly sacral sphere (Fig. 9: Stage 2). The building extends to the splitting and transport of very large building components, although these were fully enclosed by soil and as such were concealed from almost all directions. Only the forecourt provided the visitor with a clear indication that the site had been formed by humans. Impressive parts of the burial chamber only became clearly visible to those who had been permitted to enter the chamber. All the surprising and overwhelming features that can be generated by a natural cave have been transferred in this case to an artificial cavity. The original construction incorporated a subdivision of this cavity, which also provided opportunities for a boundary at which light and shadow created a further suggestive sensation (Bradley 1989a). At the same time as transforming the landscape, efforts were also made to conceal this impressive construction. The grave gifts were few in number during this period. In the monument people embodied in stone a conception that was related both to traditions—the origins of the group—and to innovations—the new forms of livelihood. It was only at a later stage that the interest was transferred to the dead and the symbols in the form of grave-goods which accompanied them to the tomb.

The building of monuments which resemble natural formations can also be seen as a symbolic act through which to subjugate the environment. By copying nature, people show how they can obtain power over it. When this is done as part of the burial ritual, it shows that the dead are a link between artificial social patterns and natural processes. Man becomes a part—but a superior part—of nature. In the earlier hunting and gathering societies, nature was an integral part of the conceptual world, but then as an equal or superior part. When people manipulate their physical environment through cultivation and animal husbandry, they feel a new need also to manifest this dominating role over those parts of nature which were not formerly directly affected by human influence.

In a later stage the passage was extended and made narrower, which made entry more difficult (Fig. 9: Stage 3). The stone setting leading to the entrance may also have come into being at this stage, as well as a narrowing of the forecourt. It was possibly at this stage that individual burial places were also produced in the form of pits excavated into the floor of the chamber. This was done during the chalkolithic period.

At a later stage the forecourt began to be used for sacrifices (Fig. 9, Stage 4). The passage was closed, but the forecourt then assumed the status of a burial place. The role of the cave as a burial chamber had expired, and interments could equally well take place in the open.

In a final phase the chamber was broken into, probably by removing the wall stones resting on the inner capstones of the passage (Fig. 9: Stage 5). Burial started again, and this involved filling with stones until the chamber was completely full. This may well have taken place during the Bronze Age.

The fact that most megalithic graves exhibit distinct traces of plundering emerges as a quite specific connecting link between megalithic graves and the axe. Ironically enough, a significant proportion of the plundering is believed to have taken place during the Roman period, when axes made of stone were very much in demand.

The fact that burials after a while were not confined to the burial chamber, but also occurred outside, as in the case of the tomb studied here, shows that the role of the megalithic tomb had changed. Archaeologists have long seen the megalithic tomb as being representative of a particular symbol—the territorial marker—in which case it would mark a petrified tradition, a picture of society which must have become antiquated after a time. If, on the other hand, megalithic tombs represent a symbolically charged role which changed form during the time when they were used, this gives us scope to see the stone group as an actor in a changeable conceptual world.

I have attempted to give deeper meaning to a number of observations in conjunction with the excavation of a megalithic tomb. This tomb relates a long and eventful story in combination with the conceptual world of generations. Some will be happy to agree with this story, whereas others will certainly adopt a sceptical view and maintain that I have over-interpreted the remains; there may even be those who believe that I am stone mad!

References

Alsaker, S. 1987. *Bømlo—Steinalderens råstoffsentrum på Sørvestlandet.* Arkeologiska avhandlinger fra Historisk museum i Bergen 4. Bergen.

Barrett, J. C. 1994. *Fragments from Antiquity. An Archaeology of Social Life in Britain, 2900–1200 BC.* Oxford.

Becker, H. 1994. Testmessung zur elektrischen Prospektion eines Megalithgrabes in Vale de Rodrigo 3, Concelho Évora, Portugal. *Madrider Mitteilungen* 35, 78–84.

Bradley, R. 1989a. Darkness and light in the design of megalithic tombs. *Oxford Journal of Archaeology* 8: 3, 251–259.

— 1989b. Death and entrances: a contextual analysis of megalithic art. *Current Anthropology* 30, 68–75.

— 1993. *Altering the Earth.* Society of Antiquaries of Scotland Monograph series 8. Edinburgh.

Dart, M. H. & Beaumont, P. 1969. Evidence of Iron Ore Mining in Southern Africa in the Middle Stone Age. *Current Anthropology* 10:1, 127–128.

Dehn, W., Kalb, P. & Vortisch, W. 1992. Geologisch-petrographische Untersuchungen an Megalitgräbern Portugals. *Madrider Mitteilungen* 32, 1991, 1–28.

Jorge, J. O. & Jorge. V. O. 1997. The Neolithic/Chalcolithic transition in Portugal: the dynamics of change in the third millennium BC. In Díaz-Andreu, M. & Keay, S. (ed.), *The Archaeology of Iberia.* London.

Kalb, P. 1981. Zur relativen Chronologie portugiesischer Megalitgräber. *Madrider Mitteilungen* 22, 55–77.

— 1989. Überlegungen zu Neolithisierung und Megalithik in Westen der Iberischen Halbinsel. *Madrider Mitteilungen* 30, 31–54.

— 1996. Megalith-building, stone transport and territorial markers: evidence from Vale de Rodrigo, Èvora, south Portugal. *Antiquity* 70, No. 269, 683–685.

Kalb, P. & Höck, M. 1994. Vale de Rodrigo 3, Concelho Évora, Portugal. Vorbericht über die Ausgrabungen 1992. *Madrider Mitteilungen* 35, 69–77.

— 1995. Vale de Rodrigo. Projecto interdisciplinar para a investição do megalitismo numa região do sul de Portugal. *Actas dos Trabalhos de Antropologia e Etnologia* 35 (2), 195–210.

Larsson, L. 1995. Stenar som förenar, stenar som betvingar. Vale de Rodrigo—en megalitbygd i södra Portugal. *Vetenskapssocieteten i Lund Årsbok* 1993, 5–31.
— 1997. Die Untersuchung des Megalithgrabes Vale de Rodrigo 2, Concelho Évora, Portugal. Vorbericht über die Ausgrabungen 1991–1995 *Madrider Mitteilungen* 38, 36–48.
L'Helgouach, J. 1983. Les idoles qu'on abat... (ou les vissicitudes des grandes stèles de Locmariaquer). *Bulletine Société polymathique du Morbihan* 1983, 57–68
Leisner, G. 1944. O Dólmen de Falsa Cúpula de Vale-de-Rodrigo. *Biblos* XX.
Leisner, G. & Leisner, V. 1943. *Die Megalithgräber der Iberischen Halbinsel. Der Süden.* Römisch-germanische Forschungen, Band 17.
— 1951. *Antas do Concelho de Reguengos de Monsaraz.* Materias para o estudo da cultura megalitica em Portugal. Lisboa.
— 1956–1965. *Die Megalithgräber der Iberischen Halbinsel. Der Westen,* 1–3. Madrider Forschungen 1.
Lubell. D, Jackes, M. & Meiklejohn, C. 1989. Archaeology and human biology of the Mesolithic–Neolithic transition: a preliminary report. In Bonsall, C. (ed.), *The Mesolithic in Europe: Proceedings of the Third International Symposium, Edinburgh 1985.* Edinburgh, 632–640.
Magnusson Staaf, B. 1996. *An Essay on Copper Flat Axes.* Acta Archaeologica Lundensia 4:21.
Morais Arnaud, J. E. 1982. La neolithique ancient et le processus de neolithisation au Portugal. *Le Neolithique Ancien Mediterraneen. Actes du Colloque International de Prehistoire Montpellier 1981.* Montpellier, 29–48.
— 1990. Le substrat mesolithique et le processus de neolithisation dans le sud du Portugal. In Cahen, D. & Otte, M. (eds.), *Rubané et Cardial. Actes du Colloque de Liège, novembre 1988.* Liège, 437–446.
Regnell, M. 1994. Paleobotaniska, kemiska och fysikaliska analyser av en jordmånsprofil från Vale de Rodrigo, Portugal. Ett diagnosticerande arbete. *Lundqua Uppdrag* 15.
Ribé, G., Cruells, W. & Molist, M. 1997. The Neolithic of the Iberian Peninsula. In Díaz-Andreu, M. & Keay, S. (ed.), *The Archaeology of Iberia.* London.
Shanks, M. & Tilley, C. 1987. *Re-Constructing Archaeology. Theory and Practice.* Cambridge.
Sherratt, A. 1995. Instruments of conversion? The role of megaliths in the Mesolithic/Neolithic transition in north-west Europe. *Oxford Journal of Archaeology* 14, no. 3, 245–260.
Silva, A. C. & Parreira, R. 1992. *A guide to the megalithic monuments of the Èvora region.* Èvora.
Strauss, L. G. 1991. The `Mesolithic–Neolithic transition' in Portugal: a view from Vidigal. *Antiquity* 65, No. 249, 899–903.
Strömberg, M. 1968. *Der Dolmen Trollasten in St. Köpinge, Schonen.* Acta Archaeologica Lundensia 8:7. Lund.
— 1971. *Die Megalithgräber von Hagestad. Zur Problematik von Grabbauten und Grabriten.* Acta Archaeologica Lundensia 8:9.
Thomas, J. 1996. *Time, Culture & Identity. An interpretiv archaeology.* London.
Thomas, J. & Tilley, C. 1993. The Axe and the Torso: Symbolic Structures in the Neolithic of Brittany. In Tilley, C. (ed.), *Interpretative Archaeology.* Oxford, 225–324.
Tilley, C. 1994. *A Phenomenology of Landscape. Places, Paths and Monuments.* Oxford.
Wymer, J. 1982. *The Palaeolithic Age.* London.

Zilhão, J. 1990. Le processus de neolithisation dans le centre du Portugal. In Cahen, D. & Otte, M. (eds.), *Rubané et Cardial. Actes du Colloque de Liège, novembre 1988.* Liège, 447–459.
— 1992. *Gruta do Caldeirão O Neolitico Antigo.* Trabalhos de Arqueologia 6. Lisboa.
— 1993. The Spread of Agro-Pastoral Economies across Mediterranean Europe: A View from the Far West. *Journal of Mediterranean Archaeology* 6:1, 5–63.

The Basic Perception of the Religious Activities at Cult-Sites such as Springs, Lakes and Rivers

By Berta Stjernquist

Colin Renfrew discusses in his work Archaeology (Renfrew & Bahn 1991) how the world-view of man is formed by sense impressions including a recollection of the world in the past and forecasts of the world in the future. It is moulded by knowledge and experiences of different kinds, a rather complicated process. An important part is, however, the environment and the symbols which appear and are active in the environment. I will return later on to the problem concerning symbols.

The environment is a network of features and energy. The understanding of the relationship between man and his environment presupposes concreteness with comprehensible elements. The landscape is such an element with stored activities by man and nature which have changed this part of the environment (Ingold 1993). Limited knowledge of the function of the nature has given fear and uncertainty which have created two aspects: dependence on the surroundings and endeavour to derive avantage from their supernatural forces.

Nature can be described as four elements: earth, water, fire, air. All these, as well as light and darkness, have been observed and animated by prehistoric man. It is a sphere of excitement where man had to orientate. In this connection I have chosen to analyse and discuss the attitude to one of these elements, water.

The concept of water as an animated part of the world seems to be a fundamental element in the world-view of perhistoric man. It appears in many ways. The attitude to water will here be illustrated by cult activities at springs and other pools of water, wet bogs and rivers. My investigation of the Röekillorna spring in Löderup Parish, south-eastern Scania, is the starting point for the discussion. The spring takes its name from the red ferriferous water (Stjernquist 1987; 1997) (Fig. 1).

The Röekillorna Spring

The reason for the excavation of the offering find at Röekillorna was the discovery of bones and some artifacts when a well was sunk at the site in 1951. When the vegetation cover was cut through, the waters of the spring broke out with great force, and bones and artifacts were washed up from the depths.

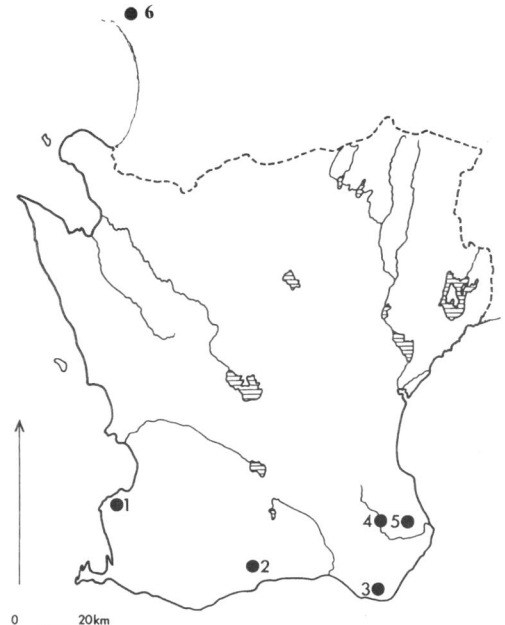

Fig. 1. Map of southern Sweden with the location of sites mentioned in the text.

1. Hinby; 2. Hassle Bösarp; 3. Röekillorna; 4. Gårdlösa; 5. Näbbe mosse; 6. Käringsjön.

Archaeological and geological investigation

Archaeological excavations were carried out between 1960 and 1962. A trial trench lm wide and in the shape of a cross, with the well as a centre-point, was laid out to establish the context of the finds and, mainly, their distribution (Fig. 2). In the following years the whole area around the spring was dug, a total of 500 m2. The spring, which had been levelled-out by layers of infill, emerged from an oval, well-marked, bowl-shaped hollow whose central part was bottomless (Fig. 3).

A pollen analytical investigation was carried out by Tage Nilsson to establish the appearance of the site in prehistoric times and to elucidate the datings of the different layers. The result of this investigation showed clearly that the now very slightly-marked depression around the spring was originally more obvious and that it began to grow over again in the Late Bronze Age at the earliest. The layers then accumulated in the Early Iron Age, and the depression was filled up before the Viking Age. The result is of very great importance for the interpretation of the archaeological evidence, suggesting that in the Neolithic period and part of the Bronze Age there was an open depression with a water-filled hole. The depression had probably been submerged at times by the water from the spring.

The basic perception of the religious activities at cult-sites 159

Fig. 2. Röekillorna. The well and the northern arm of the trial trench in the shape of a cross.

Before excavation the depression was filled up. Above the bottomless hole in the central part by the spring there were ca. 2m-thick layers of alternating turf and mud (Fig. 4). Away from the centre the layers thinned out, but a division into two layers could be discerned over virtually the whole area. The boundary between them was marked by a find-horizon. Finds also occurred in the bottom level, but were not defined to these levels as they had a consistent vertical distribution.

So the layers containing finds lay in and beside the spring and were also spread over a large area corresponding to the depression which, because of the flooding of the spring, must have been marshy (Fig. 5). Towards the south, in the direction of the flow, finds occurred in patches for about 40 m after which they become more sporadic.

Objects as a reflection of activities

The finds consited very largely of bones (about 6000 fragments). They have been identified by the late Ulrik Møhl of the Zoological Museum in Copenha-

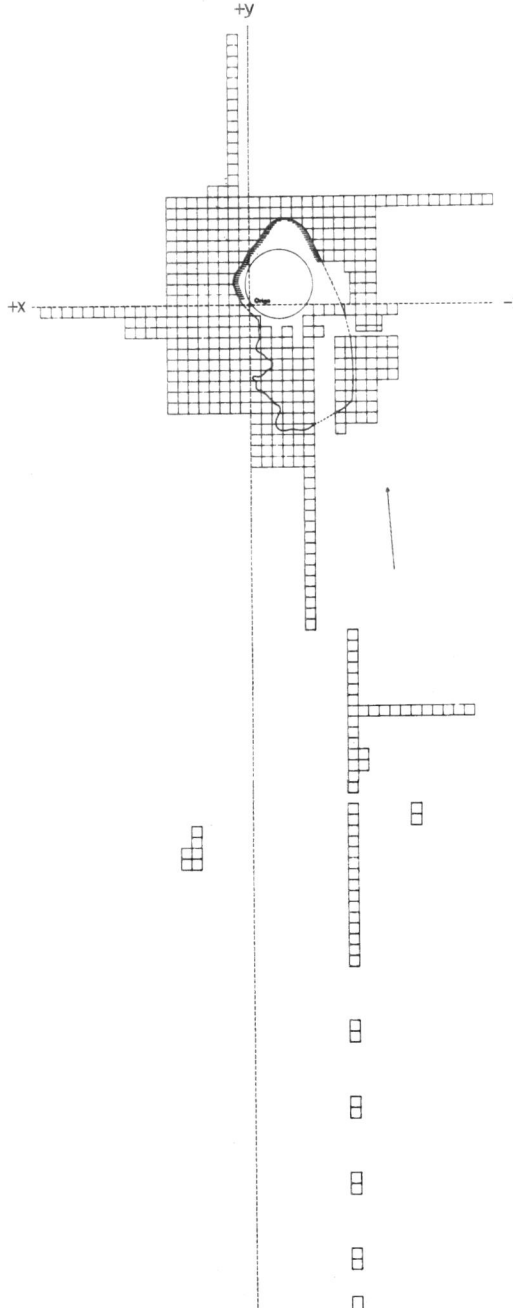

Fig. 3. Röekillorna. The excavated area with the spring at the centre.

Fig. 4. Röekillorna. The southern edge of the spring with deep layers above it.

gen. About 4000 of the fragments could be identified; they come from the common domesticated animals horse, dog, cattle, sheep/goat and pig—and there were also human bones (Fig. 6). Forty-four parts of human skeletons were discovered from at least three individuals: two adults and one child (Fig. 7).

Some of the animal bones were split, obviously to extract the marrow. They must be remains of meals. On the other hand, there were deposits of parts of all four legs of animals, a type of offering known from other finds. There is no evidence that the bones of dogs were dismembered.

The datable archaeological objects extend over a very long period of time from the early Neolithic to at least the Roman Iron Age (Fig. 8). Many axes were discovered: a thin-butted stone axe, round pecked stone axes, a thick-butted flint axe with hollow edge, two flint chisels, and some parts of flint daggers representing various phases of the Stone Age. There are no bronze objects, but there are some flints whose form dates them to the Bronze Age. Bone points, some with ring-and-dot decoration, are characteristic of the pre-Roman Iron Age. The iron objects include a fibula of pre-Roman type and some knives, to which should be added some whetstones. There is a whole sample-sheet of whetstones, crushing-stones and grinders. The pottery is badly

162 *Berta Stjernquist*

Fig. 5. Röekillorna. The bottom level with finds. A flint chisel visible to the right of the stone.

shattered and is present as large or small fragments. Parts of early Neolithic vessels were found in the spring itself. On their interior they have a dried-out layer of what appears to be a fatty substance. The same is true of sherds of later types. The innumerable very small fragments indicate that the vessels were continually trampled on. A mass of brittle-burnt stones and some carbonized fuel are of particular interest.

Worked poles. sticks and pieces of wood were found in the vicinity of the spring. There were also two wooden objects of special shape: a pole with a phallic-shaped stick (Fig. 9) and a piece with one side cut like a face, with eyes and between them a ridge as a nose (Fig. 10).

The finds may be seen to be remarkably varied. If one disregards the fibula (Fig. 11), which I believe to have been an appendage to the clothing of a human sacrifice, a large part of the tools was for cutting or for use during a meal. This fits in well with the frequency of bones split for marrow, which are clearly food remains.

The bones were spread over the whole area, but some concentrations were

The basic perception of the religious activities at cult-sites 163

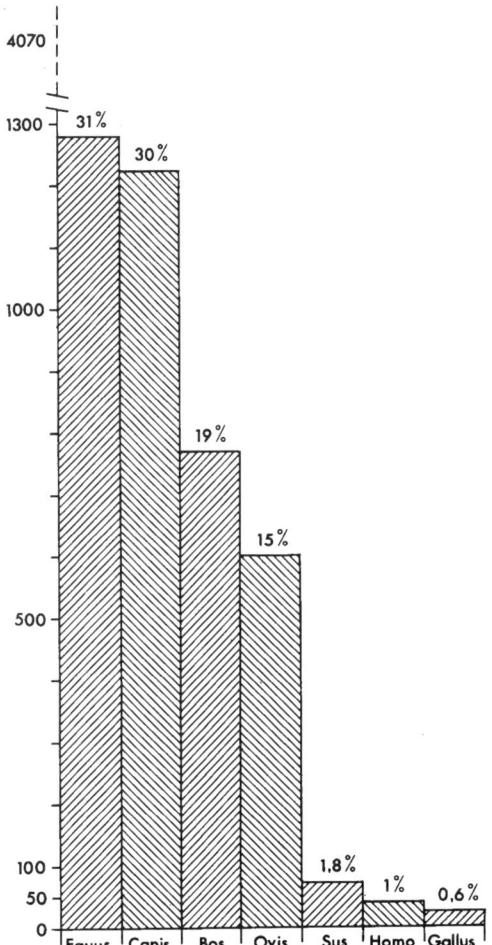

Fig. 6. Diagram showing the proportion of species of the bone fragments found during the excavation at Röekillorna.

noticeable. Some of the larger bones, particularly of horse, occurred plentifully in the spring itself and were usually not split for marrow. There were also many whole dog skeletons in immediate proximity to the spring. The bones split for their marrow occurred over the whole area. Both whole or parts of animals and the remains of meals had thus been deposited. The dogs, like the human beings, seem to have had a special position inasmuch as their bones were not split, so giving evidence that the individuals were not eaten.

The geological investigation showed that the depression had stood open for a long time. Some of the bones, heavily abraded and with toothmarks of animals, may be explained in that they had lain visible and accessible for a long time. The concentration of the finds within the bottom level where datable objects from various periods were discovered is understandable if one consid-

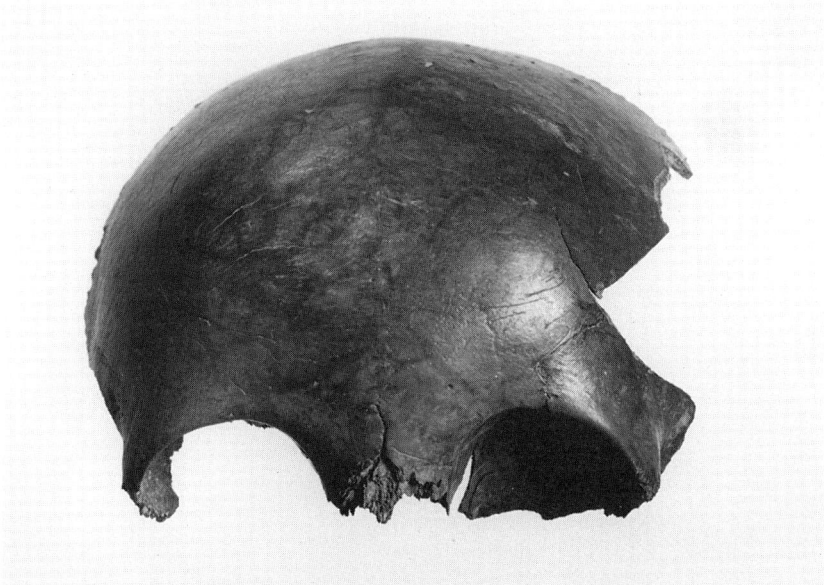

Fig. 7. A cranium of a child.

ers the character of the site in the prehistoric period. The lowest level cannot be chronologically homogeneous. Because the depression stood open, objects from different periods may be found in one and the same level. But some features, or assemblages of bone in association with tools, enable a chronological division of the lowest level to be made (Fig. 12).

Water-cult at the spring
The character and distribution of the material showed that the site had been a cult place with the spring as its centre; the water-filled holes and depressions had been the centres of activity, and fire had also played a part in the ceremonies.

Our central aim of the research has been to elucidate the functional aspects of the material. Röekillorna is a site where the role of the bones, and the tools in comparision to the bones, can be illustrated in a positive way. Organic material was central to the cult. Activity on the site can probably be associated with the everyday life of the people. The combination of the desire for assured fertility and the use of the products of the economy in the cult is therefore an essential prerequisite.

The lime-rich moraine soil in the area is some of the most easily-worked and fertile land for prehistoric cultivation. Situated in the centre of this rich prehistoric agricultural area, the cult site must be seen in connection with the simple

The basic perception of the religious activities at cult-sites 165

Fig. 8. Finds from the cult-site: an iron knife, a flint dagger, a strike-a-light, a bone point, a flint chisel, a stone axe, a grinder and a crushing-stone. Ca. 3:7.

agricultural economy of the population, with its economic aims and ambitions. The domestic animals, among which the dog had a special place, and the pottery vessels with their organic contents belong to this picture. There had been some human sacrifice. Briefly, one can outline the conditions by starting out from the actual material and the context of the finds.

The significance of this investigation lies in the fact that a long-lived cult tradition could be established and that, thanks to the well-preserved organic material, the forms of cult activity could be traced. Here there is evidence of a cult tradition which lasted from the time when agriculture was introduced in the early Neolithic period until the Roman Iron Age.

Comparative offering finds

There are in Sweden and in other parts of Scandinavia an abundance of cult sites in association with water pointing to religious activities in prehistoric times.

Fig. 9. A pole of Alnus with a phallic-shaped stick. Ca. 1:3.

Some cult places are local, like the Röekillorna spring, with cult activities in direct relationship with the social structure and economy of the agricultural population, a fertility cult. One site belonging to this category is Gårdlösa, also located in south-eastern Scania. The excavation of the Iron Age settlement revealed three hollows which were water-filled springs lying on the slope. Above the largest spring there was a construction made up of limestone slabs where fires had been repeatedly lit. The finds from the springs consisted mainly of potsherds and remains of animal bones: cattle, pig, sheep/goat, and horse. Both radio-carbon analyses and finds date the features from the period before the Birth of Christ to the Migration Period. The offering place is very interesting because of the combination with a well-investigated settlement (Stjernquist 1981b; 1993).

Another site belonging to this category was found some years ago at Hindby, Malmö. It is a bog find with much in common with the Röekillorna find with axes of stone and bronze and abundant material including human

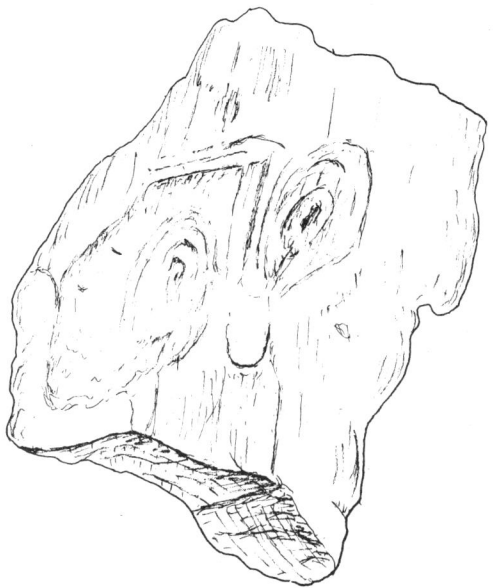

Fig. 10. A piece of wood (Ulmus) cut like a face. Drawing by the author. 1:2.

bones. It has been excavated, but not published yet (Svensson 1991; 1993) (Fig. 13).

Other cult places are the well-known Scandinavian bog-finds with votive deposits of weapons and jewellery, finds dating from the Roman Iron Age and the Migration Period. They are probably offerings after big battles. There are several large bog-finds of that category in Denmark and some in Sweden, such

Fig. 11. A fibula of iron. Ca. 1:1.

Fig. 12. A circular stone-setting with split animal bones of horse and pig, and a flint axe with hollow edge, dating from the Middle Neolithic Period.

as Hassle Bösarp in Scania—which I have excavated and published (Stjernquist 1973) (Fig. 14)—and Skedemosse on Öland, excavated and published by Ulf Erik Hagberg (Hagberg 1967). The Skedemosse find has a very rich material including 7 gold rings and a large bone material, and also human bones. Some of the bone material indicates meals and a horse cult.

There are also several smaller finds, some in wells or springs (Stjernquist 1970). Pottery vessels from bogs dating from all prehistoric periods form a large category (Becker 1970; Harck 1984; Andersen 1996). They could be offering finds, but may have had other functions as well. Becker has discussed the material and identified seven groups as offering deposits because of the circumstances. The Käringsjön lake in the south of Sweden is one of them. Many of the others are rather small. There are, however, some with an interesting combination of pottery vessels, bones and wooden objects. Forlev Nymølle, Illerup Aadal, Jutland, is one site of that kind. They have there found heaps of stones, sherds of vessels, flax, bones of horse, cattle, sheep, dog and

The basic perception of the religious activities at cult-sites 169

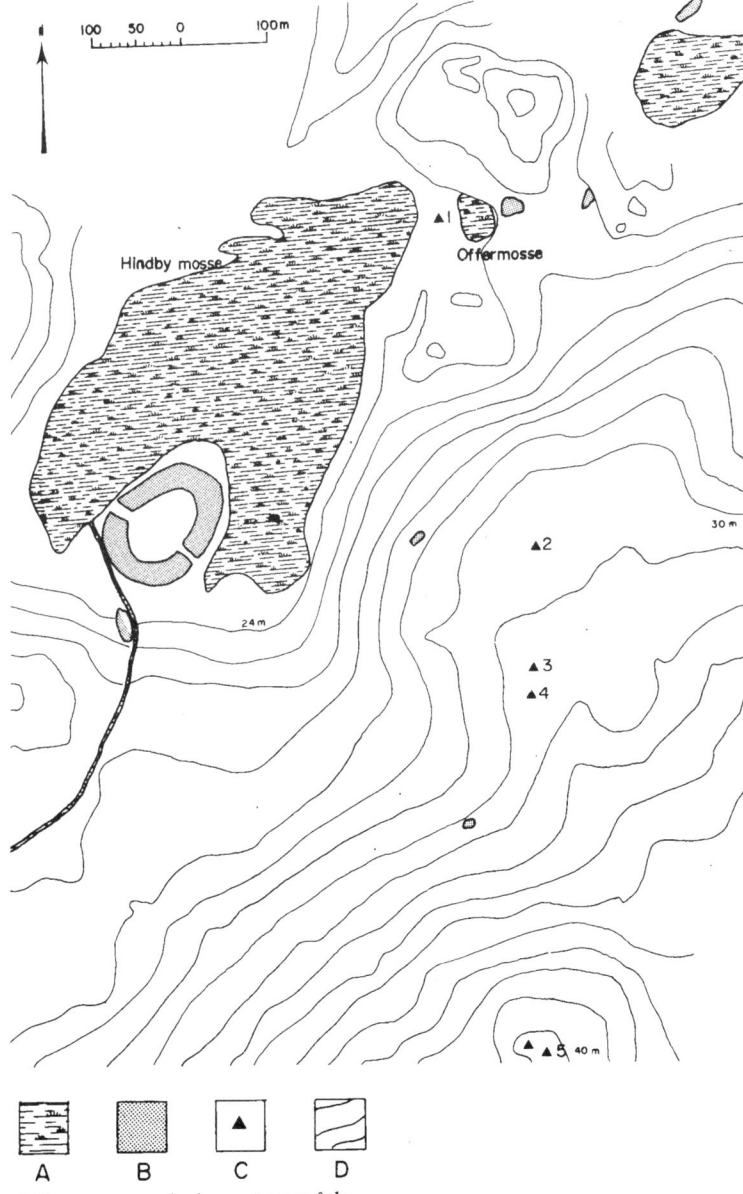

A   B   C   D

Offermossen och dess närområde.
A = Sjöar och kärr
B = Boplatser från trattbägarkulturen
C = Gravar. 1) Urnebrandgravar, 2) Stridsyxegrav, 3) Långdös, 4) Senneolitisk grav, 5) Bronsåldershögar
D = Höjdkurva

Fig. 13. The Hindby mosse bog. The small offering bog is seen at the north-eastern corner of the picture (after Svensson 1991).

Fig. 14. The Hassle Bösarp offering bog (Photo Bertil Centervall).

hare, and a wooden female figure. The ritual activities at some of these sites can be identified as a fertility cult with the water as an important element.

The Käringsjön lake, Övraby Parish, is a kettle with a diameter of about 90 x 120 m. It is a deep pool with waterflow like a spring (Fig. 15). The find material consists of pottery vessels and agricultural tools of wood. The wessels have contained food. No bones or iron objects were preserved because of the acid of the soil. The find can be dated to the Early Iron Age. This find is interesting for the interpretation of the Röekillorna cult site because of the character of the offering made by common people with agriculture as their gainful employment (Arbman 1945).

The Näbbe mosse bog, Östra Vemmerlöv Parish, is another interesting find place. Several finds dating from the Stone Age were collected during peat-cutting, such as a dug-out with swan's bones in and around it, axes (Fig. 16), bone points, a funnel beaker with a string of bast in one of the handles, and a female skeleton (Salomonsson 1958:64; Stjernquist 1981a). The bog is not excavated systematically but the items are interpreted as offering finds.

According to the identification the bones are wing portions of two mute swans and fragments of a duck. The idea behind the finds of swan's bones have been discussed. It is interesting that a swan's wing has been found below the baby in grave 8 at the Mesolithic cemetery at Vedbæk, Denmark, a double-

Fig. 15. The Käringsjön lake where offering deposits have been found (Photo ATA).

grave with skeletons of a woman and a new-born boy, who was prematurely born between the eighth and the ninth month. The grave contained red ochre. (Albrethsen & Brinch Petersen 1976). There is much evidence that swan's wings were symbols for a flight to another world. It will be noticed that the swans are associated with water.

An interesting ritual complex on the Continent is located by Lake Ried at Oberdorla in Thüringen, which is well known thanks to the excavation by Behm-Blancke (Behm-Blancke 1970). The cult site was used during the pre-Roman and Roman Iron Age by the population at a settlement in the vicinity. It is a bog with springs. There were several offering places with fences. The activities had moved between them during the time when the site was used. Several wooden idols were found (Capelle 1995). The objects were deposited at the bog, on the shore, in the lake or in the springs. The finds consisted of pottery vessels, with or without a content of organic material, and large quantities of animal bones. There were poles, possibly for hanging up hides of animals, and the extremity bones of horses. Split bones were remains of ritual meals. This was a cult site used by common people working with agriculture. There were bones of cattle, dogs, horse, pigs and sheep and some human bones (Teichert 1974).

A variant of the spring cult on the Continent is springs with offerings of jewellery or other metal items. St. Moritz in Switzerland, Pyrmont in Nieder-

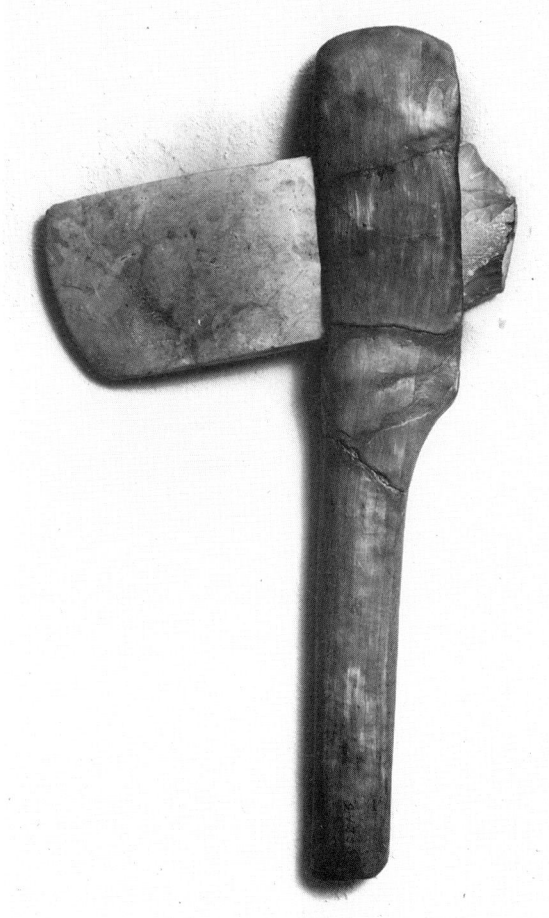

Fig. 16. The Näbbe mosse bog. A hafted thin-butted axe found in the bog. Length og the axe 19.6 cm. (Photo ATA).

sachsen and Dux (Duchcov) in Bohemia are well-known. The Budsene well in Denmark dating from the Bronze Age belongs to the same category (Stjernquist 1970). Smederup is a bog find in Denmark with lots of jewellery (rings) (Vebæk 1945; Randsborg 1995).

Aspects of the water-cult

All these categories have some kind of water-cult in common. Sometimes there are springs in the bog, and these are in some way linked to the animated springs with offerings.

The water-cult is combined not only with sacrifices but also with ritual meals. These are illustrated by remains of bone, to a great extent split for marrow, and by features with large stones and tools used in the cult to prepare the meals. Prehistoric man wanted to communicate with the divinities and tried to achieve that through the meals. The divinities got some part of the food, and the human beings had other parts. There may have been ceremonies as well, which are now difficult or impossible to trace. Widely distributed fire-cracked stones indicate some kind of ritual activities. The horse cult, with hanging up of the head, hide and feet, is another form of activity at the site probably made as a gift to the gods (Bloch 1977; Bradley 1991).

The offering of agricultural products such as animals, whole animals or meat of animals, deposited at the cult site, and corn or other kinds of food presented in pottery vessels, seems to be gifts to the divinities which demanded gifts in return. The materials at the Röekillorna cult site illustrate this basic perception of the human mind.

It is known that symbols play a great role in the thinking and doing of primitive people (Green 1986, 1989). It is said that water as a life-giving element had a symbolic value in the fertility cult. The red colour of the water may have had a special effect. Red water evokes the idea of life. It was life-giving, as can be seen from the custom of putting red ochre in the graves. The red colour was a symbol of life. Thus, the red water was an important element of the perception. The offered animals may have had a symbolic value as well. It is known that the horse was cult-animal of the Celtic deity Epona and the dog of Nehalennia. Horse, dog and bull played a role as ritual symbols over wide areas (Green 1986).

The idea in the human mind about the seat of the divinity was certainly fluid without firm boundaries. Water, and especially deep and moving and mysterious water like a spring or a stream, may have had a special place in the ritual imagination (Ninck 1921). There is abundant material at many areas which shows the veneration of water, and not only springs but also rivers and lakes. Deposits in rivers are a large category, which may have had a ritual function as offering items to the gods. The rivers and the divinities of the rivers were venerated. The deity of the river Rhein is an example (Zimmermann 1970; Torbrügge 1972; Maringer 1974; Wegner 1976; Schulze 1984; Bradley 1990; Slupecki 1994).

The source materials for our knowledge of water cults outside Scandinavia are inscriptions, place-names, reliefs, Gallic deities and Irish mythology (Alcock 1965). The water cult was especially significant in classical areas in Italy, Greece and parts of Asia (Nilsson 1967; Muthmann 1975), in Celtic areas on the Continent (Vaillat 1932; Blazquez 1957), and on British and Irish soil (Alcock 1965; Gribben 1992). This cult tradition seems to have a connection with the water cult in the Germanic areas, with the Röekillorna spring as an example.

Martin Nilsson's Geschichte der griechischen Religion gives a great deal of information about the classical cults, and note must also be taken of Muthmann's extensive synthesis of the spring-cult. Muthmann speaks about the serpent and dog as symbols of fertility. Water was also healing.

In the Celtic area the idea that water, springs as well as lakes, were populated with divinities was common. Celtic religion emphasizes man's connection to and dependence on the natural environment. Many divinities were associated with mountains, lakes and springs. There is lots of evidence of sacrifice in water or near water. Many of the divinities are known by name (Vaillat 1932; Alcock 1965; Green 1986, 1989; Brunaux 1988).

Alcock has classified the Celtic water deities in Roman Britain under three headings: deities known from inscriptions, unnamed deities of rivers and streams, and deities connected with lakes and bogs (Alcock 1965).

One of the deities known from inscription was the goddess Sulis. The shrine of Sulis Minerva beside a spring in Bath was excavated early, excavations which have been supplemented by those of Barry Cunliffe. Large quantities of finds, including about 12.000 coins, metal vessels and lead tablets, were discovered. The material came in part from the spring itself (Cunliffe 1983; Henig & King 1986). Another goddess known from inscriptions was Brigantia, who has given her name to rivers. There are also male divinities connected with water (Alcock 1965).

Unnamed deities connected with rivers are known in Roman Gaul and Britain through statues and from literary sources. Unnamed deities connected with lakes, wells and bogs are scarce in Britain, but can be evidenced through the votive deposits in lakes and other waters. They have a very long tradition going back to the Bronze and Iron Ages, which continued into the Roman period (Alcock 1965; Green 1986; Bradley 1990).

The healing cult of sacred springs was very significant in the Celtic area. A well-known example is Fontes Sequanae, the source of the Seine, where masses of wooden votives were found during the excavation of the Celtic-Roman structures which they may pre-date, partly. The pilgrims visited the healing spring and offered models of their diseases. There were two temples in the Roman period dedicated to the goddess Sequana. At Nimes and Glanum were other venerated healing springs (Green 1986).

The connection between the Celtic and the Roman traditions was very significant, for example at a site in Hochscheid near Trier, which was a shrine, where Apollo Grannus and Sirona were the principal gods. A large number of terracotta votive figurines had been placed beside the spring (Oldenstein 1984).

These examples of an abundance of ritual finds show that the Celtic and Roman traditions met, associated and changed according to environment and influences (Haffner 1995 with ref.). There is a difference between Bath and Hochscheid in the location of the deposits. At Bath deposits were put in the spring itself, which is not the case at Hochscheid, where the deposits were placed beside the spring. This deposition can also be noted at a spring at Calalzo near Cividale, northern Italy, where the votive deposits were placed in the shrine. Coins, votive statuettes and inscriptions were discovered. At many sites the offerings were, however, placed both in the spring and beside it, as at the Röekillorna spring.

There are many variations in the religious ritual. Roman offering was individual or collective, and we can assume that the Celtic offering had the same characteristic. Even the oriental Mithras-cult, which influenced the Celtic-Roman area, is found at springs.

The aim of the water-cult

This paper has called attention to fertility as an important aim of the religious activities at cult sites. There are many wooden figures which show clearly a fertility aspect (Capelle 1995). Amongst the find material from the Röekillorna spring there are the phallic-shaped wooden stick and also the face cut in wood which are mentioned above. The fertility cult was a component of the Celtic-Roman religion.

This may be a fertility for nourishment, but it also aims at an increase in human beings and animals and for the success of all kinds of industries (Slupecki 1994:163 ff.). It is known that there is a connection between the invocation of the life-giving forces and the daily effort of man. The fertility cult was practiced in the countryside, in the midst of the fields (Brunaux 1988). The cult site was seen as important for the living, and the social life of human beings. The water was central for fertility, and necessary for the crops. It played a role for life, but also for death.

The river was a boundary between the living beings and the deceased persons. The living beings had to pass this boundary. The idea that the transition from this life to another was a crossing of a river with Charon as a ferryman was widespread from the Greek and Roman world into the Germanic areas. The boat with swan's bones from the Näbbe mosse bog is another very interesting find. It is not an expression of travelling to the underworld but perhaps of a flight from the earth to another world, to heaven.

Another aim of the water cult was healing. The springs were seen as curative features. Hot springs, mineral springs and springs with red water were important for prehistoric man without knowlege of the cause and effects of illnesses. The illnesses may have been caused by bad forces. The life-giving spirits of the springs and other water-pools with moving and mysterious water could help. All the wooden votive items which have been found at spring sites such as Fontes Sequanae and Source des Roches de Chamalieres south of Clermont Ferrand speak about thanksgiving for healing. Many of the deities are known as healing divinities (Green 1986). We can also see the thanksgiving process also in modern time, for instance at Lourdes.

The aim of the water cult can be prosperity in general, which may be fertility as well as healing, but also other kinds of success and good fortune.

Conclusion

Aspects of the religious world-view are expressed in the material discussed. It is probable that prehistoric man had the idea that the water was animated. The springs had a special position because of the moving water with its mysterious depth. This water may have awoken ideas about the underworld with unknown divine forces. The idea of offering is related to the thinking behind the kind of votive deposits which are presented to the divine forces. The offering expresses the desire to get something in return.

It is possible to trace similar aims and actions of prehistoric man at different cult sites located in different countries and at cult sites venerated during different periods. The question arises whether the similarity of action means that man reacts in the same way and uses the same symbols when the conditions are the same. It has been discussed that there is a common basis for human beings' feeling, thinking and doing (Needham 1978). How far this universal applicability extends, is, however, a matter of dispute.

English revised by Roger Littleboy
ATA Antikvarisk-topografiska arkivet, Stockholm

References

Albrethsen, S. E. & Brinch Petersen, E. 1976. Excavation of a Mesolithic Cemetery at Vedbæk, Denmark. *Acta archaeologica* 47, 2–28.
Alcock, J. P. 1965. Celtic Water Cults in Roman Britain. *The Archaeological Journal* 122, 1–12.
Andersen, A.G. 1996. Frugtbarhedsofringer i Sydvestfyns ældre jernalder. *Kuml* 1993–94, 199–210.
Arbman, H. 1945. *Käringsjön. Studier i halländsk järnålder.* Kungl. Vitterhets Historie och Antikvitets Akademien. Handlingar 59:1. Stockholm.
Becker, C.J. 1970. Zur Frage der eisenzeitlichen Moorgefässe in Dänemark. In Jankuhn, H. (Hrsg.),*Vorgeschichtliche Heiligtümer und Opferplätze in Mittel- und Nordeuropa.* Bericht über ein Symposium in Reinhausen bei Göttingen vom 14. bis 16. Oktober 1968. Göttingen, 119–166.
Behm-Blancke, G. 1970. Neue Ausgrabungen germanischer Heiligtümer in Thüringen. In Filip, J. (Hrsg.), *Actes du VIIe Congrès International des Sciences Préhistoriques et Protohistoriques Prague 21–27 août 1966.* Prague, 945–949.
Blazquez, J.M. 1957. Le Culte des Eaux dans la Péninsule Ibérique. *Ogam* 9, 209–233.
Bloch, M. 1977. The past and the present in the present. *Man* 12. London, 278–292.
Bradley, R. 1990. *The passage of arms: an archaeological analysis of prehistoric hoards and votive deposits.* Cambridge.

The basic perception of the religious activities at cult-sites   177

— 1991. Ritual, time and history. *World archaeology* 23:2, 209–219.
Brunaux, J.L. 1988. *The Celtic Gauls: Gods, Rites and Sanctuaries.* London.
Capelle, T. 1995. *Anthropomorphe Holzidole in Mittel- und Nordeuropa.* Scripta Minora Regiae Societatis Humaniorum Litterarum Lundensis 1995–1996. Lund.
Cunliffe, B. 1983. The Temple of Sulis Minerva at Bath. *Archaeology* 36:6, 16–23.
Green, M. 1986. *The Gods of the Celts.* Gloucester.
— 1989. *Symbol and Image in Celtic Religious Art.* London.
Gribben, A. 1992. *Holy Wells and sacred water sources in Britain and Ireland.* New York.
Haffner, A. (Hrsg.) 1995. *Heiligtümer und Opferkulte der Kelten.* Archäologie in Deutschland. Sonderheft 1995. Stuttgart.
Hagberg, U.E. 1967. *The Archaeology of Skedemosse* I–II. Stockholm.
Harck, O. 1984. Gefässopfer der Eisenzeit im nördlichen Mitteleuropa. *Frühmittelalterliche Studien* 18, 102–121.
Henig, M. & King, A. (eds.) 1986. *Pagan Gods and Shrines of the Roman Empire.* Oxford.
Ingold, T. 1993. The temporality of the landscape. *World archaeology* 25:2, 152–174.
Maringer, J. 1974. Flussopfer und Flussverehrung in vorgeschichtlicher Zeit. *Germania* 52, 302–318.
Muthmann, F. 1975. *Mutter und Quelle. Studien zur Quellenverehrung im Altertum und im Mittelalter.* Basel.
Needham, R. 1978. *Essential Perplexities.* An Inaugural Lecture delivered before the University of Oxford on 12 May 1977. Oxford.
Nilsson, M.P. 1967. *Geschichte der griechischen Religion.* Dritte erg. Aufl. München.
Ninck, M. 1921. *Die Bedeutung des Wassers im Kult und Leben der Alten.* Leipzig.
Oldenstein, J. 1984. Opferplätze auf provinzialrömischem Gebiet. *Frühmittelalterliche Studien* 18, 173–186.
Randsborg, K. 1995. *Hjortspring: Warfare and Sacrifice in Early Europe.* Aarhus.
Renfrew, C. & Bahn, P. 1991. *Archaeology. Theories, Methods, and Practice.* London.
Salomonsson, B. 1958. Om stockbåtar. *Skånes hembygdsförbunds årsbok* 1958, 56–71.
Schulze, M. 1984. Diskussionsbeitrag zur Interpretation früh- und hochmittelalterlicher Flussfunde. *Frühmittelalterliche Studien* 18, 222–248.
Slupecki, L.P. 1994. *Slavonic Pagan Sanctuaries.* Institute of Archaeology and Ethnology. Polish Academy of Sciences. Warsaw.
Stjernquist, B. 1970. Germanische Quellenopfer. In Jankuhn, H. (Hrsg.),*Vorgeschichtliche Heiligtümer und Opferplätze in Mittel- und Nordeuropa.* Bericht über ein Symposium in Reinhausen bei Göttingen vom 14. bis 16 Oktober 1968. Göttingen, 78–99.
— 1973. Das Opfermoor in Hassle Bösarp, Schweden. *Acta archaeologica* 44, 19–62.
— 1981a. Näbbe mosse. A Mysterious Stone Age Lake. In Königsson, L.-K. & Paabo, K. (eds.), *Florilegium Florinis Dedicatum* . Striae Vol 14. Uppsala, 35–40.
— 1981b. *Gårdlösa. An Iron Age Community in its Natural and Social Setting. I. Interdisciplinary Studies.* Acta Regiae Societatis Humaniorum Litterarum Lundensis LXXV. Lund.
— 1987. Spring-cults in Scandinavian Prehistory. In Linders. T. & Nordquist, G. (eds.), *Gifts to the Gods. Proceedings of the Uppsala Symposium 1985* . Boreas 15. Uppsala, 149–157.
— 1993. *Gårdlösa. An Iron Age Community in its Natural and Social Setting. II. The Archaeological Fieldwork, the Features, and the Finds. III. Chronological, Economic, and Social Analyses.* Acta Regiae Societatis Humaniorum Litterarum Lundensis LXXX–LXXXI.Lund.

— 1997. *The Röekillorna Spring. Spring-cults in Scandinavian Prehistory.* Acta Regiae Societatis Humaniorum Litterarum Lundensis LXXXII. Lund.
Svensson, M. 1991. Hindby offermosse—en senneolitisk kultplats. *Kulturmiljövård* 1991:5–6, 32–34.
— 1993. Hindby offerkärr—en ovanlig och komplicerad fyndplats. *Fynd* 1993/2, 5–11.
Teichert, M. 1974. *Tierreste aus dem germanischen Opfermoor bei Oberdorla.* Weimar.
Torbrügge, W. 1972. *Vor- und frühgeschichtliche Flussfunde.* Römisch-Germanische Kommission Bericht 51–52, 1970–71. Berlin.
Vaillat, C. 1932. *Le culte des sources dans la Gaule antique.* Paris.
Vebæk. C.L. 1945. Smederup. An Early Iron Age Sacrificial Bog in East Jutland. *Acta archaeologica* 16, 195–211.
Wegner, G. 1976. *Die vorgeschichtlichen Flussfunde aus dem Main und aus dem Rhein bei Mainz.* Materialhefte zur bayerischen Vorgeschichte 30. Kallmünz.
Zimmermann, H. 1970. Urgeschichtliche Opferfunde aus Flüssen, Mooren, Quellen und Brunnen Südwestdeutschlands. *Neue Ausgrabungen und Forschungen in Niedersachsen* 6, 53–92.

The Cross as a Symbol of Personal Christian Belief in a Changing Religious World

Examples from Selected Areas in Merovingian and Carolingian Europe

By Michael Müller-Wille

Speaking as an archaeologist about crosses of different shape and function, mostly found in early medieval graves of Central Europe, I would like to start with the finds of Grave 23 in the cathedral of Saint-Denis near Paris, which belongs to a group of richly furnished graves of the sixth century; I remind you of the well-known Grave 49, which has been interpreted as the inhumation of Queen Aregonde (Böhme 1993:404, fig. 1).

One of the earliest inhumations with grave goods is Grave 23 of a young lady bearing two iron brooches with gold and silver inlay and cloisonné ornament and a golden cross-shaped pendant with a central garnet (Catalogue Mannheim 1996, 1:430, fig. 337; Catalogue Paris 1997: fig. on p. 89). The grave can be dated to about AD 500 and gives evidence of a Christian person of the Early Merovingian nobility at the time of the conversion of King Clovis to Roman Catholicism, in AD 496 or later.

Romania

Similar crosses of the Latin type have been found in sixth-century graves of Western Bosnia (Korita near Duvno); they were used as brooches attached to female dress (Bierbrauer 1992:7, fig. 5:1–3). Cross-shaped brooches and pendants are generally known from sixth-and seventh-century Mediterranean contexts. The earliest graves with cross-shaped brooches can be dated to about AD 400: a female inhumation, found in Onore, near Bergamo, north-east of Milan, with pairs of bracelets, earrings and finger rings and a brooch in the shape of a Greek cross (with equal arms)—a female outfit typical of the Romanic population (Bierbrauer 1992:6, fig. 4).

No grave with a cross is known from the Roman Iron Age—the first to fourth century AD—in the Mediterranean.

The custom of wearing cross-shaped brooches and of burying them with the dead is known of the periphery of the Roman world, *Romania*, as in the Adriatic coastal zone of the former Yugoslavia and in parts of the Alpine region.

Graves with cross-shaped brooches give evidence of the typical Romanic furnishings (burial custom of reduced grave goods, in German *reduzierte Beigabensitte*), with bracelets, earrings and finger rings, chains of beads; no more. As regards chronology, most of them are of sixth/seventh-century date.

A main distribution area of cross-shaped brooches is the Trentino in the central Alpine region. There are four variants of Greek crosses (Fig. 1:1–4): variant 1, simple; variant 2, with widening arms; variant 3, the same, with birds on the top; variant 4, as variant one, but with knobbed arms. The decoration mostly consists of ring-and-dot punch marks (Fig. 1).

The map shows the location of sixteen sites in Trentino (Fig. 2), the upper valley of Adige and its surroundings, after a compilation by Volker Bierbrauer (1992:21 ff.). Ten of 21 cross-shaped brooches have been found on eight sites, but no detailed records survive. There are six cross-shaped brooches from three settlement sites and five from graves or cemeteries (only one found in a female grave). The state of research is rather unsatisfactory. Some other finds of cross-shaped brooches were observed in Friuli and Veneto to the east, and Liguria to the west, further in Central Italy, but none in Southern Italy, Sardinia and Sicily.

The concentration of sites with cross-shaped brooches on the northern periphery of *Romania* means that we are dealing with a regional custom of the Romanic population. The analysed area (Fig. 3, area A) has been part of the Roman Catholic World since Roman times; the Christian "borderline" up to about AD 500 is identical with the Roman *Limes* along the Rhine and Danube in the second part of the third and the fourth century (Martin 1987:map 8; Dassmann 1993). In the second part of the sixth century Northern and Central Italy was occupied by Lombards, at first adhering to Arianism, later—at the beginning of the seventh century—converting to Catholicism. The cross, worn as a brooch or pendant, was the *signum* of the Mediterranean Romanic population from the fifth century onwards.

Alamannia and Baiuvaria

North of the Alps the situation is quite different (Fig. 3, area B). The Alamannic and Baiuvarian domains north and east of the former border (*limes*) were Christianized in later times: at the end of the sixth and during the seventh century; this is also true of the Frankish areas east of the Rhine (Main area, Mainfranken).

On a political level, all these areas were incorporated into the expanding Frankish *regnum* from the early sixth century onwards: *Alamannia, Baiora/ Baiuvaria* and the eastern parts of *Austrasia* (Dannheimer & Dopsch 1988:133, fig. 87).

In the region between the upper Rhine, upper Danube and Main nearly

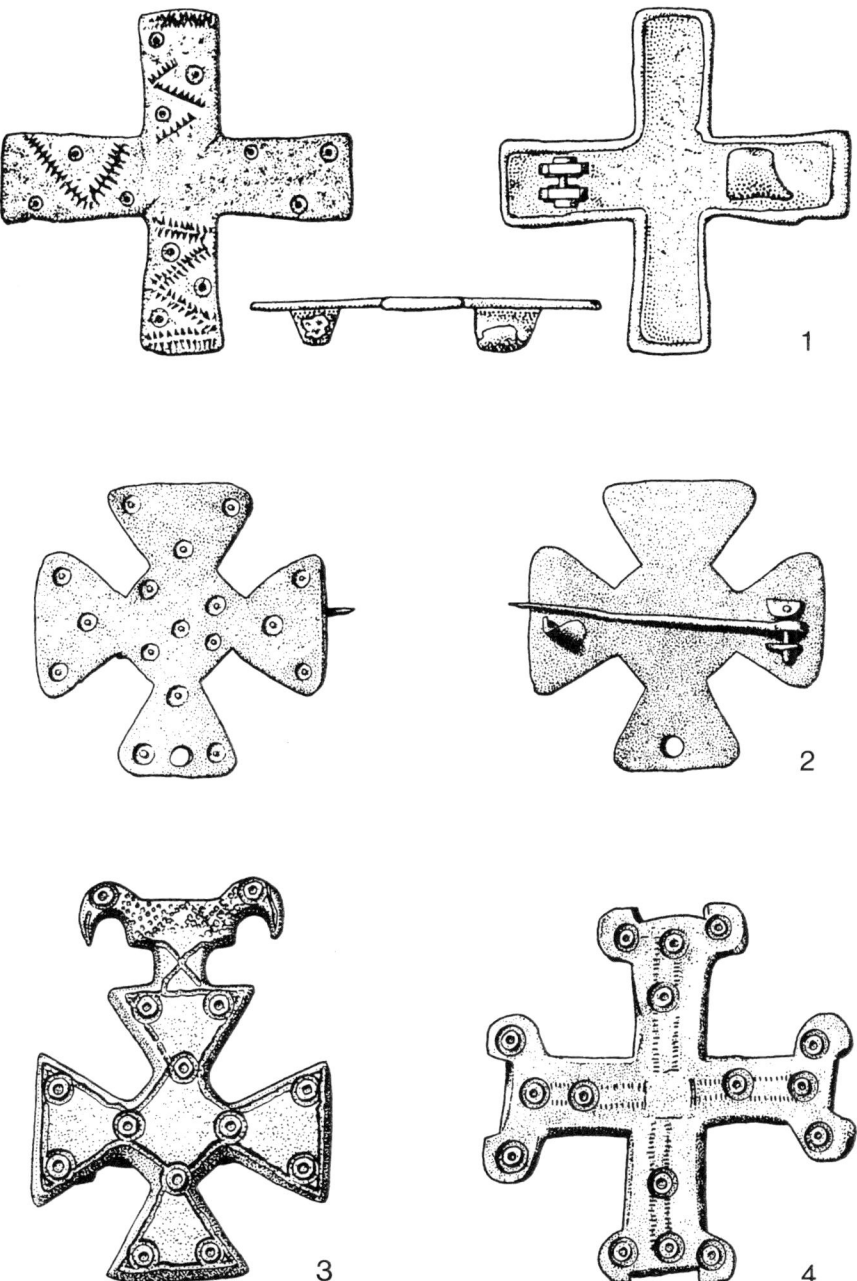

Fig. 1. Post-Roman cross-shaped brooches from Trentino. 1 Imer-Primiero (variant 1), 2 Volano (variant 2), 3 Mattarello (variant 3), 4 San Martino di Sonvico (variant 4). Bronze. Scale 1:1. After Bierbrauer 1992:3 fig. 1:1.3–4; table 1:2. (This and all the other figures are by Wolfgang Lieske, Kiel.)<

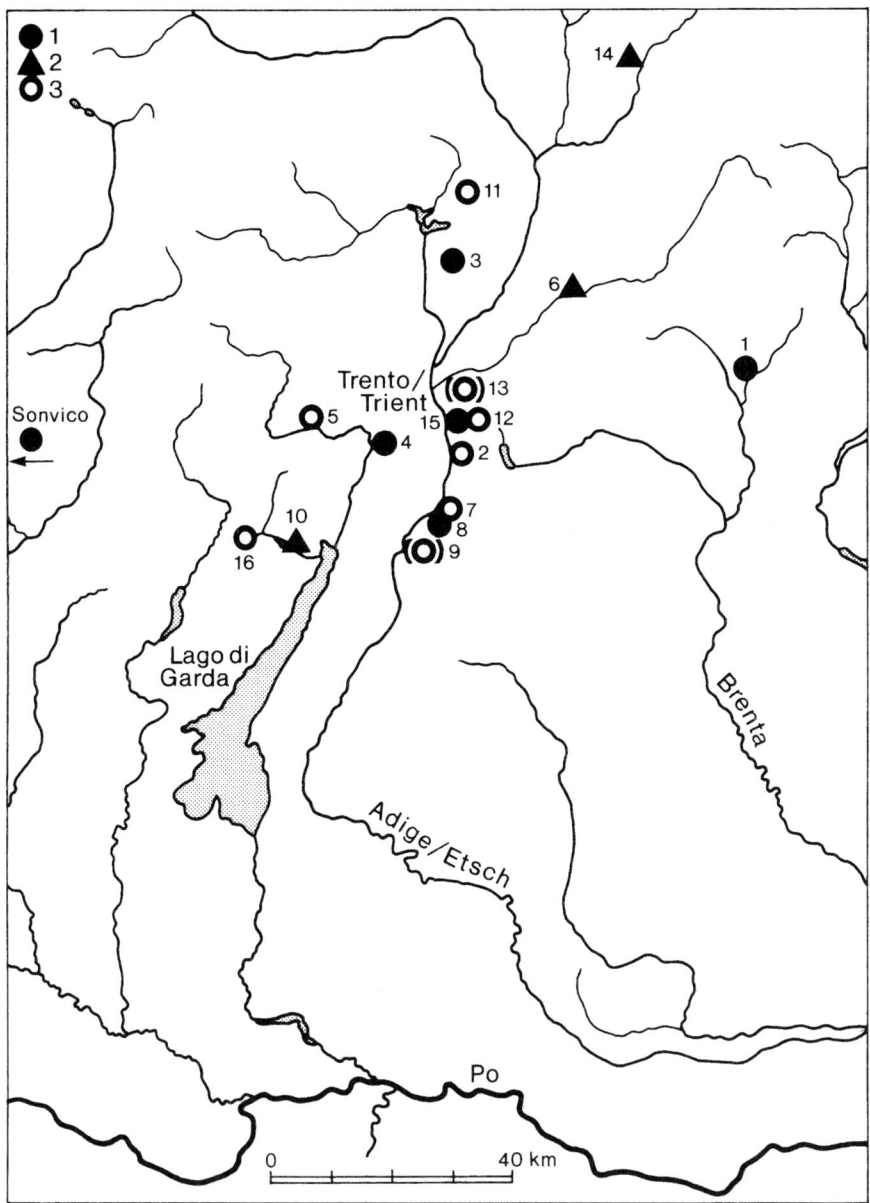

Fig. 2. Distribution of post-Roman cross-shaped brooches in Trentino. 1 grave/cemetery, 2 settlement site, 3 no excavation records. () Exact location unknown. For numbers see list 1. After Bierbrauer 1992: 8, fig. 6.

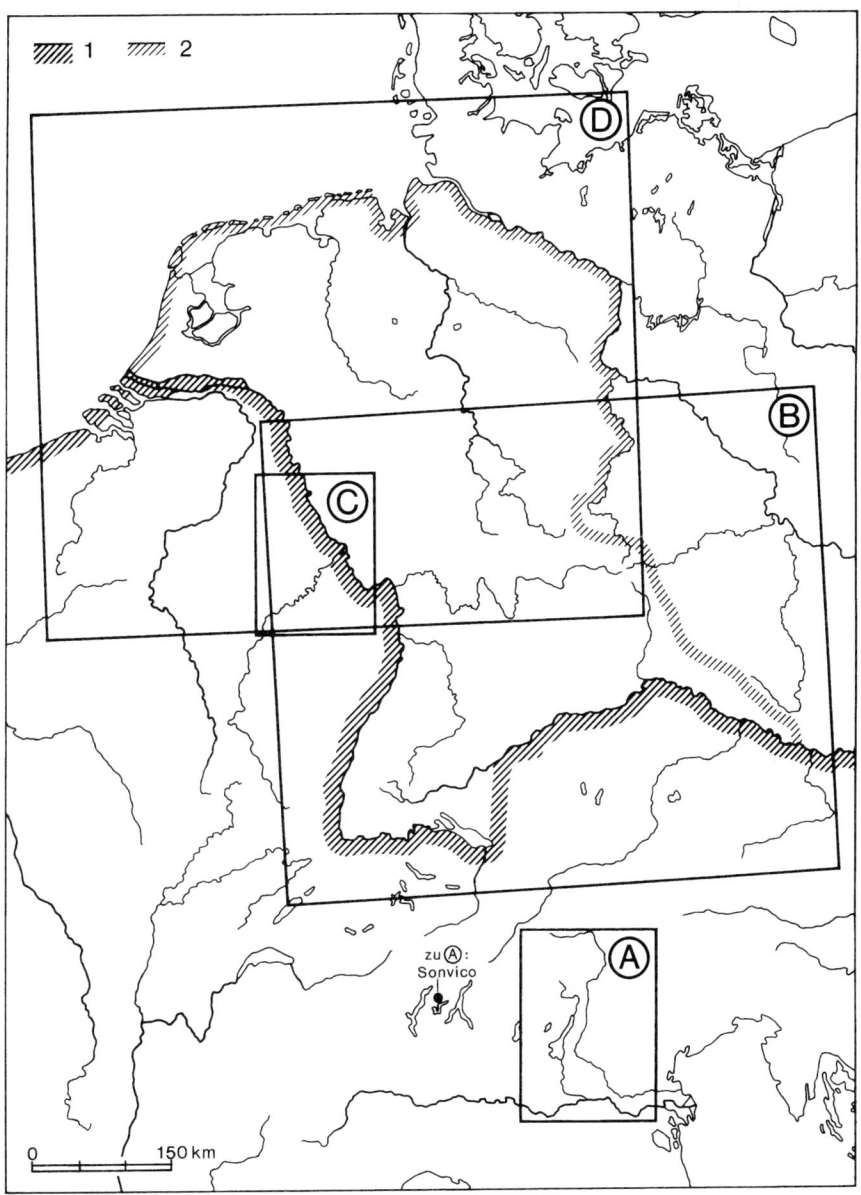

Fig. 3. Distribution of cross-shaped brooches in Merovingian and Carolingian Europe, selected areas: A Trentino (see Fig. 2). – B Southern Germany and neighbouring areas (see Figs. 5–8). – C Central Rhine and Mosel area (see Fig. 11). – D Netherlands, north-western Germany and neighbouring areas (see Figs. 13–14). "Borderline" of Christianity: 1 about AD 500, 2 about AD 800. After Martin 1987:map 2 & 25 C-D.

twenty sites with cross-shaped pendants (*Pektoralkreuze, Kreuzanhänger*) were registered by Rainer Christlein (1975) and by Mathias Knaut (1994). There are some Mediterranean examples, such as the Byzantine cross found in Friedberg near Augsburg (Fig. 4:1), but most of the crosses probably are local products and imitations of Mediterranean prototypes (Fig. 4:2–5).

Some of these crosses (eight or more) were found in graves of the late sixth and seventh centuries, as part of the female dress. Decorated examples, such as those from Wittlingen and Gammertingen (Fig. 4:3–5), can be dated to the seventh century. As shown by the distribution map, the crosses were recorded in the Alamannic and—east of the River Lech—in the Baiuvarian region, as well as in the Frankish region east of the Middle Rhine (Fig. 5).

Christlein (1975a:82) thought that the distribution of cross-shaped pendants—he numbered ten sites—is different from that of gold-foil crosses (see below). He believed that "diese Art, sein Glaubensbekenntnis offen zur Schau zu tragen, eine romanische Angelegenheit [war]" (Christlein 1978:120). Knaut (1994:328 ff., fig. 6, 1996:305, fig. 244; cf. Böhme 1996:495, fig. 5) however—referring to about twenty sites—was able to demonstrate a comparable distribution of cross-shaped pendants and gold-foil crosses.

Much more impressive—also with respect to the quality and decoration of the objects—is the distribution of so-called gold-foil crosses (*Goldblattkreuze*) between the upper and central Rhine valley and the River Lech, which mirrors the location of seventh-century Christian Alamannia; some examples are known also from the Frankish Rhineland and—in a greater number—from Baiuvaria (Fig. 3, area B). Nearly sixty sites with gold-foil crosses are presently known from Southern Germany and neighbouring areas (Fig. 6).

The crosses were usually made of thin gold sheets, which were sewn on very fine cloth and placed on the face of the dead; a very few are made of silver.

More than 260 gold-foil crosses are known from Italy, where they are mostly found in Lombard graves of the seventh century (Menghin 1985:174 ff.; Knaut 1994:317; Riemer 1997); the earliest date to about AD 600. They are cut as Greek crosses with perforations in the points or ends of their arms. Crosses from Milan, Cividale and Benevent may be shown as examples with repoussé decoration (human and animal figures, cross-hatching, impression of a coin) (Menghin 1985:table 40).

Those crosses have been found in often well and richly furnished Lombard female and male inhumations, some of them children's graves. The latest date is the first half of the eighth century (Menghin 1985:tables 36–39). The custom is supposedly connected with the deposition of votive crosses in church treasures, as was the practice of the Romanized population.

The same date can be shown to apply to Alamannia: the earliest examples are from graves of the end of the sixth century and about AD 600, most of them from the seventh century and a few from the beginning of the eighth century

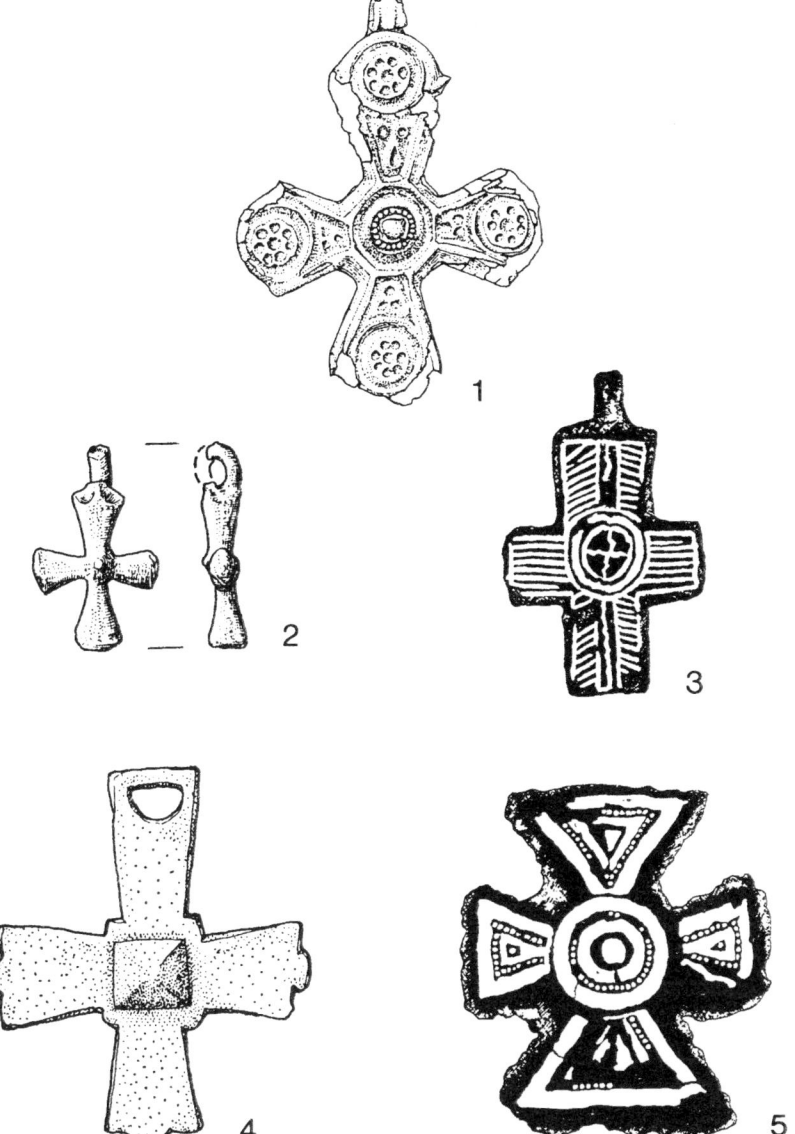

Fig. 4. Merovingian cross-shaped pendants from Southern Germany. 1 Friedberg, 2 Oberstotzingen, 3 Wittlingen, 4 Dittigheim, 5 Gammertingen. Silversheet (1), bronze (2, 4), iron with silver inlay (3, 5). Scale 1:1. After Christlein 1975a:82 fig. 9,1–2; 1978:120 fig. 97,1–3.

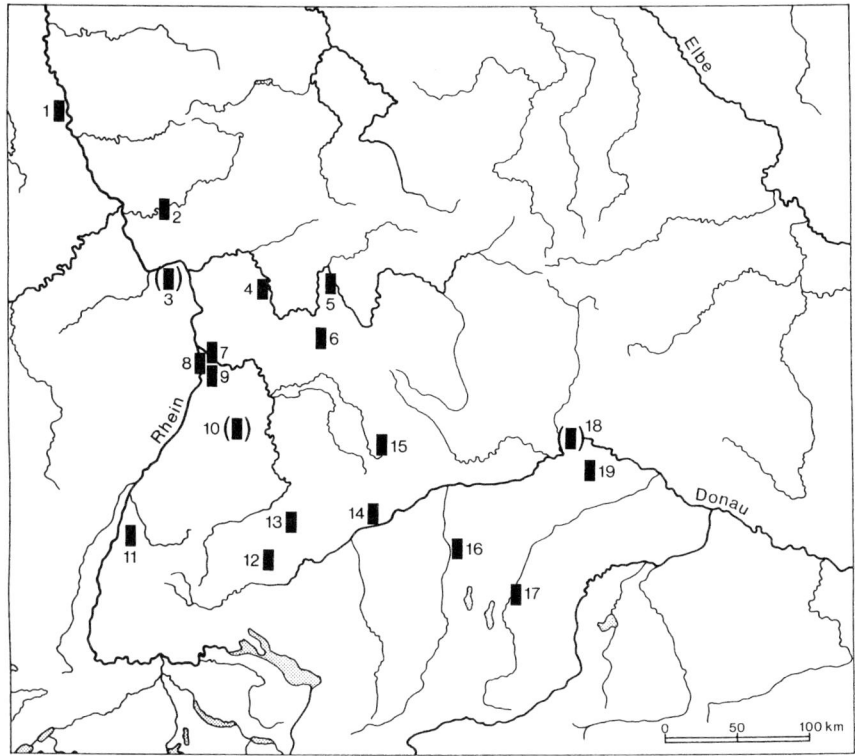

Fig. 5. Distribution of Merovingian cross-shaped pendants in Southern Germany. () Exact location unknown. For numbers see list 2. After Christlein 1975a:83, fig. 8; Knaut 1994:329, fig. 6.

(Fig. 7). Most of the early finds are from the inner part of Alamannia (see list 3, Nos. 3, 4, 6, 8, 12, 13, 17, 19, 20, 24, 27, 29, 36). A collection of Alamannic gold-foil crosses of different sizes and with varying ornamentation demonstrates the great variety of the material (Christlein 1978:table 87). Three crosses may serve as examples of different dates: Ebingen-Lautlingen, Grave 1/1910 from the late sixth century (Müller & Knaut 1987:37, fig. 7), Hintschingen, a grave from the middle of the seventh century (ibid. fig. on p. 25) and Walda, a grave from the late seventh century (Dannheimer & Dopsch 1988:277, fig. 186).

The great variation of the gold-foil crosses can also be demonstrated by those pieces which Knaut published quite recently as newly discovered and rediscovered finds (Knaut 1994:319 ff., figs. 1–3).

As in Lombard Italy, the gold-foil crosses from Southern Germany, mainly Alamannia, have been found in graves of male and—in a smaller number—of female adults and also of male children. Apparently they are restricted to well

The cross as a symbol of personal Christian belief 187

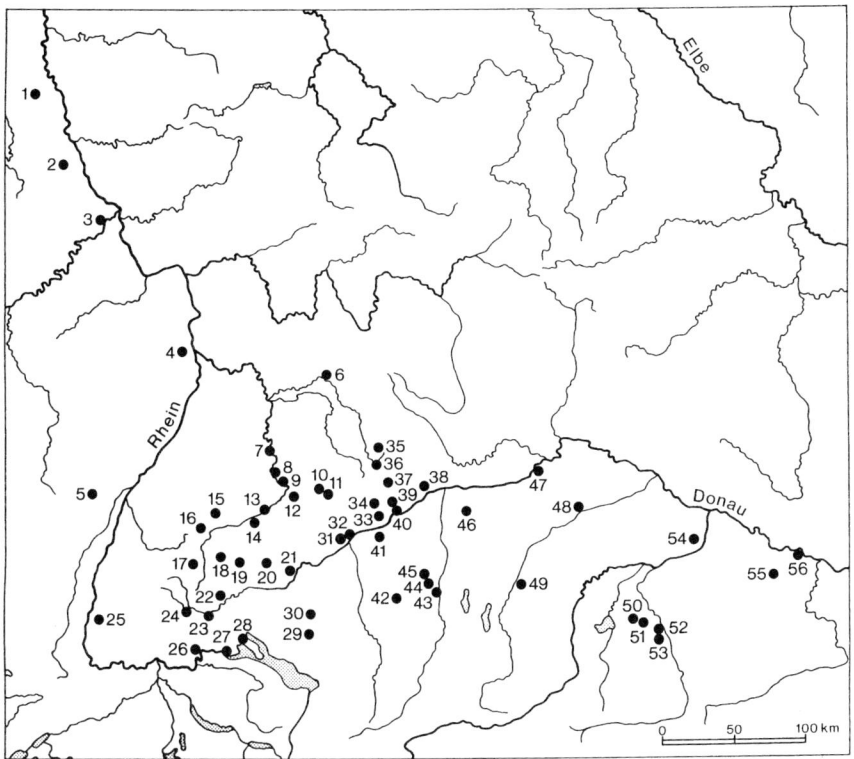

Fig. 6. Distribution of Merovingian gold-foil (and silver-foil) crosses in Southern Germany and neighbouring areas (France, Switzerland, Austria). For numbers see list 3. After Christlein 1975b; Müller & Knaut 1987; Knaut 1994.

and richly furnished graves, as Rainer Christlein has shown by including them in his quality groups B and C (Christlein 1975a:78 fig. 5).

Nearly all finds of gold-foil crosses come from graves or cemeteries, mostly—as I said—associated with males (Fig. 8). On some cemeteries up to four or six graves with gold-foil crosses have been found, demonstrating a long-lasting custom from about AD 600 to the early eighth century, as in Gammertingen and in Lauchheim (see list 3, Nos. 20 & 36). In Gammertingen two female inhumations from the seventh and early eighth century were found (Grave 6, 1903, and 57 A, 1904), one male inhumation from about AD 600 (Grave 21, 1904) and an inhumation of unknown sex from the seventh century (Grave 9, 1904). In the large row cemetery and the separate burial group of a mansion (*Hofgrablege*) at Lauchheim, six graves with gold-foil crosses were discovered, four of them by recent excavation: all are male inhumations of the early seventh to the early eighth century (Graves "O"/1986, 38, 450, 458,

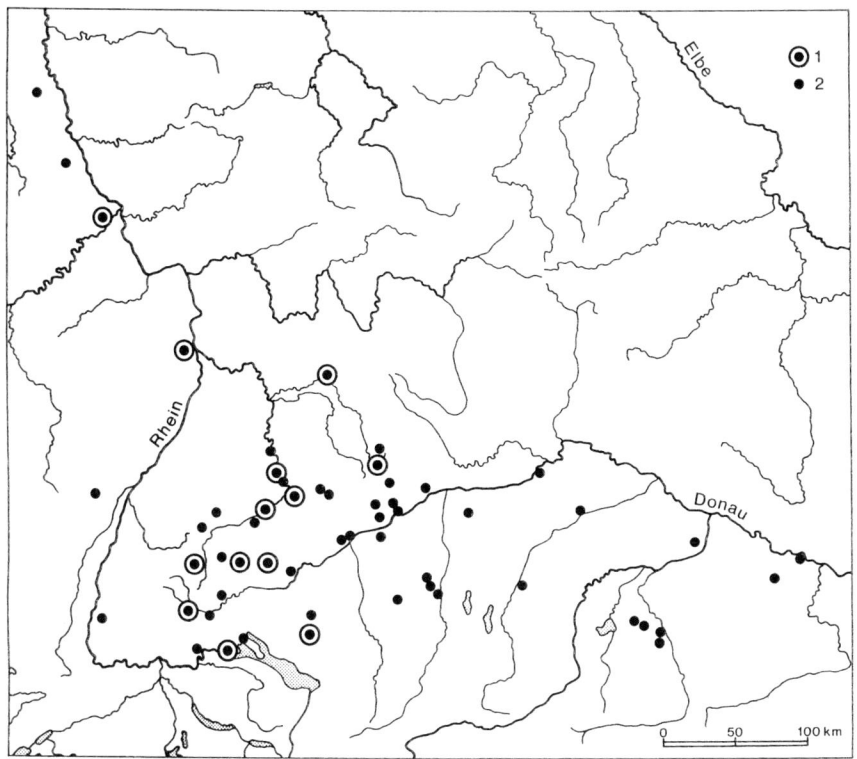

Fig. 7. Chronology of graves with gold-foil (and silver-foil) crosses in Southern Germany and neighbouring areas. 1 late sixth century/about 600, 2 seventh and early eighth century. After Böhme 1996:495, fig. 5.

burial group Graves 25 & 27), two of them with five crosses each (burial group Graves 25 & 27) (Stork 1997:301, 306 ff.).

It is generally believed that the leading families (*nobilitas*) in the Alamannic region took over the custom of gold-foil crosses from Lombard Italy. As Horst Wolfgang Böhme (1996) suggested in a recent article, there may have been a Mediterranean mission, perhaps from Milan and Aquileia, in Alamannia which unfortunately is not known from historical sources. Maybe the bishoprics of Constance and Augsburg were involved.

Interestingly, in Alamannia none of the gold-foil crosses were found in connection with the earliest churches, which often bear the names of the Frankish patrons Martin and Remigius (Müller & Knaut 1987:fig. on p. 6). Therefore, the archaeological source material possibly indicates two missions, a Mediterranean and a Frankish one.

But the subject is more complicated than that. Grave 13, a boy's grave, in the newly discovered row cemetery at Klepsau, Baden-Württemberg, with a

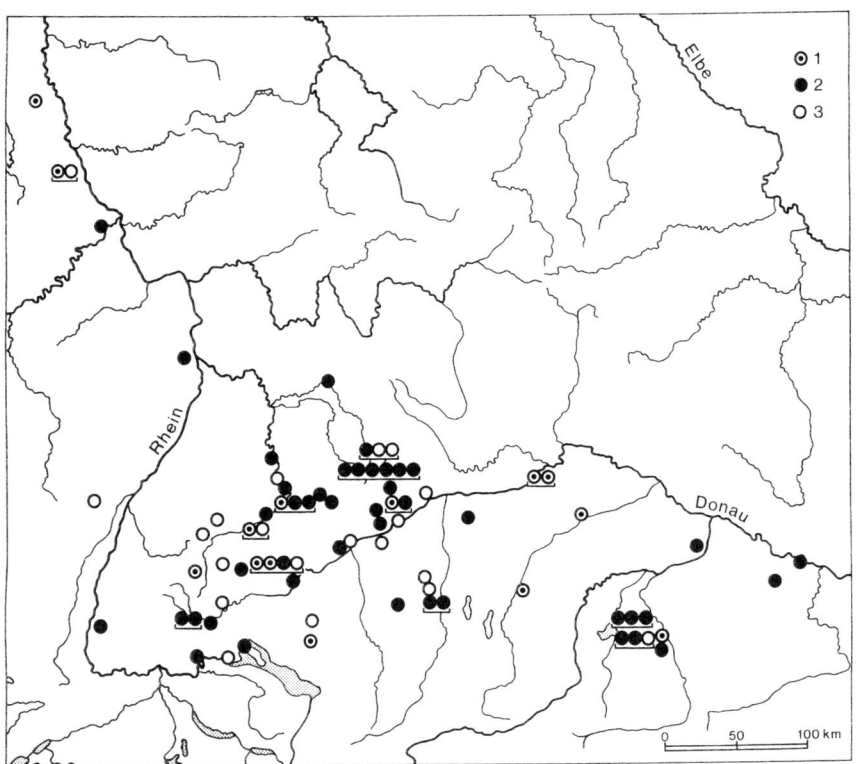

Fig. 8. Graves with Merovingian gold (and silver) foil crosses in Southern Germany and neighbouring areas. 1 Female inhumation, 2 Male inhumation, 3 Inhumation/ probable inhumation. After Christlein 1975b; Müller & Knaut 1987; Knaut 1994.

silver-foil cross (without perforations), dates to the middle of the sixth century—before strong Lombard influence can be discerned in Alamannia. According to Ursula Koch (1990:249): "Diesen Brauch hatte ein Familienangehöriger im Mittelmeerraum, vermutlich in Italien kennengelernt, lange bevor ihn die Langobarden übernahmen" (cross: Koch 1990:table 16, 10; Catalogue Mannheim 1996:1, 321, fig. 261; see below list 3, No. 6).

Francia

In the Frankish area gold-foil crosses never became part of the burial custom, as we have seen. There are few exceptions, as two richly furnished grave finds from the end of the seventh century prove: Rommerskirchen near Cologne with several pieces of jewellery, gold and silver (Catalogue Mannheim 1996:2, 743, fig. 612; see below list 3, No. 1) and the grave of a young girl in a chamber grave under Frankfurt Cathedral, probably inside a seventh-century

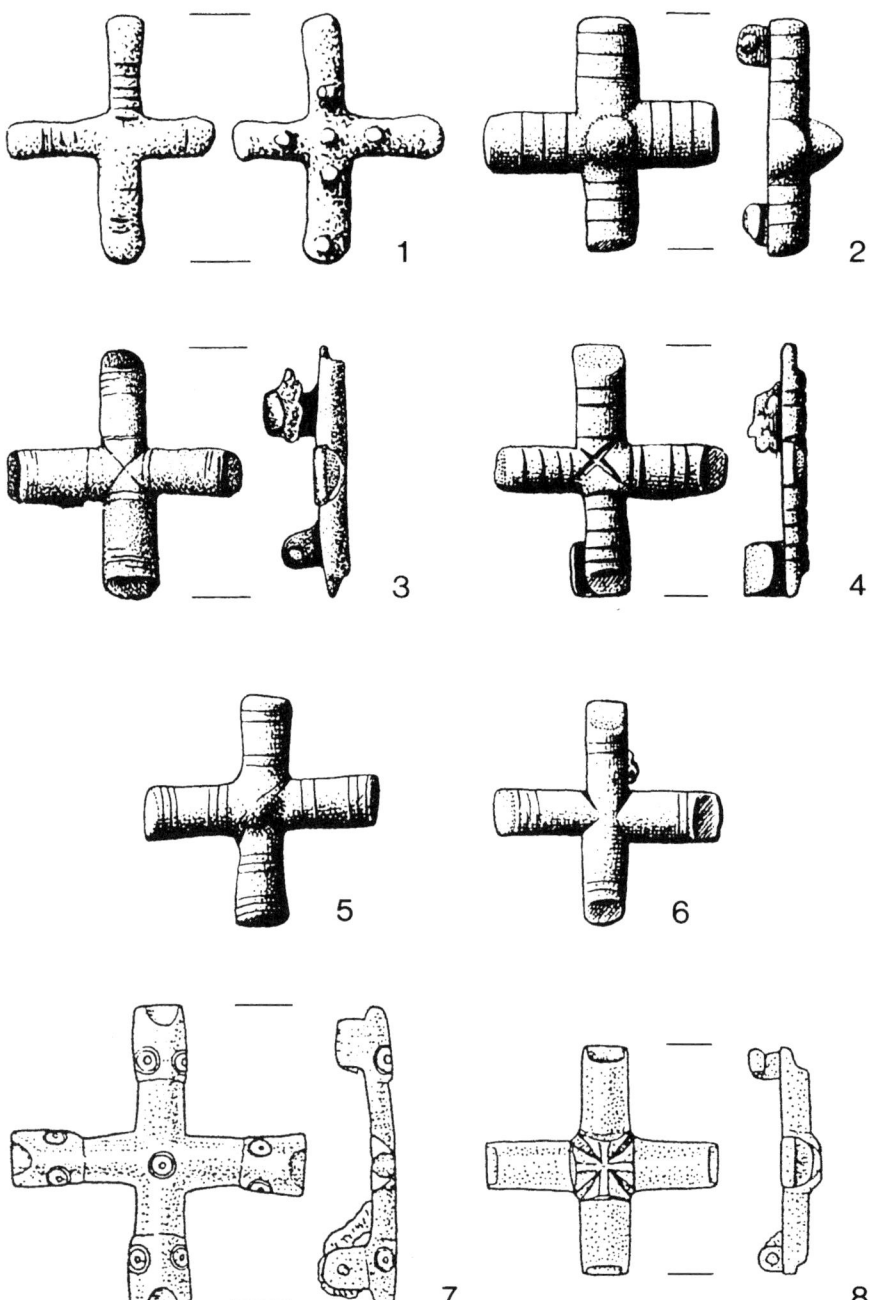

Fig. 9. Late Merovingian cross-shaped brooches from central Rhine and Mosel area. 1–6 Gondorf, 7–8 Iversheim. Bronze. Scale 1:1. After Schulze-Dörrlamm 1990:table 37,1–6; Neuffer-Müller 1972:tables 11,61(5); 26,141(3).

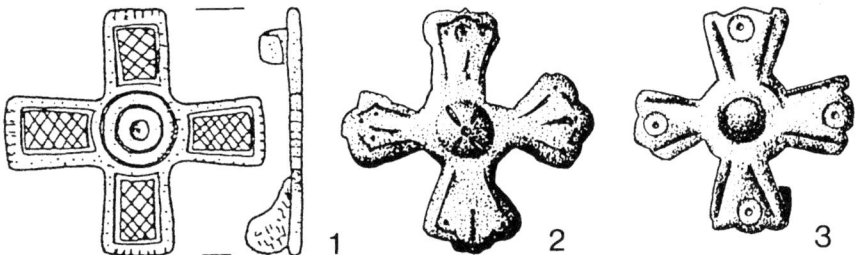

Fig. 10. Late Merovingian cross-shaped brooches from central Rhine and Mosel area. 1 Iversheim. 2–3 Gondorf. Bronze. Scale 1:1. After Neuffer-Müller 1972:table 5,45 (1); Schulze-Dörrlamm 1990:tables 23,4/1890 (3); 37,7.

church, with many grave goods, among them a cross made of gold braid (Hampel 1994:119, fig. 71, No. 14).

In one Frankish area—the central Rhine and the Mosel area—the Mediterranean type of cross-shaped brooch was apparently adopted in the second part of the seventh century (Fig. 3, area C; 11). We know about twenty sites, mostly female graves or cemeteries with cross brooches, which are interpreted as evidence of, I am quoting Egon Wamers (1994:135), "Übernahme einer mediterranen Kreuzfibelsitte mit plakativem Bekenntnis zum Christentum". In the seventh century, however, Christianity was long-established in the area between Trier and Cologne (Böhme 1996:477 ff., fig. 1; Päffgen & Ristow 1996:407 ff., fig. 321). Why, then, this late evidence?

The cross-shaped brooches of the Middle Rhine and Mosel region are mainly made of bronze, have simple shapes (Greek cross) and bear simple ornamentation (Figs. 9–10).

There is a group of crosses with small raised arms and ornamentation with incisions and punchmarks, sometimes a boss or an X-shaped decoration in the centre (Fig. 9). Christiane Neuffer-Müller (1972:21 ff. with map fig. 2) mentioned some parallels in the Rhineland and in Switzerland, and Mechtild Schulze-Dörrlamm (1990:153) added some examples from Burgundy and Eastern and Northern France. The most recent contribution is by Herrmann Ament (1993:55 ff.; map: 96. fig. 87,3). There are apparently no prototypes in the Mediterranean area. The cross-shaped brooches are regarded as local products.

Another group of cross-shaped brooches is characterized by widening arms (with straight, floral or corrugated ends), which are decorated with crosshatches or ring-and-dot design. They always have a central boss or circle (Fig. 10).

At twelve of twenty sites graves have been found which contain cross-shaped brooches (Figs. 11; list 4, Nos. 3, 6, 9, 10, 11, 12, 13, 14, 16, 17, 19, 20).

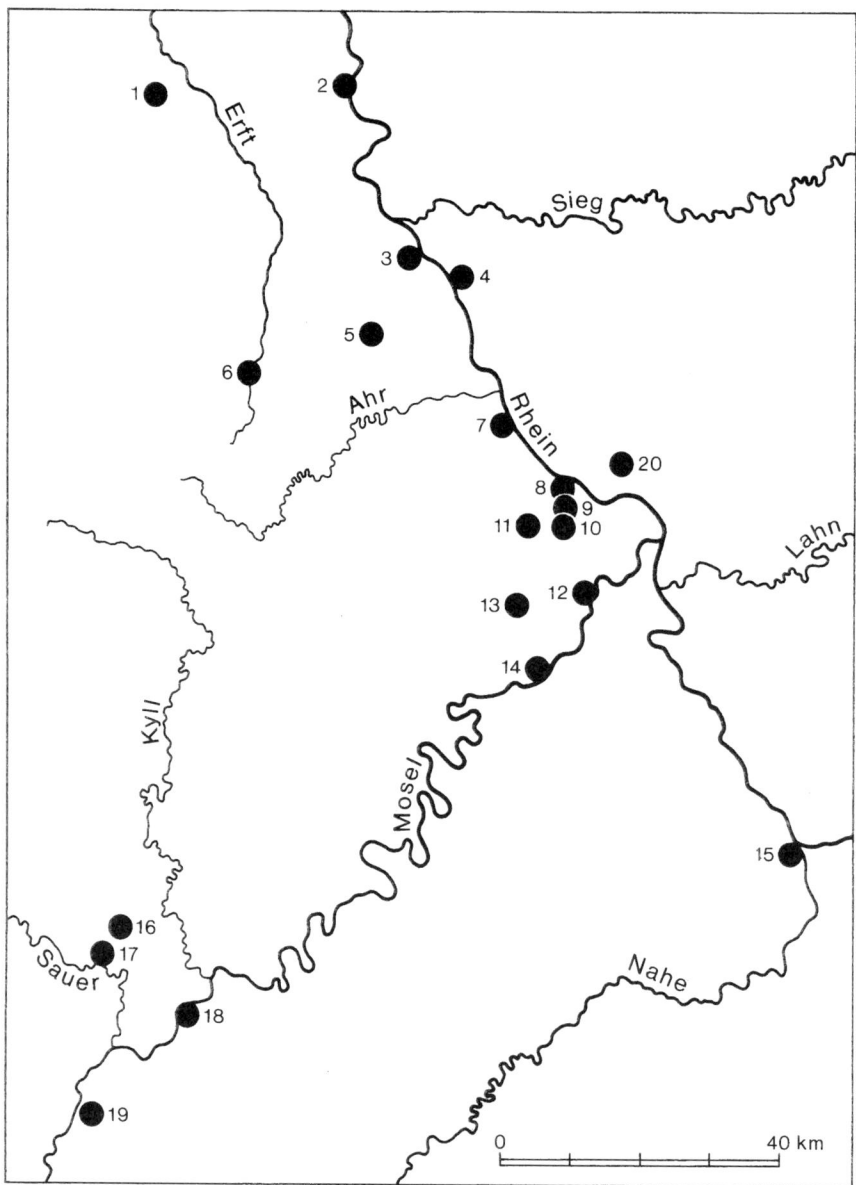

Fig. 11. Distribution of late Merovingian cross-shaped brooches in the central Rhine and Mosel area. For numbers see list 4. After Neuffer-Müller 1972:24, fig. 2 (with additions).

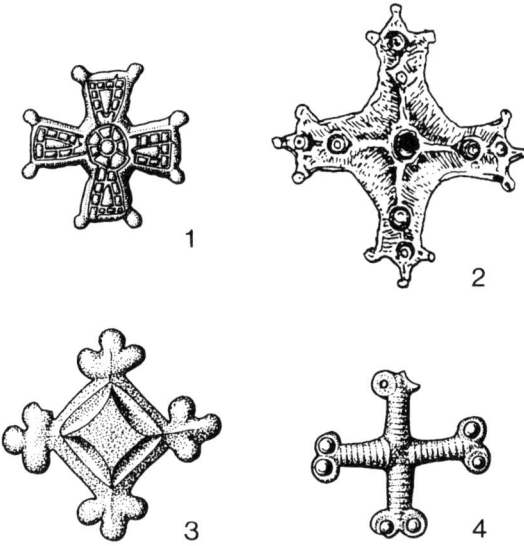

Fig. 12. Carolingian cross-shaped brooches with knobs at the points of their arms from the area between Rhine, Main and Elbe. 1 Drantum, Grave 192 (variant a). 2 Hamburg (variant b). 3 Wulfsen, Grave 414 (variant c). 4 Schinna, grave (variant d). Bronze. Scale 1:1. After Ahrens 1978:556, figs. 40–41; Schindler 1957:101, fig. 34; Busch 1987:162 f. with fig..

These female inhumations were modestly furnished, as was the late Merovingian custom in the second half and at the end of the seventh century; it may be sufficient to refer to graves at Iversheim and Gondorf (Neuffer-Müller 1972:tables 5,45; 11,61; 26,141; Schulze-Dörrlamm 1990:table 23,4/1890) and to the two graves of girls at Saffig (Melzer 1993:tables 8,35; 9,33).

Saxonia and Frisia

There remains the fourth and last area which we have selected for our analysis: the region between the Central/Lower Rhine, Main, Saale/Elbe and the coastal zones of the North and the Baltic sea (Fig. 3, area D), an area which was first Christianized during the Carolingian period and the northern expansion of the Carolingian Empire in the eighth and ninth centuries (Angenendt 1990:233 ff.). The borderline of Christianity about AD 800 ran along the Northern part of the Elbe and along the Saale in the south (Fig. 3).

At the end of the eighth century and the beginning of the ninth century many bishoprics were founded in the region between the Rhine and the Elbe, among others Bremen and Hamburg (Angenendt 1990:297, fig. 50).

As in the central Rhine and Mosel area, you can observe a reception of the Mediterranean custom of wearing cross-shaped brooches on the northern periphery of the Carolingian Empire during the ninth and tenth centuries.

One prominent form—amongst others—is the cross with small knobs at the points of the arms (*Kreuzfibel mit Eckrundeln*). Several variants can be distinguished, as Egon Wamers (1994:138 ff.) has done in recent work on

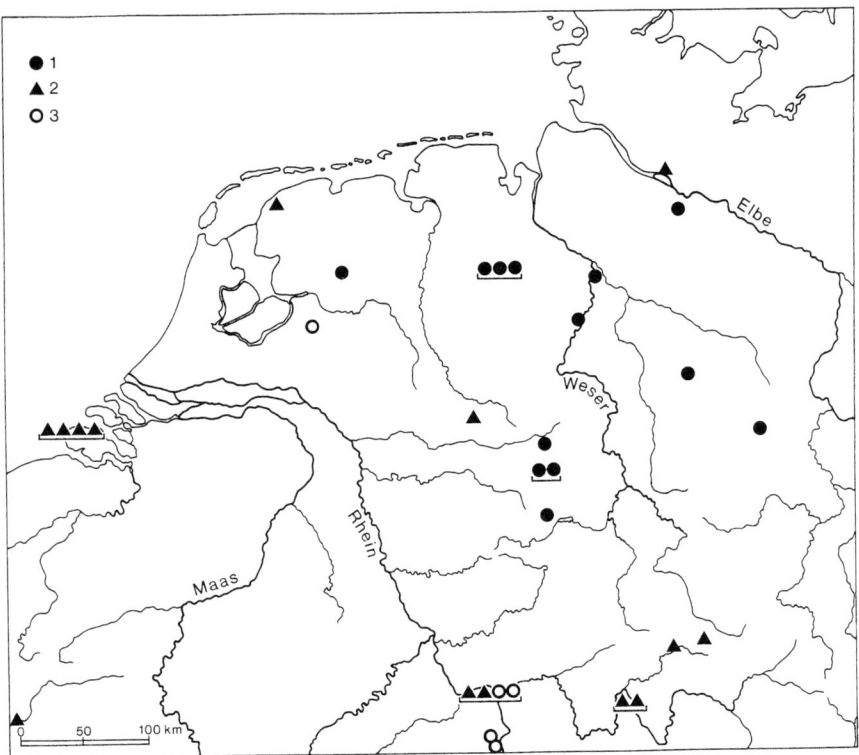

Fig. 13. Distribution of Carolingian cross-shaped brooches (variants a–d) from the area between the Rhine, the Main and the Elbe. 1 Grave/cemetery, 2 Settlement, 3 Without context. For identification of the sites see list 5. After Wamers 1994:140, fig. 83.

Carolingian and Ottonian metalwork. According to the shape of the arms and the number and arrangement of the knobs at the points he calls them variants a–d; an example of each variant may be shown from sites in Lower Saxony and Hamburg (Fig. 12). Variant a (Fig. 12:1) can be dated to the second half of the eighth to the first half of the tenth century; there are Mediterranean prototypes such as variant 2 in Trentino (Fig. 1:2). Variant d in the North (Fig. 12:4), which dates to the period from the late eighth to the second half of the ninth century, likewise has a Mediterranean prototype, variant 4 in Tessin (Fig. 1:4). The distribution of those cross-shaped brooches extends from the Alps to the coastal zone; most finds are known north of the Main (Wamers 1994:140, fig. 83; most recently with additions: Schulze-Dörrlamm 1997:344, fig. 3).

When looking at the archaeological sources, you have to observe that finds of the Carolingian cross-shaped brooches with knobs at the points come partly from settlement sites, partly from graves (Fig. 13).

The cross as a symbol of personal Christian belief 195

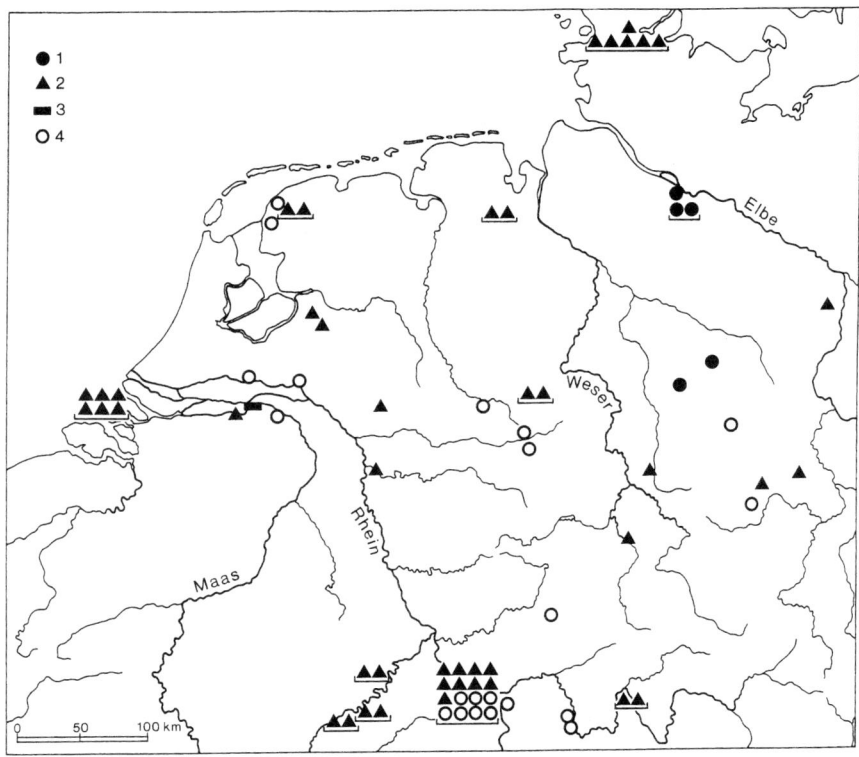

Fig. 14. Distribution of Carolingian enamelled disc brooches with cross ornament from the area between Rhine, Main and Elbe. 1 Grave/cemetery, 2 Settlement, 3 River, 4 Without context. For identification of the sites see list 6. After Wamers 1994:60, fig. 34.

If you add enamelled disc brooches with cross ornament (type 3) as further examples of Christian symbols in context with female (and male) dress,—the distribution map shows a clear concentration between Rhine and Elbe (Fig. 14)—it is obvious that the greatest part of the finds are from settlements, and only a small part from graves. There may be a chronological reason: the custom of furnishing graves with grave goods was abandoned in the course of the ninth century. As Wamers supposes, I think correctly, many of the cross-shaped brooches and disc brooches with Christian symbols (cross, bust of a saint) are later than the phase of mission in about AD 800.

Conclusion

If you compare the four areas selected for analysis, you have to bear in mind cultural, ethnic, social, religious and chronological differences. In Trentino (Fig. 2; 3 A) and other North Italian and Adriatic regions cross-shaped brooches and pendants were worn by female members of the Romanic population, from about AD 400 and into the seventh century, as far as we know from graves which are—according to Romanic tradition—poorly furnished. Roman Catholicism was long-established in these regions.

The same custom can be observed in the central Rhine/Mosel region (Figs. 3 C; 11). There cross-shaped brooches were observed in female graves of the second half of the seventh century, in graves with reduced grave goods—quite the rule at that time—on row cemeteries. As in the *Romania* of northern Italy, Christianity in the Mosel and Rhine area was deeply rooted in Roman tradition (Fig. 3). In contrast to these areas, the two others are mission areas, which were converted during the late sixth and seventh centuries—the Alamannic and Baiuvarian regions (Figs. 3 B; 5–8) and the Frisian and Saxon regions (Figs. 3 D; 13–14) during the late eighth and the ninth centuries.

While the cross-shaped pendants from female graves (Fig. 5) have to be connected with the Romanic tradition south of Alps, the gold-foil crosses, mostly known from Alamannia (Figs. 6–8), are visible signs of a strong Italian Lombard influence. Individuals of both sexes and all age groups were buried with gold-foil crosses; undoubtedly the custom was restricted to the leading group of the population—the gold-foil cross was the symbol of the newly Christianized *nobilitas*. Finally, in the north the Mediterranean custom was adopted during Carolingian times (Fig. 13), some time after the systematic mission ordered by Charlemagne. Settlement sites are dominant in this context.

The development in Southern and Central Scandinavia—crosses, crucifixes and encolpia from graves, hoards, settlement sites and as single finds of the Viking Age and the Early Middle Ages—has been studied by Jörn Staecker (1995) in his doctoral thesis. More than 120 finds are known, partly from Denmark (including Schleswig and Scania), partly from Eastern (including Öland and Gotland) and Central Sweden. In contrast to the analysed areas in Continental Europe, hoards play an important role as an archaeological source (Staecker 1995:31 ff. with map 3).

I greet you, Gad Rausing, and congratulate the subject of this celebration, on the way from Trentino to the North; you all know the work two Lundensians have done in Birka, one of them present here, the other still present through his important publications, among others *Die Grabfunde Birkas,* with the publication of cross-shaped pendants from several graves and the well-known pendant in the form of a crucifix from Grave 660 (Arbman 1940:Taf. 102,2a; Holmqvist & Granath 1979:fig. p. 121). But that is another story.

Figures: Wolfgang Lieske, Kiel.

References

Ahrens, C. (ed.) 1978. *Sachsen und Angelsachsen*. Veröffentlichungen des Helms-Museums 32. Hamburg.

Ament, H. 1976. *Die fränkischen Grabfunde aus Mayen und der Pellenz*. Germanische Denkmäler der Völkerwanderungszeit. Serie B, Die fränkischen Altertümer des Rheinlandes 9. Berlin.

— 1993. *Siedlung und Gräberfeld des frühen Mittelalters von Mertloch, Künzerhof (Kreis Mayen-Koblenz)*. Wissenschaftliche Beibände zum Anzeiger des Germanischen Nationalmuseums 9. Nürnberg.

Angenendt, A. 1990. *Das Frühmittelalter. Die abendländische Christenheit von 400 bis 900*. Stuttgart, Berlin, Köln.

Arbman, H. 1940. *Birka I. Die Gräber*. Tafeln. Stockholm.

Back, U. 1989. *Frühmittelalterliche Grabfunde beiderseits der unteren Mosel*. BAR International Series 532. Oxford.

Bierbrauer, V. 1992. Kreuzfibeln in der mittelalpinen romanischen Frauentracht des 5.–7. Jahrhunderts: Trentino und Südtirol. *Archivio per l'Alto Adige. Rivista di Studi alpini* 86, 1–26.

Böhme, H. W. 1993. Adelsgräber im Frankenreich. Archäologische Zeugnisse zur Herausbildung einer Herrenschicht unter den merowingischen Königen. *Jahrbuch des Römisch-Germanischen Zentralmuseums Mainz* 40, 1993, No. 2, 397–534.

— 1996. Adel und Kirche bei den Alamannen der Merowingerzeit. *Germania* 74, 477–507.

Böhner, K. 1958. *Die fränkischen Altertümer des Trierer Landes*. Germanische Denkmäler der Völkerwanderungszeit. Serie B, Die fränkischen Altertümer des Rheinlandes 1. Berlin.

Busch, R. (ed.) 1987. *Von den Sachsen zur Hammaburg: Bilder aus Hamburgs Frühzeit*. Veröffentlichung des Helms-Museums 50. Neumünster.

Catalogue Mannheim 1996. *Die Franken. Wegbereiter Europas. Vor 1500 Jahren: König Chlodwig und seine Erben*. Vol. 1 & 2. Mainz.

Catalogue Paris 1997. *Les Francs, précurseurs de l'Europe*. Musée du Petit Palais. Paris.

Catalogue Stuttgart 1997. *Die Alamannen*. Archäologisches Landesmuseum Baden-Württemberg. Stuttgart.

Christlein, R. 1975 a. Der soziologische Hintergrund der Goldblattkreuze nördlich der Alpen. In Hübener 1975, 73–83.

— 1975 b. Verzeichnis der Goldblattkreuze nördlich der Alpen. In Hübener 1975, 105–112.

— 1978. *Die Alamannen. Archäologie eines lebendigen Volkes*. Stuttgart-Aalen.

Dannheimer, H. & Dopsch, H. (ed.) 1988. *Die Bajuwaren. Von Severin bis Tassilo 488–788*. Korneuburg.

Dassmann, E. 1993. *Die Anfänge der Kirche in Deutschland. Von der Spätantike bis zur frühfränkischen Zeit*. Urban-Taschenbücher 444. Stuttgart.

Hampel, A. 1994. *Der Kaiserdom zu Frankfurt am Main. Ausgrabungen 1991–1993*. Nußloch.

Holmqvist, W. & Granath, K.-E. 1979. *Swedish Vikings on Helgö and Birka*. Värnamo.

Hübener, W. (ed.) 1975. *Die Goldblattkreuze des frühen Mittelalters*. Veröffentlichung des Alamannischen Instituts Freiburg i. Br. 37. Bühl/Baden.

Knaut, M. 1994. Goldblattkreuze und andere Kreuzzeichen. Gedanken zu einer süddeutsch-italischen Beigabensitte. In Dobiat, C. (ed.), *Festschrift für Otto-Herman Frey zum 65. Geburtstag*. Marburger Studien zur Vor- und Frühgeschichte 16. Hitzeroth, 317–330.

— 1996. Die Alamannen. In *Die Franken* 1996, Vol. 1, 304–307.
Koch, U. 1990. *Das fränkische Gräberfeld von Klepsau im Hohenlohekreis*. Forschungen und Berichte zur Vor- und Frühgeschichte in Baden-Württemberg 38. Stuttgart.
Martin, J. (ed.) 1987. *Atlas zur Kirchengeschichte. Die christlichen Kirchen in Geschichte und Gegenwart*. Freiburg.
Melzer, W. 1993. *Das fränkische Gräberfeld von Saffig, Kreis Mayen-Koblenz*. Internationale Archäologie 17. Buch am Erlbach.
Menghin, W. 1985. *Die Langobarden. Archäologie und Geschichte*. Stuttgart.
Müller, W. & Knaut, M. 1987. *Heiden und Christen*. Kleine Schriften zur Ur- und Frühgeschichte Südwestdeutschlands 2. Stuttgart.
Neuffer-Müller, C. 1972. *Das fränkische Gräberfeld von Iversheim*. Germanische Denkmäler der Völkerwanderungszeit. Serie B, Die fränkischen Altertümer des Rheinlandes 6. Berlin.
Päffgen, B. & Ristow, S. 1996. Christentum, Kirchenbau und Sakralkunst im östlichen Frankenreich (Austrasien). In *Die Franken* 1996, Vol. 1, 407–415.
Riemer, E. 1997. Im Zeichen des Kreutzes. Goldblattkreuze und andere Funde mit christlichem Symbolgehalt. In *Catalogue Stuttgart* 1997, 447–454.
Schindler, R. 1957. *Ausgrabungen in Alt-Hamburg*. Hamburg.
Schulze-Dörrlamm, M. 1990. *Die spätrömischen und frühmittelalterlichen Gräberfelder von Gondorf, Gem. Kobern-Gondorf, Kr. Mayen-Koblenz*. Germanische Denkmäler der Völkerwanderungszeit. Serie B, Die fränkischen Altertümer des Rheinlandes 14. Berlin.
— 1997. Unbekannte Kreutzfibeln der Karolingerzeit aus Edelmetall. *Archäologisches Korrespondenzblatt* 27, 341–354.
Staecker, J. 1995. *Rex regum et dominus dominorum. Die wikingerzeitlichen Kreuz- und Kruzifixanhänger als Ausdruck der Mission in Altdänemark und Schweden*. Dissertation, University of Kiel.
Stork, I. 1997. Friedhof und Dorf, Herrenhof und Adelsgrab. Der einmalige Befund Lauchheim. In *Catalogue Stuttgart* 1977, 290–310.
Wamers, E. 1994. *Die frühmittelalterlichen Lesefunde aus der Löhrstraße (Baustelle Hilton II) in Mainz*. Mainzer Archäologische Schriften 1. Mainz.

Lists

List 1. Post-Roman cross-shaped brooches in Trentino. See Fig. 2. After Bierbrauer 1992.

1 Imer-Primiero. – 2 Mattarello (2 spec.). – 3 Vervò, Nonsberg. – 4 Madruzzo. – 5 Valle d'Algone, near Stenico. – 6 Cavalese, dosso S. Valerio. – 7 Volano. – 8 Rovereto – S. Ilario. – 9 Rovereto (or surroundings?). – 10 Ledro B – volta di Besta (4 spec.). – 11 Seio, Nonsberg. – 12 Sprè di Povo (2 spec.). – 13 Site unknown, Trentino. – 14 Villanders-Plunacker. – 15 Trento/Trient. – 16 Tiarno di Sotto.

List 2. Merovingian cross-shaped pendants in Southern Germany. See Fig. 5. After Christlein (= C) 1975 a: 82 note 47 with numbers; Knaut (= K) 1994: 328 note 44 with numbers.

1 Köln, St. Severin, Grave P 73 (C 1). – 2 Diez an der Lahn (K 20). – 3 Site unknown, central Rhine area? (C 2). – 4 Niedernberg, Grave 32 (K 13). – 5

Karlburg (K 14). – 6 Dittigheim (C 3). – 7 Mannheim-Seckenheim, Grave 5 (C 4). – 8 Mannheim-Vogelstang (K 15). – 9 Schwetzingen, Grave 5 (K 16). – 10 Freudenheim or Freudenstein (K 17). – 11 Lahr-Burgheim, Grave 10 (K 18). – 12 Gammertingen (K 12). – 13 Wittlingen (K 11). – 14 Oberstotzingen (C 8). – 15 Pfahlheim (C 6). – 16 Friedberg, Grave 15 (C 9). – 17 München – Giesing, Grave 224 (C 10). – 18 Großprüfening? (K 19). – 19 Sallach, Grave 6 a (C 7).

List 3. Merovingian gold-foil (and silver-foil) crosses in Southern Germany and neighbouring areas. See Fig. 6. After Christlein (= C) 1975 b with numbers; Müller & Knaut (= M/K) 1987: 48–51 with numbers; Knaut (= K) 1994, with additions (unnumbered).
1 Rommerskirchen (C 47). – 2 Meckenheim (C 46, K p. 320). – 3 Gondorf (K p. 320). – 4 Eppstein (K p. 320). – 5 Odratzheim, France (C 49). – 6 Klepsau (M/K 22). – 7 Freiberg-Geisingen (M/K 10). – 8 Stuttgart-Untertürkheim (C 26, M/K 34). – 9 Esslingen-Sirnau (C 9, M/K 9). – 10 Eislingen/Fils (C 8, M/K 8). – 11 Donzdorf (C 4, M/K 4). – 12 Kirchheim u. Teck (C 16–18, M/K 19–21). – 13 Pliezhausen (C 23–24, M/K 31–32). – 14 Tübingen-Derendingen (C 27–28, M/K 35–36). – 15 Nagold (M/K 25). – 16 Oberiflingen (C 19, M/K 27). – 17 Dunningen (C 6, M/K 6). – 18 Dotternhausen (C 5, M/K 5). – 19 Ebingen-Lautlingen (C 7, M/K 7). – 20 Gammertingen (C 10–12, M/K 11–13, K p. 319). – 21 Andelfingen (C 1, M/K 1). – 22 Wurmlingen (C 31, M/K 40). – 23 Hintschingen (C 15, M/K 16). – 24 Hüfingen (C 17–18). – 25 Buggingen (C 3, M/K 3). – 26 Beringen, Switzerland (C 51). – 27 Burg, Switzerland (K p. 322). – 28 Güttingen (C 14, M/K 15). – 29 Weingarten (C 30, M/K 39). – 30 Aulendorf (C 2, M/K 2). – 31 Ulm-Ermingen (M/K 38). – 32 Ulm (C 29, M/K 37). – 33 Sontheim an der Brenz (C 25, M/K 33). – 34 Giengen an der Brenz (C 13, M/K 14). – 35 Pfahlheim (C 20–22, M/K 28–30). – 36 Lauchheim (M/K 23–24, K p. 319 f.). – 37 Neresheim (M/K 26). – 38 Ebermergen (C 33). – 39 Wittislingen (C 44–45). – 40 Lauingen (C 37). – 41 Kötz-Großkötz (C 35). – 42 Mindelheim (C 38). – 43 Spötting (K p. 321). – 44 Langerringen (C 36). – 45 Schwabmünchen (C 40). – 46 Walda (C 43). – 47 Staubing (C 41–42). – 48 Altheim (K p. 320). – 49 Aschheim (K p. 321). – 50 Waging (K p. 321). – 51 Petting (K p. 321). – 52 Freilassing (C 34). – 53 Ainring – Feldkirchen (C 32). – 54 Pocking – Inzing (C 39). – 55 Wels, Austria (K p. 321). – 56 Linz-Zizlau, Austria (C 50). – Not shown: Lezéville, France (C 48); Oyes, France (K p. 322).

List 4. Late Merovingian cross-shaped brooches in the central Rhine and Mosel area. See Fig. 11. After Neuffer-Müller 1972: 23 ff.; with additions.
1 Elsdorf. – 2 Köln (Back 1989: 58 note 151, date?). – 3 Bonn, Münster, Grave 29. – 4 Oberdollendorf. – 5 Meckenheim. – 6 Iversheim, Graves 45, 61, 141. – 7 Niederbreisig. – 8 Andernach. – 9 Miesenheim, Grave 134 (Ament 1976: 66 f.). – 10 Saffig, graves 33 & 35 (Melzer 1993: 43). – 11 Kruft, grave (no

context?) (Ament 1976: 66 f.). – 12 Gondorf, graves (no context) (Schulze-Dörrlamm 1990: 153 f.). – 13 Mertloch, grave (no context) (Ament 1993: 55 ff.). – 14 Moselkern, grave (no context) (Back 1989: 22). – 15 Bingerbrück. – 16 Eisenach, Grave 41. – 17 Minden, grave 3. – 18 Trier, Porta Nigra. – 19 Söst, Grave 9. – (For Nos. 16–19 and two cross-shaped brooches from unknown sites see Böhner 1958: 110 f.). – 20 Neuwied-Gladbach, Grave 39 (Catalogue Mannheim 1996: 2, 1027 fig. 12).

List 5. Carolingian cross-shaped brooches in the area between the Rhine, the Main and the Elbe. See Fig. 13. After Wamers 1994: 140 fig. 83 and list 32 a–d p. 242ff., with numbers, here in brackets.
Variant a (ibid. 242 f. list 32 a)
(No. 4) Boxhornschanze (grave). – (Nos. 6–7) Domburg (settlement). – (No. 8) Drantum (Grave 192). – (No. 10) Goddelsheim (Grave 23). – (Nos. 12–13) Mainz (settlement). – (No. 14) Paderborn (Grave 154). – (No. 15) Quiercy (settlement). – (No. 18) Wünnenberg-Fürstenberg (Grave 47).
Variant b (ibid. 244 list 32 b)
(No. 1) Abenheim (without context). – (No. 2) Altenburg (settlement). – (No. 4) Hamburg (settlement). – (No. 5) Karlburg (settlement). – (No. 7) Wijnaldum (settlement). – (No. 8) Woltwiesche (Grave 1). – (No. 9) Worms (without context).
Variant c (ibid. 244 f. list 32 c)
(No. 1) Wünnenberg-Fürstenberg (grave 37). – (No. 2) Herxen (without context). – (No. 3) Karlburg (settlement). – (No. 4) Mainz (without context). – (No. 5) Neustadt an der Saale (settlement). – (No. 6) Wulfsen (Grave 414). – (No. 7) Balhorn (settlement).
Variant d (ibid. 245 list 32 d)
(No. 1) Dörverden (Grave 128 a). – (No. 2) Mainz (without context). – (Nos. 3–4) Domburg (settlement). – (Nos. 6–6 a) Drantum (Grave 306, grave near 306). – (No. 7) Schinna (grave). – (No. 8) Looveen (Grave 5).

List 6. Carolingian enamelled disc brooches with cross ornament (type 3) in the area between Rhine, Main and Elbe. See Fig. 14. After Wamers 1994: 60 fig. 34 and list 5, p. 208 ff. with numbers.
Nos. 1–14, 14 a, 15–20, 20 a–20 b, 21–26, 26 a–c, 27–45, 46–47, 49–59, 60–64, 71–73.
Grave/cemeteries: Nos. 5, 26, 63–64, 72.
Settlement: Nos. 2–3, 4, 6, 9, 10, 11, 12, 13, 15, 16–20, 20 a–b, 21, 22, 23, 24, 25, 26 a–b, 27–35, 49–53, 54, 55, 60–61.
River: No. 43
Without context: Nos. 1, 7, 8, 14, 14 a, 26 c, 36–42, 44, 45, 46, 47, 56, 57–58, 59, 62, 71, 73.

Vingen Revisited
A Gendered Perspective on "Hunters" Rock Art
By Gro Mandt

The conventional androcentric interpretation of Scandinavian rock art is challenged here, and the rock art is re-evaluated from a gendered point of view. The study focuses on a large rock-art site, Vingen, on the north-western coast of Norway, ascribed to Late Mesolithic/Early Neolithic hunter-gatherers. Chronological, chorological and contextual analyses of the carvings indicate that the site was used over a considerable period of time. Different parts of the area may have been used for different purposes, exclusively for women or men respectively. Other parts may have been used by both sexes. Several motifs may be associated with female symbolism. In addition, some topographical features, such as "passages" in a rock-strewn slope and a characteristic mountain formation associated with witches, may be seen to emphasize a gendered perception of the site.

Background

Since the turn of the century it has been common practice in Scandinavia to differentiate between two categories of rock art, assumed to represent separate chronological stages and cultural traditions. The distinction has been based partly on differences in the selection of motifs, partly on variations in the geographical distribution. This dichotomy was emphasized by Gutorm Gjessing in the 1930s, when he introduced the terms "hunters'" rock art and "agrarian" or "farmers'" rock art to signify the alleged economies of the people who had made the pictures (Gjessing 1932, 1936).

The concept of "hunters'" rock art identifies depictions of big game, primarily elk, reindeer, red deer and sea mammals. The pictures have been explained as a reflection of hunting magic performed in hunter-gatherer societies, mainly in the Stone Age. The concept of "agrarian" rock art, on the other hand, identifies a complex of motifs comprising human representations, man-made objects and abstract patterns. These rock pictures have been interpreted as a manifestation of religious practice in an agrarian society, presumably in a Bronze Age cultural setting. Alternatively they have been explained as territorial markers, symbols of an élite or expressions of power relations and ideological information.

It is only during the past two decades that this dichotomy—characterized as a strait-jacket (Helskog 1993)—has been challenged. In order to gain new insight into the interpretation and semantic content of Scandinavian rock art, serious rethinking and new approaches are called for.

Point of Departure

My point of departure is that information about social life and human interrelation in the past is embedded in rock art. Thus, I assume that the rock pictures hold "messages" about the relationship between women and men, their potential conflicts and negotiations. This point of view has hitherto been downplayed in rock-art research, due to the prevalent androcentric bias in the research tradition. My aim, therefore, is to challenge the traditional interpretations, and demonstrate how a gendered perspective—focusing on gender relations and making women and female symbolism visible—may extend our understanding of rock art. My main object of study is a large rock-art site on the north-western coast of Norway, called Vingen. I believe this site has a great potential when it comes to exploring gender aspects in material culture.

Approaches

My approach is based partly on contextual and spatial analyses, partly on comparative symbolism. I suggest that a study of the context and combination of the various motifs, as well as their distribution and location in the landscape, are meaningful in explaining human relations and interaction. As an interpretative model, I will draw attention to an analysis of gender relations in Australian rock art. My interpretation of the various rock-art motifs and their meaning content is based on comparison partly with cross-cultural analogies relating to universal symbols, partly with material culture remains from different cultures and periods of time.

The Male Bias

In recent years women archaeologists have drawn attention to the male bias prevalent in rock-art research all over the world. Even in Australia, where both female and male representations are easily identified in rock art, Julie Drew has demonstrated androcentrism. Although a large proportion of the human representations is sexually undifferentiated, they have been classified as males, while the fairly abundant female representations have been more or less overlooked (Drew 1995:105). As to the interpretation of the Palaeolithic rock art of Europe, Pamela Russel has suggested that much of the biased thinking may stem from the fact that research on this subject began in the

Victorian era, a period when there were no women in the profession (Russel 1991:346).

The interpretations of Scandinavian rock art, put forward primarily by male researchers during the past 150–200 years, have focused on male activities, with regard to the making as well as to the use, function and symbolic meaning of the rock art. It has been assumed that the production of rock pictures and the ceremonies associated with them were a male domain, and, more or less unconsciously, the "artists" have been considered male shamans or priests.

Gjessing's explanation of "hunters'" rock art was in accordance with the early twentieth-century interpretation of Palaeolithic rock art. In order to explain the symbolic and social meaning content and function of the rock pictures, he used ethnographic material from different parts of the world for analogical comparison (Gjessing 1936:138 ff.). His main focus was on hunting magic and shamanism. Considering descriptions of hunting rituals among Native American groups, for example, he explained body decorations occurring in Scandinavian animal representations as "life-line" and "heart". These elements he interpreted as symbols of the living animal (Gjessing 1936:142). The ethnographic example was seen as a direct illustration of magic practice in Stone Age Scandinavia: prior to the hunt, the shaman, at the request of the hunter, painted the life symbols on a picture of the potential game.

Gjessing and his successors have also been concerned with aspects of a potential fertility symbolism in "hunters'" rock art. On the basis of ethnographic analogies describing hunting rituals involving women, Gjessing explained female representations and phallic males in rock art as expressions of fertility rites associated with hunting magic (Gjessing 1936:154 f.). He also explained the geometric patterns within this frame of thought, and suggested that they represented some kind of magic force related to the prey animals (Gjessing 1936:146 ff.).

Some 40 years later Egil Bakka, under the influence of French structuralistic analyses of Palaeolithic cave art, emphasized the fertility aspects of "hunters'" rock art. Among other things, he identified some abstract-geometric patterns as representations of the female sexual organ (Bakka 1973). But he did not develop this explanation any further than stating that the sexual elements should be understood in relation to the psychology of hunting. The central themes were the prey animals and the abundance of food they represented. In this situation the hunters experienced uncertainty, suspense, ferocity, gluttony and sexual excitement (Bakka 1973:157).

Thus, both functionalistic and structuralistic explanations have demonstrated the existence of female representations and fertility symbols in "hunters'" rock art. However, the female and fertility elements have only been considered as functional by-products of the hunting, and not as social symbols in their own right. The "Man-the-Hunter" model has long since established hunting as an exclusively male occupation (Russel 1991; Slocum 1975). It is no wonder, therefore, that the society considered responsible for "hunters'" rock art appears to have been populated by ferocious male hunters, conducting their hunting and their magic in splendid isolation from women and children.

In order to impart nuances to this picture one should look more closely into the totality of the context of the rock art. This includes, among other things, variations in motifs and motif combinations, the landscape and topographical features surrounding the sites, as well as the spatial distribution patterns of rock art and related culture elements.

Gender and Material Culture

Ever since feminist thinkers established gender as a main structuring principle in human society (e.g. Harding 1986, 1991), the gender question has been a hot issue on the agendas of disciplines concerning themselves with human culture—past as well as present. Anthropological research has demonstrated the pluralism and complexity of gender relations among living people (e.g. Rosaldo & Lamphere 1974; Reiter 1975; di Leonardo 1991), and archaeologists are beginning to probe into gender relations of cultures long dead (e.g. Bertelsen *et al.* 1987; Claassen 1992; Conkey 1991; Conkey & Gero 1991; Conkey & Spector 1984; Engelstad 1991; Gero 1983; Gero & Conkey 1991; Hodder 1991; Walde & Willows 1991). It is advocated that past gender arrangements may be traced in the archaeological evidence by investigating situations in which gender relations are mediated through material culture (Sørensen 1992:34). The basic assumption for making the "mute" material culture elements "speak" is that human beings create, use and manipulate material objects and their symbolic capabilities, in order to signify their identity as individuals or group-members. Because objects link generations and mediate traditions, material culture is seen as an important factor in social reproduction (ibid.).

All aspects of material culture patterning are thought to be produced according to a set of rules expressing the underlying logic of a society, and transmitting the ideological message of the society (Moore 1986; Larsson 1986). In its broadest and most general sense the concept of "ideology" may be understood as a sort of mental infrastructure: the ideals, beliefs and values of a certain population, designating "social formulas" for human interrelation and for the socio-political, economic and religious activities of the society.

The underlying ideological structure of a society is inherent, in particular, in its artistic expressions. The image has the power of ideological conviction or persuasion. Due to its capacity of looking real and natural, the figurative image makes people believe that it represents the only possible reality (Arsenault 1991). At the same time, different procedures may be used to reflect a distorted aspect of reality, such as a selection of the represented subjects, organization of the pictorial space, and so on. When people become conscious of the power of imagery, they will begin to control and manipulate the content of the pictures, because control allows a better promotion of one's own interests.

Iconography and art are some of the most distinct activities involved in communicating gender categories (Sørensen 1992). Past gender relations, therefore, may be easier to trace in rock art than in other material culture remains. In certain types of art—as well as in burials and costumes—women are clearly visible from the outset. Art can have a mediating function in periods of social and political stress (Hesjedal 1994; Prescott & Walderhaug 1995, Walderhaug 1995). This applies to relations between groups of people as well as between individuals, e.g. women and men.

On Explaining Symbols

In order to explain the meaning of images and signs occurring in a prehistoric context, one may turn to the phenomenology of religions (e.g. Eliade 1958, 1961, 1969), and look for universal similarities in symbolic expressions. This primarily applies to abstract patterns, which are not immediately identifiable with living objects. Such motifs may be explained as archetypal symbols, given identical visual shape, and even the same meaning content, because the human brain is supposed to work in the same way irrespective of time and place. The model refers to the Jungian notion of prototypic phenomena, which forms the content of the collective unconscious, and which are assumed to reflect universal human thought found in all cultures.

Related to this model, in the sense that it is based on the universality of being human, is a neuropsychological model, put forward by David Lewis-Williams and Thomas A. Dowson (1988). It explains the abstract-geometric rock art motifs found worldwide as representations of entoptic phenomena, experienced by the human mind in altered states of consciousness. Although complex and diverse, these visual phenomena take on geometric forms, such as zigzags, spirals, grids, dots, etc. Such percepts may be induced by a variety of means, for example, flickering light, drugs, fatigue, sensory deprivation, intense concentration, migraine, hyperventilation, rhythmic movement. It has been suggested that the contexts in which these visual percepts may be brought about fit shamanistic activities (Lewis-Williams & Dowson 1988).

Both archetypes and entoptic phenomena represent important subjects of study with respect to an overall understanding of rock art symbolism. In my search for interpretative models for explaining Scandinavian rock-art motifs, I have also turned to the extensive empirical material collected by Marija Gimbutas (1989, 1991). She has drawn attention to a multitude of signs and images which occur on objects from all over Europe during the whole time-span from the Palaeolithic to the Bronze Age. Her research is based on interdisciplinary studies, including archaeology, comparative mythology, early historic sources, linguistics and folklore (Gimbutas 1989:xv). The symbols which are of particular interest to rock art include chevrons, zigzags, meanders, wavy lines, spirals, circles, multiple arcs, triangles, eye- and net-motifs, crescents, horns, vulvas and snakes. According to Gimbutas these images should be seen as manifestations of a universal female symbolism based on such basic concepts as birth, death and the renewal of life. From my point of view this material may be considered a visual counterpart to the archetypes of the phenomenology of religion, thus constituting the basis for what may be called "comparative visual symbolism".

An Australian Analogy

As a model for interpreting Scandinavian rock art in a gendered perspective, I will draw attention to an analysis by Julie Drew of women and gender relations in Australian Aboriginal rock art (Drew 1991, 1995). In order to re-evaluate the material and make women visible to archaeology, she has introduced the terms "exclusive" and "inclusive" gender relations. Gender-exclusive activities, which exclude one or the other sex, highlight the status of either women or men. Gender-inclusive relations, which include both sexes, show a balanced or complementary relationship, recognizing independent activities, for example, initiation rites.

Through an examination of rock art and relevant ethnographic accounts Drew demonstrates that there is great variation in Australian rock art as to the sex of the human representations. In some regions women are well represented and the ratio of males to females depicted is balanced. In other areas there is a predominance of neutral human representations, and in yet other areas male depictions dominate. Drew claims that these variations relay messages about the gender relations in different societies, periods or situations in which the rock art was made. An examination of the contexts in which the human representations occur shows that the women are depicted in the same type of scenes as men, and engaged in the same kind of activities, whether secular or ritual.

This kind of contextual analysis, and, in particular, the distinction between "gender-exclusive" and "gender-inclusive" activities, appears to be a most fruitful approach, applicable in other rock art regions as well. In the following I will try to demonstrate this with regard to the rock art at Vingen.

The Rock Art at Vingen

Vingen is the largest rock-art site in southern Norway, comprising approximately 2,000 figures. It is located on the north-western coast, in Sogn og Fjordane county, by a tiny and narrow fiord surrounded by steep thousand-

Fig. 1. View from Vingen, with a rock-art site in the foreground, towards the headland Vingeneset and the mountain formation Hornelen (*axis mundi*?) in the background (Photo: G. Mandt).

metre- high hillsides rising almost vertically from the sea (Fig. 1). The majority of the carvings comprise red deer, but even human representations and various abstract-geometric patterns also occur frequently (Fig. 2). They are scattered along the beach, on large sloping rocks, on boulders and on smaller stones. On the basis of stylistic variations in the animal representations, as well as shoreline dating, it is assumed that the rock art at Vingen covers a time span of about 2000 years, from the transition Late Mesolithic/Early Neolithic—c. 5000/4000 BC—to the beginning of the Late Neolithic—c. 2500/2000 BC (Bakka 1973, 1975, 1979; Walderhaug 1994, 1995).

The carvings have been ascribed to a hunting-gathering population, using the site for magic, and even practical, purposes. According to the earliest interpretation, put forward at the beginning of this century, and based on a historic analogy, Vingen functioned as a huge natural trap for drift-hunting (Brøgger 1925; Bøe 1932; Hallström 1938). In recent years, under the influence of symbolic and contextual archaeology, the site has been explained as a ceremonial gathering place, where different rituals were performed, for example, initiation rites or cult activities related to the reproduction of social bonds (Mézec 1989; Mandt 1991).

Fig. 2. Section of a panel with a number of deer representations, human figures, a hook and a vulva (below to the left). The majority of the deer lack horns and therefore probably picture hinds (Tracing: E. Bakka).

Vingen Reviewed: The Motifs

A new perspective on the rock art at Vingen may bring about a more in-depth understanding, not only of Vingen, but of "hunters'" rock art in general. Various aspects of the carvings at Vingen indicate that a gendered perception of the site might be valid. This applies not only to the human representations and the abstract-geometric motifs. Even the animal figures may be included in a gendered interpretation. I suggest that a contextual analysis of the carvings, surveying similarities and differences in the combination of motifs and including temporal and spatial variables, may reveal gender systems and gender ideologies as well as changes in social interaction during the time-span in which Vingen was in use. The variety of motifs, the great stylistic variation indicating chronological differences, and the distribution of a large number of carvings over an extensive area, make the site well suited for this kind of analysis.

The most abundant motif at Vingen is the red deer, occurring in a variety of different shapes (Figs. 2 and 15). A great deal of the animals are endowed with abstract-geometric body decorations, often resembling the free-standing geometric patterns. According to the presence or absence of horns, both stags (Fig.

Fig. 3. The representation of a large stag, either in a grazing or a mating position. (Photo: G. Mandt.)

3) and hinds appear to be depicted. If absence of horns is accepted as a characterization of the female of the species, hinds are in majority (Fig. 2). Of other animal representations, a few birds and sea mammals should be mentioned, along with some snake figures.

As demonstrated above, the abundant representations of big game have been the major argument for the hunting magic interpretation. No doubt the red deer represented a valued resource for the Stone Age hunter-gatherers of western Norway, although it was probably not their basic means of subsistence. However, the wish to bring down game may have been only one reason for depicting the animals. The strength and beauty of the animals, and the excitement, effort and potential danger associated with hunting them, may have rendered them an aura of mysticism and supernatural status (Fig. 4).

The red deer, therefore, may be considered a complex symbol encompassing a variety of concepts associated with the cosmology and ritual practice of the community.

This is the case, for example, with the eland in South African San bushman rock art and folklore, as demonstrated by Lewis-Williams (1981). The eland is not only "good to eat", but it is "good to think". It is a central symbol in initiation rites, such as the menarcheal rite, the rite of a young hunter's first eland kill, and the marriage rite, and it plays a vital part in rain-making ceremonies.

Fig. 4. The representation of a hind with body decorations, surrounded by hooks and a geometric pattern (Photo: G. Mandt).

Fertility symbolism, then, is prominent in the rituals associated with the eland in South Africa. Several arguments may likewise be put forward to interpret the deer representations in Scandinavian "hunters'" rock art within the frames of a fertility symbolism, where aspects of life-death-rebirth are the dominating themes. In folklore, legends and songs from all over Europe we find traces of ancient rituals centred on horned animals, mainly deer, and in particular hinds (Storm 1995). The European cervine tradition often manifests itself in the shape of song games: "the Hind Game". The main themes are life, death and sexual love, and the deer is frequently associated with water, trees and snakes (ibid.). In a number of legends and myths the deer is connected to supernatural or heroic human beings, primarily women (ibid., 121 ff.). In many cases the relationship between deer and woman is so close that it verges on full identification with the cervine species (ibid., 158). This is of particular interest when it comes to interpreting some motif combinations at Vingen. On some panels there is such a close relationship between deer and human representation, presumably female, that a symbolic affiliation between the two appears to be intentional (Fig. 5).

Both the human representations and the abstract-geometric motifs at Vingen may be explained in terms of a fertility symbolism. The sexual identification of the human representations is in many cases difficult to assess. This is partly

Vingen revisited 211

Fig. 5. A composition presenting a close affiliation between a hind and a human being—presumably a woman (due to the rounded shape of the body)—which may be explained in relation to the "Hind Game" (Photo: G. Mandt).

Fig. 6. Section of a panel with deer and human representations. The three human figures to the left are interpreted as females, due to their rounded shapes and the vulva-like markings in their abdomens (Tracing: E. Bakka).

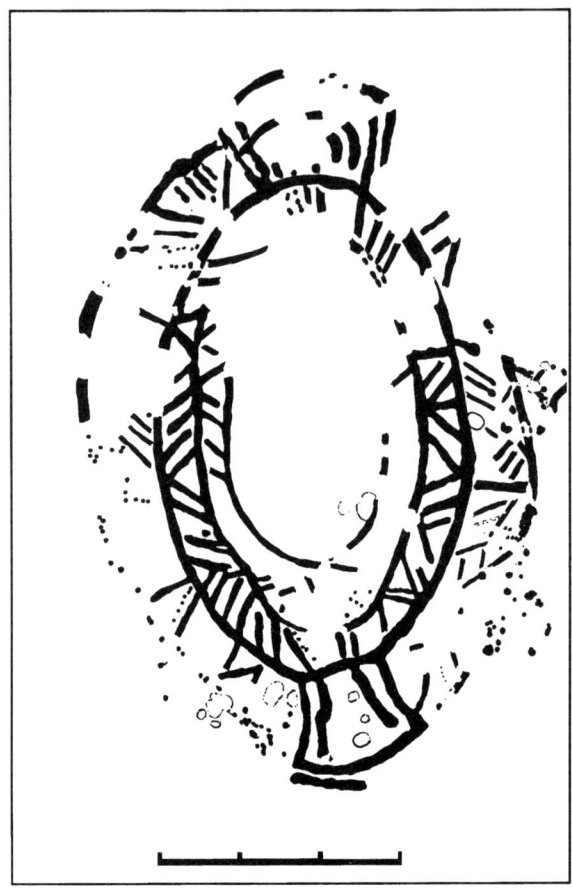

Fig. 7. An oval-shaped figure interpreted as a vulva (Tracing: E. Bakka).

because a number of the humans appear to be non-sexed, partly because the sexual characteristics are often somewhat ambiguous. For example, a line placed between the legs may be explained as a penis, but may just as well be seen as a representation of the female sexual organ. However, several human figures can indisputably be identified as women, due to a vulva-like marking in their abdomen (Fig. 6). Even single vulva representations occur (Fig. 7), as has been demonstrated by Bakka (1973).

A variety of the abstract-geometric motifs may be seen as symbols of women or femininity. These are motifs which—according to Gimbutas (1989, 1991)—may be associated with a system of female symbols in prehistoric Europe, such as eye- and mask-motifs (Fig. 8), multiple arcs, zigzags and wavy lines (Fig. 9), ladders, fringes and hooks (the latter sometimes referred to as "scythes", Fig. 10).

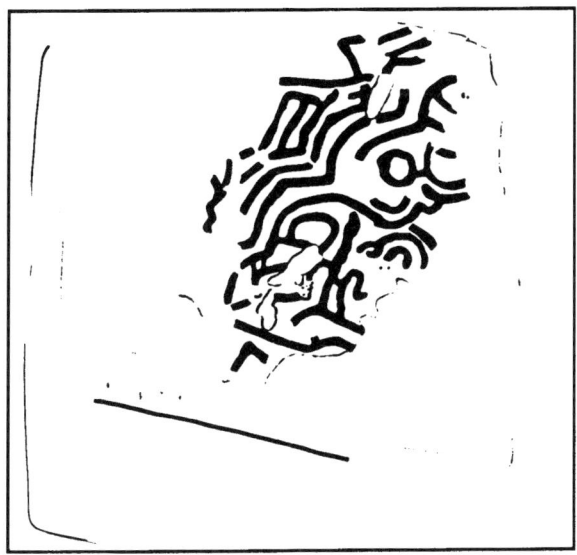

Fig. 8. Eye- or mask-motif on a small, loose stone (Tracing: E. Bakka).

Decorations similar to the geometric rock art motifs appear on some contemporary artefacts which may also be associated with women, for example star-shaped mace-heads (Fig. 11), and clay figurines interpreted as idols (Bakka 1973:170; Hagen 1969:87). The mace-heads are assumed to be weights for digging sticks, and it has been suggested that they were produced as well as used by women in food collecting (Vinsrygg 1979, 1987).

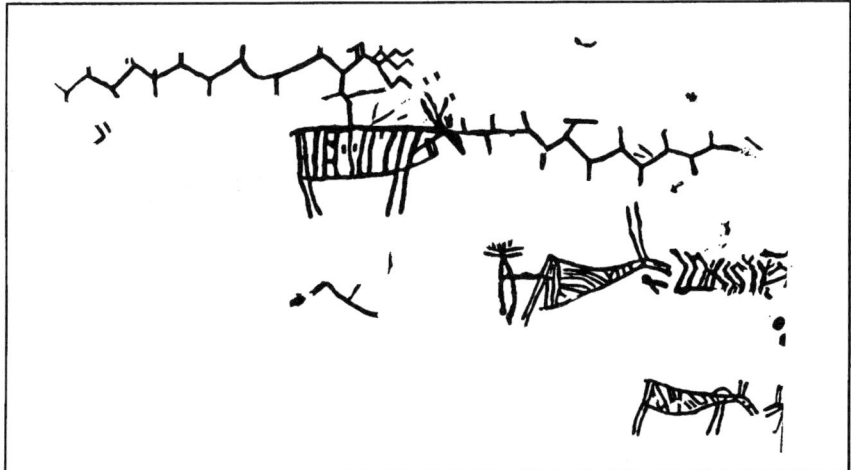

Fig. 9. Section of a panel with animal and human figures in combination with zigzags or snake-like representations (Tracing: E. Bakka).

Fig. 10. A composition of hooks and (possibly) an ambiguous animal to the right (Photo: G. Mandt).

The occurrence of snakes and snake-like patterns among the motifs at Vingen is of particular interest. Apart from free-standing zigzags, the motif is incorporated in the body decorations of the deer, and some of the human figures, primarily those I identify as women, have arms or legs shaped like multi-

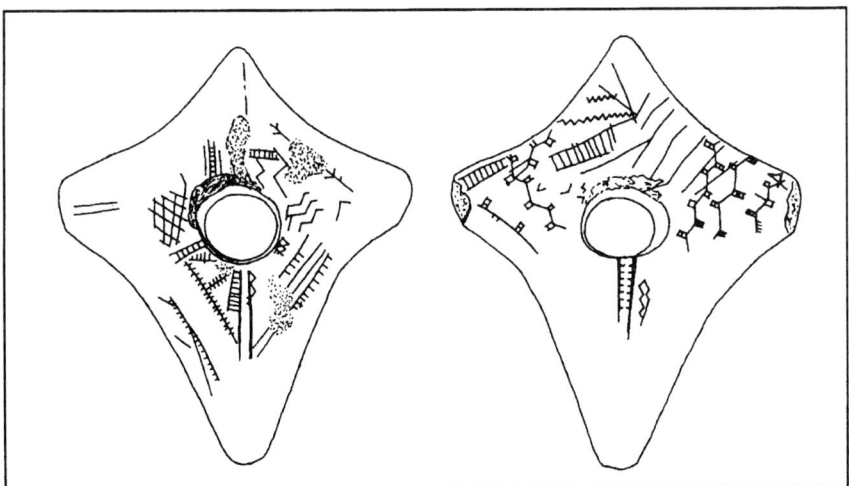

Fig. 11. Star-shaped mace-heads decorated with ladders, net-patterns and zigzags, the latter similar to the rock art motif shown in Fig. 9 (After Bakka 1973).

Fig. 12. A female representation with arms and legs shaped like zigzags (Photo: G. Mandt).

ple zigzags (Fig. 12). A connection between deer and snakes has been reported both in European literary texts and myths (Fig. 13) and in material culture from prehistoric and early historic times (Mandt 1996; Storm 1995:219). Worldwide the snake appears as an ambiguous symbol, encompassing both positive and negative qualities. Due to its hibernation periods and the shedding of its skin the snake is often associated with death and renewal, and therefore an important fertility symbol (Gimbutas 1989:121).

This brief survey of the motifs at Vingen indicates that the animal and human representations as well as the abstract-geometric motifs may be explained as expressions of female and fertility symbolism, accentuating aspects of life-death-rebirth. Instead of focusing on "Man-the-Hunter" and his hunting-related activities, the perspective has been shifted to an overall social and ideological explanation of the site. The red deer are no longer looked upon exclusively as prey animals and food supply. They have been "transformed" into

216 *Gro Mandt*

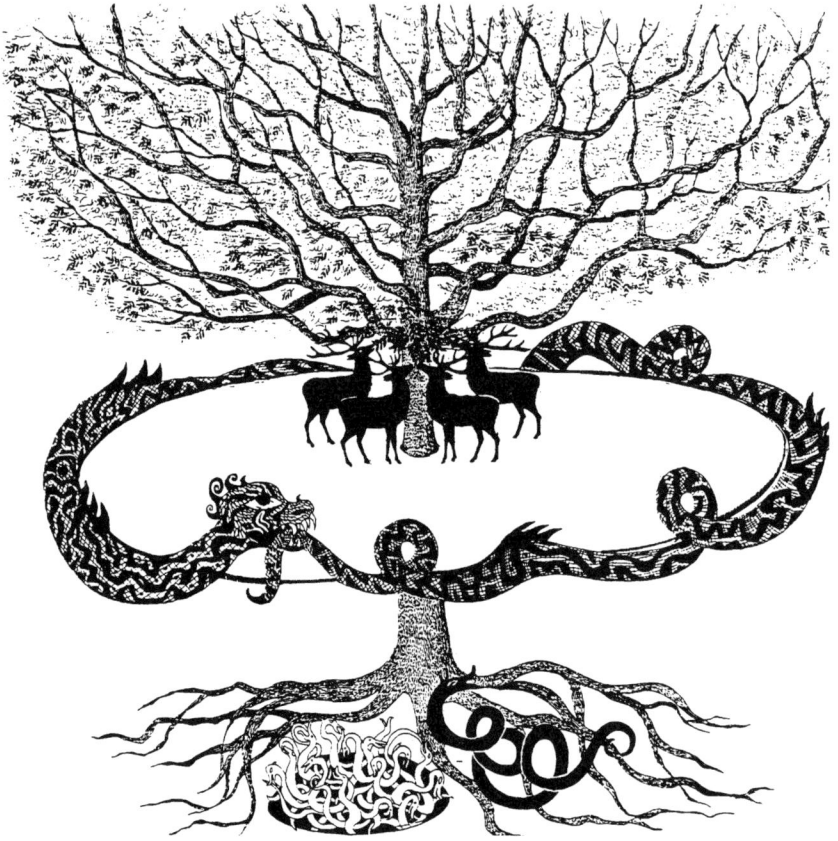

Fig. 13. A visualization of the Norse cosmology known from myths written down in the 11th century AD, but relating traditions several hundred years older. The World Tree—*Yggdrasil*—grows from the underworld, through the realm of the living and reaches into the firmament. A giant snake—*Midgardsormen*—encircles the realm of the living and keeps chaos at bay. Another snake gnaws at the roots of the World Tree, while four deer eat at its leaves (Drawing: E. Hoff.).

central symbols in the cosmology of the community, and are seen as metaphors for cyclical renewal, sexual love, vitality, and supernatural heroic women and men (Storm 1995:252f.).

Vingen Reviewed: Context and Combinations

The impression of Vingen as a site for rituals concerned with fertility and the reproduction of society is emphasized when the combination of the motifs and their spatial distribution are taken into consideration.

In order to carry out a contextual and spatial analysis of the vast body of rock pictures at Vingen, I have divided the area into sections, based on topographical characteristics (Fig. 14). Within each section I have studied the combination of motifs on the various panels, in relation to a typological-chronological sequence of the deer representations previously established by Bakka (1973). He has identified four main animal types, which represent stages in the production of rock art at Vingen (Fig. 15). I have made a preliminary classification of the human representations, and studied the distribution patterns of the various motifs and motif combinations within the overall Vingen space.

Most of the carvings at Vingen are found on panels along the southern shore of the narrow fiord. Only a limited number of panels occur on the northern side, on a headland at the mouth of the fiord. The majority of the typologically earliest animal representations occur *in the outermost (western) part of the area,* on the southern side of the fiord, and they are located close to the Mesolithic shoreline. Only a few human representations appear in this topographical section, and they are either neutral or possibly males. The panels in this section, then, appear to be "gender-exclusive", including only or primarily potential males. Only few abstract-geometric motifs are found in this context.

In *the central part of the area* the two "middle" types of deer occur, together with a variety of abstract-geometric motifs and human representations, a majority of which can be identified as women. Since both females and males appear in this topographical section, it should be classified as "gender-inclusive". However, a closer examination of the various panels may reveal variations within this central area.

In *the innermost (eastern) part of the area* is a foaming waterfall originating in the mountains, which is the natural habitat of the red deer. In this section the later type of deer occurs most frequently. Only a few human representations are found, none of them indisputably male. This possibly indicates that the section is "gender-exclusive": for women only?

Of particular interest in this topographical section is a rock-strewn slope with huge boulders, many of which are decorated with animal figures, a few female and neutral human representations, and various enigmatic abstract-geometric patterns. In between the boulders are a multitude of narrow passages, some decorated with abstract patterns. It is tempting to associate these with passages or tunnels used in initiation rites, imitating the birth canal (e.g. Turner 1967).

At *the headland on the northern side* of the fiord the two later animal type occur most frequently, in combination with some potentially female representations and a few abstract-geometric patterns. In this area too, there are lots of large boulders and rock-strewn slopes. So far no carvings have been found on these rocks, probably because they consist of conglomerate, which is not favourable to pecking. All the other carvings at Vingen occur in sandstone.

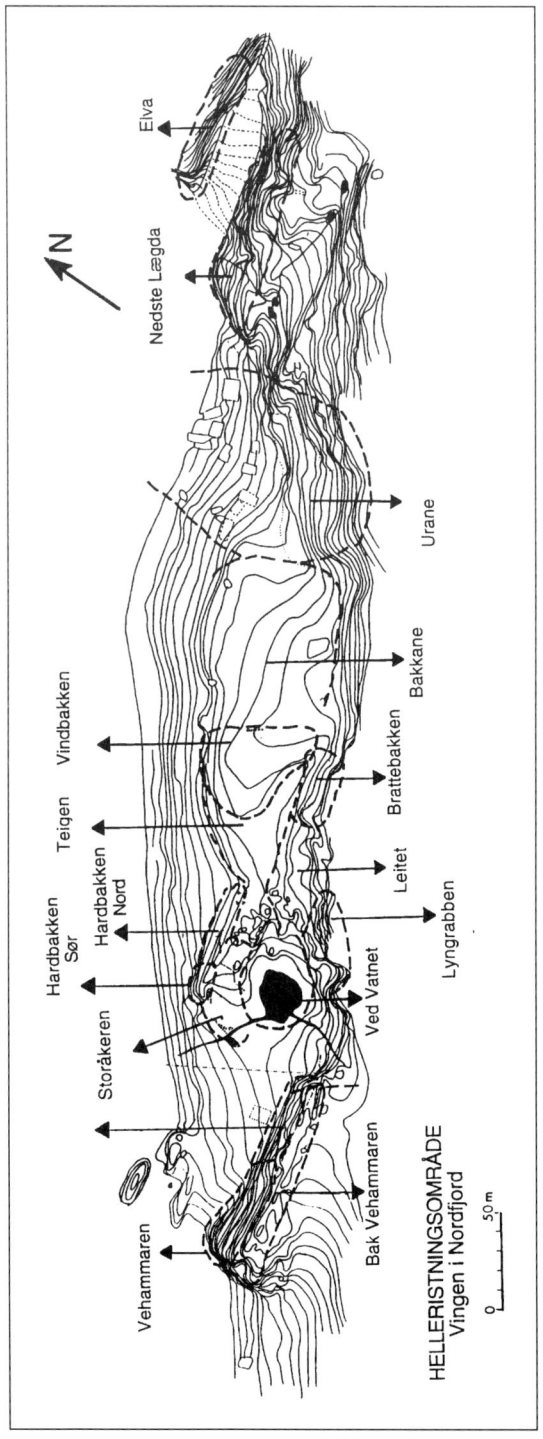

Fig. 14. Map of part of the Vingen rock-art area with the different topographical sections marked.

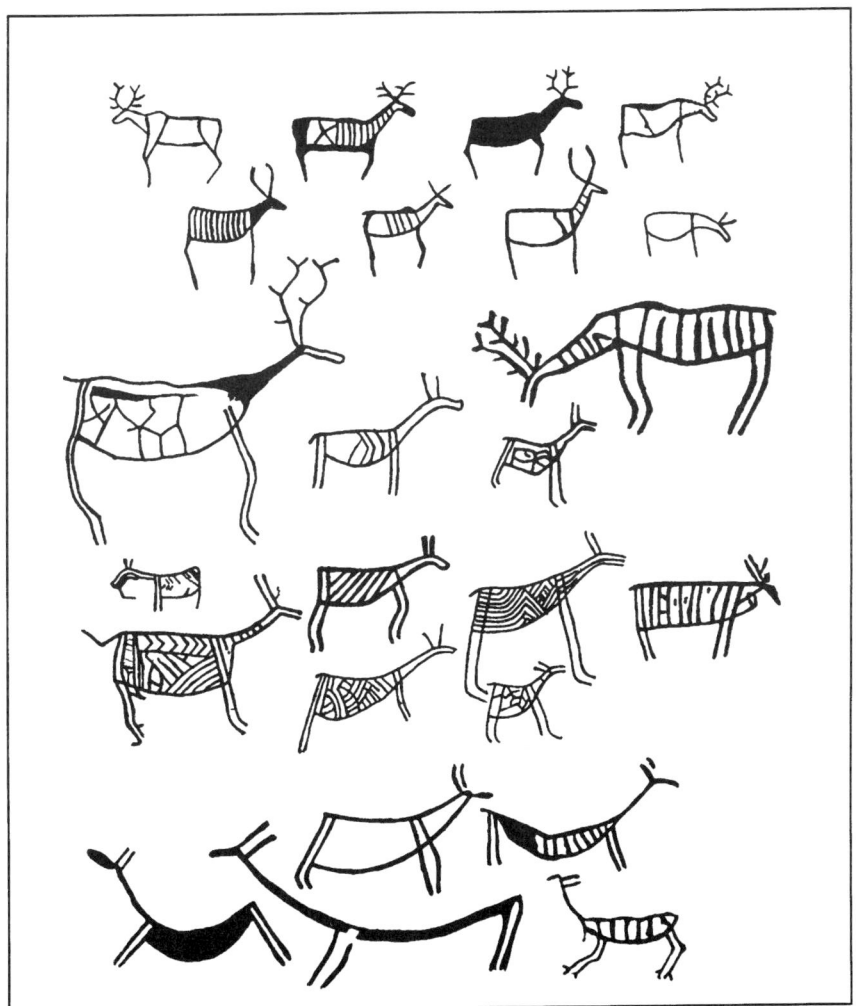

Fig. 15. Egil Bakka's typological-chronological sequence of the deer representations at Vingen. The two upper rows—the "Hammaren" type—represent the earliest stage. The middle rows—the "Hardbakken" and "Brattebakken" types respectively—represent the intermediate stages. The two lower rows—the "Elva" type—represent the latest stage (After Bakka 1973).

My conclusion so far is that the spatial and contextual pattern of the rock carvings indicates a sexual differentiation of the different topographical sections at Vingen. Some loci were reserved for women and their ritual activities, namely, the innermost section, including the rock-strewn slope, and the headland to the north. Other loci were exclusive for men, namely, the outermost sections along the southern shore. Yet others may have been used by both sexes, namely, the central part of the Vingen space. A temporal change in gender relations seems to be involved as well. Human figures in general and the assumed female representations in particular, and also abstract-geometric patterns, occur more sparsely together with the earlier animal figures than with the later ones.

Vingen Reviewed: The Landscape

The multitude and variety of rock pictures, their scattered location along the narrow beach, and their potential time-depth contribute to the impression of Vingen as a very special place. This impression is emphasized by the dramatic landscape: the narrow fiord, the steep and unapproachable mountains. But is the landscape impressive only in a modern, Western sense? Could it be that the landscape itself—the whole scenario of the surroundings—holds the clue to understanding why Vingen was chosen as a site suitable for the production of rock art in the first place?

The concept of "sacred space" is discussed by Mircea Eliade, who demonstrates how it is constituted through hierophanies, and how this again constitutes the world, *cosmos* (1969:13 ff.). The sacred space is a place where the three cosmic levels—earth, heaven and underworld—meet, an opening where transcendence from one cosmic region to another is made possible. This connection may be expressed in different metaphors, such as ladders, trees, mountains, and the like, symbolizing the centre of the world, *axis mundi* (Eliade 1958:375, 1969:23). The sacred space is never "chosen" by men, it is discovered by them, or revealed to them by some divine intervention (ibid. 1958:369). It involves the repetition of the primeval hierophany which consecrated the place by marking it out (Eliade 1958:368).

How, then, is a sacred place revealed? How does the sacred manifest itself to people? According to Eliade the sacredness of a place may be signified by a particular incident which has happened there, by a dream associated with the place, by mythical beings related to the site, by special qualities or characteristics ascribed to it, and so on. (1969:17). When it comes to explaining Vingen as a potential "sacred space" in Eliade's sense of the concept, I will draw attention to two aspects of the landscape which may have characterized it as a powerful and potent place.

In the first place, there is *a large mountain formation,* called Hornelen, which is a most characteristic landmark along this part of the coast (Fig. 1). It towers above the main ships' channel, right across the fiord from Vingen. The easternmost part of the mountain ends in a peak, nearly 1,000 metres high, rising precipitously from the sea. The peak is reported to have been even higher in earlier times, ending in a point or "horn", but this fell down at the turn of the century. It does not seem too far-fetched to suggest that this mountain peak may have constituted *axis mundi*—the centre of the world—reaching literally from the underworld up to the sky.

Even in later periods Hornelen has been considered something special, and also a little awe-inspiring. According to local folklore the witches gathered at the mountain each Midsummer Night. It is tempting to ascribe a long-term tradition to this alleged "use", and see it as a reminiscence of rituals associated with the rock art at Vingen.

Secondly, *the entire layout of the Vingen landscape* may have distinguished the site as something different from the profane world. When approaching Vingen by boat—which is and was the only and "natural" way to get there—the tiny fiord, Vingepollen, is not visible from a distance. As one comes closer, however, an opening appears between the mainland to the south and the headland to the north. One has the feeling of passing through a "gate", of being let into a secluded, almost secret, and rather awe-inspiring, space: the narrow fiord surrounded by the steep hillsides, and, at the bottom of the fiord, the waterfall cascading from the high mountains. The whole scenario could be construed as a hierophany, as nature's representation of the female body: the narrow fiord imitates the birth canal between the woman's "thighs"—the hillsides—and the water of life is streaming from above. And in clear view from the enclosed Vingen space is Hornelen, its peak (like a phallos) stretching right into the firmament.

A further investigation of the distribution of specific motifs and motif combinations, as well as a more thorough analysis of the landscape, may throw light on how the various panels and special environments within the overall Vingen area were used through time. However, I will not at this stage draw any further conclusions about the implications of temporal variations in gender relations and gender symbolism, as seen in the rock art. This calls for an indepth analysis of the rock art in relation to the contemporary society, and such an analysis is now in progress at the University of Bergen, conducted by Eva M. Walderhaug.

Concluding Remarks

Throughout the history of archaeological research various attempts at explaining rock art have been put forward, influenced by the shifting theoretical trends of the discipline. The researchers are of necessity children of their own time, and their inferences have been based on their own social, political and ideological background, and—not least—their gender.

Within the realm of material culture rock art holds a special position. It conveys not only the material aspects of a society, but spiritual values and human interrelations as well. Embedded in the rock pictures are ideas and beliefs that were important for maintaining the social order and reproduction of the community. This does not imply that all rock-art sites were necessarily "sacred" in a modern, Western notion of the concept. There is probably not one single explanation that fits all rock-art sites, but a variety of different usages may be discerned. Some sites may have functioned in initiation rites, for women and men respectively, and these may have been secret or "sacred" places. Other sites may have served the purpose of educating the young in the customs and traditions of their society. Others, again, may have been used in communal rituals where the purpose was to create a sense of group solidarity and unity. Whatever the purpose of the different sites, it is my assumption that one of the most important "messages" of rock art relates to gender ideology and the potential conflicts and negotiations between women and men.

References

Arsenault, D. 1991. The Representation of Women in Moche Iconography. In Walde, D. & Willows, N. D. (eds.), *The Archaeology of Gender: Proceedings of the 22nd Annual Chacmool Conference*, 313–326. Calgary.
Bakka, E. 1973. Om alderen på veideristningane. *Viking 37*, 151–187.
— 1975. Geologically dated Arctic rock carvings at Hammer near Steinkjer in Nord-Trøndelag. *Arkeologiske skrifter. Historisk museum. Universitetet i Bergen*, 2, 7–48. Bergen.
— 1979. On Shoreline Dating of Arctic Rock Carvings in Vingen, Western Norway. *Norwegian Archaeological Review*, 12:2, 115–122.
Bertelsen, R. , Lillehammer, A. & Næss, J.-R. (eds.). 1987. *Were they all men? An examination of sex-roles in prehistoric society*. AmS-Varia 17. Stavanger.
Bøe, J. 1932. Felszeichnungen im westlichen Norwegen I. Vingen und Henn øya. *Bergens Museums Skrifter* 15. Bergen.
Brøgger, A. W. 1925. *Det norske folk i oldtiden*. Oslo.
Claassen, C. 1992. Questioning Gender: An Introduction. In Claassen, C. (ed.), *Exploring Gender Through Archaeology: Selected Papers from the 1991 Boone Conference*, 1–10. Monographs in World Archaeology. Madison.
Conkey, M. W. 1991. Does it Make a Difference? Feminist Thinking and Archaeologies of Gender. In Walde, D. & Willows, N. D. (eds.), *The Archaeology of Gender: Proceedings of the 22nd Annual Chacmool Conference*, 24–34. Calgary.
Conkey, M. W. & Gero, J. M. 1991. Tensions, Pluralities, and Engendering Archaeology: An Introduction to Women in Prehistory. In Gero, J. M. & Conkey, M. W. (eds.), *Engendering Archaeology: Women in Prehistory*, 3–30. Cornwall.
Conkey, M. W. & Spector, J. D. 1984. Archaeology and the Study of Gender. In Schiffer, M. B. (ed.), *Advances in Archaeological Method and Theory* 7. New York.
Drew, J. 1991. Women and Gender Relations in Australian Aboriginal Rock Art. Unpubl. B.A. thesis. University of Sydney.
— 1995. Depictions of women and gender relations in Aboriginal rock art. In Balme, J. & Beck, W. (eds.), *Gendered archaeology: The second Australian Women in Archaeology Conference*. ANH Publications. RSPAS. Canberra, 105–113.
Eliade, M. 1958. *Patterns in Comparative Religion*. London.
— 1961. *Images and symbols*. London.
— 1969. *Det hellige og det profane*. Oslo.

Engelstad, E. 1991. Images of Power and Contradiction: feminist Theory and Post-processual Archaeology. *Antiquity 65*, 502.
Gero, J. M. 1983. Gender Bias in Archaeology: A Cross-Cultural Perspective. In Gero, J. M., Lacy, D. & Blakey, M. L. (eds.), *The Socio-Politics of Archaeology*. Amherst: University of Massachusetts. Department of Anthropology. Research Report 23, 51–57.
Gero, J. M. & Conkey, M. W. 1991. (eds.), *Engendering Archaeology. Women in Prehistory*. Cornwall.
Gimbutas, M. 1989. *The Language of the Goddess*. London.
— 1991. *The Civilization of the Goddess: The World of Old Europe*. London.
Gjessing, G. 1936. *Nordenfjeldske ristninger og malinger av den arktiske gruppe*. Instituttet for sammenlignende kulturforskning. Serie B. 30. Oslo.
Hagen, A. 1969. Studier i vestnorsk bergkunst. Ausevik i Flora. *Årbok for Universitetet i Bergen*. Humanistisk serie 3.
Hallström, G. 1938. *Monumental Art of Northern Europe from the Stone Age: The Norwegian Localities*. Stockholm.
Harding, S. 1986. *The Science Question in Feminism*. Milton Keynes.
— 1991. *Whose Science? Whose Knowledge? Thinking from Women's Lives*. Milton Keynes.
Helskog, K. 1993. Fra tvangstrøyer til 90-åras pluralisme i helleristningsforskning. In Prescott, C. & Solberg, B. (eds.), *Nordic Tag. Report from the third Nordic TAG conference 1990*. Historisk museum, Universitetet i Bergen, 70–75.
Hesjedal, A. 1990. Helleristninger som tegn og tekst. En analyse av veideristningene i Nordland og Troms. Unpublished M.A. thesis. University of Tromsø.
— 1994. The Hunters' Rock Art in Northern Norway. Problems of Chronology and Interpretation. *Norwegian Archaeological Review*. 27:1, 1–14.
Hodder, I. 1991. Gender Representation and Social Reality. In Walde, D. & Willows, N. D. (eds.), *The Archaeology of Gender. Proceedings of the 22nd Annual Chacmool Conference*, 11–16. Calgary.
Larsson, T. B. 1986. *The Bronze Age Metalwork in Southern Sweden: Aspects of Social and Spatial Organization*. Papers in Northern Archaeology. Archaeology and Environment 6. Umeå.
di Leonardo, M. (ed.). 1991. *Gender at the Crossroads of Knowledge: Feminist Anthropology in the Postmodern Era*. Berkeley.
Lewis-Williams, D. 1981. *Believing and seeing: Symbolic meanings in Southern San rock paintings*. New York.
Lewis-Williams, D. & Dowson, T. A. 1988. The Signs of All Times: Entoptic Phenomena in Upper Paleolithic Art. *Current Anthropology* 29:2, 201–245.
Mandt, G. 1991. Vestnorske ristninger i tid og rom. Kronologiske, korologiske ogkontekstuelle studier. Bd. 1–2. Unpublished Dr. Philos. thesis. University of Bergen.
— 1996. Material culture and myth: snake symbolism in Nordic prehistory. *K.A.N. Kvinner i arkeologi i Norge*. 21, 33–50.
Mézec, B. 1989. A Structural Analysis of the Late Stone-Age Petroglyphs at Vingen, Norway. Unpubl. dissertation. University College, London.
Moore, H. L. 1986. *Space, Text and Gender: An Anthropological Study of the Marakwet of Kenya*. Cambridge.
Prescott, C. & Walderhaug, E. M. 1995. The last frontier? Processes of Indo-Europeanization in Northern Europe. The Norwegian case. *The Journal of Indo-European Studies* 23. 3 & 4, 257–280.
Reiter, R. R. (ed.) 1975. *Toward an Anthropology of Women*. New York.
Rosaldo, M. Z. & Lamphere, L. (eds.) 1974. *Women, Culture and Society*. Stanford.

Russel, P. 1991. Men Only? The Myths About European Paleolithic Artists. In Walde, D. & Willows, N. D. (eds.), *The Archaeology of Gender: Proceedings of the 22nd Annual Chacmool Conference*, 246–351. Calgary.

Slocum, S. 1975. Woman the Gatherer: Male Bias in Anthropology. In Reiter, R. R. (ed.), *Toward an Anthropology of Women*, 36–50. New York.

Sørensen, M. L. S. 1992. Gender Archaeology and Scandinavian Bronze Age Studies. *Norwegian Archaeological Review*. 25, 1, 31–49.

Storm, L. 1995. *The Hind Game—seen in the light of European cervine tradition*. Bergen.

Turner, V. 1967. *The Forest of Symbols: Aspects of Ndembu Ritual*. Ithaca.

Vinsrygg, S. 1979. Reiskapar til sanking/primitivt jordbruk? Analyse av steinkøller med bora hol frå Rogaland. *Viking* 42, 27–68.

— 1987. Sex-roles and the division of labour in hunting-gathering societies. In Bertelsen, R., Lillehammer, A. & Næss, J.-N. (eds.), *Were they all men? An examination of sex roles in prehistoric society*, 23–32. AmS-Varia 17. Stavanger.

Walde, D. & Willows, N. D. (eds.). 1991. *The Archaeology of Gender. Proceedings of the 22nd Annual Chacmool Conference*. The Archaeological Association of the University of Calgary.

Walderhaug, E. M. 1994. "Ansiktet er av stein". Ausevik i Flora—en analyse av bergkunst og kontekst. Unpublished M.A. thesis. University of Bergen.

— 1995. Rock Art and Society in Neolithic Sogn og Fjordane. In Helskog, K. & Olsen, B. (eds), *Perceiving Rock Art: Social and Political Perspectives*. Institute for Comparative Research in Human Culture. Novus.

Man-Made Boundaries of World Views
Long-Distance Ramparts
By Torsten Capelle

Introduction

Just as the Berlin Wall in modern times, as a part of the Iron Curtain, was a border between cultures or at least between two different political systems—almost without any possibility of a passage through from the east—there were a great many long-distance demarcation lines especially during the Iron Age which in some cases may even have looked similar to the Berlin Wall. But not all of them had the same function, as will be shown in the following.

Other long-distance borders of more recent times, with a similar appearance, which should be identifiable by later archaeologists are the different forms of noise barriers along motorways—separating noise from silence. And of course the impressive coastal dykes dating from the medieval period and those built up to the present must be mentioned—separating water from the mainland or islands, and indeed for non-swimmers forming the borders of their world.

But here we have to deal with the long-distance ramparts dating from the Iron Age. These are the largest prehistoric monuments on earth. They were planned by authorities and raised with enormous manpower. Often they were built with such a height and such dimensions that their remnants are still visible along their entire length. Two main forms can be distinguished throughout the centuries: single permanent defence lines connecting two points on the one hand, and enclosures of large areas on the other hand.

Enclosures

From the late medieval period in central Europe countless territorial boundaries of dioceses, counties, townships or other zones are known from contemporary written sources and evident in the landscape (cf. Grimm 1958). Normally they consist of one to three parallel earthen ramparts which were surmounted by a very dense hedgerow. These lines were supposed to make passage more difficult or even impossible. Such medieval constructions had merely a minor defensive character. Their main purpose was rather to enable easier tax-collecting at the gates.

A similar controlling effect was produced by broad wasteland zones with bushes, shrubs and forest instead of linear earthworks. Such zones surrounded settlement areas of Germanic tribes in the Roman Iron Age (Capelle 1971:11). They are identifiable on distribution maps and were reported by contemporary authors such as Caesar, Tacitus and Mela. Above all these guarded zones were to secure the rural settlements from sudden attacks by neighbouring peoples.

Comparable to these zones is the Heidengraben on the outer hills of the Black Forest in south-western Germany, which dates from the Latène period (Fischer 1971). The Heidengraben encloses an area of 1,662 hectares, that is, more than six square miles. Here the area is not completely secured by ramparts. Sometimes natural topographical features were used in parts of its construction, as for example deep valleys. The Heidengraben was not an oppidum in the common sense, because it surrounded a whole settlement area which isolated itself from the rest of the Celtic world.

Some Scythian fortifications are even larger, namely the Gorodisce from Bel'sk in the forest-steppe (Rolle 1980:124 ff.). Here a 33 km long rampart enclosed an area of nearly 4,000 hectares to secure settlement places, as well as pasturelands, so all activities throughout the year including the important cattle-breeding could be done in peace and without violent surprises.

Finally we have a reference to an immense mythological enclosure. It is Snorri himself who tells us in the *Edda* that even the northern Gods intended to surround their territory named Asgard by a strong defensive rampart so that the giants could not enter and do any harm (Page 1990:20 f.).

Some of these more or less ring-shaped constructions may have been real fortifications. But as they could not be manned completely and were not particularly high, they mostly just marked borderlines between neighbouring areas and separated districts from each other with throughpasses at special gates. So territories of some thousand hectares were enclosed but not completely sealed off.

Dykes

More efficient than real borders, in contrast to these enclosures, were long-distance linear ramparts running in one direction with a beginning and an end, and bounding whole countries or regions of power. These sometimes worked as lines of death where an unauthorizied trespass indeed could be fatal, as these linear earthworks or walls mostly separated nations.

From medieval sources the *Limes Saxoniae* (Fig. 1:2) is known to have stretched from the Elbe near Lauenburg to the Baltic Sea near Kiel, or more than 100 km (Jankuhn 1957:137 ff.). This *limes* included earthworks, forts, rivers, wetlands and even dense forest zones. It was a border between intruding Slavonic peoples coming from the south-east and the Saxons in Holstein. The

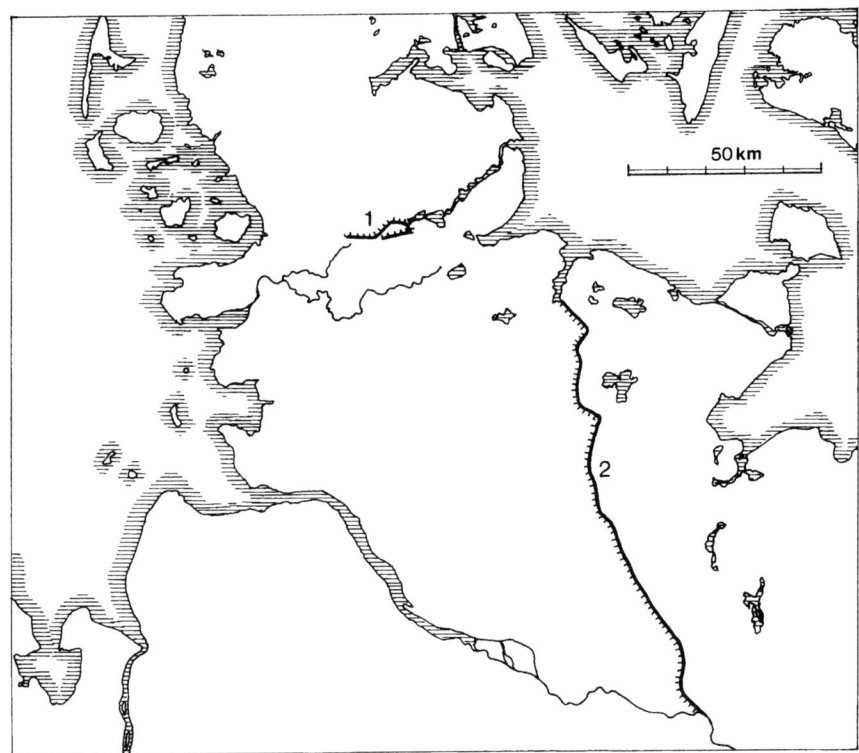

Fig. 1. 1 The Danewerk, 2 *Limes Saxoniae*.

Limes Saxoniae must have worked well for a long time because cultural and material exchange between both peoples was minimal, as archaeological investigations indicate.

More impressive as an architectural structure is the well known Danewerk (Fig. 1:1) which crosses the Jutish peninsula at a strategically important location with a length of about 14 km at the narrowest place (Andersen 1977). As a link in a larger system it uses rivers and wetlands in the west and the Schlei cutting into the land in the east as prolongations (Fig. 2). The oldest parts are dated by dendrochronology to AD 737, but it was later rebuilt and enlarged several times. Even king Valdemar still boasted of having erected the brick-wall part, which was 3.7 km long and up to seven metres high. The Danewerk was particularly strongly developed under Harald Bluetooth, because it became an important place during his struggles with the German emperor Otto II.

Since then it has always been a powerful symbol of Denmark's independence from the German Empire (Axboe 1995:221 f.). Its military significance is again emphasized by the fact that it was refortified in the middle of the nineteenth century. For the astonishing time of more than one thousand years this

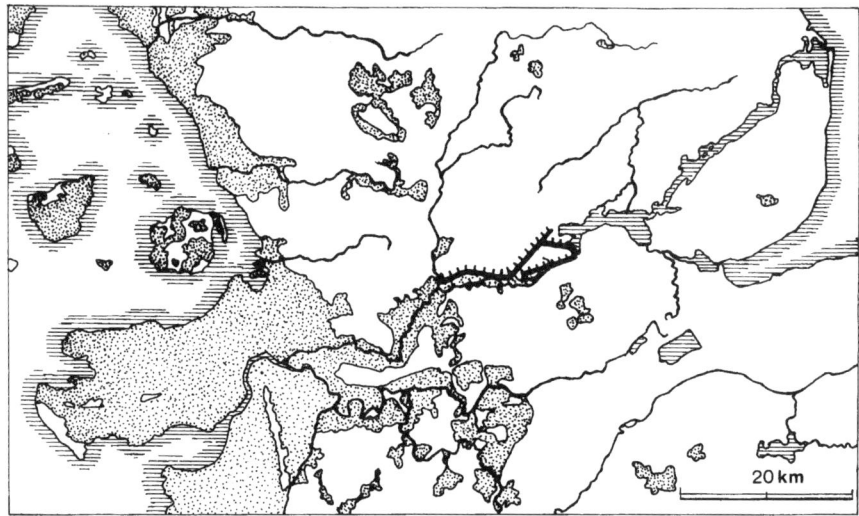

Fig. 2. The Danewerk.

area at the "Schleswig pass" divided German and Danish spheres of power. Even today it is still a border region between the North and the Continent.

In Britain, Offa's Dyke had a similar function (Wormald 1982:120f.). This famous dyke runs from Basingwerk in the north to the Severn in the south (Fig. 3:3) with a length of 192 km or more, including rivers, marshlands, firths and hills. In the ninth century Asser mentions it as "vallum magnum" from sea to sea. It separated the Anglo-Saxon lowlands in England from the Celtic-inhabited highlands in Wales and must have been built by Offa of Mercia to defend his nation against Celtic invaders. For at least two centuries this was successful. At the same time the dyke marked the end of Anglo-Saxon westward expansion, which means that it literally was the end of the Germanic world.

Limites

Even earlier Germanic people on the continent had similar experiences with tribes being separated from one another by long-distance ramparts. Tacitus reports the Angrivarian rampart (Mildenberger 1978:146), now probably identified, with a length of only two kilometres, nearby the Steinhuder Meer in north-western Germany, but prolonged by wetlands and rivers to a total security line of about 20 km. Among the Volkevolde in Denmark the Olgerdige north of the Anglians must also be mentioned, which includes third-century oak palisades dated by dendrochronology in two phases: AD 219 and 278 (Neumann 1982). This dyke may have been an effective military barrier as well as a formal and economic border marker.

Man-made boundaries of world views 229

Fig. 3. 1 Hadrian's Wall, 2 The Antonine Wall, 3 Offa's Dyke.

Best known in Europe of course, is the Roman *Limes* in Germany (Baatz 1974). But the Roman Empire erected limites in other regions as well (Elton 1996), from Palestine in the east and Africa in the south, to Scotland in the north in order to secure their civilization against foreign influences. In such a way they established an inner and an outer world by a firm demarcation line which separated Roman civilization from the barbarians.

The uninterrupted fortification line of the *limes* in Germany has a length of 548 km (Fig. 4). It linked the Rhine and Danube lines with their forts. In most parts this *limes* is made of ditches, ramparts and palisades alone, but in some

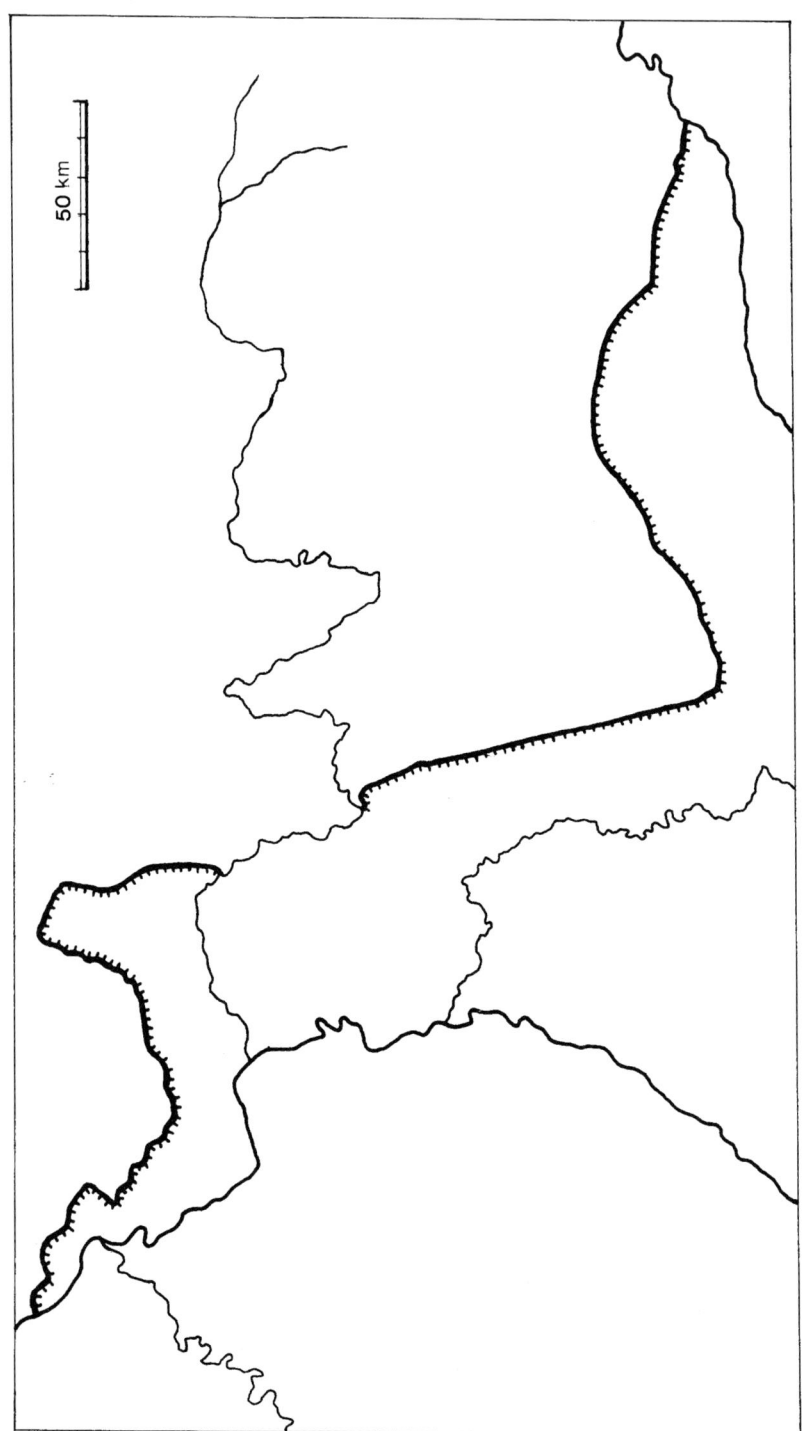

Fig. 4. Limes between the Rhine and the Danube.

parts there is a real stone-built wall up to three metres high. This continental limes was a hindrance with very few passageways and with the permanent effect of frightening strangers away. The Roman culture could reach the regions outside and so it did, but it took centuries until Germanic lifestyle got inside.

How the Romans selected the topographically most suitable areas to erect their limits is best demonstrated by Hadrian's Wall (Fig. 3:1) and the Antonine Wall (Fig. 3:2) in northern Britain (*Hadrian's/Antonine Wall* 1975/1969). In both cases firths which cut far into the land were incorporated. With a minimum of manpower the northern Celtic inhabited zone was cut off from the Romanized south of Britain.

Even some of the long-distance ramparts still visible in Hungary and Romania are supposed to be of Roman origin (Balás 1963). As parts of short-term defensive systems they may have been used later too by Germanic tribes during the Migration Period. But these ramparts have not yet been completely investigated.

The Great Wall

The oldest, the largest and the most impressive example of a completely constructed borderline of course is the Great Wall of China (Zhewen & Luo 1986). This famous wall (Fig. 5) stretches like a snake between the sea in the east and the desert in the west with a total length (considering all parts) of nearly 10,000 km. But the Great Wall was not just one line. Instead, it fell into disrepair, was maintained, enlarged, renewed and even removed several times. Various old walls were neglected and left to ruin, whilst others were kept in constant repair throughout the ages.

The earliest single parts from the sixth century BC were built as earthen ramparts. The first combined long-distance line originates from the Quin dynasty at the end of the third century BC. During the Han dynasty the wall was enlarged at several places from the second century BC to the second century AD. Again it was extensively repaired in the Tang dynasty from the seventh to the ninth century AD. Finally it was transformed into an architectural monument in the Ming dynasty from the fourteenth to the seventeenth century. The modern appearance in most parts dates back to this last enterprise.

The Great Wall does not run in a straight line at any location but often follows hilltops. In contrast to the smaller but comparable European monuments, suitable natural features were included only very rarely. So for centuries the Great Wall was nearly altogether a totally artificially built monument, intended to survive many generations.

Just as the Mississippi in North America marked the boundary between the white mans civilization and the so-called savagery during the nineteenth century, the Great Wall was a far more visible demonstration of power and a

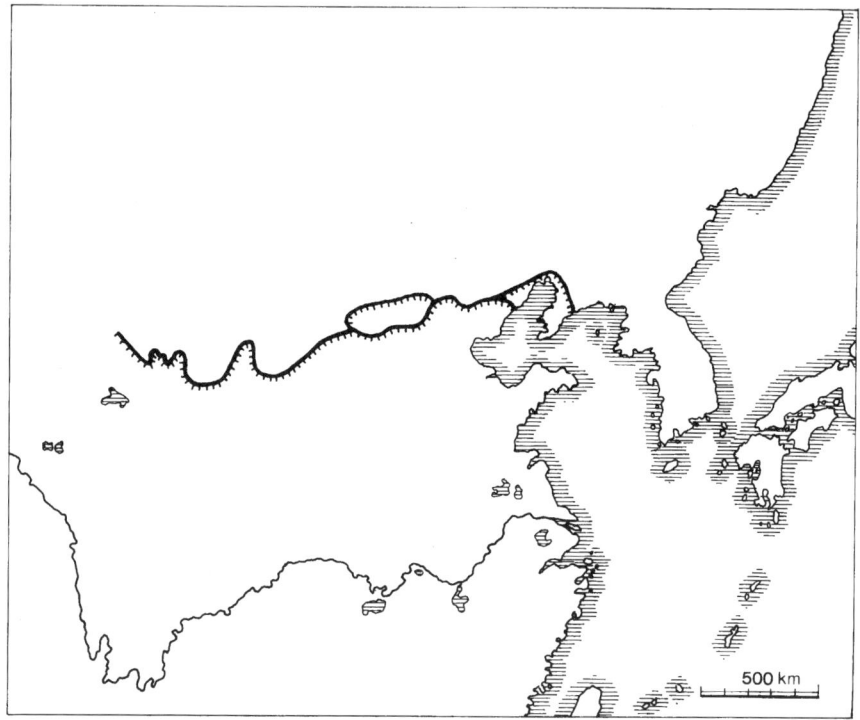

Fig. 5. The main part of the Great Wall of China.

demarcation line between the Chinese civilization in the south and the barbarian nomads in the north. With this dragon-like fortification China marked off itself for a long time from the rest of the world.

The Great Wall is the largest constructional work ever produced by man. The amount of bricks and stones used would be enough for a dyke of one to five metres high around the whole globe.

The reason for building, maintaining and guarding the immense size of this wall curling through and across the mountains was not fear of invasion alone. It was rather fear of foreign influence of all kind. But it worked in both directions, so that China became an isolated world for itself.

Conclusion

Of all the long-distance constructions named here, at least the oldest, i.e. the Great Wall in China, and the youngest, i.e. the Berlin Wall, and perhaps also parts of the Roman European limites as well as Offa's Dyke, *Limes Saxoniae* and the Danewerk, sometimes really made up the ends of a world view created by a deliberate decision of the builders.

References

Andersen, H. 1977. *Jyllands vold.* Copenhagen.
Axboe, M. 1995. Danish Kings and Dendrochronology. In Ausenda, G. (ed.), *After Empire—Towards an Ethnology of Europe's Barbarians,* 221ff. San Marino.
Baatz, D. 1974. *Der römische Limes.* Berlin.
Balás, V. 1963. Die Erdwälle der Ungarischen Tiefebene. *Acta Archaeologica Hungarica* 15, 309ff.
Capelle, T. 1971. *Studien über elbgermanische Gräberfelder in der ausgehenden Latènezeit und der älteren römischen Kaiserzeit.* Hildesheim.
Elton, H. 1996. *Frontiers of the Roman Empire.* London.
Fischer, F. 1971. *Der Heidengraben bei Grabenstetten.* Stuttgart.
Grimm, P. 1958. *Die vor- und frühgeschichtlichen Burgwälle der Bezirke Halle und Magdeburg.* Berlin.
Hadrian's/Antonine Wall. 1975/1969. Ordnance Survey maps. London.
Jankuhn, H. 1957. *Die Frühgeschichte: Geschichte Schleswig-Holsteins* 3. Neumünster.
Mildenberger, G. 1978. *Germanische Burgen.* Münster.
Neumann, H. 1982. *Olgerdiget—et bidrag til Danmarks tidligste historie.* Haderslev.
Page, R. I. 1990. *Norse Myths.* London.
Rolle, R. 1980. *Die Welt der Skythen.* Luzern.
Wormald, P. 1982. The Age of Offa and Alcuin. In Campbell, J. (ed.), *The Anglo-Saxons,* 101–128. Oxford.
Zhewen, L. & Luo, Z. 1986. *Chinas Grosse Mauer.* Beijing.

The Mutilated Image
"We" and "They" in History—and Prehistory?
By Carl Nylander

A couple of years ago a student entered Akademiska Föreningen in Lund not to have a cup of coffee or to chat with his girl friend but to cover the face of King Charles XII and his sister with white spray (Fig. 1). At about the same time another student slashed the brand new painting of Princess Diana in the National Gallery in London with a knife, and in Washington D.C. a visitor to the Museum of American art looked at Winslow Homer's well known "The Visit of the old Mistress" to her former slave family and destroyed her face (Freedberg 1985 & 1989). Can such strange happenings be meaningfully connected with the problems of "world view of ancient man", historic or prehistoric? I believe they might.

In a chapter on "Primitive World View and Civilization" Robert Redfield writes that "it is probably safe to say that among the groupings of people in every society are always some that distinguish people who are my people, or are more my people, from people who are not so much my people. The *We-they* difference, in some form, arranges the human elements on the universal stage." (Redfield 1963:92 f.). Such a basic polarity of *We* and *they* probably always will have been a structural and structuring fact of life and action on that grand stage and, consequently, it will also have been an important part of any "world view" of ancient man. Many strategies, ideological and practical, will have been elaborated to strengthen and enforce the *We*-dimension and, as far as possible, to contain and control the *they*-aspect. Whether inside a group or society or between groups and societies, such a *We-they*-relation will mostly have been assymetric and inegalitarian, based on assumed or real superiority, in origins or race or lineage or closeness to the gods, in morals, power, status or authority, superiority more or less subtle and unseen or crudely manifest and tangible. Its expressions, in the past as well as in the present, will have been manifold though for the archaeologist less easy to document and analyze than for the social anthropologist. Yet we are beginning to have some insight into the possibilities as well as the complexities of the so called "archaeology of social relations" and of the "archaeology of power" (Herring *et al.* 1991).

Material manifestations of superiority and power and of resulting inequality are often found in the archaeological record. To the archaeologist of hierarchi-

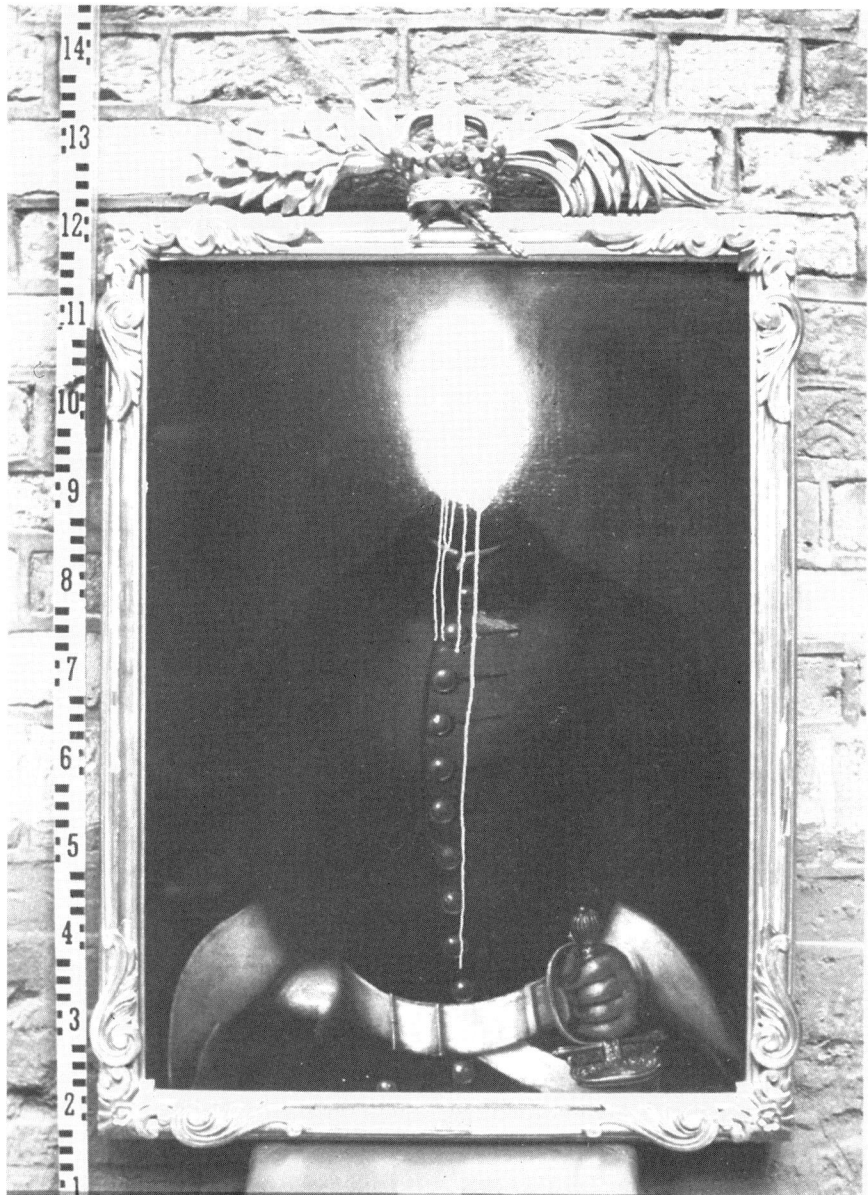

Fig. 1. Charles XII. Akademiska Föreningen. Lund.

cal, urbanised societies the *We*'s tend to become those who have spoken with the louder voice, while as to *they* their material silence makes them harder to perceive; with Brecht: "die im Schatten sieht man nicht". The *We*'s, the vociferous victors, the powerful and the upperhands, have achieved a high visibility by eloquently stating "their case", either through ample display of status and surplus or by means of triumphal or propagandistic words or images. Less easy is finding out how such *We-they* dialectics were felt and lived by the *they*'s, by the victims and the vanquished, by the underdogs the unprivileged, by the marginal barbarians, who were often demeaningly depicted just as such by the victorious *We*'s. It is my purpose here briefly to discuss a possible way somehow redress the balance and to learn more about the reactions and feelings of those elusive *they*'s, the people in the shadow, who often share, as it were, in a kind of "prehistoric" condition in the sense that they mostly lived without writing and left no words for us to use in the old sense of the Roman law: *audiatur et altera pars*—let us hear also the other side!

The Mutilated Image

My starting point is the damaged, fragmentary state of much, or even most of ancient art that has come to us. This has mostly been ascribed to the ravages of time and attrition or, occasionally, to vandalism. Such fragmentation has thus been of scant interest to scholars as caused, apparently, by forces more related to nature or to psycho-pathology than to history. I believe, on the contrary, that such damage to ancient art was not rarely intentional and functional and that selective mutilation of art may be a *We-they* statement in reverse, sometimes even a "language", that can, at least in part, be deciphered. This seems to be true for quite some art from historical periods and stratified societies. It is an interesting problem whether similar phenomena can be observed also in prehistoric contexts. And if not, why?

Let us first look at three assumptions that underlie my argument.

First: art is communication and message. When an old Oriental statue was finished in the workshop there occurred a ceremony called "the opening of the mouth" (Jacobsen 1987). This was a magical enabling the statue to convey the patron's or donor's message to the gods of the upper or nether worlds or to whomever else concerned. The statue thus had a *message*. In a sense, the statue itself *was* the message which was expressed by means of particular combinations of iconographic symbols. Not rarely the message was made more explicit by means of an inscription on the statue itself or on its base. This messenger aspect of ancient monumental art has long been neglected. Today however, to a generation all too familiar with the manipulation of the media by "hidden persuaders" and mindful of Umberto Eco's dictum that "all cultural processes are 'processes of communication'", there is a growing interest in the communicative, propagandistic, messenger function of ancient public art, the dominant medium of the times, as well as in the subsequent question as to how those messages were received and understood (Hölscher 1984, 1987).

Secondly, what were those messages? The question is fundamental but complex. But we may safely say that much or most of ancient oriental and classical, major art had particula functions that could be termed "ideological", "status expressive", "political" or "propagandistic". It is art produced, often by anonymous craftsmen, on behalf of patrons in power and in control of society's resources in order to reflect and make more explicit their status, their achievements and their pretensions. Even when such people turn to the gods with votive gifts in much visited sanctuaries or when they elaborate their tombs and those of their family, the piety theme has a counterpoint in a more or less obvious show off and status propaganda, a conveying of messages of power and prestige to rivals within the broader, competing *We* group, and also to the multitude of the powerless *they*.

Thirdly, a central issue is obviously the notion of power. Power means pressure, and an excess of power will easily produce counter-pressure of some kind, ranging from silent and sullen opposition to open rivalry, revolt or revolution. One very particular type of reaction to the authority and domination of the powerful has always been to ridicule, to mutilate or to destroy their messages of status, power and intimidation as expressed by public art or, perhaps better, art in public, a reaction witnessed not least all over eastern Europe as recently as 1991 and after (Warnke 1973; Bredekamp 1975).

But there is more to this than just ridicule, haphazard nocking off of noses or impulsive overturning and destruction of public sculpture (Reuterswärd 1962; Bahrani 1995). The ancient view of the particular relation between certain types of art and the human reality depicted is crystallized in two well-known passages by St. Basil and Artemidorus: "The honour rendered to the image passes to the prototype" (*De Spiritu Sancto* XVIII,45) and the negative inversion "There is no difference whether you trample or hit the emperor himself or his image." (*Onirocriticon* IV,31). Image and prototype are thus to some extent "identical" and what happens to the image somehow affects or reflects on the prototype/sender. I therefore believe that the fragmented, mutilated state of much ancient art may then, at times, be explained as the consequence of a wilful, purposive reaction to those provocative messages of power and persuasion expressed by the particular iconography, by the precious material and by the prestigious setting of the work of art. A close look at the detailed pattern of damage found on ancient sculpture may thus reveal something of otherwise elusive problems such as the nature of its message and the way this was received and reacted upon by the recipients. As we will see, the partial mutilation of a messenger of power may have a precise semiotic function and become a negation of the original statement, a *counter*-message. The resulting palimpsest character of message and superimposed *counter*-message may then add something to our understanding of the dialectics of power and anti-power, of the interaction of the *We*'s and the *they*'s.

Noseless in Nineveh

My brief demonstration of the potential of this way to look at damage on ancient sculpture begins far away. In August in the year 612 B.C., when Tarquinius Priscus, the Etruscan, reigned in Rome and when the Scandinavians enjoyed their incipient Iron Age, a momentous event in the distant Near East saw the dramatic end of the old and much-hated empire of the Assyrians (Zawadzki 1988). Its evil capital Nineveh fell to the onslaught of a coalition of Medes, Babylonians and Elamites who, after much plundering and triumphal feasting, eventually destroyed the city. But before doing so, the conquerors toured the royal palaces and looked very carefully at the splendid series of bas-reliefs with scenes of hunting, war and victory, now in the basement of the British Museum (Barnett & Lorenzini 1975). And the victors reacted to these pictorial chronicles of Assyrian heroic toil and triumph in very interesting, telling ways. In scenes particularly hateful to the conquerors crucial figures were singled out and systematically mutilated by well directed and precise strokes of pointed tools (Barnett & Lorenzini 1975: pls. 76, 92, 104, 116, 118, 122, 131; Matthiae 1994:63 ff.). In the great slaughter scene at the Ulai river of 639 B.C., no doubt the most sophisticated representation of a battle in pre-Greek art, the Assyrian soldier who cuts off the head of the Elamite king has had his face hacked away (Fig. 2; cf. Strommenger 1962:Pls. 238, 240). So has the Elamite Quisling and puppet ruler Ummanigash when introduced to his kneeling subjects by an Assyrian officer (Reade 1976). The Elamites thus seem to have destroyed figures who were central in the triumphal depiction of their defeat and humiliation some 25 years earlier. There are several more instances of such selective mutilation in otherwise extremely well preserved scenes: for instance, the hated Sennacherib, the destroyer not only of Lachish but also of Babylon, is mutilated, alone among his many men (Matthiae 1994:fig. II.10).

The most striking case of such selective iconoclasm is the well known, apparently idyllic "garden party" of king Assurbanipal and queen Assur Sharrat under the grape loaden pergola with wine and music, incidentally the very first of thousands of reclining banquet scenes in ancient art (Fig. 3; cf. Strommenger 1962:Pl. 241; Barnett 1976; Dentzer 1982). While the rest of the scene is perfectly well preserved, the face of the king and his right hand with the wine cup have been damaged by pointed chisel strokes. In addition the lower part of the face of his queen has been mutilated. The maltreatment of this peaceful and relaxed scene may, at first sight, seem surprising and unmotivated. But to the enemies the "garden party" was probably the most provocative scene in the entire Nineveh and meant much more than just a festive imbibing of wine at an assumedly relaxed and happy family scene away from the duties of kingship (Nylander 1998). Why?

Fig. 2. Battle at Ulai 631 B.C. Assyrian soldiers, cutting off the heads of the Elamite king and crown prince, have had their heads mutilated.

At first sight the answer may seem easy: no Elamite could remain cold at the sight of defeated and captive Elamite nobles forced to serve the carousing king and queen and, above all, the sight of the severed head of the their king Te-Umman hanging in a tree close by. This fact would be, we might think, enough of a provocation to account for the mutilation of the royal couple. But it does not quite explain why the king's right hand with the cup and the particular act of drinking have been singled out and treated as particularly odious, while the cup of the queen has not been touched. This fact indicates that the gesture of the king holding his wine cup may have had, to the Assyrians and to their enemies, some particular significance.

Gods drinking have long been one of the recurrent, powerful images of the ancient Near East with connotations of sacred marriage, fertility and abundance but also judgement and, probably, the peaceful maintenance of the cosmic order, all basic elements in the world view of oriental man (Dentzer 1982; Michalowski 1994). This motif of exalted drinking of "leicht lebende Götter" was also extended to the gods' representatives on earth, rulers and kings who appear holding a precious vessel, alone, with a woman or at the grand banquet in innumerable images, from miniatures on seals, ivories and drinking bowls to monumental rock reliefs (Reade 1995). They are not rarely coupled with scenes of victory in war, of success in hunting and of piety in temple building,

Fig. 3. The royal couple at the "garden party" and the grape-loaden pergola. Both faces and the king´s rigth hand and the wine cup have been mutilated.

all to be understood as emblems of high moments of the king's stewardship under the gods. The rich potential of the emblem of "the king and the cup" is testified to by its very long life far into the Middle Ages in the poetic imagery of both East and West (e.g. Gabrieli & Scerrato 1979: figs. 44 & 45).

But the significant motif of the king drinking here in Nineveh has a further dimension. We are well aware of the great importance of wine and the vine in the rich and complex symbolism of Near Eastern kingship. Chares of Mytilene and Athenaeus refers to the Persian Great King's bed chamber where "a golden wine, jewel studded, extended over the bed" (*Deipnosophistai* XII, 514). And we may remember the huge golden vine with grape clusters symbolizing Israel hanging down from the ceiling beams of the Temple of Jerusalem (Stendahl 1963). Herodotus (I,108) tells of king Astyages's dream of how a vine grew from the womb of his daughter Mandane and covered the whole of Asia. Through this *somnium imperii* was foretold the advent and rule of Cyrus: the vine is often the tree of life but equally so a symbol of power, kingship and empire. It is surely no coincidence that the Andokides Painter of Athens depicted Heracles's apotheosis through the image of the now immortal hero banquetting on a couch, cup in hand and waited on by Athena, all under a vine rich with clusters of grapes (Fig. 4; Pfuhl 1923:Abb. 265 & 315). And the Etruscan grandees in their eternal subterranean feast were probably also somehow aware of the glorious and high status associations of the vine and grape clus-

Fig. 4. Andokides-Painter (ca. 520/510 B.C.): Heracles feasting under the vine after his *apotheosis*.

ters above their heads(Steingräber 1984:Tavv. 166 & 167). This oriental vision of the "Glückseligkeit des Universalherrschers" under the vine with its many associations had thus rapidly spread far to the west. But recent research has shown that the image of exalted drinking under the grape vine was indeed not a Nineveh invention but had a long oriental past and particularly so in Elam where a number of cylinder seals of the 2nd millennium display ceremonial or cult scenes with divinities and royal couples drinking under a vine rich with grapes (Porada 1990; Aruz 1992:74 f.).

We now understand better why precisely this scene with the drinking cup was thus maltreated: it is obviously a potent emblem of semidivine kingship at its highest level, rich in significance and associations, not least for an Elamite conscious of its Elamite background. To mutilate it on crucial points meant the total negation of its propagandistic Assyrian *We*-message and the superimposition of a counter-message by the new *We*'s, i.e. the former *they*'s. Such a counter-effect is interestingly heightened by the curious mutilation of the lower part of the face of the queen which is intriguingly reminiscent of the Assyro-Babylonian law codes' cruel and demeaning treatment of unfaithful wives by cutting off their lips (Jelitto 1913; Driver & Miles 1955, 1975, index "mutilation"; but cf. Bahrani 1995).

Such selectively destructive reaction to the still painful Assyrian triumphal messages is most probably the explanation for the enigmatic treatment of the splendid royal copper head found in 1931 by Max Mallowan in what was

Fig. 5. Mutilated ruler´s head, Nineveh: one eye, nose and both ears.

probably the same late seventh century Nineveh context (Fig. 5.; Nylander 1980). We note a strange and particular damage pattern oddly contrasting with the otherwise excellent preservation. One eye has been gouged out, the nose has been damaged by a series of right hand blows with a hammer like tool and both ears chiselled off. This curious treatment remained unexplained until seen in the context of the other mutilations just referred to and until the mutilation pattern—one eye, both ears and the nose—was compared to what another Iranian victor did and told less than a hundred years after the fall of Nineveh. In his great trilingual inscription at Behistun from about 520 the Great King Darius tells what he did to two particularly hateful vanquished enemies: "Then I cut off his nose, his two ears, his tounge and blinded one eye of his. He was held in fetters at my gate. All the people could see him. Afterwise I impaled him at Ecbatana." (Kent 1953:124).

The Nineveh and Behistun configuration of mutilation facts and the reasonable conclusions drawn therefrom have a certain paradigmatic value because of the rich and well preserved background context of the selective and rather easily interpreted mutilations. In addition, there is, as we have seen, an important hint of a possible bridge between iconoclastic mutilation of propagandistic art and the demeaning corporeal disfigurements so common among punishments in ancient Near Eastern legal codes (*contra* Bahrani 1995). Such a link constitutes another interesting indication of a semantic precision in the mutilation formulae used on sculpture. And in these very selective mutilations of the old enemy's triumphal messages we do strongly sense, I believe, the cold, calculated fury and the rhetoric of hatred acted out by the long suffering *they*'s.

Wounded in Venice

Leaving aside a good number of similar, though less clear cases of intentional mutilation of sculpture in the Near East (Beran 1988) and an interestingly scarce documentation from Greece and Etruria, we may however briefly note what has happened to the grave stela of a young Athenian noble (Fig. 6) and that the busts of the Etruscan lord and lady in the otherwise extremely well preserved Tomba dei Rilievi at Cerveteri have been destroyed (Richter 1961:figs. 66–68; Steingräber 1984:Tav.1; Blanck 1986:Tav.X.). Let us then move on to Rome. The importance and the strongly political and ideological dimension of Roman public art should make it a promising field for testing the hypothesis of selective mutilation of sculpture as a means of creating propagandistic counter-messages to those intended by the patrons/makers. It is worth while to remember that one Roman term for "making revolution" is *imagines detrahere,* to throw down the images. And amongst the textually documented reactions to public sculpture we find such activities as smashing, braking, dismembring, melting, mutilating, pelting with stones, whipping and

The mutilated image 245

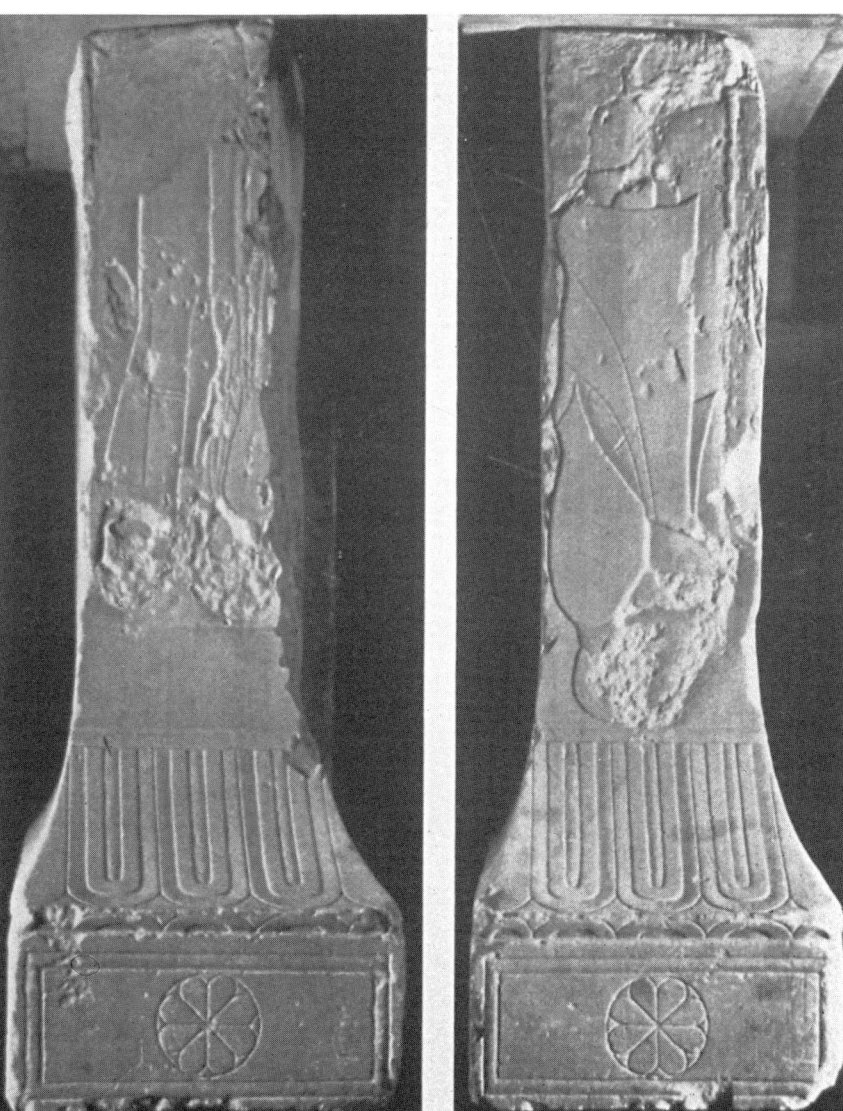

Fig. 6. Attic gravestone (ca. 550 B.C.): mutilated mourners.

scourging, smearing with mud, painting black, urinating and emptying chamber pots on and throwing in the sewers (Lahusen 1984; Gregory 1994). No wonder that public sculpture often had to be guarded. This is then the background atmosphere in which the investigation has to move. Disregarding chronological order we will begin in Venice with what I believe is a good case of the very same thing we have just met in Nineveh. The porphyry Tetrarchs outside San Marco need no presentation, well known and, because of the great

Diocletianus und Maximianus Herculius.

Fig. 7. Tetrarchs (ca. 300 A.D.): noses and imperial fibulae destroyed.

Fig. 8. Mutilated Victories (early 1st cent. B.C.).

hardness of the stone, very well preserved (Fig. 7; Delbrueck 1932:Pls. 31–34). But all four have lost their noses. This, *per se,* may not be significant-it is an ageold pass-time to knock off noses on sculpture just for the fun of it. Matters get serious, however, when we note that the imperial fibulae have also been cut away. In Late Antiquity fibulae denoted rank and hierarchy and had important ceremonial and symbolical functions, and for the very special imperial fibulae there was even a particular, high court charge to handle them, the *praepositus a fibulis*. The iconoclastic combination of nose and imperial fibula becomes highly significant when we consider the great symbolical importance of the fibula and the fact of increasing judicious savagery in Late Antiquity with its numerous physical mutilations, including, above all, the horrible, demeaning *rhinokopía,* the public "cutting off of the nose", practised not much later on pretenders and imperial rivals (Delbrueck 1914; Breckenridge 1981). It is a reasonable guess that somebody in opposition has subjected the stone Tetrarchs to a combined degradation from their imperial rank and a demeaning treatment forever impairing their ability and right to rule.

Moving backwards to Late Republican and Augustan times with their many political tensions, there are a number of interestingly damaged stones which may or may not be relevant here. In ancient iconoclastic contexts it is understandably rare to find mutilated divinities-people's polemics mostly is not with gods but with men. Yet a particular problem is raised by a number of mutilated Late Republican and early Augustan winged Victories (Fig. 8). This is interesting in view of the close and strongly personalized relationship with the god-

Fig. 9. Augustan altar, Carthage: mutilated *Dea Roma.*

dess Victoria claimed, in the 1st. century B.C., by a number of successful generals and politicians, not least by such controversial personalities as Marius and Sulla (Hölscher 1967). There is thus a particular *Victoria Sullana,* Victory of Sulla, a *Victoria Caesaris,* and a *Victoria Augusta* and so on. Such close relationships were then elaborated and propagandistically paraded on the triumphal monuments which, according to our sources, were sometimes destroyed or damaged by adversaries and rivals (e.g. Hölscher 1979, Schäfer 1979). Such an apparent, iconoclastic "war on the Victories" may thus find an explanation in the goddess's particularly strong and very personal relationship with prominent and much hated politicians of the day.

Let us remember, for a moment, Cicero's words: *Difficile est dictu, Quirites, quanto in odio simus apud exteras nationes!*—"It is hard to tell, o Romans, how much we are hated by the foreign nations!". We should therefore raise the question of the situation of Roman monuments in the conquered provinces now ruled by foreign military might and a regime not necessarily much liked. It is not inconceivable that, at times, the inhabitants, the local *they*'s, may have reacted aggressively on the monumental *We*-proclamations or statements of Roman rule, be they official or private. It is thus tempting to note the mutilations on the otherwise fairly well preserved altar of the *gens Augusta* in Tunis (Fig. 9; Poinssot 1929; Kraus 1967:fig. 187). On one side *Dea Roma,* surrounded by a rich array of symbols of the victorious and beneficent rule of

Rome, has had her face mutilated. On the other side the same thing has happened to the head of Aeneas, while his father and son appear to have been spared. The combination *Dea Roma* and Aeneas would make good iconoclastic sense in any context but becomes particularly poignant when we consider the origin of the piece: Rome's former enemy No. One, Carthage, where Aeneas once abandoned Queen Dido to a sad suicide to engender the people and the city of Rome that was eventually to completely destroy the city of Dido and Hannibal. Here, however, some caution is necessary: there are also other mutilations on the monument which may cast doubt on this tempting combination.

On the provincial Trajanic monument celebrating the Dacian War at Adamklissi in Romania the figure of Trajan seems to have had his head mutilated every time he appears, and on the Arch at Orange in France figures have been purposively damaged (Florescu 1965:Abb. 214 & 226; Picard *et al.* 1962:138). However, the precise nature and meaning of such mutilations have yet to be ascertained. Above all, a great many Roman funerary monuments in the provinces show mutilations all of which can hardly be accidental. On their grave stones the faces of legionaries, once proud members of the occupation forces, have often been damaged (Wood 1994:16). And so, not rarely, have the faces of the participants in the funerary banquets, mutilated, maybe, by those who were not invited but who, in the end, had to pay for the feast.

With the examples mentioned, which could be multiplied, I hope to have demonstrated the potential interest and importance of the fragmented, mutilated state of much ancient sculpture and other art. Not rarely may we hear in such damage the voices of the great silent majority of the *they*'s and catch a glimpse of the other side of the coin of history. The mutilated image, carefully and critically studied, may thus become a new, so far neglected historical source and, also, another little key to the world view of man, ancient and modern.

Before *We* and *they*?

This seems to be true for the "the mutilated image" in the historical context of urbanized, hierarchical and polarized societies marked by power and class struggles and of their conflictual "interface" with a more or less "prehistoric" world. But do we find the same kind of evidence and can we apply the same reasoning in the realm of real, deep prehistory?

It is not for me to answer that question. But amongst innumerable representations in prehistoric art of caves and rocks in various continents and countries I have found no trace of a polarity of a human *We-they* -difference, nor of the Mutilated Image. I find instead a homogeneous world of images peaceful rather than conflictual, a world where the *they* seems to become a divine *Thou,* a world dominated by the mystic majesty of the wild animal and by man's harmonious interaction with Nature, hunting and herding, plowing the earth and the sea, worshipping Nature's enigmatic and powerful divine forces, dancing, fighting ritual combats, performing mysterious sacrifices and ceremonies, or joining in that eternal *unio mystica,* the sacred marriage, which, in all world views, is the seed and flower of all life.

In short, is this the reflection of a paradisiac world of innocence before the fatal, devastating discovery of the *We–they* -difference with all its terrible, dehumanizing consequences?

References

Aruz, J. 1992. Seals of the Old Elamite Period. In Harper, P.O., Aruz, J. & Tallon, F. (eds.), *The Royal City of Susa. Ancient Near Eastern Treasures in the Louvre.* New York, 106 120.

Bahrani, Z. 1995. Assault and Abduction: the Fate of the Royal Image in the Ancient Near East. *Art History* 18, 1995, 363 382.

Barnett, R. D. & Lorenzini, A. 1975. *Assyrian Sculpture in the British Museum.* Toronto.

Barnett, R. D. 1976. *Sculptures from the North Palace of Ashurbanipal at Nineveh (668 627 B.C.).* London

Beran, T. 1988. Leben und Tod der Bilder. In Mauer,G. & Magen. U. (eds.), *Festgabe für Karlheinz Deller.* Neukirchen Vluyn, 55–60.

Blanck, H. 1986. *La Tomba dei Rilievi di Cerveteri.* Studi di Archeologia pubblicati dalla Soprintendenza Archeologica per l'Etruria Meridionale 1. Roma.

Breckenridge, J.D. 1981. Again the "Carmagnola". *Gesta* (International Center of Medieval Art) XX, 1–7.

Bredekamp, H. 1975. *Kunst als Medium sozialer Konflikte. Bilderkämpfe von der Spätantike bis zur Hussitenrevolution.* Frankfurt a.M.

Delbrueck, R. 1914. Carmagnola (Porträt eines byzantinischen Kaisers). *Mitteilungen des Kaiserlich Deutschen Archologischen Instituts. Roemische Abteilung,* XXIX, 1914. Rom, 70–89.

Delbrueck, R. 1923. *Antike Porphyrwerke.* Studien zur spätantiken Kunstgeschichte 6. Berlin.

Dentzer, J. M., 1982. *Le Motif du Banquet Couché dans le Proche Orient et le Monde Grec du VIIe au IVe Siècle avant J. C.* Rome.

Driver, G.R. & Miles, J.C. 1952,1955. *The Babylonian Laws* I,II. Oxford.

— 1975. *The Assyrian Laws.* Oxford.

Florescu, F. B. 1965. *Das Siegesdenkmal von Adamklissi Tropaeum Traiani.* Bukarest.

Freedberg, D. 1985. *Iconoclasts and their motives* (The second Gerson Lecture held in memory of Horst Gerson, 1907–1978, in the aula of the University of Groningen on October 7. 1983), Maarsen, Netherlands.

— 1989. *The Power of Images. Studies in the History and Theory of Response.* Chicago.

Gabrieli, F. & Scerrato, U. 1979. *Gli Arabi in Italia. Cultura, contatti e tradizioni.* Milano.

Gregory, A.P., 1994. "Powerful images": responses to portraits and the political uses of images in Rome. *Journal of Roman Archaeology* 7, 80–99.

Herring, E.,.Whitehouse, R.& Wilkins, J. (eds). 1991. *Papers of the Fourth Conference of Italian Archaeology. The Archaeology of Power* 1 & 2. London.

Hölscher, T. 1967. *Victoria romana. Archäologische Untersuchungen zur Geschichte und Wesensart der römischen Siegesgöttin von den Anfängen bis zum Ende des 3.Jhs.n.Chr.* Mainz.

— 1979. Römische Siegesdenkmäler der späten Republik. In Cahn, A. & Simon, E. (eds.), *Tainia. Roland Hampe zum 70. Geburtstag am 2.Dezember 1978 dargebracht.* Mainz, 351–371.
— 1984. *Staatsdenkmal und Publikum. Vom Untergang der Republik bis zur Festigung des Kaisertums in Rom.* Xenia. Konstanzer althistorische Vorträge und Forschungen, Heft 9. Konstanz.
— 1987. *Römische Bildsprache als semantisches System.* Abhandlungen der Heidelberger Akademie der Wissenschaften, Phil. hist. Klasse 1987:2. Heidelberg.
Jacobsen, Th. 1987. The Graven Image. In Miller Jr., P. D., Hanson, P. D. & McBride, S. D. (eds.), *Ancient Israelite Religion: essays in honor of Frank Moore Cross.* Philadelphia, 15–32.
Jelitto, J. 1913. *Die peinlichen Strafen im Kriegs und Rechtswesen der Babylonier und Assyrer.* Breslau.
Kent, R. G. 1953. *Old Persian—Grammar, Text, Lexicon.* New Haven.
Lahusen, G. 1984. *Schriftquellen zum römischen Bildnis I.Textstellen. Von den Anfängen bis zum 3. Jahrhundert n. Chr.* Bremen.
Matthiae, P. 1994. *Il sovrano e l'opera. Arte e potere nella Mesopotamia antica.* Roma.
Michalowski, P. 1994. The Drinking Gods. Alcohol in Mesopotamian Ritual and Mythology. In Milano, L. (ed.), *Drinking in Ancient Societies. History and Culture of Drinks in the Ancient Near East.* Padova, 27 44.
Nylander, C. 1980. Earless in Nineveh: Who Mutilated "Sargon's" Head? *American Journal of Archaeology* 84, 329 333.
— 1988. Imago Mutilata: Iconoclasm as a Counter-language.*Center 8. Research Reports and Record of Activities June 1987 May 1988.* National Gallery of Art. Center for Advanced Study of the Visual Arts. Washington, 73–74.
— 1998. Breaking the King's cup A Note from Nineveh. In *Festschrift David Stronach* (in preparation).
Pfuhl, E. 1923. *Malerei und Zeichnung der Griechen* III. München.
Picard, G. Ch. 1962. In *L'Arc d'Orange.* XVe Supplément à *Gallia.* Paris
Poinssot, L. 1929. *L'Autel de la Gens Augusta à Carthage.* (Notes & Documents publiés par la Direction des Antiquités et Arts.X). Tunis.
Porada, E. 1990. More Seals of the Time of the Sukkalmah. *Revue d'Assyriologie* 84, 171–178.
Reade, J. E. 1976. Elam and Elamites in Assyrian Sculpture. *Archäologische Mitteilungen aus Iran* N.F. 9, 97–106.
— 1995.The *Symposion* in Ancient Mesopotamia: Archaeological Evidence. In Murray, O. & Tecusan, M. (eds.), *In Vino Veritas.* London, 35–56.
Redfield, R. 1963. *The Primitive World and Its Transformations* (7th ed.). Ithaca.
Reuterswärd, P. 1962. De avslagna näsorna. *Kontakt med Nationalmuseum.* Stockholm, 35–40.
Schäfer, T. 1979. Das Siegesdenkmal vom Kapitol. In Horn, H. H. & Rüger, C. H. (eds.), *Die Numider. Reiter und Könige nördlich der Sahara* . Bonn, 243–250.
Steingräber, S. 1984. *Catalogo ragionato della pittura etrusca.* Milano
Stendahl, K. 1963. Vinträdet. *Svenskt Bibliskt Uppslagsverk* II. Stockholm, 1405.
Strommenger, E. 1962. *Fünf Jahrtausende Mesopotamien. Die Kunst von den Anfängen um 5000 v.Chr. bis zu Alexander dem Grossen.*München.
Warnke, M. 1973. *Bildersturm. Die Zerstörung des Kunstwerks.* München.
Wood, M. 1994. *In Search of the Dark Ages.* London
Zawadzki, S. 1988. *The Fall of Assyria and Median-Babylonian Relations in Light of the Nabopolassar Chronicle.* Delft.

Ethnology as Archaeology
By Nils-Arvid Bringéus

Point of departure in Lund

Fifty years ago, when I started to study ethnology at Lund University, only a very small circle of students attended the lectures and took part in the seminars. But Lund was small then, and there were lively contacts with neighbouring subjects. These were of course mainly determined by ties of personal friendship, but they were also channelled through the Ethnological Society.

The society had been founded in 1903 on the initiative of three young scholars, the archaeologist Knut Stjerna (1874–1909), the botanist Johan af Klercker (1866–1929), and the zoologist Hans Wallengren (1864–1938). The first chairman to be appointed was a scholar who already belonged to the establishment, the professor of anatomy Carl Magnus Fürst (1854–1935). The intention was "to bring about an association of people from the subjects of anthropology, ethnography, archaeology, linguistics, and psychology, who had common bonds in their interest in man and human cultural phenomena". According to the statutes, the society was to unite people "in southern Sweden who nourish a scholarly interest in any of the branches of knowledge belonging to the area of ethnology".

There can scarcely be any doubt that Knut Stjerna, despite his youth, was the leading figure in the birth of the Ethnological Association. In his research he combined archaeology, history, literature, philology, and folklore studies. In his doctoral dissertation on Iron Age burials on Bornholm he tried to show how archaeological finds and the Anglo-Saxon epic *Beowulf* could shed light on each other.

There was great enthusiasm when the society was founded. The only one who was sullen about it was Georg Karlin, curator of Kulturen, the Museum of Cultural History in Lund. Twenty years previously he had founded an association with what he felt to be a similar purpose (Bringéus 1992). He therefore declined the invitation to be elected as a member.

The panorama of lectures to the society was broad, to say the least. Professor Fürst could speak about a clay liver with a cuneiform inscription found in Baghdad, Otto Rydbeck about Olaus Magnus. Lauritz Weibull lectured on Finn the Giant in 1905, Evert Wrangel on the oldest Christian cult in Småland,

Martin P:n Nilsson on the origin of coins, Carl Wilhelm von Sydow on Central European farms, Gotthard Gustafsson on "Contributions to the History of the Scanian Farm", to select just a few examples. Martin Nilsson and von Sydow were particularly frequent lecturers, and they also served periods as secretary to the society.

The Ethnological Association was far from being a society for mutual admiration. It should suffice to point out the differences of opinion between C. W. von Sydow and Lauritz Weibull in the interpretation of the legend of Finn, and later on the heavy blows exchanged by von Sydow and Martin P:n Nilsson (Swahn 1996:100 ff.). What united them was evidently a basic positivist stance inspired by the empirical approach and the quest for regularity that characterized the natural sciences. Weibull was an exponent of critical empiricism with a positivist outlook (Torstendahl 1964; Odén 1975). Von Sydow took his own folkloristic taxonomy from botany (Swahn 1996:106). The Ethnological Association was an expression of the open scholarly climate that prevailed in Lund at the start of the twentieth century.

The living past

Ethnology was thus the spreading umbrella under which all these disciplines were thought to be able to shelter. How was it possible for so much importance to be ascribed to the concept of ethnology? It had been introduced to Sweden by the zoologist and archaeologist Sven Nilsson, whose statue stands in Lundagård, just south of the university building. The subject was continued by Gunnar Olof Hyltén-Cavallius, whose *magnum opus* on the Värend district of Småland bore the subtitle "An Essay in Swedish Ethnology" (1863–68). This work was distinguished by its focus on people and the author's holistic view of their spiritual, material, and social culture, and the method of using modern-day survivals in these spheres to reconstruct life in prehistoric times (Bringéus 1966).

Hyltén-Cavallius had applied a continuity perspective to folk culture by comparing modern and prehistoric artefacts. In 1879 he sent a bone needle to Artur Hazelius. Needles like this were still used here and there in Småland to make thick socks and woollen mittens. Hyltén-Cavallius sent a sample to accompany the needle, pointing out that similar needles had been found from the Late Iron Age, for example, at Björkö (Bringéus 1966:216 f.).

A similar outlook was shared by the superintendent of antiquities Gabriel Djurklou. In 1870 he visited Södra Unnaryd in Finnveden, Småland, and when he published his book on the customs of the people there (1874), he described the district as a living antiquity. He felt "intensely moved by the remarkable remains of ancient belief and ancient custom to be perceived there" (p. III). The book ends with the exhortation: "Let us therefore try diligently, while there is still time, to gather these scattered remains of ancient belief and ancient customs" (p. 76).

Hyltén-Cavallius' endeavours were driven by a powerful national passion, which led to the creation of our first museum of cultural history in Växjö. Here, however, we shall ignore the nationalism and concentrate on the prehistoric projection, which was expressed in the newly founded museums (many of which were given names contains words with the prefix *forn-* "ancient": *fornhem, fornsal, fornstuga*) and archaeological associations (*fornminnesföreningar*) The archaeological association founded by Gabriel Djurklou in Örebro in 1856 was followed by many others elsewhere in Sweden, and in 1870 they were federated in a national association, Svenska Fornminnesföreningen (Arcadius 1997).

The rune stone became the classic logotype on books and journals (Bringéus 1972:10; Arcadius 1997:60). Newly carved rune stones were erected on the graves of the scholars of antiquity (Tornehed 1996:4). Journals were given Old Norse names, such as *Runa*, published by Hazelius, *Ymer*, a journal of anthropology and geography (1881), *Rig*, a journal of Swedish cultural history (1918), called after a figure in an eddic poem, and of course there was the archaeological journal *Fornvännen*.

The infatuation with prehistory at the turn of the century also spread to the general public in the form of trade marks such as rune-marked butter and rune-marked eggs (1904). Boats and babies were given Old Norse names, and when children reached school age they learned to write in exercise books bearing the name Runa. In the decorative arts, winding ribbons of runes went well with the scrolls of *art nouveau*.

Some time into the twentieth century there was criticism of the concepts of *fornminne* (ancient monument) and *fornkunskap* (archaeology, literally, knowledge of antiquity), since they were considered too woolly. Despite this, the subject of archaeology continued to be designated as *Nordisk och jämförande fornkunskap* (Nordic and Comparative Archaeology) at universities until 1968, when it was changed to *Arkeologi, särskilt nordeuropeisk* (Archaeology, especially Northern European). A little later the term *fornminnesvård* (the care of ancient monuments) was replaced by *kulturmiljövård* (care and protection of the cultural environment), but ancient finds are still referred to as *fornfynd*.

Education and field research

Both archaeology and ethnology developed earliest at the central museums in Stockholm, the Historical Museum and the Nordic Museum. The two museums were closely linked. The director of the Nordic Museum, Bernhard Sahlin (1861–1931), ended his career as Director-General of the Central Board of

National Antiquities. It was only later that the two museums set up a chronological dividing line for their collecting policies.

Ethnology was established as an academic discipline in 1918 with the creation of the Hallwyl Professorship at the Nordic Museum. The first occupant of the chair, which was called Nordic and Comparative Folklife Studies, was Nils Lithberg (1883–1934), an archaeologist by training. He had once been an assistant to Georg Karlin at Kulturen. His successor, Sigurd Erixon, had also studied archaeology. In 1912, for example, he published an essay on the Stone Age in Blekinge and in 1915 an article about runic inscriptions in Dalarna. As late as 1934, Sigurd Erixon could still compare the construction of modern church-boats and Viking Age boats, arguing that there was continuity.

The heavy initial emphasis on prehistory in the research of both Lithberg and Erixon was due to the fact that they had attended university in Uppsala, where archaeology had some brilliant representatives. Also in Uppsala was Gustaf Hallström (1880–1962), the leading scholar with an ethnological or anthropological outlook among those who devoted their research to archaeology. Evert Baudou has shown how Hallström was distinguished by a holistic ethnological view which comprised the present and the past; in addition, he was an exceptional field researcher, who documented Saami culture with his camera and notebook, even working as a participant observer (Baudou 1997:153 f.). Hallström's concentration on field research was undoubtedly a model for Sigurd Erixon.

For this first generation of scientifically schooled researchers, there was thus no real boundary between ethnology and archaeology—they were both concerned with knowledge of the past, *fornkunskap*, the indigenous equivalent of the term *archaeology*. Both ethnologists and archaeologists contributed to the same journal, *Rig*.

As the last representative of a combined archaeological and ethnological perspective <i>I would regard Harald Hvarfner (1926–1975). He had a licentiate degree in both subjects, and the building of the big dams in Norrland meant that this became his chief research field. I accompanied him a couple of times on long journeys, and I don't think I have ever experienced the closeness of archaeology and ethnology so vividly. One had the feeling that prehistory came into the open here. Hunting and fishing were the indicators of this. One of Hvarfner's books is characteristically entitled *Hunting and Fishing: Nordic Symposium on Life in a Traditional Hunting and Fishing Milieu in Prehistoric Times and up to the Present Day*. Outside Sweden as well, there were scholars with similar perspectives, such as Helmer Tegengren in Åbo, who incidentally addressed the Ethnological Society in Lund in 1951 on the subject of "Wild Reindeer Trails and Seasonal Settlement". By that time, however, interest in the society was waning. The last meeting was held in the spring of 1956.

Shared theoretical paradigms

The primary scientific paradigm that made the prehistoric perspective possible was evolutionism. This had been developed in geology and comparative research, and it was the method introduced by Sven Nilsson and continued by Hyltén-Cavallius and his friend Nils Månsson Mandelgren. In Mandelgren's pictorial atlas we can see the evolutionist perspective applied to house construction and boat building (Bringéus 1990:29 ff.). The leading light in archaeology, Oscar Montelius, was also an evolutionist. Hazelius was more oriented to environments and provinces, which went hand in hand with his educational ambitions. But in the Nordic Museum, as in other museums of cultural history, artefacts in the permanent exhibitions were arranged on the model of the typological method, just as they were in the historical museums (Nilsson 1996:32).

When functionalism then made its entry, ethnology could still be combined with archaeology. The archaeologists were responsible for prehistoric finds, but they were often bewildered by them. Ethnologists could explain the function, especially of the objects found in medieval archaeological contexts, drawing on their knowledge of modern artefacts and techniques. Gösta Berg (1974), for example, showed that certain medieval pottery finds from urban excavations had been completely misunderstood and designated as fish dishes whereas in fact they were used for catching the fat from food being grilled on a spit over an open fire. Another example of the misinterpretation of medieval objects has been pointed out by the art historian Oscar Reutersvärd (1975). He argues convincingly that the round stones that are called "bread-stones", assumed to have served as shewbread in churches, were in fact used in the winter to heat the water in baptismal fonts.

Diffusionism also served as a shared theory for ethnology and archaeology. This era is easily recognized by its diffusion and distribution maps. Diffusionism in ethnology, under the influence of Sigfrid Svensson and the geographer Torsten Hägerstrand, resulted in an interest in innovations (Bringéus 1990:39 ff.), and there are examples of their theories being applied by archaeologists.

Ein Kopfsprung in die Urzeit

Folklorists also focused their research on the ancient past. The leading scholar at the Nordic Museum was Nils Edvard Hammarstedt (1861–1939). In the early 1920s he set up an exhibition in the museum on the subject of ancient belief. In 1939 C. W. von Sydow in Lund published an essay entitled "Folktales and Archaeology", and two years later he published a popular work entitled "Our Folktales and What They Say about Prehistoric Beliefs and Customs". As late as 1945, von Sydow lectured to the Ethnological Society in Lund on "Archaeology and Folklore Studies". He said, for example, that the distribution of the tale of the Swan Maiden (Aa 400) and the tale of the Magic Flight from the Ogre (Aa 313, 314) corresponded to the occurrence of megalithic graves, basing his claim on some diffusionist archaeologists and anthropologists from the 1930s. "This hypothesis about the occurrence of 'megalithic sagas' was von Sydow's definitive *Kopfsprung in die Urzeit* and was much ridiculed by the archaeologists," writes Jan Öjvind Swahn, adding, "I would regard these ideas as an instance of failing judgement and uncritical assimilation of notions that favoured his hypothesis from scholars in sciences that he did not master" (Swahn 1996:105). In combining folk traditions and archaeology, however, von Sydow was not alone. I have pointed out above how Knut Stjerna had associated Iron Age finds with *Beowulf*. Einar Nermann likewise combined the list of Swedish kings in the Icelandic *Ynglinga saga* with the same Old English poem (Baudou 1997:164).

Philologically oriented folkloristics had a similar prehistoric perspective. Dag Strömbäck (1935) wrote a dissertation about *Sejd*, ancient magical spells. My own teacher of history of religion, Carl-Martin Edsman, still an active scholar, published an article with the characteristic title "Folk Customs with Roots in Pagan Times" (1946). Folklore opened a peephole deep into the well of time, the deeper the better. "Tradition tells the truth" could have been the title of a large number of local studies. An aura of folklore surrounded the ancestral barrows. Living tradition could even serve as a kind of divining rod for archaeologists, telling them where they should dig.

The prehistoric perspective survived longest in the lists of required reading for undergraduates. Although Sigfrid Svensson was really the first to bring ethnology into the present day, for example, in his study of black and white confirmation dress, he did not forget the prehistoric perspective. In his introductory ethnological textbook from 1966, *Introduktion till folklivsforskningen*, the first chapter is entitled "Folk Culture and Prehistoric Culture". This is illustrated with a number of examples representing both material and non-material culture: Odysseus and Polyphemus, where Svensson uses legendary material; rubbing sticks together to produce fire as a cure for disease in cattle; the oldest settlements of the Finns; skis through the ages. One of the subtitles is characteristic: "The Continuity of Artefact Forms". The criterion of form played an important role in archaeology, and it was applied not just in archaeological but also ethnological investigations.

The abandonment of the prehistoric perspective

How was the prehistoric perspective in Swedish ethnology broken? Evert Baudou argues that the holistic view of the past began to weaken as soon as separate university subjects were established. Gustaf Hallström was rather alone among archaeologists as a defender of the concept of "the living past".

When the archaeologists began to abandon the journal *Rig* in the early 1930s, it was a sign that the journal's temporal perspective on cultural history had become shorter, and perhaps that the two sciences had begun to go their separate ways. Medieval research was represented somewhat longer in the journal.

Bo G. Nilsson, in a recent doctoral dissertation (1996) on workers' memoirs, has some interesting retrospective glances at the history of scholarship. He singles out von Sydow and Sigurd Erixon in particular. C. W. von Sydow did not only represent the prehistoric perspective; he was also deeply impressed by psychology. There were therefore several different—even mutually incompatible—lines in his research. For Sigurd Erixon on the other hand, it was the influence of sociology that led to a change in course. However, his new signals in the journal *Folkliv* in 1938, where he tried to lead ethnology in the direction of sociology were not accepted by everyone.

Critique of ideology

In Germany in the Third Reich, this prehistoric projection had been converted into a kind of practical folk knowledge and folklorism, the ultimate aim of which was to show the primacy of the Aryan race.

C. W. von Sydow, who, like most academics at the time, had good contacts with German scholars, levelled harsh criticism already in 1939 at the Nazi henchman Hermann Wirth and his attempt to construct a Germanic religion and national cult. At the ethnological congress in Heidelberg in 1934, von Sydow himself was able to listen to John Meier's criticism of Wirth, and he also saw how Meier had to pay a high price for his outspokenness (Bringéus 1991:14 f.). Among Swedish archaeologists, Nils Åberg in Stockholm seems to have been the only one to react to Wirth's glorification of the Nordic race. Yet this did not prevent Wirth from being invited to Sweden in 1935, where he gave lectures, for instance, to the Swedish Society of Medicine in Stockholm. It was not until the German occupation of Denmark and Norway on 9 April 1940 that the Nazi sympathizers in Sweden lowered their voices (Baudou 1997:231 ff.).

Many German ethnologists were seriously tainted, and when a new generation of scholars took over after the war, those in Tübingen in particular were highly critical of the criterion of continuity. Their chief representative, Hermann Bausinger, steered ethnological research into the age of technology. "Gegenwartsvolkskunde" even became a technical term. The pendulum always swings to its maximum extent. In many places, ethnology was transformed from a study of the distant past into a modern social science.

Critique of element studies

Following Hyltén-Cavallius, ethnologists to large extent devoted their efforts to finding traces or indicators as evidence in their scholarly argumentation. For comparative studies in time and place, it became necessary to focus on individual elements of culture, whether fairytales or threshing flails. These often became so central that the people who had created and used them were left in the background. This was particularly the case in diffusionist studies, and as a result, there was harsh criticism of diffusionist research—in Scandinavia represented chiefly by the Finnish school—which combined chronological and chorological studies and which sought to reconstruct ur-forms and archetypes. Orvar Löfgren writes: "Yet here the perspective was mostly temporal. It was ahistorical in the sense that the scholar was usually not interested in relating the studied cultural element to the various social contexts through which it passed. It was the journey of the custom or the artefact through time, not through history or society, that was in focus. There was rarely any attempt to see the transformation of the custom in relation to the transformation of society in different eras" (Löfgren 1996:82).

In opposition to ethnological studies of elements, the early sixties saw the coming of studies of cultural laws, systems, and societies of various kinds (Bringéus 1990:173 ff.).

Two new concepts helped to divert interest from the study of elements. One was ecology, the other was context. Evert Baudou has shown how the concept of ecology runs like a theme through Gustaf Hallström's archaeological research. Hallström was not interested in museum objects (Baudou 1997:288); instead he was an assiduous field researcher, chiefly in Norrland. Among the ethnologists, Phebe Fjellström, professor in Umeå, continued to plead for ecology in virtually all contexts after she completed her dissertation on Saami silver in 1962.

The concept of context also had a heavy impact on ethnology and folklore studies. In single-level studies or studies of an era, it is a matter of course to study the context. The combination of diachronic and synchronic analysis, on the other hand, was problematic. Harald Hvarfner tried to find a method for a dissertation that he unfortunately never completed, on Christian names in a parish in Västergötland. He depicted it graphically as a spiral coiling through time, with continuous shifts in space and time. It is easier, however, to do this in a model than in a full-scale study. I think it was chiefly the methodological difficulty of combining the synchronic and diachronic axes that made scholars abandon the diachronic and opt for synchronic studies. Structuralism particularly encouraged this kind of study. Temporal depth was sacrificed, and nowadays it is only ethnological dissertations oriented to cultural history that go back in time more than a hundred years.

The influence of the social sciences

Ethnology as the study of prehistory focused on the countryside. It was there, especially in remote relict areas, that prehistoric traces of both material and non-material culture could be found. But when the term *folkminne* was replaced by *folkliv* "folklife", this opened up the possibility of doing research in towns and among other social categories than the peasantry. While ethnology in the 1960s was still chiefly the study of rural peasants, this is now a very small sector of the subject. Ethnologists have thus followed the migration from the countryside to the towns, from agrarian society to the modern industrial and service society.

In Sweden it was the new anthropological influences in particular that were mainly responsible for the change of paradigm. This time, however, they did not come from physical anthropology but from cultural and social anthropology. The door was first opened by Börje Hanssen; Orvar Löfgren (1993) calls his work "a tacit cultural revolution". While Hanssen still concentrated on the countryside and earlier historical periods, Åke Daun (1969) brought ethnological research into the present and into industrial society, inspired by the Norwegian social anthropologist Fredrik Barth. From then on, ethnology increasingly had a social orientation, which is too well known to need any further presentation.

Increased source-critical awareness

Another factor that led to the abandonment of the prehistoric perspective in ethnology and folklore studies was an increased awareness of source criticism. The evidence adduced for continuity had many weak links. Seemingly primitive forms of houses, such as the *backstuga*, a crofter's shack built into a hillside, proved not to be particularly old; they were necessitated by poverty in the modern period, built in times of excess population (Bringéus 1966:196 ff.).

Montelius' article "The Sun God's Axe and Thor's Hammer" (1900) was a stage in his archaeological thesis on the significance of the doctrine of evolution. It was long believed that the Nordic Saint Olaf had taken over the pagan god Thor's role as killer of giants and trolls. Olaf's axe was interpreted as a Thor's hammer, his red beard as Thor's beard. The idea of a hypostatic similarity between Thor and Olaf has been criticized by several scholars (Odenius 1949; Lidén 1997).

Sometimes the terminology has been misleading. I myself have criticized the practice among folklorists of speaking of magic spells (*trollformler*), a term that arouses associations with pagan magic when they are in fact chiefly medieval blessings (Bringéus 1995). Another seductive term is "medieval ballad". The ballad scholar Anne-Marie Häggman has pointed out the sources of error in this (Arvidsson 1996:12 ff.). There are even scholars who question the concept of the medieval ballad.

A fresh example of source criticism comes from Birgitta Odén (1997) in a study of the alleged ancient practice of liquidating old people when they grew too feeble and sickly; folklorists have cited traditions of a cliff from which the old people were hurled, and a club from Tidersrum has even been presented as evidence. As a historian, Odén is able to show that the tradition derives from the Icelandic *Gautreks saga*, a jocular saga which has spread to become a schoolbook truth.

Source criticism is never wrong, no matter what angle it comes from. In combination with the other arguments that I have put forward, it has meant that ethnologists have deserted some of their old fields of study. It is no small area that has been left to lie fallow; in fact, it is the whole of Swedish folk culture before 1850, or even before 1900. What was the reason? In part it was the new methods. Ethnologists used to record folklife and lore, but now it became a matter of reconstructing life-courses, and soon there will be no one left who was born before 1900. Ethnology became an interviewing science, with refined interview techniques. But only living people can be interviewed, which limits the temporal perspective to a thin section comprising at most three generations living at the same time.

Ethnology loses its role as vocational training

Both the first and the second generation of professors in ethnology were museum men (Lithberg, Erixon, Svensson, Granlund, Rehnberg). Some of the teaching was done among the museum collections, and the students were geared to a future career in the museum system. The situation was similar in archaeology and art history which, together with ethnology, made up the so-called museum subjects. Field studies in ethnology and archaeology were an important part of the education of would-be museum workers.

The education explosion at the universities at the end of the 1960s mean that students of ethnology had to seek careers outside the museums. This in turn meant that ethnology lost its role as vocational training and that the courses became more general and anthropological in character. New partners for dialogue were chosen, which can of course be positive. But it is nevertheless the focus on a shared professional career that brings young people together, whether they are budding lawyers, theologians, or medics. The museums could also attach priority to other combinations of subjects when employing new staff, so it was no longer relevant to speak of the three museum subjects. It should be added, however, that the development in our neighbouring countries did not have such radical consequences. In Denmark, where cultural history has traditionally had a strong position, historical anthropology has helped to retain a deeper historical perspective. In Norway, on the other hand, the ethnologists have found a new labour market in the field of cultural conservation.

The divergence between archaeology and ethnology has already had damaging effects. Archaeologists and ethnologists simply are not familiar enough with each other's research.

Let me take an example. In 1950 Brita Egardt gave a lecture to the Ethnological Society in Lund on "Problems concerning Horse Skulls". In 1962 she defended her doctoral dissertation on taboos surrounding the knackers who slaughtered horses, in which she referred to both learned and popular perceptions about the taboo on horse meat in Scandinavia in early and recent times.

In 1995 Raimond Thörn published an essay on Viking Age horse sacrifices in the village of Oxie, without even listing Egardt's dissertation in the bibliography. This is serious, since even a superficial comparison shows a similar geographical pattern. The horse sacrifices that he charts are southern Swedish and Danish, and it is precisely in south-west Sweden that Egardt found the densest distribution of taboos. Thörn's thorough analysis of finds of horse sacrifices, the most important of which have been discovered since Egardt's dissertation was published, makes it necessary, in other words, to take up the question of horse sacrifices once again. Egardt tried to show that the taboos emanated from German cultural contacts from the late Middle Ages. This is no doubt essentially correct, but the main question about attitudes to the horse and to horse meat should obviously be taken much further back in time.

Continued separation or new contacts?

What about the future? Will archaeology and ethnology continue to go their separate ways? New scientific methods in archaeology—such as radiocarbon dating, dendrochronology, osteology—suggest this. Yet there is at the same time a new human perspective in archaeology. The archaeologists' focus on artefacts is beginning to shift towards a greater interest in the people who used the artefacts, their social organization, and even their religious conceptions.

An interesting symptom is that the term archaeology is acquiring a new meaning, and the archaeological excavation technique has taken on a kind of symbolic meaning. An excavator begins on the surface, penetrating deeper and deeper into the strata. The ethnologist Birgitta Svensson, who is profoundly inspired by Michel Foucault, speaks—albeit with quotation marks—about Foucault's "archaeology" and adds, without quotation marks this time: "I have used this combination of genealogy and archaeology in my search for knowledge of how the manner of maintaining norms changed, by looking back in time at the encounter of the tinkers with justice" (Svensson 1993:61 f.).

On the other hand, archaeologists have once again begun to take an interest in ethnological and anthropological questions, having introduced the concept of "ethnoarchaeology" (Kramer 1979). This can be regarded in a way as a revival of Sven Nilsson's comparative method, by which he compared ancient finds with the cultures of distant peoples in the present. The difference is that the comparison no longer concerns formal similarities but complete networks of relations. The pedagogical usefulness of the method has been shown above all by the Stockholm archaeologist Göran Burenhult. A recent example comes from the Uppsala archaeologist Helena Knutsson with her dissertation from 1995 about the change from mobile to permanent settlement. Her hypothesis is that the ethnographically observed relations between hunter-gatherers and farmers can also be detected in archaeological remains. Other scholars have criticized or dismissed what such ethnographic analogies can tell us about prehistory (Petersson 1997).

An important factor for a rapprochement between ethnology and archaeology is that the task of archaeology is not confined to revealing the supposed original meaning of ancient remains but also the multitude of meanings that have been ascribed to them through the centuries. This outlook was forcefully expressed by the Stockholm archaeologist Mats Burström when the Royal Academy of Letters held a symposium a few years ago on the seventeenth-century antiquarian investigations. He ended by saying: "These records show ... that the material cultural heritage—the antiquities—and the immaterial cultural heritage—the conceptions about the antiquities—are indissolubly united" (Burström 1995:77). As an example I may refer to my small local study of pilgrimages to the village and church of Sankt Olof in Österlen. I try to show how the attitude to the cult of St Olaf's Well and the healing ceremony using St Olaf's axe has gradually changed from the late Middle Ages to the present day, ultimately because of the changed social context (Bringéus 1997).

Both ethnology and archaeology study man as a cultural being, although in different epochs. They have in common the elementary questions of what people eat, how they dress, how they build, how they organize their societies, and how they relate to supernatural powers. The comparative method is and remains central in this. In peripheral areas especially, foodways show highly archaic features. Yet it is important to bear in mind, as the Danish ethnologist Bjarne Stoklund (1988) has shown in his study of work and gender roles on the island of Læsø in the period 1200–1900, that the long temporal perspective may also contain discontinuities or "readjustment phases".

I mentioned Harald Hvarfner as the last scholar who combined ethnology and archaeology in his own research. Today a combination like this is scarcely possible at the individual level, but it can be achieved in interdisciplinary projects. It is pleasing that one of the latest and biggest humanistic research projects in our country has an interdisciplinary orientation, with both ethnology and archaeology represented. It is being coordinated by the Lund ethnologist Ella Johansson, now research assistant in Umeå. The project is entitled

"Flexibility as Tradition: Patterns of Culture and Livelihood in the Norrland Forests over a Thousand Years". The hypothesis is that flexibility in the utilization of resources has been combined with strong continuity as regards lifemodes and cultural values. Scholars from a number of disciplines, including ethnology and archaeology, have selected Ängersjö in Härjedalen as their meeting-place, where they are now studying conditions from interdisciplinary angles in a *longue durée* perspective. "The members have high expectations of a turbulent encounter between—to put it simply—the decidedly materialist outlook of the natural sciences and ecology on the one hand, and the decidedly symbolic, cultural, and mental outlook on the other hand," as the project is presented. An example is one study to be conducted as part of the project, entitled "Technical Competence among People in the Forest Region in a Long Temporal Perspective", by the archaeologist Gert Magnusson of the Central Board of National Antiquities. He intends to cover the period 1200–1800 to see "how different technical changes in iron production—both improvements and failures—have affected the social, economic, and gender organization of the communities in the region."

Turning the clock back and transforming ethnology back into a study of the distant past is neither desirable nor possible. But it would undoubtedly be fruitful to prolong the *longue durée* perspective—backwards in the case of ethnology, forwards in the case of archaeology, especially with an increased awareness of the pluralism of meaning. Perhaps we will once again need a joint forum for discussion, corresponding to the Ethnological Society in Lund.

References

Unpublished

Historiska museet, Lund: Etnologiska sällskapets handlingar.

Published

Arcadius, K. 1997. *Museum på svenska: Länsmuseerna och kulturhistorien.* Stockholm.
Arvidsson, A. 1996. Individhistoria som social konstruktion: Tema med variationer. In Jacobsson, R. & Lundgren, B. (ed.), *Oväntat: Aspekter på etnologisk kulturforskning.* Stockholm, 11-24.
Baudou, E. 1997. *Gustaf Hallström: Arkeolog i världskrigens epok.* Stockholm.
Berg, G. 1974. De s.k. fiskfaten och deras användning. *Kulturen,* 103-116
Bringéus, N.-A. 1966. *Gunnar Olof Hyltén-Cavallius som etnolog: En studie kring Wärend och wirdarne.* Stockholm.
— 1972. Artur Hazelius och Nordiska museet. *Fataburen,* 33-56.
— 1990. *Människan som kulturvarelse: En introduktion till etnologin.* Stockholm.
— 1992. Karlin och Kulturen. *Kulturens årsbok,* 7-186.
— 1995. "Ben mot ben, led mot led." 25 gotländska signelser. In *Sæt ikke vantro i min overtroes stæd: Studier i folketro og folkelig religiositet: Festskrift til Ørnulf Hodne på 60-årsdagen 28. september 1995.* Oslo, 60-80.

— 1997. *Vallfärder till S:t Olof.* Lund.
Burström, M. 1995. Fornlämningarnas meningspluralism. Ett arkeologiskt perspektiv på fornlämningsuppteckningar. In Baudou, E. & Moen, J. (red.), *Rannsakningar efter antikviteter—ett symposium om 1600-talets Sverige.* Kungl. Vitterhets Historie och Antikvitets Akademien Konferenser 30, 73–77.
Daun, Å. 1969. *Upp till kamp i Båtskärsnäs: En etnologisk studie av ett samhälle inför industrinedläggelse.* Oskarshamn.
Djurklou, G. 1874. *Unnarsboarnes Seder och Lif.* Stockholm.
Edsman, C.-M. 1946. Folklig sed med rot i heden tid. *Arv,* 145-176.
Egardt, B. 1962. *Hästslakt och rackarskam: En etnologisk undersökning av folkliga fördomar.* Lund.
Erixon, S. 1912. Stenåldern i Blekinge. *Fornvännen,* 125-212.
— 1915. Runinskrifter från Dalarna. *Fataburen,* 147-162.
— 1938. *Svenskt folkliv: några kapitel svensk folklivsforskning med belysande av dess arbetsuppgifter och metoder.* Stockholm.
Hazelius, A. 1868. *Fosterländsk läsning för barn och ungdom.* Stockholm.
Hvarfner, H. (ed.). 1965. *Hunting and Fishing: Nordic Symposium on Life in a Traditional Hunting and Fishing Milieu in Prehistoric Times and up to the Present Day.* Luleå.
Hyltén-Cavallius, G. O. 1863–68. *Wärend och wirdarne: Ett försök i Svensk Ethnologi.* Stockholm.
Knutsson, H. 1995. *Slutvandrat? Aspekter på övergången från rörlig till bofast tillvaro.* Uppsala.
Kramer, C. (ed.) 1979. *Ethnoarchaeology: Implications of Ethnography for Archaeology.* New York.
Lidén, A. 1997. Bilden av Sankt Olav—en ikonografisk studie. *Helgonet i Nidaros: Olavskult och kristnande i Norden.* Mitt-Nordens historie- och arkivdagar i Östersund maj 1995, in press.
Löfgren, O. 1993. På John Granlunds tid. Lusthusporten 1955-1969. In Hellspong, M. (ed.), *Lusthusporten: En forskningsinstitution och dess framväxt 1918–1993: Festskrift till den Hallwylska professuren i folklivsforskning i Stockholm vid dess 75-årsjubileum,* Stockholm, 94-107.
— 1996. Ett ämne väljer väg. In Ehn, B. & Löfgren, O. (eds.),*Vardagslivets etnologi: Reflexioner kring en kulturvetenskap.* Stockholm, 5-87.
Montelius, O. 1900. Solgudens yxa och Tors hammare. *Svenska fornminnesföreningens tidskrift* 10, 277-296
Nilsson, B. G. 1996. *Folkhemmets arbetarminnen.* Stockholm.
Odén, B. 1975. *Lauritz Weibull och forskarsamhället.* Lund.
— 1997. Ättestupan—myt eller verklighet. *Scandia,* 221-234.
Odenius, O. 1949. Till frågan om hypostaslikhet mellan Tor och Sankt Olof. *Credo* 29/30, *Katolsk tidskrift.*
Peterson, H. 1997. En kritisk kommentar till Helena Knutssons avhandling Slutvandrat? och till etnografiska analogier som ett slags episteme för arkeologiska kulturer. *Fornvännen,* 216-219.
Reutersvärd, O. 1975. De "liturgiska stenarna" från medeltidskyrkan i Tryde. *Tomelilla hembygdskrets årsbok,* 25-34.
Stjernquist, B. 1983. Sven Nilsson som banbrytare i svensk arkeologi. In *Sven Nilsson: En lärd i 1800-talets Lund.* Studier utgivna av Kungl. Fysiografiska Sällskapet i Lund, 157-212.
Stoklund, B. 1988. *Arbejde og kønsroller på Læsø o. 1200–1900.* Fredrikshavn.
Strömbäck, D. 1935. *Sejd: Textstudier i nordisk religionshistoria.* Lund.

Svensson, B. 1993. *Bortom all ära och redlighet: Tattarnas spel med rättvisan.* Kristianstad.
Svensson, S. 1966. *Introduktion till folklivsforskning.* Stockholm.
Swahn, J.-Ö. 1996. Arvet från von Sydow. *Rig,* 97-116.
von Sydow, C. W. 1939. Folksagor och fornkunskap. *Saga och sed,* 19-29.
— 1941. *Våra folksagor och vad de berätta om forntida tro och sed.* Stockholm.
Thörn, R. 1995. Vikingatida hästoffer i Oxie by. *Elbogen* 63, 11-36.
Tornedalens historia II utgiven av Tornedalskommunernas historiebokskommitté, 1993. Juväskylä.
Tornehed, S. 1996. Hyltén-Cavallius minnesvård kom från trollberg i Hulevik. *Kulturspridaren i Värend och Sunnerbo.* Växjö, 9-11.
Torstendahl, R. 1964. *Källkritik och vetenskapssyn i svensk historisk forskning 1820–1920.* Stockholm.

Bibliography—Gad Rausing

1949 Three Bronze Age Mounds at Barkåkra in Skåne. *Meddelanden från Lunds Universitets Historiska Museum* 1949, 33–68.
1955 Some Notes on the Preservation of Bone, Antler and other Organic Materials. *Meddelanden från Lunds Universitets Historiska Museum* 1955, 158–161.
1956 On the Climate of North China in Earlier Times. *Meddelanden från Lunds Universitets Historiska Museum* 1956, 155–167.
1958 *Arkeologien och Naturvetenskaperna*. Från Forntid och Medeltid 3. Lund 1958.
1960 *Lars Lawskis Vapensamling*. Norrköpings Museums skriftserie nr 1.1960.
1962 On the Polymerization of Hydrocarbons on Cellulose fibers.*Tappi. Journal of the Technical Association of the Pulp and Paper Industry,* vol 45, No. 1, 1962, 203A–206A.
1963 Fra Arkeologiens Laboratorium. *Skalk* 1963 nr 1, 20–29.
1967 *The Bow. Some Notes on its Origin and Development*. Acta Archaeologica Lundensia 8:6. Lund 1967.
– Bågen i äldre tid. *Limhamniana* 1967, 7–14.
1968 Stavkyrkor. *Fornvännen* 63, 1968, 229–244.
1969 Neanderthals förfäder i Skandinavien. *Limhamniana* 1969, 26–36.
1971 *Arkeologien som Naturvetenskap*. Från Forntid och Medeltid 5. Lund 1971.
– Dalby, King Canute and Lund. *Meddelanden från Lunds Universitets Historiska Museum* 1969–1970 (1971), 280–284.
1973 The Earliest Date in History? *Orientalia Suecana* vol XXI, 1972 (1973), 113–118.
– The Ancestry of the Unicorn. *Meddelanden från Lunds Universitets Historiska Museum* 1971–1972 (1973), 188–197.
1976 Några skånska fornborgar. *Ale. Historisk tidskrift för Skåneland* 1976 nr 1, 13–16.
– et al. Gold traces on wedge-shaped artefacts from the Late Neolithic of southern Scandinavia analyaed by proton-induced X-ray emission spectroscopy. *Archaeometry* No. 18:1, 1976, 39–49.
1977 Bronzealderens Columbus. *Skalk* 1977 nr 1, 9–10.
– together with Lars Larsson. Pilhaken, en stenåldersboplats under Öresund. *Ale. Historisk tidskrift för Skåneland* 1977 nr 2, 1–3.
1978 Den der kommer allersidst. *Skalk* 1978 nr 5, 18–26.
1979 Moving Large Blocks of Stone in Pakistan. *Antiquity,* vol. 53, No. 208, 1979, 43–44.
– Grubehuse. *Skalk* 1979 nr 1, 16–17.
1980 Beowulf—Saga eller verklighet? Statens Historiska Museer, *Historiska Nyheter* nr 13, 1980, 15.
– Iceland—the Island of the Smiths, Ironland. *Fornvännen* 75, 1980, 201–202.

1981 Ecology, Economy and Man. Från Forntid och Medeltid 7. Lund 1981.
1984 Review of Nordens Guld. By J. Jensen. 1982. Fornvännen 78, 1983 (1984), 280–282.
- De foro vida... Fornvännen 79, 1984, 1–3.
- Bernstein und Weihrauch in der Bronzezeit. Mannus. Deutsche Zeitschrift für Vor- und Frühgeschichte Band 50, 1984, 293–297.
- Handel och städer i förhistorisk tid. Populär Arkeologi nr 2:2, 1984, 26–28.
- Förfader, kusin, ättling. Populär Arkeologi nr 2:3, 1984, 24–26
- Prehistoric Boats and Ships of Northwestern Europe. Some reflections. Från Forntid och Medeltid 8. Lund 1984.
1985 Beowulf, Ynglingatal and the Ynglinga Saga. Fiction or history? Fornvännen 80, 1985, 163–178.
1986 Medeltida skånska slagfält. Meddelande från Skånes Vapenhistoriska Förening nr 155 & 157.
1987 Silberschätze und Greshams Gesetz. Ein Fallbeispiel der Wirtschaft zur Wikingerzeit. In Festschrift für Dieter Korell, Mannus-Bibliothek, NF XXVIII, 1987, 797–819.
- Patronhylsan, en förpackning. Kulturen 1987, 118–125.
- Nordbor och Skrälingar, koppor och tuberkulos. Sydsvenska medicinhistoriska sällskapets årsskrift 1987, 15–16.
- Charcoal, Wheat and History. Opuscula Romana XVI:6, 1987, 121–124.
- Barbarian Mercenaries or Roman Citizens? Fornvännen 82, 1987, 126–131.
1988 Black Powder Through the Centuries. Gun Digest 42nd edition. 1988, 209–215.
- Bättre foder med ringbarkning. Populär Arkeologi nr 6:1, 1988, 14.
- Världens äldsta skyttegravar. Meddelande från Skånes Vapenhistoriska Förening nr 163, 1988, 29–32.
- The Silk Road. Some Reflections during two Short Walks in the Karakorum in 1963 and in 1986. In Hårdh, B., Larsson, L., Olausson, D. & Petré, R. (eds.), Trade and Exchange in Prehistory. Studies in Honour of Berta Stjernquist. Acta Archaeologica Lundensia 8:16. Lund 1988, 177–185.
- More on the ard marks. Antiquity vol. 62, No. 235, 1988, 285.
- Om Du vill ha fred, rusta Dig för krig. Meddelande från Skånes Vapenhistoriska Förening nr 164, 1988, 22–32.
- Några tankar om förhistoriska städer, skånska och andra. Ale. Historisk tidskrift för Skåneland 1988 nr 1, 15–22.
- The Elgin Marbles syndrome. Fornvännen 83, 1988, 109–111.
1989 Review of. "The Maldive Mystery". By T. Heyerdahl. Fornvännen 84, 1989, 197–200.
- Review of Stones, Ships and Symbols.The picture stones of Gotland from the Viking Age and before. 1988. By E. Nylén & J.P. Lamm. Fornvännen 84, 1989, 178–181.
- Soma. Orientalia Suecana XXXVI–XXXVII, 1987–1988 (1989), 125–126.
- Månstorps gavlar—vår yngsta fornborg. Ale. Historisk tidskrift för Skåneland 1988 nr 4 (1989), 26–29.
- Dahlgren Guns and Ericsson Ships... They changed our world. Gun Digest 43rd edition, 1989, 17–21.
- Vägar och vadställen, kungar och kanoner. Meddelande från Skånes Vapenhistoriska Förening nr 167, 1989, 4–9.
- Vadstället vid Raus kyrka. Kring Kärnan 18, 1989, 7–17.
- Zum geschichtlichen Hintergrund altnordischer Dichtung. Mannus. Deutsche

Zeitschrift für Vor- und Frühgeschichte Band 55, 1989, 283–310; Band 56, 1990, 329–348.
1990 Löddeköpinge, Lund and Lödde Kar. *Meddelanden från Lunds Universitets Historiska Museum* 1989–1990 (1990), 143–148.
- The "Bulwark" at Tingstäde. *Fornvännen* 85, 1990, 122–124.
- Fanns ren i Skottland under vikingatid? *KUML* 1988–89 (1990), 325–363.
- Vitis pips in Neolithic Sweden. *Antiquity* vol. 64, No. 242, 1990, 111–122.
- When did man become man? *Forntid och Framtid*, 1990, nr 4, 5
- Tjuv fastnade i Rausings fälla. *Hänt i Travellers'Club i Malmö*, 1990 nr 2, 11.
- Några notiser om bågen. *Forntida Teknik,* 1990, 3–11.
1991 Bears, Boars and Burials. *Fornvännen* 86, 1991, 73–77.
- Hunters and Agriculture. *Fornvännen* 86, 1991, 255–258.
- Kalthoff's repeating rifles. *Gun Digest 45th edition*, 1991, 62–64.
- Hjemrejse. *Skalk* 1991 nr 4, 29.
- The chariots of the Petroglyphs. In Jennbert, K., Larsson, L., Petré, R. & Wyszomirska-Werbart, B. (eds.), *Regions and Reflections, in Honour of Märta Strömberg.* Acta Archaeologica Lundensia 8:20. Lund 1991, 153–162.
1992 The Oldest Guns in the World. *Gun Digest 46th edition*, 1992, 71–73.
- Stone age man, anemia and iron oxide. *Fornvännen* 87, 1992, 127–128.
- Over sø og land. *Skalk* 1992 nr 2, 9–12.
- Where Columbus did not find China. *The Mariner's Mirror. The Journal of the Society for Nautical Research,* vol 78, 1992 no 1, 76–80
- Något om Logistiska problem i äldre tid. *Meddelande från Skånes Vapenhistoriska Förening* nr 178, 1992, 37–40.
- Arkeologi från Luften. In Hansson, L. (red.), *Flygspaning efter historia.* Institutet för Kulturforskning. 1992, 9–15.
- On the Origin of the Runes. *Fornvännen* 87, 1992, 200–205.
- Kivik. *Jul i Simrishamn,* 1992, 24–27.
1993 Ynglinga Saga. *Medieval Scandinavia. An Encyclopedia,* 1993, 739–740.
- Öresundsbron—en fråga för hela Skandinavien. *Forskning och Framsteg,* 1993 nr 1, 46–47.
- Review of Archaeology, Theories, Methods and Practice. By C. Renfrew & P. Bahn. 1991. *Fornvännen* 88, 1993, 39–50.
- Rapporter och uppsatser. *META. Medeltidsarkeologisk tidskrift* 1993 nr 1, 39–42.
- Mounds, Monuments and Social Mobility. In Larsson, L. (red.), *Bronsålderns gravhögar. Rapport från ett symposium i Lund 15. XI –16. XI 1991.* University of Lund, Institute of Archaeology. Report series No. 48. Lund 1993, 191–196.
- Kanonerna i Filipstad. *Svenska Vapenhistoriska Sällskapets Skrifter, Nya serien* XVI, 1993, 29–37.
- *Emperors and popes, kings and bishops: Scandinavian history in the "Dark Ages".* H.M. Chadwick Memorial lectures No 4.1993. First published 1994 by the Department of Anglo-Saxon, Norse, and Celtic, University of Cambridge.
- together with A.Stellan Karlsson. Skogen skadas av överdriven dikning. *Forskning och Framsteg,* 1993 nr 8, 55–56.
- Where Did the Reindeer Go? *Sources and Resources. Studies in Honour of Birgit Arrhenius.* PACT 38, 1993, 201–210.
- The Way of an Invention from the Laboratory Bench to the World Market. The Case of Tetra Pak. In Gustafsson, L., Howard, S. & Niklasson, N. (eds.), *The Creative Process.* Stockholm 1993, 49–78.

1994 Därför bör Vega bärgas ! Varför och varthän seglade Columbus? Varför år 1492? *Hänt i Travellers' Club i Malmö,* 1994 nr 2, 4–6.
- A company meets foreign cultures. *Meeting Foreign Cultures. A special arrangement to celebrate the 75th anniversary of the Royal Society of Letters at Lund* . Studier utgivna av Kungl. Humanistiska Vetenskapssamfundet i Lund 1993–1994: 2 (1994), 62–74.
1995 A modern murus gallicus. *Antiquity* vol 69 No. 262, 1995, 6.
- Brev till redaktör Ulla Hagberg. *Populär Arkeologi* nr 13:1, 1995, 33.
- A comment on "Beowulf—Gutarnas nationalepos" by Tore Gannholm. *Fornvännen* 90, 1995, 50–53.
- The days of the week and Dark Age politics. *Fornvännen* 90, 1995, 229–238.
- Akademien granskar arkeologi. *Saga och Sed,* Kungl. Gustav Adolfs Akademiens årsbok, 1995, 95–103.
1996 The Leather Guns of the 17th Century. *Gun Digest 50th Edition,* 1996, 234–240.
- Kings, Emperors, Missionaries and Diplomats. Northern Europe in the 9th Century. *En Kreatörs Tankevärld, vänbok till Hans Rausing,* 1996, 147–167.
- Några tankar och frågor kring dåtid och nutid. *Limhamniana ,*1996, 45–52.
- Roman Reflections. *Roman Reflections in Scandinavia,* Roma 1996, 21–24.
- *China and Europe. Some notes on communications in early times.* Tetra Pak International AB. Värnamo 1996. Edition in Chinese 1996.
1997 Riflessi di Roma. In *Riflessi di Roma. Impero Romano e Barbari del Baltico.* "L'ERMA" di Bretschneider, Roma 1997, pp. 21–24. (Edition in Italian of Roman Reflections in Scandinavia, 1996).
- The wheeled cauldrons and the wine. *Antiquity* vol. 71, No. 274. 1997, pp. 994–999.

Bibliography revised by Berta Stjernquist

Addresses of the Authors

John C. Barrett
Department of Archaeology
Northgate House
West Street
Sheffield S1 4ET
United Kingdom

Richard Bradley
Department of Archaeology
Whiteknights
PO Box 218
Reading RG6 2AA
United Kingdom

Nils-Arvid Bringéus
Department of European Ethnology
Finngatan 8
S-223 62 LUND
Sweden

Torsten Capelle
Seminar für Ur- und Frühgeschichte
Westfälische Wilhelms-Universität
Domplatz 20-22
D-48143 Münster
B R D

Bo Gräslund
Department of Archaeology and Ancient History
S:t Eriks Torg 5,
S-753 10 UPPSALA
Sweden

Alf Hornborg
Human Ecology Division
Finngatan 16
S-223 632 LUND
Sweden

Lars Larsson
Institute of Archaeology
Sandgatan 1
S-223 50 LUND
Sweden

Gro Mandt
Arkeologisk institutt
Bergens museum
Haakon Sheteligs plass 3
N-5007 Bergen
Norway

Michael Müller-Wille
Institut für Ur- und Frühgeschichte
Christian-Albrechts-Universität zu Kiel
D–24098 Kiel
B R D

Evzen Neustupny
Archeologicky Ustav
Ceskoslovenska akademie ved
Malá Strana
Letenská 4
118 01 PRAHA 1
Czech Republic

Carl Nylander
Swedish Institute of Classical Studies in Rome
Via Omero 14
Valle Julia
00197 ROMA
Italy

Ulf Näsman
Department of Prehistoric Archaeology
Moesgård
DK-8270 Højbjerg
Denmark

Addresses of the authors

Berta Stjernquist
Institute of Archaeology
Sandgatan 1
S-223 50 LUND
Sweden

Ezra Zubrow
Department of Anthropology
Faculty of Social Sciences
380 MFAC, Ellicott Complex
Box 61005
Buffalo, New York 14261-0005
U S A

Kungl. Vitterhets Historie och Antikvitets Akademiens serie *Konferenser*

1 Människan i tekniksamhället. Föredrag och diskussioner vid Vitterhetsakademiens konferens 25–27 januari 1977. 1977
2 Människan i tekniksamhället. Bibliografi. 1977
3 Swedish-Polish Literary Contacts. 1979
4 Människan, kulturlandskapet och framtiden. Föredrag och diskussioner vid Vitterhetsakademiens konferens 12–14 februari 1979. 1980
5 Människan, kulturlandskapet och framtiden. Bibliografi. Ed. Arnold Renting. 1980
6 Safe Guarding of Medieval Altarpieces and Wood Carvings in Churches and Museums. A Conference in Stockholm, May 28–30 1980. 1981
7 Tolkning och tolkningsteorier. Föredrag och diskussioner vid Vitterhetsakademiens symposium 17–19 november 1981. 1982
8 Research on Tropes. Proceedings of a Symposium Organized by the Royal Academy of Letters History and Antiquities and the Corpus Troporum, Stockholm, June 1–3 1981. Ed. Gunilla Iversen. 1983
9 Om stilforskning. Föredrag och diskussionsinlägg vid Vitterhetsakademiens symposium 16–18 november 1982. 1983
10 J. V. Snellman och hans gärning. Ett finskt-svenskt symposium hållet på Hässelby slott 1981 till 100-årsminnet av Snellmans död. 1984
11 Behövs "småspråken"? Föredrag vid Vitterhetsakademiens konferens den 22 november 1983. 1984
12 Altaistic Studies. Papers Presented at the 25th Meeting of the Permanent International Altaistic Conference at Uppsala June 7–11, 1982. Eds. Gunnar Jarring and Staffan Rosén. 1985
13 Att vara svensk. Föredrag vid Vitterhetsakademiens symposium 12–13 april 1984. 1985
14 Samhällsplanering och kulturminnesvård. Föredrag och diskussionsinlägg vid Vitterhetsakademiens symposium 28 mars 1985. 1986
15 Runor och runinskrifter. Föredrag vid Riksantikvarieämbetets och Vitterhetsakademiens symposium 8–11 september 1985. 1987
16 The Slavic Literatures and Modernism. A Nobel Symposium August 5–8 1985. Ed. Nils Åke Nilsson. 1987
17 Nubian Culture: Past and Present. Main Papers Presented at the Sixth International Conference for Nubian Studies in Uppsala, 11–16 August, 1986. Ed. Tomas Hägg. 1987
18 "1786". Vitterhetsakademiens jubileumssymposium 1986. 1988
19 Polish-Swedish Literary Contacts. A Symposium in Warsaw September 22–26 1986. Eds. Maria Janion and Nils Åke Nilsson. 1988
20 Sverige och Petersburg. Vitterhetsakademiens symposium 27–28 april 1987. Red. Sten Carlsson och Nils Åke Nilsson. 1989
21 Tradition and Modern Society. A Symposium at the Royal Academy of Letters History and Antiquities, Stockholm, November 26–29, 1987. Ed. Sven Gustavsson. 1989
22 Die Bronzezeit im Ostseegebiet. Ein Rapport der Kgl. Schwedischen Akademie der Literatur Geschichte und Altertumsforschung über das Julita-Symposium 1986. Ed. Björn Ambrosiani. 1989

23 Bilden som källa till vetenskaplig information. Föredrag vid Vitterhetsakademiens symposium 13–14 april 1989. Red. Allan Ellenius. 1990
24 Att tala utan ord. Människans icke-verbala uttrycksformer. Föredrag vid symposium i Vitterhetsakademien 25–26 oktober 1989. Red. Göran Hermerén. 1991
25 Boris Pasternak och hans tid. Föredrag vid symposium i Vitterhetsakademien 28–30 maj 1990. Red. Peter Alberg Jensen, Per-Arne Bodin och Nils Åke Nilsson. 1991
26 Czesław Miłosz. A Stockholm Conference. September 9–11, 1991. Ed. Nils Åke Nilsson. 1992
27 Contemplating Evolution and Doing Politics. Historical Scholars and Students in Sweden and in Hungary Facing Historical Change 1840–1920. A Symposium in Sigtuna, June 1989. Ed. Ragnar Björk. 1993
28 Heliga Birgitta – budskapet och förebilden. Föredrag vid jubileumssymposiet i Vadstena 3–7 oktober 1991. Red. Alf Härdelin och Mereth Lindgren. 1993
29 Prehistoric Graves as a Source of Information. Symposium at Kastlösa, Öland, May 21–23, 1992. Ed. Berta Stjernquist. 1994
30 Rannsakningar efter antikviteter – ett symposium om 1600-talets Sverige. Red. Evert Baudou och Jon Moen. 1995
31 Religion in Everyday Life. Papers given at a symposium in Stockholm, 13–15 September 1993. Ed. Nils-Arvid Bringéus. 1994
32 Oscar Montelius 150 years. Proceedings of a Colloquium held in the Royal Academy of Letters, History and Antiquities, Stockholm, 13 May 1993. Ed. Paul Åström. 1995
33 August Strindberg och hans översättare. Föredrag vid symposium i Vitterhetsakademien 8 september 1994. Red. Björn Meidal och Nils Åke Nilsson. 1995
34 The Aim of Laboratory Analyses of Ceramics in Archaeology, April 7–9 1995 in Lund, Sweden. Ed. Anders Lindahl and Ole Stilborg. 1995
35 Qumranlitteraturen. Fynden och forskningsresultaten. Föreläsningar vid ett symposium i Stockholm den 14 november 1994. Red. Tryggve Kronholm och Birger Olsson. 1996
36 Words. Proceedings of an International Symposium, Lund, 25–26 August 1995. Ed. Jan Svartvik. 1996
37 History-Making. The Intellectual and Social Formation of a Discipline. Proceedings of an International Conference, Uppsala, September 1994. Eds. Rolf Torstendahl and Irmline Veit-Bruse. 1996
38 Kultursamanhengar i Midt-Norden. Tverrfagleg Symposium for doktorgradsstudentar og forskarar. Førelesingar ved eit symposium i Levanger 1996. Red. Steinar Supphellen. 1997
39 State and Minorities. A Symposium on National Processes in Russia and Scandinavia, Ekaterinburg, March 1996. Eds. Veniamin Alekseyev and Sven Lundkvist. 1997
40 The World-View of Prehistoric Man. Papers presented at a symposium in Lund, 5–7 May 1997, arranged by the Royal Academy of Letters, History and Antiquities along with The Foundation Natur och Kultur, Publishers. Eds. Lars Larsson and Berta Stjernquist. 1998